The Making of
NEW DEAL
DEMOCRATS

The Making of NEW DEAL DEMOCRATS

Voting Behavior and Realignment in Boston, 1920–1940

Gerald H. Gamm

The University of Chicago Press
Chicago and London

Gerald H. Gamm is a Ph.D. candidate in a joint program in history and government at Harvard University.

The University of Chicago Press, Chicago 60637
The University of Chicago Press, Ltd., London

Printed in the United States of America

98 97 96 95 94 93 92 91 90 89 54321

Library of Congress Cataloging-in-Publication Data

Gamm, Gerald H.
The making of new deal Democrats : voting behavior and realignment in Boston, 1920–1940 / Gerald H. Gamm.
p. cm.
Bibliography: p.
Includes index.
ISBN 0–226–28060–8 (alk. paper). — ISBN 0–226–28061–6 (pbk. : alk. paper)
1. Voting—Massachusetts—Boston—History—20th century.
2. Minorities—Suffrage—Massachusetts—Boston—History—20th century. 3. Party affiliation—Massachusetts—Boston—History—20th century. I. Title
JS617.A3 1989
324.9744′61′042—dc20

♾ The paper used in this publication meets the minimum requirements of the American National Standard for Information Sciences—Permanence of Paper for Printed Library Materials, ANSI Z39.48–1984.

For Mom and Dad

Contents

Maps, Figures, and Tables

Maps

Figures

Tables

Acknowledgments

Good teachers cannot be thanked too much. I encountered many in the public schools of Sharon, Massachusetts, and many in the years I have been at Harvard. This book is a debt I owe to those teachers. Of them, two deserve special mention. One is Duane Draper. The other is Sidney Verba, who was a constant source of support during the research and writing of this book and who, gently but adamantly, continues to show me how to listen and learn.

Most of the basic research was conducted in libraries and office buildings across Greater Boston. I am particularly grateful to the United Community Planning Corporation, the unlikely depository for some of the census documents central to this study, and the Government Documents room at the Boston Public Library in Copley Square. Hundreds of hours were spent poring over maps and documents in that room in the library, and the task was eased by the patience and dependable, expert assistance of Lloyd Jameson, Mary Kercz, and Miriam Seltzer. A number of other people shared their time and accumulated knowledge with me: Michael Tyner and Paul Hunt, of the United Community Planning Corporation; C. Vincent Haynes; Ralph Melnick; James M. O'Toole and Tim Meagher, of the Boston archdiocesan archives; Alexander Ganz and Anne Hafrey, of the Boston Redevelopment Authority; John R. Cronin, of the *Boston Herald;* and George Cushman, of the city's Election Department.

Easing the writing of the final chapters of this book was the financial assistance of three sources. At Harvard my senior thesis, on which this work is based, was awarded the Thomas T. Hoopes Prize and Philo Sherman Bennett Prize. Also, I have been the recipient of a National Science Foundation Graduate Fellowship.

Many people read the manuscript in one or more of its various stages. For their time and effort on my behalf, I thank them: Kristi Andersen, MaryAnne Borrelli, Henry E. Brady, Nancy E. Burns, John DiIulio, Andrew S. Goloboy, Gary King, Drew R. McCoy, Norman H. Nie, Gary R. Orren, H. Douglas Price, Lillian Savage, Stephan Thernstrom, and, especially, Walter Dean

Burnham and the two anonymous readers for the University of Chicago Press. I have profited from their advice and instruction, and this is a better work for their scrutiny.

In some real sense, this book is a team effort. It was begun and completed during my years in Mather House, and all my friends there deserve a large measure of credit for it. Among them are Andrew B. Bloomer, Michael Cavuoti, Paul Kent, William C. Stevens, and Cody Weston, who helped me to collect and review data for each of the tables, and Brian P. Burns, Anthony Gellert, Travis Metz, Joseph A. Sweeney, and Mary Velasquez, who offered generous assistance in the final stages of production. My deepest gratitude is reserved, however, for two others. Christopher Arbery prepared the maps. And Barbara Looney proofread with me the entire text of the book. I am fortunate to have such friends.

At the end, the duty to thank my parents, Stephen and Sandra Gamm, my brothers, Ben and Dan, my sister, Shanna, and my grandparents, Lillian and Louis Feinstein and Dorothy and Louis Gamm, is utterly natural. To now express my deep love and respect for all that they are is the sweetest task I can know.

Cambridge, Massachusetts — G.H.G.
January 3, 1989

The Making of
NEW DEAL
DEMOCRATS

1

Introduction

Once in this century, and probably for the last time in this nation's political history, there was an intense moment of realignment in the American party system. In the 1930s, the Democratic party took control of the federal and most state governments and gained the loyalty of a majority of voters, reclaiming a position in the political system which it had not enjoyed since before the Civil War. Its ascendancy proved lasting at nearly all levels of government; the presidency was, of course, a notable exception. The party system remade in the Great Depression and nurtured by Franklin Delano Roosevelt endured into the 1960s, when partisanship and voter participation resumed a general and serious decline, and the shadow of that earlier moment continues still to haunt the contours of party divisions as we enter the 1990s. Only two other times since the establishment of mass politics have such decisive realignments occurred: at the birth of the Republican party in the 1850s, and in the 1890s, when the Republicans reconfigured their electoral coalition and consolidated political control. For the twentieth century, then, the New Deal realignment stands in sharp relief.

Political scientists since the mid-1950s have focused on those past moments of unusual change and activity in their accounts of party evolution. Electoral eras of seemingly abrupt change have been designated periods of critical realignment, qualitatively distinct from the more stable years lying between such realignments. That approach represented a reaction to the older accounts of the party system, which denigrated the place of change and growth in American political parties and argued that lines of cleavage had barely changed since the establishment of the first federal government. This book, like nearly all other work done on the subject in the last generation, has its roots in the newer tradition; that its focus is the era of change in the late 1920s and 1930s, commonly and so here called the New Deal realignment, is evidence of its origins. But one of the conclusions reached in these pages, expressed most forcefully in the final chapter, is that party change is more gradual and more constant than realignment theory allows. Our parties were neither thoroughly transformed in one great upheaval nor do they persist for any length of time with their bases of voter support wholly intact. The changes of the 1930s differed only in degree, not in kind, from the realignments in the electorate in the decades before and since.

In this book we examine the electoral underpinnings of the New Deal realignment. Our task is to trace the movement of adults into and out of the pool of active political participants and to relate that movement to the relative increase of Democratic supporters within that pool. As early as election night 1932 Americans became aware of the sudden gains made by the Democratic party in its contests with the Republican party at all levels of the political system. But it was only after the passage of many years that the permanence of those Democratic gains became apparent and the historic importance of that shift in the party system was appreciated. Efforts to describe the significance of that era in American political history led scholars to define and locate comparable realignments in the nation's past. Implicit in nearly all of these studies is the assumption that such a drastic change in the relative position and composition of the two major parties is of significant consequence to the political system. Some students of the field have explicitly investigated that assumption, looking at the relationship between party realignment and policy-making or between realignment and changes in institutional structures. Most scholars, however, have focused on the electoral aspect of party realignment; they have attempted to identify critical elections and to characterize the regional, ethnic, and socioeconomic groups composing party coalitions. That issue, the realignment as it occurred in the electorate, is the primary concern of this book.

What distinguishes this book, though, is the effort to approach as nearly as possible the behavior of individual political actors. The enterprise of locating and naming the few realignments in our past is spent. Other scholars have taught us much about the nature of and changes in electoral coalitions, while still others have constructed models to explain such widespread changes in terms of issues or overarching theory. In this book those important achievements form the basis of a deeper probing of the mechanics of realignment. My analysis is grounded in the belief that a party system existed in 1940 which was different in basic ways from the 1920 party system, that a realignment occurred sometime in the course of those two decades, and that Boston is an acceptable laboratory for studying that realignment. From those propositions I examine the New Deal realignment as it was effected by the myriad decisions of individual men and women in the electorate. I describe, from data collected for ethnically and socioeconomically homogeneous voting precincts, the most likely scenarios for individual behavior that collectively resulted in vast systemic change. Thus the book investigates the timing of electoral decisions, the linkages between the votes cast for different levels of political offices, the ties between those voting patterns and patterns of partisan registration, and the sources of the majority coalition formed in those years. Specifically, the new Democratic voters could have come from two very different sources. On the one hand, former Republican voters could have crossed party lines and become Democrats. On the other, Republicans could have remained Republicans while the new Democrats came from the massive pool of previous nonvoters. Determining the roles played by voter conversion and by voter mobilization in the New Deal realignment, as part of a larger inquiry into voter mechanics, should help us in the effort to understand more recent changes in the party system.

The political upheaval of the 1930s was a peculiar realignment. It has had no equal in this century and, in important ways, it did not entirely resemble the initial alignment of mass parties and subsequent realignments of the nineteenth century. Changes in the party system in the 1830s, 1850s, and 1890s occurred in an era of widespread participation in political life and of intense partisanship. By the early 1930s, in contrast, voter turnout and partisan loyalty had declined sharply. Whereas the older critical elections dramatically shaped and reshaped highly mobilized electorates, the New Deal realignment could only temporarily slow the drift from political parties, a drift which by 1930 was already more than a generation old.

In "The Changing Shape of the American Political Universe," a 1965 article, Walter Dean Burnham suggested that the "system of 1896" had inaugurated a new era in American politics. "The late 19th-century voting universe was marked by a more complete and intensely party-oriented voting participation among the American electorate than ever before or since," wrote Burnham. "This earlier political order . . . was eroded away very rapidly after 1900. Turnout fell precipitately from 19th-century levels. . . . As turnout declined, a larger and larger component of the still-active electorate moved from a core to a peripheral position, and the hold of the parties over their mass base appreciably deteriorated." Those great changes he attributed to the effects of the 1890s realignment.[1]

What Burnham could not explain was why the New Deal realignment had not been sufficient to permanently reverse, or even greatly slow, the changes which had begun by 1900. "If, as seems more than likely, the political regime established after 1896 was largely responsible for the marked relative decline in the active voting universe and the marked increase in peripherality among those who still occasionally voted," Burnham noted, "it is all the more remarkable that the dramatic political realignment of the 1930s has had such little effect in reversing these trends." He found, in fact, that the realignment of voters and parties in the 1930s had had little lasting impact: "These trends were overwhelmingly prominent between about 1900 and 1930, were only very moderately reversed following the political realignment of 1928–1936, and now seem to be increasing once again along several dimensions of analysis.'' While he offered important insights and laid the foundation for further study of American political development, Burnham failed to address adequately the relationship between the realignments of the 1890s and the 1930s and longer-term changes in the American party system. The ''unidirectional, post-1900 trends toward the degeneration of party linkages in our system of electoral politics'' that are examined in his 1970 book, *Critical Elections and the Mainsprings of American Politics,* Burnham tied directly to the 1896 realignment. ''This revolutionary contraction in the size and diffusion in the shape of the voting universe was,'' he wrote in the earlier article, ''almost certainly the fruit of the heavily sectional party realignment which was inaugurated in 1896.'' Yet, Burnham admitted, the New Deal realignment had not been able to revitalize the party system: by the standards of past realignments, it ''has been both incomplete and transitional.''[2]

Burnham's substantial contribution was in recognizing the profound transformation of American politics since the turn of the century. His analysis was limited, however, by the basic assumption that lines of causation ran principally from the electorate and parties to the government and the larger political system. Hence Burnham explained changes in the political system after 1900 as results of the 1896 electoral realignment, and his analysis was stunted by the refusal of the political system to respond in equally significant ways to the New Deal realignment.

Not for several years was another student of the period able to recognize the limits imposed by that assumption and attempt to transcend them. It is Richard L. McCormick who has argued most forcefully that the political system can determine the terms of party competition, that it might reward certain forms of party behavior and punish others, and that such a system of incentives has changed over time. Specifically, realignments, rather than changing any basic rules of the political game, might themselves conform to and be restricted by existing guidelines. In the nineteenth century, McCormick suggested, parties had to adapt to a system of mass democracy; in the twentieth century, they have had to adapt to a government which has grown more complex and closer to its citizens, to the demands placed on that government by an industrial society, and to a revolution in communications. Thus, he argued, the framework within which the American party system operated was itself fundamentally transformed at the turn of the twentieth century.[3]

From the birth of mass democracy in the 1830s, and until the early 1900s, according to McCormick, ''parties dominated political participation and channeled the flow of government policies.'' Distinct from the decades which preceded it, during which the institutions and attitudes of a competitive, mass-based political system were still being developed, and the many decades which have followed, this was the great age of political parties in the United States. It was, wrote McCormick, ''the 'party period' of American political history, when voting was more partisan and more widespread than ever before or since.'' Twice during the ''party period'' major realignments occurred, in the 1850s and the 1890s. Three basic party orders organized political competition in that era: the second party system, whose origins in the 1830s coincided with the advent of mass democratic institutions, and thus with the origins of the ''party period'' itself; the Civil War party system, which emerged in the 1850s after the disintegration of the second system; and the first few years of the ''system of 1896.'' The ''party period'' ended early in the twentieth century, victim to the assaults of Progressive reformers and the growing demands on government to regulate the economy, as well as to the enervating impact of the 1890s realignment, which had destroyed true two-party competition in most areas of the country.[4]

Even so, parties themselves and the coalitions supporting parties did not immediately wither away. Not, in fact, until the 1960s were parties in full retreat, supported by shrinking shares of a shrinking electorate. That retreat, which had begun in the early 1900s, was slowed just once, in the realignment of the 1930s and its immediate aftermath. ''In some ways,'' McCormick argued, ''the emergence of the New Deal coalition restored nineteenth-century-style party politics.'' For a brief moment, the ''party period'' lived again: ''Voter turnout rose, partisan competitiveness increased . . . , and a rising generation of men and women signed on to do party work.''[5] But the revival was temporary. The ''party period'' was dead. And all that lasted beyond the 1930s, 1940s, and 1950s were new party groupings, new voter coalitions giving the relative advantage to the Democratic party—but in a framework in which both parties grew inexorably less relevant to the peopling and direction of government.

Things had changed at the turn of the century. McCormick, expanding on Burnham's insight, showed that that radical restructuring of the American party system had been the result of many factors, only some of which were related to the realignment of the 1890s. The only subsequent large-scale realignment of party forces occurred in the New Deal period. If realignment is indeed still possible, then the 1930s provide the most fertile ground for attempts to understand the nature and consequences of that process. But if, as is more likely, the political environment has evolved so much that no realignment similar to that of the 1930s or to earlier realignments could again occur—if party organizations have lost control over their own nominations, if only a bare majority of eligible voters participate in elections, if party identification ceases to be an important voting cue even to members of the active electorate, if split tickets are become commonplace—then it is to the 1930s that this and future generations of scholars must look for the moment which defined the partisan complexion of a still-young era, the "post-party period" in which our politics are now conducted.

The study of political realignment traces its origins to the 1950s scholarship of Samuel Lubell, V. O. Key, Jr., and E. E. Schattschneider. Published in 1955, Key's article, "A Theory of Critical Elections," was certainly the most important work of the era. That article was the first to posit the existence of realigning elections and to suggest methods for identifying such elections. The article is not without shortcomings: it relies solely on presidential election returns as a measure of partisanship; it focuses on a single "critical election" rather than a longer period of realignment; it identifies 1928 as the year of that critical election for the New Deal era, at least in New England. But Key's article still commands the attention of scholars for creating an important field of academic inquiry. Decades later, political scientists and political historians continue to study American political development and the evolution of American political parties through the prism of realignment. Key's perspective remains a dominant one in our attempts to organize the past and understand the present.[6]

No coherent concept of realignment existed before the publication of Key's article. Until the 1950s, historians and political scientists had stressed the continuity of the American party system. Accounts of the party system traced the persistence of certain cleavages and themes running throughout American history and assumed that the last significant political upheaval had occurred in the 1850s, when the Republican party had emerged. Only slowly, beginning in the 1940s, did scholars begin to ascribe an unusual importance to the elections that had catapulted Franklin Roosevelt into and returned him to the presidency. But extrapolation from that era was limited; a theory of realignment was slow to emerge.

Writing in 1942, V. O. Key himself accepted the traditional view of the party system as the obviously correct one. The history of American political parties, argued Key, was best divided "into periods marked by changes in party names"; thus, in the terminology of the day, a single "great party alignment," the third such alignment since the founding of the Republic, had persisted substantially unchanged from its formation in 1856. "Although the names of the major parties have been changed from time to time," Key explained, "there has been a high degree of continuity in the party system in that similar cleavages have prevailed, and each party has, back through its predecessors, relied primarily on the same sources of support." The events of the 1930s and early 1940s did not cause Key to revise this scheme of party competition. "In terms of the distribution of the popular vote, the Democratic victories of 1932 and 1936," he believed, " 'show only slight changes from the normal as reflected in the prevailing American political climate'." And, he continued, there was a general "swing to the Republican banner from 1936 to 1940." Despite three consecutive Democratic victories, Key argued in 1942 that there had been no fundamental change in the party system.[7]

Probably the most concise and influential work on the development of the American party system written in the earlier, prerealignment tradition was Charles A. Beard's *The American Party Battle,* published in 1928. Key called the book "the best brief history of American political parties." The thesis of Beard's book was that, throughout American history, the division of voters into two parties was rooted in "the possession of different kinds and amounts of property." It was Beard who noted that it had become "customary to separate American political history into three periods, using changes in party names as the basis of the division." In such a scheme, the first period was identified with Federalists and Republicans and lasted from 1789 to 1816; the second period, running from 1830 to 1856, was identified with Whigs and Democrats; and the third period, the present-day era of Republicans and Democrats, had begun in 1856. "But this division is arbitrary and only for convenience," argued Beard. "In fact, there has been no sharp break in the sources of party strength, in policy, or in opinion. On the contrary, these three alignments have been merely phases of one unbroken conflict originating in the age of George Washington and continuing without interruption to our own time." That conflict pitted "the Hamilton-Webster-McKinley-Coolidge party" against "the frank alignment of agricultural interests made by Jefferson, continued by Jackson (who added an army of mechanics), solidified by the slave-owning planters, and marshaled anew by Bryan after division in the Civil War." Even as power in the Democratic party was shifting from its agricultural wing to its urban "mechanical wing" by the 1920s, Beard did not qualify his argument that the basic lines of cleavage in American politics had remained undisturbed from the adoption of the Constitution through the present.[8]

By the 1940s, however, the view began slowly to emerge that the 1932 election of Roosevelt had been an extraordinary event, a watershed. Cortez A. M. Ewing, in his 1940 work, *Presidential Elections,* expressed the belief that the American party system had changed significantly in the 1930s. "The 1932 election represented a major realignment of party membership," Ewing argued. "Only 1856 and 1896 can be regarded as approximating it in intensity, but the numbers involved in 1932 were far greater. The new administration took its mandate for intervention seriously, equaling, if not surpassing, the record of Woodrow Wilson's first two years in the White

House.'' Like other contemporary observers, Ewing grouped the 1932 election with other major shifts in voting, such as those of 1856 and 1896, and with other major shifts in policy, such as that following the election of 1912. He also made a crude attempt to classify elections more rigorously and to develop a model for distinguishing between periods in the history of American parties. Toward that end, Ewing argued first that ''the political history of the United States may be roughly divided into two periods separated by the Civil War.'' Then he attempted to describe, in some detail, four distinct periods which structured party competition since the Civil War: 1864 to 1876, 1880 to 1892, 1896 to 1916, and 1920 to 1936. His basis for the division was the relative success of the two parties in presidential elections. The last period, ''the post-war period,'' was an especially odd grouping, composed of three Republican landslides followed by two Democratic landslides. Indeed, Ewing admitted that ''throughout these sixteen years, there was threat of party realignment.'' For one who spoke so forcefully of the importance of the 1932 election at another point in his book, Ewing still clung to a classification of elections that took no account of the 1932 election as a marker of great change.[9]

Wilfred E. Binkley, in his *American Political Parties: Their Natural History,* published in 1943, drew heavily on Beard's work and on the basic premises of existing scholarship. In Binkley's view, ''The fact that almost from the beginning of the national period two major interests, the mercantile-financial on the one hand and independent farming on the other, have contended for supremacy has undoubtedly provided the basis of our two-party alignments.'' Since Binkley offered no basis for dividing that history into identifiable periods, he apparently believed that the stability of the lines of political division were of greater long-term relevance than changes in party labels and in party coalitions. He understood that the election and reelections of Franklin Roosevelt had transformed the existing political balance. Referring to the election of 1932, Binkley wrote that ''there could be no doubt about it that the old days of party regularity were gone when the balloting revealed the most notable reversal in any four years of our party history.'' And, describing the supporters of Roosevelt and Alf Landon in 1936, Binkley asserted that there was ''an almost revolutionary change in the group structure of our major parties.'' But that hyperbole did not obscure Binkley's emphasis on the continuity in the American party system, albeit a continuity punctuated by elections that suddenly upset the status quo. He realized that the vast electoral shifts of the 1930s were of historic importance, but he did not extend that insight to a more general statement of the place of change and realignment in the system's evolution. For parallels to the three Roosevelt elections, Binkley looked to 1912 and 1916, to the coalitions that had elected Woodrow

Wilson and to the legislative program enacted under Wilson's leadership. ''Despite the one-sidedness of the 1940 presidential election,'' Binkley wrote, ''it was evident that, for the first time since World War I, the balloting revealed a decisive shift toward the restoration of a balance between the major parties.'' In the evolution of political science, there was still in the 1940s little sense that the elections of 1856, 1896, and 1932 were qualitatively different from those of 1912, when Democrats won the presidency, or 1920, when Republicans decisively won it back.[10]

Samuel Lubell was the first to propose that the 1930s was a period of political change of enormous and permanent consequence. His 1952 book, *The Future of American Politics,* was a great breakthrough in the development of a concept of political realignment. As he argued:

> Some historians have pictured the New Deal as the latest round in . . . the ''ceaseless conflict between man and the dollar.'' But the distinctive feature of the political revolution which Franklin D. Roosevelt began and Truman inherited lies not in its resemblance to the political wars of Andrew Jackson or Thomas Jefferson, but in its abrupt break with the continuity of the past. If, as Charles A. Beard contended, the Civil War was the ''Second American Revolution,'' then the toppling of the dominance held by the Republicans for nearly three-fourths of a century can be considered as the Third American Revolution.

Lubell understood that American politics had changed in the 1930s, that a new alignment of party forces had supplanted the traditional order. Where he broke with existing scholarship was in his insistence that there would be no restoration of Republican dominance—that the ''normal,'' which had been able to accommodate two victories by Wilson in the 1910s, was no more, and that a new era had begun.[11]

The force with which Lubell struck at older accounts of party history signaled the dawn of a realignment scholarship. A great ''political revolution,'' he wrote, had ''rema[de] the politics of our time . . . —namely, the transformation of the United States from a nation with a traditional Republican majority to one with a normal Democratic majority.'' What characterized that realignment was not a Democratic monopoly on the presidency; indeed, Lubell realized that as early as 1952 Republicans could win the office. Rather, ''the significance of the Democratic rise to majority standing lies in the fact that with it has come a wholly new orbit of political conflict—an orbit as controlling upon the Republicans as upon the Democrats, and one which is likely to govern the course of American politics as long as the animosities and loyalties of the New Deal remain in the memories of the bulk of voters.'' Other students of political parties had classified party history according to labels, but Lubell rejected that approach. ''The mistake is being made,'' he argued, ''to assume that the labels of one political age are applicable to a quite different political era.'' In fact, Lubell asserted, the crucible of the 1930s had created two substantially new political parties.[12]

Not only did Lubell assess the significance of the New Deal realignment for national policy and for the course of party politics, but he was sensitive to its origins in the behavior of individual actors in the mass electorate. He did not believe that the new Democratic majority could be attributed simply to the conversion of former Republicans. He proposed, instead, that a massive infusion of new voters into the active electorate, principally those of foreign stock who were concentrated in the cities, had contributed heavily to the political realignment. ''The really revolutionary surge behind the New Deal lay in [the] coupling of the depression with the rise of a new generation, which had been malnourished on the congestion of our cities and the abuses of industrialism,'' wrote Lubell. This generation's invasion of the active electorate, ''this revolt of the city,'' he argued, ''furnished the votes which re-elected Roosevelt again and again—and, in the process, ended the traditional Republican majority in this country.'' As Lubell observed in 1952: ''Today this same big-city generation still stands like a human wall between the Republicans and their past dominance.'' Many of those new Democrats cast their first votes in 1928; Al Smith had a special appeal to the first- and second-generation Americans of the nation's cities. ''Before the Roosevelt Revolution there was an Al Smith Revolution,'' noted Lubell. ''Smith may be today's 'Forgotten Warrior' but the line he drew across the map of American politics has never been erased.'' As Smith attracted foreign-stock voters to the Democratic party in 1928, so Roosevelt by 1936 consolidated those gains and added to them additional voters. Lubell concluded that 1936 was ''the year of realignment in which the Democrats became the nation's normal majority party. The traditional dominance which the Republicans had enjoyed since the Civil War was washed away and a new era in American politics began.'' And that realignment was driven in large part by the newly mobilized voters of the cities.[13]

The great contribution of V. O. Key, Jr., lay in his ability to extract from his own observations as well as from the work of Lubell and others a more precisely defined concept of political realignment. That concept was developed and refined in three articles published in 1952, 1955, and 1959. By the late 1950s, Key had succeeded in creating a general model of American political conflict out of the peculiar circumstances of the New Deal era.

''The Future of the Democratic Party,'' which appeared in 1952, closely paralleled the arguments that Lubell was making at the time. In the article, Key suggested that the American party system had changed radically in the

1930s. For Key, as for Lubell, the last change of such magnitude had occurred in the 1850s and 1860s. ''A catastrophe, the War of the Rebellion, as our Yankee friends call it,'' wrote Key in a Virginia journal, ''burned into the American electorate a pattern of partisan faith that persisted in its main outlines until 1932. The impact of that crisis created Democratic—and Republican—loyalties that maintained themselves generation after generation. . . . It remained for a second catastrophe, the Great Depression, to produce a major alteration in the pattern of partisan division within the voting population.'' A long age of Republican hegemony, which had survived ''the crucial election of 1896,'' had finally ended in a spasm of national economic despair. No longer was the country '' 'normally' Republican.''[14]

Key attributed the triumph of the new Democratic coalition in the 1930s largely to the mobilization of new voters. Because of the substantial increases in the active national electorate during that decade, Key believed, like Lubell, that any attempt to understand the sources of the Democratic majority would have to examine the impact of changes in voter turnout. ''The chances are that Roosevelt and the New Deal converted to the Democrats comparatively few old-line Republicans,'' wrote Key in 1952. ''Rather, the Democrats gained the allegiance of persons who had not been enough concerned with public affairs to vote and of persons coming to voting age.'' While many of those new voters had entered the active electorate in the 1930s, many others, Key argued, had been attracted to the Democratic party as early as 1928. Concentrated in the cities, these men and women ''had been accumulating under the effects of long-term demographic trends and were awaiting political activation.'' The forces of industrialization, immigration, and urbanization had created a huge pool of ''potential Democrats,'' suggested Key. ''Al Smith's campaign of 1928 had initiated the process of activation by tying to the Democratic party substantial numbers of Catholics, notably in Massachusetts and Rhode Island.'' But it was not until Roosevelt's first reelection that the Democratic coalition was consolidated. ''The polling of 1936,'' Key concluded, ''signalized the formation of a new majority combination among the voters.''[15]

In 1955, with the publication of ''A Theory of Critical Elections,'' Key argued that the upheaval of the late 1920s and 1930s was part of a larger class of realigning elections. He conceived ''of an election type in which the depth and intensity of electoral involvement are high, in which more or less profound readjustments occur in the relations of power within the community, and in which new and durable electoral groupings are formed.'' Such critical elections decisively alter ''the pre-existing cleavage within the electorate'' and represent a fundamental realignment of the system of party competition. While, as Key admitted, ''these notions ha[d] been put forward in fragmentary form elsewhere''—such as in Lubell's book and in Key's own 1952 piece, ''where the argument is stated unencumbered by supporting data''—it was in the 1955 article where, for the first time, the realignment approach was explicitly stated and defended. We should note, too, that, from its birth, realignment theory has partaken of both a short- and a long-term dimension. ''Central to our concept of critical elections,'' Key explained, ''is a realignment within the electorate both sharp and durable.'' Thus we distinguish the realigning, or critical, election from the particular ''party system'' that it inaugurates.[16]

Key suggested two specific cases of critical elections: the presidential elections of 1928 and 1896 in the New England states. His fullest discussion is of the 1928 election in Massachusetts. As he found, using language reminiscent of Lubell, ''In New England, at least, the Roosevelt revolution of 1932 was in large measure an Al Smith revolution of 1928, a characterization less applicable to the remainder of the country.'' A sharp shift from earlier patterns occurred in 1928 in the distribution of votes cast for president. And, Key stated, ''the cleavage confirmed by the 1928 returns persisted. At subsequent elections the voters shifted to and fro within the outlines of the broad division fixed in 1928.'' He speculated that the mobilization of a large number of foreign-stock city residents, especially in Massachusetts and Rhode Island, accounted for the impact of Al Smith's candidacy on the timing of the realignment. ''What probably happened to a considerable extent in New England,'' Key thought, ''was that the 1928 election broke the electorate into two new groups that would have been formed in 1932 had there been no realignment in 1928.'' After discussing the 1928 election, Key proceeded to demonstrate that the election of 1896 was, too, a critical election. Unlike 1928, when realignment exposed a sharp cleavage along socioeconomic and ethnic lines, in 1896 the realignment ''reflected more a sectional antagonism and anxiety, shared by all classes, expressed in opposition to the dangers supposed to be threatening from the West.'' While there were, of course, important differences between the two realignments, ''in terms of sharpness and durability of realignment both elections were of roughly the same type, at least in New England.'' Key argued that the party system that emerged in 1896 ''persisted in its basic form until 1928,'' attributing the Democratic victory of 1916 to ''a short-term desertion of the Republican Party'' rather than to any basic changes in the relative strength of the two parties.[17]

Although the emphasis in ''A Theory of Critical Elections'' was on identifying realignments and examining their role in the development of the American political system, Key also understood the importance of studying the sources of realignment in the behavior of individual men and women. Consequently, he alluded to the probable mechanics of the realignments of

1896 and 1928, expanding on the ideas relating to the New Deal realignment first propounded in 1952 by himself and Lubell in their separate pieces. The electoral realignment of 1928, Key stated, was ''reflective of the activation by the Democratic candidate of low-income, Catholic, urban voters of recent immigrant stock.'' He obviously believed, based on his review of aggregate returns from presidential elections, that the mobilization of new voters was crucial to the 1928 realignment, but that the critical election of 1896 depended more heavily on conversion within the existing electorate. That case is made in an extensive footnote:

> The 1896 voting evidently involved a great deal of crossing of party lines by Democrats while it seems probable that in 1928 the Democratic gain came in considerable measure from the attraction of new voters into the active electorate. . . . From 1892 to 1896 in New England the total presidential vote increased only 3 percent, while the Republican vote grew by 35.8 percent and the Democratic vote declined by 37.7 percent. Such figures point toward a large scale conversion of Democrats to the Republican cause. . . . In 1928, the total New England presidential vote grew by 34.6 percent over 1924, an unusually high rate of growth between elections. . . . The absolute Democratic gain was of the general order of magnitude of the gain in the total vote. A substantial proportion of the new Democratic vote probably came from accretions to the active electorate.

It was Key's hypothesis that different electoral mechanisms had produced the realignments of 1896 and 1928 in New England. The consolidation of Republican dominance in 1896 occurred, he argued, within a stable electorate; it was the consequence of a large-scale conversion of allegiances from the Democratic to the Republican party. In 1928, in contrast, according to Key, realignment had resulted from the massive influx of new voters into the political system. That mobilization had expanded the active electorate and transformed its partisan composition, as its former majority of Republicans was overwhelmed by hordes of invading Democrats.[18]

As Key was grounding a theory of realignment on sharp, decisive electoral changes and describing the voting behavior behind those changes, E. E. Schattschneider offered a different perspective on the field. His 1956 article explored the consequences for the political system of particular party alignments. Much of what Schattschneider wrote regarding the relationship between party competition, public policy, and the political environment in the nineteenth century anticipated Richard L. McCormick's later discussion of the ''party period''; Schattschneider, though, ascribed too much importance to the effects that electoral realignments, in particular that of the 1930s, could have on the underlying political system. He believed, for example, that the "whole family of antiparty ideas and devices" which prevailed from the turn of the twentieth century until the New Deal realignment had been a temporary phenomenon which had been reversed by the events of the 1930s. That "attitude toward the party system," Schattschneider explained, was "a product of the sectional alignment following the election of 1896." And he concluded: "The destruction of the old sectional alignment is likely to . . . produce a re-examination of the characteristic antiparty concepts and measures of the first third of the century." The task of dispelling that assumption fell a decade later to Burnham.[19]

Nevertheless, Schattschneider's perspective on realignment contributed greatly to the attempt to define the contours of change in the American party system. The 1956 article provided perhaps the earliest instance of a scholar dividing American political history into distinct periods of party alignment, into periods still recognizable today both for the divisions themselves and the reasons for making those divisions: "a very simple kind of party system" of elite Federalist and Republican parties; a locally based system of mass parties which emerged with Andrew Jackson; "the great period of Republican supremacy from 1860 to 1932," of which Schattschneider said that "the Republican system after 1896 is one of the masterpieces of American politics"; the "revolution of 1932" and the new party alignment that it ushered in. Schattschneider considered the 1896 election to be "one of the decisive elections in American history," determining the basic alignment of American politics until 1932. That election placed business interests firmly on the Republican side of the party divide, giving the Republican party a stoutly conservative cast. The triumph of conservatism over its populist foes was reflected not only in the Republican party but in the establishment of an alliance, a new alignment which "turned the country over to two powerful sectional minorities: (1) the northern sectional business-Republican minority and (2) its southern Bourbon Democratic sectional counterpart." Party competition was stifled, political activity began to decline, and a national opposition to conservatism became impossible against the power of two entrenched regional powers. The New Deal realignment, Schattschneider believed, promised to restore parties to their former positions of prominence in the political system. As the political upheaval of those years raised the Democratic party to majority status and redefined the agenda of the national government, so too did it create an environment again conducive to strong political parties. "The elections of the 1930's," wrote Schattschneider, "substituted a national political alignment for an extreme sectional alignment everywhere in the country except in the South." What he could not see was that the assault on parties and the declining level of political participation after the turn of the century was more than the residue of the 1896 alignment, that what had been ''normal'' before 1896 would not return even with the events of the 1930s. Still, what Schattschneider did understand was the extent to which politics had changed since the turn of the century. And he saw, too, that the political system had been nationalized with the New Deal realignment, discerning some, if not all, of the consequences of that nationalization.[20]

By the late 1950s, a concept of critical realignment and applications of that concept to the development of the American party system had developed. It is no exaggeration to state that the concept was born in the effort of scholars to understand the events of the 1930s. For V. O. Key, Jr., the critical change in New England politics had occurred in 1928; for most other scholars and also for Key, the critical elections with national scope had been in the 1930s. More important than dating the advent of the new party system, though, was the realization that basic forces in American politics had, in fact, changed in the 1930s, and that such fundamental change occurred only rarely in the nation's history.

In ''Secular Realignment and the Party System,'' published in 1959, Key placed those rare instances of critical realignment into a larger context. He supposed ''the existence of processes of long-term, or secular, shifts in party attachment among the voters.'' Voters were mobilized into the active electorate or converted to another political party not only in periods of sudden political change but at all times:

> Events and communications of political import play upon the electorate continuously; election returns merely record periodic readings of the relative magnitudes of streams of attitudes that are undergoing steady expansion or contraction. Some elections may be ''critical'' in that they involve far wider movements and more durable shifts than do other elections. Yet the rise and fall of parties may to some degree be the consequence of trends that perhaps persist over decades and elections may mark only steps in a more or less continuous creation of new loyalties and decay of old. . . . Only events with widespread and powerful impact or issues touching deep emotions produce abrupt changes. On the other hand, other processes operate inexorably, and almost imperceptibly, election after election, to form new party alignments and to build new party groupings.

Key suggested that such secular change was due to ''both relative increases in the numbers of some sectors of the population and declines in others as well as the gradual growth in political consciousness and solidarity of the swelling population categories.'' For the mechanics of secular realignment, as of critical realignment, Key looked both to the mobilization and demobilization of voters and to conversion within the active electorate.[21]

The theory of realignment, then, was a reaction of scholars in the 1950s to the peculiar events of the 1930s. As it was conceived, the new field was composed of several strands. One strand emphasized changes in government policy. Another focused on consequences of the realignment for political participation and for the societal rules governing party competition. Another attempted to identify critical elections. Another stressed the composition of party coalitions, investigating the process by which certain groups entered and deserted each party. And, on the electoral side again, yet another strand of analysis described the sources of the new party alignments in terms of individual political behavior.

Textbooks, by the late 1950s and early 1960s, were revised to reflect the insights provided by a realignment perspective. As Wilfred E. Binkley noted in 1958, Franklin Roosevelt ''did something with the Democratic party that no other leader since Andrew Jackson had quite managed to do.'' Binkley continued, explaining: ''Publicists had long been accustomed to observe that the United States was normally a Republican nation. Before the 1930's most American voters evidently regarded themselves as Republicans. . . . At the end of twelve years a majority of Americans had formed the habit of voting the Democratic ticket and doubtless considered themselves Democrats.'' While Binkley did not speak explicitly of the concept of realignment, he did, at least in his treatment of the 1930s, share some of the basic assumptions of that concept. Still he did not change the organization of his text, which continued to stress the importance of individual elections and to downplay the significance of especially critical periods. Neither did he abandon his belief that the lines of cleavage separating the party coalitions had barely changed over time. V. O. Key, Jr., in the final edition of his textbook, published in 1964, more thoroughly reflected the impact of a realignment approach to American party history. An entire chapter, in fact, was devoted to ''The Party Battle, 1896–1960.'' In the chapter, Key asserted that growing national tensions ''came to a head in the election of 1896 and led to a realignment of the old political cleavages by which the Republican combination gained new strength.'' That party system, in turn, was overthrown in the 1930s. ''The presidential election of 1932 marked a turning point in American party history,'' wrote Key. ''Under the impact of the Great Depression, the Republican following disintegrated and the circumstances were created for the formation of a new Democratic party.'' Key then studied the sturdiness of the party coalitions created in that era.[22]

As scholars began to evaluate the realignment perspective for the study of politics and to refine it as a tool, they pursued many of the strands suggested by the early literature. Key and Lubell, in their consideration of one of those strands, the voter mechanics of realignment, both suggested that the New Deal realignment relied heavily on an infusion of new voters into the active electorate, on a process of voter mobilization rather than on the conversion of existing voters. To investigate that particular hypothesis and to explore more fully the electoral dynamics of realignment is the purpose of this book. We return to the 1920s and 1930s to determine where all those men and women who voted for Roosevelt had been in the decade before, to understand the mechanisms by which so many persons who had never before cast Democratic ballots suddenly came to do so. Key, in his 1955 article, wrote that ''a re-examination of elections with an eye to the bearing on the results of sharp increases in the electorate . . . might produce significant reinterpretations of episodes in the American party battle.''[23] To that issue both he and Lubell gave considerable attention, but it is an issue which the next generation of scholars in the field generally neglected. Of much greater interest were topics which probably seemed broader: the consequences of periodic realignments for the political system, the coalitions formed by realignments and the issues that cemented those coalitions, the identification and categorization of critical realignments, and the relationship between electoral realignment and governmental changes. Since the 1950s, most scholars have simply taken ballots for granted. They have been concerned not with where those new Democrats in the 1930s came from but rather with what effect the emergence of the New Deal Democratic coalition had on the American system of parties and elections. It is worth recalling some of those efforts, especially studies of realignment in the electorate.

Toward the end of their 1960 work, *The American Voter,* Angus Campbell, Philip E. Converse, Warren E. Miller, and Donald E. Stokes devoted eight pages ''to develop a more generalized system of classification of presidential elections.'' They suggested ''three basic types'' of elections: ''maintaining'' elections, such as 1948, when the vote for president reflects the underlying system of party attachments; ''deviating'' elections, such as 1916 and 1952, when the majority party's candidate is defeated although ''the basic division of partisan loyalties is not seriously disturbed''; and ''realigning'' elections or electoral eras, such as 1896 and the 1930s, when ''the basic partisan commitments of a portion of the electorate change.'' This classification grew naturally out of the writing of the 1950s and helped to clarify the emerging field. Since the emphasis in *The American Voter* was on individual voting behavior, Campbell et al. also, unlike most other scholars, addressed the question of electoral mechanics. Referring to critical realignment, they argued "that the changes of such an era arise not alone from changes in the party loyalties of those who are past the age of socialization to politics. It comes as well from the relative advantage of the party that dominates the era in recruiting new identifiers from among those who are first developing their political values." Campbell et al., drawing their conclusions from the particular realignment of the 1930s and, more exactly, from retroactive survey questions, shared with Key and Lubell the belief that voter mobilization was crucial to the process of realignment. But other writers tended to recall the discussion of realignment in *The American Voter* principally for its classification of elections—as indeed did Campbell et al. themselves, in their 1966 book, *Elections and the Political Order.* Gerald Pomper wrote a 1967 article which added a fourth category to the three outlined in *The American Voter.* Pomper distinguished "realigning" elections, when a new majority party emerges, from "converting" elections, when the old majority party is "endorsed by a different electoral coalition." In Pomper's scheme, "the elections of 1836, 1896, and 1960–64 are classified as Converting, and those of 1864 and 1928–32 as Realigning."[24]

Probably the most influential studies of realignment since the 1950s have been *The American Party Systems,* a 1967 volume edited by William Nisbet Chambers and Walter Dean Burnham, and Burnham's 1970 book, *Critical Elections and the Mainsprings of American Politics.* Together, the books expanded on the insights of earlier realignment theorists and established a sturdy foundation for continued inquiry.

Chambers, in the first chapter of *The American Party Systems,* remarked that recent scholarship proved the worth of studying party development over time. He rejected the "older historiography," which viewed parties "as a continuous flow from colonial times to the present, with little more than variations in dominant leaders and political labels." In its place, Chambers argued that American political parties had developed in a series of stages between the late eighteenth century and mid-nineteenth century. By the 1860s, Chambers wrote, the basic forms of party structures had been set. Chambers as well as the other contributors to the book distinguished such long-term trends in the evolution of the system from changing alignments of partisan competition. The articles in the volume—and its plural title—emphasized the belief of the authors that American political development was best characterized not as a single evolving "party system" but as a series of distinct and successive "party systems." Steps in political development tended to coincide with the transition from one party system to another. Burnham, returning to themes in his 1965 article and presaging his forthcoming book, argued that the modern system of mass political parties in the

United States had emerged by the 1840s and that the only major changes in party organization since that time had occurred between 1900 and 1915. "All of the available evidence," wrote Burnham in 1967, "suggests that the American party systems, viewed comparatively, have exhibited an arrested development which stands in particularly striking contrast to the extraordinary dynamism of the nation's socio-economic system." He concluded by identifying critical realignments in the American past and suggesting that those realignments and the five distinct party systems mark crucial episodes in the nation's political development.[25]

It was this thesis which stood at the center of Burnham's 1970 work, *Critical Elections*. The contribution of that book lay not just in its rigorous classification of elections, but in its explication of the role periodicity has played in the occurrence of critical realignments and what effects those realignments themselves have had on the larger political system. Burnham offered statistical support for his division of American history into party systems. And, as he constructed a framework of analysis for critical elections, he suggested that attempts by men such as Pomper to distinguish between "converting" and "realigning" elections had served only to obscure the general importance of all critical realignments. What impressed Burnham was "the periodic rhythm of American electoral politics, the cycle of oscillation between the normal and the disruptive." American political institutions, he argued, have not evolved gradually in reaction to socioeconomic developments. Rather, only rare political crises punctuating the nation's past have shocked American politics into long overdue reconciliation with changes in the underlying social and economic structure. "Critical realignment," in Burnham's view, "may well be defined as the chief tension-management device available to so peculiar a political system." He designed a place for critical elections in American political development; he also knew that American politics had changed decisively at the turn of the twentieth century, a change he attributed principally to the 1896 realignment. This dual insight, and especially the rich treatment of political realignment, makes the book the most important work in its field written since the 1950s.[26]

Much else, of course, has been written. There has been a vigorous debate to identify the election or elections which spawned the New Deal party system. Curiously, the 1928 election, which Key had termed "critical" only in reference to the realignment in New England, has been most closely analyzed. Duncan MacRae, Jr., and James A. Meldrum, in a 1960 article, argued that "in Illinois major and lasting reorientations of the electorate centered about the Presidential elections of 1928 and 1896." While adopting the 1928 election as a crucial part of a longer "critical period," MacRae and Meldrum also noted that "it was not until 1936 that the Roosevelt coalition assumed the form that it has had since.'' John M. Allswang, in his 1971 study of nine Chicago ethnic groups, argued ''that what was true in other cities emerges as true for Chicago also: the 1928 election was certainly the most critical of the period.'' In his 1964 analysis of the role of urban voters in periods of realignment, Carl N. Degler termed 1928 the year of the decisive shift in voting patterns. ''The forces which would consummate the Roosevelt revolution were,'' Degler wrote in reference to the nation's cities, ''already in motion in 1928 in behalf of Alfred E. Smith.'' John L. Shover declared in 1967 that the answer to the question, ''Was there an Al Smith revolution in California?'' was a definite ''No.'' Rather, Shover concluded from his study of presidential elections, ''the election of 1928 in California was a backward step in the process that led in 1932 to the emergence of a Democratic constituency whose existence was presaged in the elections of 1916 and of 1924.'' A valuable contribution to this debate was made in 1969 by Jerome M. Clubb and Howard W. Allen. They emphasized that any assessment of the 1928 election must examine the vote for lesser offices than the presidency and must recognize that the timing of that era's realignment might have differed for different parts of the country. With that approach, Clubb and Allen determined that, in many cities, there was no ''Al Smith Revolution.'' And, they continued, even in those cities where the vote cast for the Democratic nominee rose dramatically in 1928, it did not follow necessarily that ''major and lasting partisan realignment'' had occurred in that year; ''indeed, shifts in this vote seem equally consistent with the view that realignment came primarily in the 1930's.''[27]

Other scholars have rejected the effort to classify particular elections and have focused on broader patterns of continuity and upheaval in the party system. Thus Allan J. Lichtman, in a 1976 article, denied that ''the presidential election of 1928 was either a critical election or an important component of a realigning era of electoral change.'' He then offered a deeper criticism of the entire realignment perspective. ''No election between 1916 and 1940 qualifies as a critical election,'' Lichtman argued, ''and taken together these presidential contests form a more intricate pattern of stability and change than is predicted by critical election theory.'' Although his data are restricted to the presidential vote and some party registration figures and although he did not account for changes in voter turnout, Lichtman did help correct the tendency to focus on one or more critical elections. As V. O. Key had quickly modified his theory of critical realignment in the 1950s with an article on secular realignment, so two decades later the concept of secular change began rippling through a discipline which had long focused on more dramatic moments of political upheaval. Writing in 1978, Burnham, Clubb, and William H. Flanigan argued that ''realignments should be viewed as parts of a longer sequence which is marked by more or less considerable electoral variability at all times''; they believed, though, that the concept of critical realignment remained essentially accurate and useful as a tool for studying American party development. Lee Benson, Joel H. Silbey, and Phyllis F. Field, also in 1978, observed that ''each state may be a *separate* political system with its own individual behavior pattern'' and that, even at the state level, voting patterns for different offices may not realign in tandem. From their study of New York's party history, Benson, Silbey, and Field concluded that the past was not neatly divided into stable party systems separated by sudden realignments. ''The real pattern of electoral 'order' in the American past,'' they wrote, ''is actually a high degree of disorder.'' That thesis was developed further in a 1980 book by Clubb, Flanigan, and Nancy H. Zingale. Their work explored the links between electoral behavior and the direction of government. And, without rejecting the importance of critical realignments, Clubb, Flanigan, and Zingale argued that ''both long-term and short-term electoral change is a more constant property of American politics than much of the relevant literature would indicate.''[28]

One subject on which all students of the period generally concur is the composition of the coalition that elected and reelected Roosevelt. The Democratic party which emerged from the 1920s had ''transformed itself from an institution largely rural in its orientation and leadership to one that embodied the aspirations of the American city dweller—and most notably, the urbanite of immigrant stock,'' wrote David Burner in 1967. After the late 1920s and 1930s, the whites of the South shared power in the party not only with Irish voters in the North but with blacks, Jews, Poles, and many other residents of the nation's great cities, with blue-collar workers, with liberal reformers. James L. Sundquist, in his 1973 survey of party history, *Dynamics of the Party System,* remarked that the new Democrats ''were concentrated in the industrial cities of the North.'' Democratic support was, Sundquist showed, ''far higher among Catholics, Jews, and blacks than among white Protestants,'' and the new party adherents ''were predominantly of the working class.'' Similar findings were presented in 1975 by Everett Carll Ladd, Jr., and Charles D. Hadley. The ''submerged, inarticulate urban masses,'' whose role in the realignment Lubell had described so vividly in his 1952 book, were crucial to the establishment of a new Democratic majority.[29]

Whence, though, did all those Democratic voters come? Lubell argued, of course, as did Key and the authors of *The American Voter,* that much of the new Democratic majority, especially in the cities, was composed of new voters. ''Industrialization, the growth of cities by migration from rural areas, and the gradual assimilation into the political order of the last great wave of immigrants and their children had built a reservoir of potential Democrats,'' wrote Key in 1952. It was the mobilization of those men and women, the transformation of that vast "potential electorate" into part of the active electorate, rather than any large-scale partisan conversion within the active electorate, that resulted in the New Deal realignment. Or so, on the basis of their limited evidence, did these scholars believe. Thus Carl N. Degler asserted in 1964 that the massive vote for Al Smith had been made up principally of those "voters of immigrant stock" who were casting votes "for the first time. . . . These same people," Degler continued, "backed by even greater numbers, would come out in 1932 to vote for Franklin Roosevelt and consummate the Roosevelt Revolution in politics." Charles Sellers made the same point in a 1965 article, grounding his argument in the stability of party attachment recently demonstrated in *The American Voter.* "Realignment," he wrote, "seems not to be caused mainly by permanent changes on the part of people with established identifications . . . , but rather by a strong shift to the advantaged party by younger people and other new voters still in the process of forming their identifications." Returning to the specific context of the 1920s and 1930s, David Burner stated that "the Smith victory was not a conversion of Republicans." An expansion of the electorate fueled the Democratic success in the cities. "The massive immigration of 1900 to 1914," wrote Burner, "was apparently paying dividends in votes in 1928."[30]

But scholarly discussion of this strand, of the behavior of voters and nonvoters undergirding the New Deal realignment, has nearly always been tangential to the main streams of realignment research. Whether Democrats were created through Republican conversion or through the mobilization of new voters has been an afterthought in most studies of the era since the 1950s. That it was not an issue given serious consideration is apparent from internal contradictions in otherwise important works. Burnham, for example, in his 1970 book, argued that "large blocks of the active electorate . . . shift their partisan allegiance" during critical elections. Yet, at another point in the same text, he suggested that in the 1930s, at least, realignment occurred by a very different process. Rather than arising from decisions made by those already in the active electorate, the New Deal realignment emerged from the actions of newly mobilized participants. That political upheaval, contended Burnham, "began from an extremely low base of political participation and rested very largely upon an unevenly distributed ingestion of poor and immigrant-stock whites into the active electorate." Sundquist, too, while relying on Lubell's description of the 1928 election, made no mention of the role played by new voters; neither, though, did he explicitly reject the scenario of voter mobilization in accounting for the realignment. Careless rhetoric, more than careful decision, was probably what led Sundquist to attribute the Democratic urban gains in 1928 to "the heavy movement across party lines." That characterization of the 1928 election remained intact even after Sundquist had revised his text in 1983. Elsewhere in the revised text, however, Sundquist admitted that "both conversion and mobilization play substantial parts in realignment." Just two pages after ascribing Al Smith's urban success to voter conversion, Sundquist proceeded to argue that the Roosevelt coalition had resulted when millions of voters permanently changed parties and when "millions of citizens who had not voted were impelled to enter the electorate."[31]

Sundquist had been prompted to consider more carefully the sources of the new Democratic majority because the long-neglected issue began to receive some attention in the mid-1970s. Writing in 1975, Ladd and Hadley recalled the early belief of realignment theorists that the New Deal realignment had resulted from the mobilization of new voters and then summarily dismissed the scenario. Their analysis rested on survey data for the generation of voters "who came of age during the New Deal." There was, Ladd and Hadley concluded, "little indication . . . of any bulge in Democratic support among new members of the electorate." Kristi Andersen, who studied survey data for those who cast their first vote during the years of realignment rather than just those who grew old enough to vote in those years, reached the opposite conclusion. In a 1976 piece, Andersen argued that "the shift to a Democratic majority occurred largely through the entry of new groups into the active electorate between 1920 and 1936. These entrants," Andersen explained, "consisted of young voters entering the electorate and older (largely immigrant or second generation) Americans voting for the first time. The conversion of long-time Republicans played a far less significant role."[32]

That argument was expressed more fully in Andersen's *The Creation of a Democratic Majority, 1928–1936,* published in 1979. In it, Andersen dealt explicitly with that major strand of realignment theory which had previously been relegated to the realm of assumption and hypothesis, not of sustained inquiry. She drew on survey data and on voting returns from some Chicago wards and precincts to demonstrate the importance of new voters to the New Deal realignment. "The mobilization of groups outside the core electorate," Andersen stated, "played a more important role than the conversion of loyal Republicans in creating the Democratic majority that emerged from the realignment."[33]

There was, though, something peculiar in Andersen's approach to the topic. While the book is important as the first extensive treatment of the electoral mechanics of the New Deal realignment, Andersen took her primary task to be the discrediting of voter conversion as an important explanation for political change in the 1930s. Conversion within the active electorate "is virtually the only explanation given for the massive realignment which took place in the 1920s and 1930s,'' she asserted. The ''literature,'' Andersen wrote in 1976, ''conveys an image of party switching by individuals on a grand scale. . . . The urban, predominantly ethnic voters who became the backbone of this new Democratic majority were converted from Republicans to Democrats between 1928 and 1936 'and stayed switched'.'' As she argued in 1979, this was the existing ''popular mythology of the New Deal realignment: Bad times caused Republicans by the millions to become Democrats.'' The language of voter conversion was indeed used by Sundquist—and Andersen quoted him liberally. Ladd and Hadley also argued that voter conversion was more significant than the mobilization of new voters, but Andersen cited only another piece by Ladd, one in which he ''appear[ed] to subscribe to the idea of 'mobilization,' rather than 'conversion,' as the mechanism of change.'' Apart from those scholars, few political scientists had suggested that the New Deal Democratic coalition had been fashioned primarily out of disaffected Republicans. Consequently, the following became the props upon which Andersen built her argument:

> . . . [C]ritical election theory, at base, assumes that partisan change occurs when large numbers of individuals decide, at a particular time, to change their habitual patterns of voting. . . . The picture drawn of a high intensity, high salience, polarized politics leads one almost inevitably to consider individual partisan ''conversion'' as the basis of realignment.
>
> In Key's study of New England as well as in Burnham's study of Pennsylvania, sharp changes in the habitual electoral behavior of citizens are more or less taken for granted. . . .
>
> . . . [B]oth authors (and they are by no means unique) view the volume of participation and the new bases of party support as two independent phenomena. . . . In the specific context of the 1930s many historians and political scientists have recognized the advantage Democrats gained from the mobilization of immigrant groups, but a solid theoretical connection between realignment and the mobilization of nonparticipants has not been made.

Andersen at one point qualified her characterization of the literature, admitting ''that in general both Key and Burnham ignore the issue of the actual behavior of individual voters in critical realignments.'' Immediately, however, she again asserted that Burnham did indeed make ''the assumption of individual change in behavior more than implicit.''[34] The basis for such assertions was not clearly established by Andersen. And the present study suggests an alternate reading of the literature: Key considered the issue carefully and Burnham did not; Key emphatically argued that the New Deal realignment resulted from the mobilization of new voters; Burnham, in the context of that realignment, made a similar argument, although inconsistencies elsewhere in his book suggest that the argument was not carefully constructed. From the earliest work in the field—in the writing of Key, of Lubell, of Campbell et al.—"a solid theoretical connection between realignment and the mobilization of nonparticipants" was most definitely made, if not suitably investigated, and that connection was sustained in most of the occasional references to the subject made in the subsequent literature. Andersen must be applauded for recovering that strand in realignment theory. Ironically, though, her approach not only minimized the fact that she had reclaimed an important question for political science but caused her to focus on voter mobilization as the correct mechanism for change, as if that were not already the widely accepted explanation. Andersen's primary concern was to rebut the presumed bias for the conversion scenario when what was needed was to examine with quiet detachment the individual political decisions leading to the realignment in the 1930s.

To reconstruct the mechanics of that electoral realignment, the voting and registration behavior of small, homogeneous groups of Bostonians is examined in these pages. The data allow us to track the influx of former nonvoters into the active electorate, to determine the partisan composition of the body of voters, to study the relationship between patterns of registration and patterns of voting for several offices, and to better describe the timing of the realignment. Much more is learned than the relative importance of mobilization and conversion. Our study of that issue through Boston voting precincts gives us entrée into a richer, fuller inquiry into the mechanics of the electoral upheaval.

Precinct lines in Boston were drawn and redrawn throughout the 1920s and 1930s to reflect changes in the number of registered voters in each precinct. Therefore, an attempt to follow particular precincts over any significant period of time would be impossible; such an attempt might also be undesirable, given the likelihood that even the population within fixed lines would change over time. Instead, this study examines the behavior of clusters of precincts, small areas which were ethnically and socioeconomically homogeneous and, in most cases, geographically continuous. The individuals and families living in those precinct clusters certainly changed over the two decades studied: some of the residents died, some were born, some moved into the area, some moved out. What did remain constant in each cluster was its particular ethnic and socioeconomic homogeneity and its geographic location. The same types of individuals persisted in these precincts between 1920 and 1940, even if individuals themselves were entering and exiting the universe of potential voters. In fact, the geographic mobility of individuals and of families probably served to reinforce the continuing homogeneity of each precinct cluster. Lower-middle-class Jewish areas, for example, stayed homogeneous in part because some upper-middle-class or working-class Jews left and were replaced by entering lower-middle-class Jews. Thus could residential mobility result in continued homogeneity for a given area.

A basic assumption of this study is that these homogeneous precinct clusters afford us a window on individual voting behavior. Because the New Deal realignment occurred before the advent of public opinion polling, any conclusions regarding individual behavior in those years must be inferential. We can do no more, even from small groups of precincts, than establish parameters of individual behavior. But parameters of likely behavior are fortunately narrow when the data are derived from homogeneous precincts. As Kristi Andersen argued, "In times of political change or crisis the general partisan movements of small, homogeneous areas would be in a single direction."[35] It is very likely, and at times assumed in the course of this book, that individual behavior is reflected, albeit partially and imperfectly, in the aggregate behavior of homogeneous districts. In such districts, then, which shifted generally toward the Democratic party, three of four possible accretions to the active electorate are considered important—the mobilization of new Republicans, the mobilization of new Democrats, and the conversion of existing Republicans to the Democratic party. The fourth possibility, the conversion of existing Democrats to the Republican party, is viewed as relatively minor in homogeneous precincts whose general movement is in the opposite direction. When this assumption is made in the text, it is stated explicitly so the reader can evaluate the validity of any conclusions drawn from it.

But clusters of homogeneous precincts also prove useful for what they reveal about the actual behavior of small groups of political actors. At times, inferences are made regarding the bounds of individual behavior; I look much more often, though, to the precincts as aggregate units. When I track changes in turnout, in voting behavior, and in patterns of voter registration for the precincts under study, I infer nothing and state only fact. And it is that accumulation of fact and detail which helps to illumine the political realignment of the 1930s.

Precincts are recommended as a unit for such a study by many scholars. Andersen, whose study of Chicago was primarily at the ward level, remarked that it would have been preferable to look at "voting patterns of precincts rather than wards . . . , but the amount of work involved . . . and the impossibility of obtaining demographic data for such areas make the present [ward] method more desirable." Similarly, Lawrence H. Fuchs, in his study of the political behavior of American Jews, admitted that his own ward-level analysis was "a rough instrument"; it precluded, for example, "a subdivision of the Jews into rich Jews and poor Jews.'' In his discussion of the debate over conversion and mobilization, Sundquist called for a study of the issue at as local a level as possible. A precinct study, he expected, would reduce ''the proportion of the Democratic gains that can be explained by mobilization,'' since surges in Democratic support in some areas would not overwhelm voter conversion and Republican mobilization in other areas. Clubb and Allen, too, believed that our understanding of the party system would be advanced by such a study. They hesitated to conclude that no cities were realigned in 1928, in part because of limitations imposed by their data. The areas they studied were ''of large size, and it is possible that voting patterns at the county level conceal rather than reveal significant trends and changes.'' For that reason, Clubb and Allen considered it ''quite conceivable that investigation of voting patterns at the level of wards and precincts would reveal evidence of lasting partisan change in 1928.'' It is clear that the voting precinct stands as an important frontier, and that the frontier demands exploration.[36]

The large literature on the New Deal realignment contains no extensive precinct-level analysis of the electoral mechanics of that upheaval. This is due partially to the paucity of data usually available for voting precincts and to the difficulty of assembling that data and reconstructing precinct boundaries. It is due at least as much, though, to the relative inattention paid by the discipline to this strand of inquiry. If most scholars have failed to examine the extent of voter conversion in the 1930s and to quantify the level of mobilization of new voters, if they have considered the electoral underpinnings of the realignment as beyond the limits of their work, then they could utilize bulkier units of voters in the service of their analysis. Studies of states or counties or major cities afford data which are more easily accessible and collected; such data also generate conclusions immediately applicable to whole regions or to the whole country. Precinct-level data, on the other hand, are necessarily restricted in geographic scope. Their great advantage lies in generating a more thorough and detailed picture of the mechanics of realignment.

Lubell formed his impressions of the New Deal realignment by visiting Americans in the nation's cities and towns. ''I have deliberately swung the spotlight away from Washington out into the country,'' he wrote in 1952. ''It is there, among the people themselves, that the real drama of political realignment is being acted out.'' He began his research by sorting through election returns in order to locate ''the major voting streams and trends in the country,'' but his text contained no systematic study of voting patterns. Rather, Lubell emphasized what voters were communicating through the returns. Those messages were the fruit of his time spent ''traveling through the country, visiting strategic voting areas and talking firsthand to voters in every walk of life''; in those conversations lie the most memorable parts of the book. Thus Lubell gave real vividness to the class cleavages exposed in the 1940 election: "When I asked one auto unionist in Detroit why the third-term issue had made so little difference he replied, 'I'll say it even though it doesn't sound nice. We've grown class conscious.' " As he walked through cities, Lubell discovered that in neighborhoods where rents were below a certain average level, Roosevelt's "pluralities were overwhelming"; above that level, "they faded away." The main exceptions to this class-based voting, observed Lubell, "came on the basis of ethnic background." Roosevelt, he found, generally did poorly in German and Italian areas and received strong support among even wealthy Jews. Young voters, especially those who had found employment in programs sponsored by the New Deal, expressed their gratitude in votes. William Galvin, a ward leader in the Charlestown section of Boston, helped Lubell realize the importance of jobs to the development of party loyalties. Before then, Lubell had regarded the New Deal with skepticism. But, he discovered, "when one translated its benefits down to what they meant to the families I was interviewing in 1940, the whole Roosevelt program took on a new consistency." It was in this relatively unscientific fashion, then, that Lubell expounded the many valuable insights he had into American political behavior.[37]

V. O. Key illustrated his 1955 discussion of critical elections with votes cast for president in selected New England cities and towns. His study of secular realignment, published in 1959, also relied heavily on local election returns. In the latter article, Key isolated the presidential vote in a series of communities, tracing it over time. He looked also at a series of presidential elections in an Ohio county and at changing patterns of voter registration in a Jewish ward in Boston. An eclectic collection of data was scattered throughout the two articles to buttress his developing thoughts on political realignment. The connections he made between the mobilization of new voters and the New Deal realignment were based on analyses of national and regional voting returns for the presidency. At no point did Key conduct an extensive ward-level or precinct-level investigation of the subject.[38]

One study that did attempt some analysis of precinct-level returns was David Burner's *The Politics of Provincialism*. That 1967 book examined the struggle for control of the Democratic party that culminated in the 1920s and 1930s, a struggle pitting the agrarian white South against the immigrant neighborhoods of Northern cities. To show the support that Al Smith received in the North in the 1928 presidential election, Burner examined election returns between 1916 and 1932 for "homogeneous election districts" in New York, Chicago, and Boston. For each city, he claimed to have isolated precincts on the basis of ethnic homogeneity and to have then reported the total vote cast for president by all such districts of a given ethnic group. But the value of his data is limited. They are, first, at least for Boston, imperfect representations of the ethnic voting they purport to describe. Burner reported only an ''Italian vote'' for Boston, explaining that the Irish had already been sufficiently studied and that, based on his understanding of a 1930 census report, none ''of the other ethnic groups in Boston . . . [was] numerous enough in the government lists to assure accurate measurement''; those claims, obviously, are contested here. What is more baffling is the list of precincts chosen by Burner and identified as homogeneously Italian. Votes are reported for 1916 and the early 1920s for areas that did not become Italian until at least the late 1920s, all on the basis of a 1930 census. And his identification of Italian precincts was odd even for 1932. Burner reported as Italian the vote cast in seven precincts that year: according to the composition of first- and second-generation Americans living in those areas and reported in the 1930 census, four of the precincts included were at least 75 percent Italian (Burner's criterion for homogeneity) but three of the precincts were not, and an additional precinct which was not included at all was nearly 85 percent Italian. Equally important, even if the data had more obviously reflected the voting behavior of homogeneous districts, their utility to a study of the electoral sources of realignment would be limited. They report only the vote for president, they give no indication of levels of turnout or of the portion of the potential electorate actually casting votes, and the time series ends in 1932. While interesting, Burner's precinct data can tell us little about the mechanics of the New Deal realignment.[39]

A more impressive use of precinct data is made in *A House for All Peoples*, a 1971 work by John M. Allswang. The book examines the nature of ethnic politics in Chicago between the 1890s and 1930s, emphasizing the role of ethnic groups ''in the rise to unprecedented power of the Democratic party'' in that city in the years after the First World War. Allswang sought to understand the transformation of urban politics and took as his central questions: ''What was the role of ethnic groups in Chicago's politics, and to what extent was the changing political balance of power attributable to their political behavior?'' In seeking answers, Allswang, of course, studied the ties between Chicago politics and a realignment that affected all levels of the political system, but throughout the book he focused firmly on the question of urban political arrangements. Since he was concerned particularly with the behavior of ethnic groups and their relationship to each other, Allswang isolated and studied ethnically homogeneous precincts. The voting behavior of those precincts is described well, but there are real limitations to the data presented. Party registration figures before 1928 were not available for Chicago. Of greater importance, though, is that votes are reported only as shares of the total numbers cast; there is no indication given of changing levels of turnout, of the number of adults actively participating in the political system. Although one might argue that those issues were tangential to the study Allswang was conducting, their consideration is crucial to any investigation of the electoral underpinnings of the national political upheaval in the late 1920s and 1930s.[40]

Andersen began such an investigation with her 1979 book, but did not pursue it far. To demonstrate the importance of voter mobilization to the New Deal realignment, Andersen relied heavily on retrospective survey data. She expressed understandable concern, though, over "the questionable nature of these recall data." So, combining that concern with a positive interest in describing the realignment as it occurred in a major city, Andersen examined aggregate data from Chicago. Aiming to isolate small sections of the city which were "sufficiently homogeneous demographically," Andersen chose three sets of wards—"the six wards, or groups of wards, with the highest foreign-born population; two middle-class, lakefront, predominantly native-born wards; and a ward that was (and is) largely black." Andersen's criteria for categorizing wards, as well as the identity of the wards selected, were somewhat vague. Left unanswered were questions about the ethnic and socioeconomic profiles of the ward groupings and, especially in the case of the "foreign-stock" wards, their bulky size. The "foreign-stock" category was not only large; it also presumably encompassed a wide spectrum of immigrant groups, so Andersen proceeded to divide the "foreign-stock" wards along ethnic lines. One ward resulting from that division was characterized as Polish, Italian, and Russian, yet little ground exists for supposing that the voting behavior of such disparate groups moved in unison. Andersen, in analyzing ward-level partisan data, reported election returns as fractions of the potential electorate, not simply as fractions of all votes cast; that technique is essential to measuring the impact of new voters on electoral change, and its use nicely demonstrated the shortcomings of older studies that had examined only active voters. Still, the importance of that approach is nearly eclipsed by questions about the study. The group of "foreign-stock" wards, from the limited information we are given, may well have included an electorate nearly as large and as heterogeneous as that of the entire city of Boston. And Andersen's accompanying precinct analysis, which took advantage of the lists of ethnically homogeneous precincts generated by Allswang, was itself wanting. To estimate the relative roles played by voter conversion and mobilization in those precincts, Andersen constructed a model for which she had measures of the active electorate only. She was forced to silently assume that the size of the potential electorate, the total number of adults in the precincts eligible to vote, did not change between 1920 and 1936—that, over a period of sixteen years, neither slight changes in precinct boundaries nor larger movements of individuals resulted in an expansion or diminution of the base population. That assumption is not patently reasonable, and no evidence is offered to support it. Her analysis, too, for wards as well as for precincts, was restricted to the votes cast in presidential elections.[41]

The study presented in this book is rooted in a set of Boston precincts which have been identified as ethnically and socioeconomically homogeneous. Five broad ethnic divisions organize the book. Chapters 2 through 6 deal, in turn, with Jewish, Italian, black, Yankee, and Irish precincts; no other ethnic groups lived in Boston in tightly massed and large enough pockets to permit precinct study for the period between 1920 and 1940. Three of the chapters further divide precincts along socioeconomic or geographic lines. In all five chapters, only precincts of like ethnic and socioeconomic composition are grouped together. How those precincts were chosen is discussed in Appendix 1, and the list of precincts is contained in Appendix 2. In Appendix 3, the method used to compile raw voting and party registration data and to convert it into the forms reported in the text is reviewed. And Appendix 4 addresses questions of data presentation and statistical techniques.

The process of selecting precincts for this study was a lengthy and difficult one. As should be apparent in each of the chapters as well as in Appendix 1, much of the research involved locating ethnically homogeneous neighborhoods that existed in Boston between 1920 and 1940, establishing the boundaries of those neighborhoods and the ways in which the boundaries changed over time, and reconstructing the neighborhoods within the ephemeral lines of voting precincts. Several sources were used to verify the ethnic homogeneity of sections of the city and of specific precincts. Perhaps the most important were the published and unpublished summaries of the federal censuses of 1920, 1930, and 1940; depending on the year, summaries were available at the level of the ward, the census tract, or the city block. Settlement house studies, government studies, community studies conducted by religious or ethnic organizations, and personal accounts of a given neighborhood all proved important supplements to the censuses. Precinct boundaries changed several times, and for all but a few of those changes the only records are the verbal descriptions of the changes contained in official city documents. Once reconstructed, precinct maps were superimposed over ethnic maps for each of several moments in time. For blacks, the final determination of precincts was based on the accumulation of records and, especially, on settlement house reports and a 1940 census describing the racial composition of each of Boston's city blocks; for white ethnic groups, precincts were finally chosen after a review of the annual "police list," a list of city residents by precinct.

Ethnic homogeneity was the ultimate criterion for the selection of voting precincts for this study. Those precincts whose populations contained at least 80–85 percent of a single ethnic group were considered homogeneous;

precincts for which such high levels of ethnic concentration could not be shown have not been included in this study. While available sources have permitted the accurate identification of homogeneous precincts, they do not, unfortunately, allow measures of degree of homogeneity. It is not possible to give exact profiles of each precinct at a given point in time because, with the exception of the "police list," none of the sources reported any information at the level of the voting precinct; thus precincts could be identified only as subunits of one or more larger ethnic pockets. It is not possible, either, to give precise comparative measures of ethnicity for even clusters of precincts across time. The documents used to study ethnicity were extremely valuable for describing residential patterns at single points in time, but almost none of them applied identical methods of study to an earlier or later period. Certainly the federal censuses suffered from these limitations: they did not report information at the level of the voting precinct; they reported information for census tracts only in 1930 and 1940 and at the block level only in 1940; they reported different measures of ethnicity in different censuses; and, at best, they reported ethnicity in terms of racial distinctions and, for white immigrants, in terms of country of birth, resulting in the classification of Boston's Irish descendants as, simply, American-born. As rich as they were, the federal censuses obviously could not have been used on their own to locate ethnic neighborhoods. And even combined with other sources, they did not permit the calibration of degree of ethnicity for individual precincts or for groups of precincts across time.

That all the voting and registration data contained in this book are derived from precincts chosen, first, for their ethnic homogeneity, and then clustered according to socioeconomic or geographic variables, requires that any broad claims for the representative nature of these results be immediately disavowed. For a group like Boston's Irish, many of whom by the 1920s no longer lived in homogeneous neighborhoods, homogeneous precincts described only a minority. At the other extreme, homogeneous precincts encompassed a large majority of the city's Jewish population, which was packed tightly into one large district. It is fair to think that, since Boston's Jewish community was characterized by a high level of residential segregation, the votes of Jews in such areas more nearly represented their community than did the votes of Irish in homogeneous precincts. In neither case, however, is it claimed that entire ethnic groups were represented by those members living in ethnic neighborhoods. The men and women resident in ethnically and socioeconomically homogeneous districts were exposed to different influences and probably acted in different ways than their counterparts in more heterogeneous sections of the city.

I have chosen to isolate homogeneous voting precincts because of the better insights they can give into individual electoral behavior. Since we have no access to individual voting records from the 1920s and 1930s and since the period predates all but the most primitive public opinion surveys, the closest we can get to the individual is the homogeneous precinct—a small aggregate unit of individuals who, by a number of criteria deemed relevant for studies of voting and partisanship, look very much alike. We can never know for sure if they indeed acted politically so alike. But we can infer much about individual decisions from these precincts and learn even more about the actual behavior of small groups of similarly situated men and women.

Detailed information about the voting behavior and registration patterns of these Boston precincts has been well preserved. At the level of the precinct, there were regular counts of the total population of adults, reported separately for men and for women. The problems of generational change and residential mobility, which are not directly visible in such counts, are discussed in Appendix 4. There were counts made every two years of the total number of registered voters by precinct, listing the number of registered Democrats and the number of registered Republicans; again, all of this information was reported separately for women and for men. And, of course, there were election returns. For this study, votes were tallied for three offices. Reported in this book are votes cast for senator in the General Court of the Commonwealth of Massachusetts, a position more commonly known, especially in states whose legislatures are not referred to as ''general courts'' and whose polities make no professed claims to be ''commonwealths,'' as state senator; for representative in the United States Congress; and for electors of the president and vice-president of the United States. Appendix 3 contains the method used for translating data from these raw sources into the finished form in which it is presented in the text.

Most registration and voting statistics are reported in this book as proportions of the whole potential electorate of a given group of precincts. As an example, the adult population for each precinct cluster is broken down into those registered as Democrats, those registered as Republicans, those registered to vote without a party identification, and those not registered to vote at all. In order to gauge the extent of nonvoting and its possible impact on the party system through mobilization, we must measure it as carefully as we measure the relative percentages of a two-party vote.

It is, then, essential to distinguish the active electorate from the potential electorate. The active electorate includes all men and women registered to vote; one smaller group within the active electorate is the body of voters at any particular election. Most previous scholars have studied change only within the active electorate. But that electorate is itself only a portion of the potential electorate. ''The potential electorate includes both the naturalized and the nonnaturalized, the registered and the unregistered,'' wrote Andersen. ''These attributes can be seen as the result of political decisions; like the decision to vote or not to vote, they are affected by the candidates, issues, and campaigns at a particular time.''[42] Residential and generational change aside—both, it is argued in Appendix 4, are processes of population replacement which, especially in consistently homogeneous areas, should not of themselves upset the existing partisan balance—the potential electorate represents the pool from which the active electorate draws new members. Every adult in the potential electorate could conceivably exercise her franchise, but many do not today and did not in the 1920s and 1930s. It does, of course, take considerably longer for a recent immigrant to be naturalized than for a native-born citizen to register to vote, but each, at least in a long-term perspective, is part of the potential electorate. Excellent measures of the potential electorate were made in the frequent counts of adult women and men in each of Boston's voting precincts. Those regular tabulations represented the exertions of city government to obtain precise figures of the potential electorate of Boston, the number of its residents of voting age. As I have already mentioned, there were in cities like Boston many members of the potential electorate who were not participating in the political system in the 1920s. Long-term trends toward a demobilization of the electorate since the turn of the century had shrunk the size of the active electorate relative to the potential electorate. Those trends in the general population were exacerbated by the many men and women whose introduction to active political participation was still recent in the 1920s: immigrants and their children and, of course, all women.

Throughout the book, questions of timing are central. It is one conclusion of this book that the timing of political change varied from place to place, from neighborhood to neighborhood, from individual to individual, within the same city. A generous time frame of twenty years is examined to permit some understanding of the pace of realignment and of its extent among various groups. We are concerned, above all, with the mechanics of that realignment. So we trace the relative impact of Al Smith and Franklin Roosevelt, of national politics and local politics, on the electorates we study. This book seeks, too, to understand the extent of new-voter mobilization between 1920 and 1940, of the accretions to the active electorate beyond the normal pattern of generational and residential change. To discover if voter conversion within the active electorate occurred at critical periods, certain shorter periods of time are isolated for particular clusters of precincts. In such short frames of time, mobilization would appear as a sudden surge in the size of the voting population, while conversion would explain a sudden and permanent shift in party fortunes without such a surge.

That both registration and voting records are extant permits particularly careful consideration of the relative significance of mobilization and conversion to the New Deal realignment. Two extreme cases help to illustrate their joint value. Assume, on the one hand, that conversion is the only explanation of the political upheaval. In a stable electorate, no new voters (again excepting the young and new residents) entered the active electorate even as realignment occurred. A group initially solidly Republican, even after it had realigned, would only slowly reveal that realignment in its party registration figures. Just as we cannot recognize a realignment until long after it has occurred, so voters could not have realized at the time that they had forever abandoned the Republican party with their first votes for Roosevelt. On the other hand, assume that the mobilization of new voters accounted for the entire realignment. The New Deal party system, with its attendant cleavages, was presumably able to attract new voters to the active electorate precisely because of the nature of those new cleavages. Those new voters who entered the active electorate because of Roosevelt and the party he represented would naturally, it seems, have registered as Democrats, at least if they chose a party. Where conversion was the dominant mechanism of realignment, as in the first scenario, changes in registration patterns would lag considerably behind the actual critical change in party identification. But in the second scenario, where mobilization was dominant, there would be little or no time lag between the moment of realignment and its reflection in party registration figures.

More than its rich records recommend Boston for a study of the political changes of the 1920s and 1930s. As one of the largest cities in the country and as a city with a particularly large immigrant population, Boston swayed to the appeals made by the Democratic party in that era. It, with other urban centers in the Northeast and Midwest, was a primary component of the new national Democratic coalition. Dominated by the Irish and with large Jewish and Italian populations, Boston distinguished itself for its solid support of Smith in 1928 and has continued to be a bulwark of the Democratic party in the years since. It is to Boston that V. O. Key, Jr., Samuel Lubell, and subsequent scholars have looked for the case study of the Al Smith Revolution and the seeds of the New Deal realignment.[43] If any city was realigned, if anywhere the realignment occurred in 1928 rather than in the 1930s, if anywhere the mobilization of first- and second-generation Americans overshadowed conversion within the active electorate, it was Boston. Many of the forces which helped reshape American political parties in the 1930s operated with special energy in the city on a hill.

The ethnic groups which dominated Boston have long been recognized for their roles in the politics of the era. While the Irish had been Democratic long before Smith sought the presidency, and the Yankees, those men and women of ancient stock who were building their homes on Beacon Hill when their own John Adams was moving into the White House, were unswervingly

Republican, Boston contained three newer groups whose party allegiances were affected deeply in the New Deal era. The campaign of 1928 and the elections of Roosevelt drew to the Democratic party the new immigrant groups of Jews and Italians as well as those most traditionally Republican of all Americans, blacks. Jews and Italians had begun arriving in large numbers in the 1880s and had continued to come until the First World War and the federal government imposed severe immigration restrictions. Boston's black community, much smaller than either of the two groups of recent immigrants, also began to expand in those years. Proud of their roots in the city's past, blacks born in Boston welcomed to the city migrants from the South and from abroad.

The 1920s and 1930s, though, were a relatively quiet time for Boston. Immigration was nearly ended, and, unlike many other Northern cities, Boston experienced no massive in-migration of Southern blacks. Politically, Democratic Boston was engaged throughout much of this period in a struggle with a Republican state legislature eager to impose its will on the apparently corrupt Irish Democrats who controlled City Hall. James Michael Curley was the preeminent local political figure in those years, but his power never approached that of machine bosses in other major cities. There were, to be sure, ward bosses in Boston, but their geographical influence was limited and their importance was waning, as the Irish hierarchy struggled to maintain control over a changing city many of whose voters were not Irish.[44]

Maps of Boston immediately follow this chapter. The entire city is shown in map 1. In maps 2 and 3 are shown in greater detail two sections of the city. Map 2 illustrates the core of the city, the peninsula jutting into Boston Harbor and the teeming, crowded, poor neighborhoods and elegant, upper-class areas surrounding the business district. And map 3 shows the neighborhoods of Roxbury and Dorchester, formerly independent towns annexed to the central city to accommodate its expanding population and to share in its services. Boston, at least since the 1840s, has been a city of strong ethnic divisions. Its patterns of residential districts and its politics have attested to the power of ethnicity for one full century and for half, so far, of a second century. Much of this book is devoted to a recreation of the neighborhoods and lives of the political actors whom we study. In part, of course, the history is valuable for its own sake. And in part, it is necessary to establish the objective homogeneity of the selected precincts. But, above all, history is woven into the book because of the insights it brings into the lives of those people whose registration and voting records stand at the center of this study of the time. Context does matter.

We come to Boston and we invade the memories buried in its precinct records as part of a larger design. It is our purpose to investigate the thick web of decisions, acted upon and abdicated, which occurred in the 1920s and 1930s. In many ways, of course, the New Deal realignment represented an aberrant moment in American political history. Aspects of the time proved anachronistic. What occurred in the 1930s and in the decade or two which followed was a sudden flaring up of a way of conducting politics which had lain dormant since the turn of the century. That political upheaval was the final legacy of the nineteenth-century "party period," peculiar to its own century and to all other realignments because it occurred three full decades after the drift from parties had begun.

Yet for all their strangeness, something about the events of that era lingers on in us. Their impact on scholarship, as much as on contemporary politics, remains profound. The upheaval of the 1930s, the only realignment in the "post-party" years after 1900, became the model and prototype of the concept of political realignment that emerged in the 1950s. In its aftermath, political scientists concluded that events of equal significance had occurred in the alignment formed in the 1830s and in the realignments of the 1850s and 1890s. No matter that the 1930s and our time are part of a new age: not since before the nation was rent asunder in civil war, after all, has a wholly new major political party been invented—in that respect, the events of the 1830s and 1850s were quite different from the events of the 1890s and 1930s, since realignment was probably more profound when all bases of continuity had evaporated—and the 1930s has been the only realignment in the age after the dissolution of the "party period." But that new and peculiar age is our age. The New Deal realignment was one of the great formative experiences of the "post-party period." It gave renewed, if temporary, vigor to political parties and helped create fierce party attachments which have corroded only slowly. Not since has the party system been so suddenly and thoroughly transformed.

We look at the behavior underlying that realignment to understand the mechanisms of past political change and the prospects for current and future change. One of the most important findings of this book is that there was no single realignment in the 1920s or 1930s. American politics, of course, changed in those years, and that change is etched deep into the records of homogeneous voting precincts in Boston. But, as we shall see, the New Deal realignment was a rubric for a broad number of smaller changes. That those smaller events all happened in a compressed period of time, that many resulted from issues with national scope, and that most of the change was in the direction of a single political party all have contributed to the deeply held impression that a massive upheaval occurred in that era. But the realignment was effected by delicate decisions independently arrived at. Many voters switched parties and many entered the active electorate for the first time during this period. Yet many more voters—including most of Boston's Irish and upper-class Yankees and such vast national groups as white Southerners—passed through the 1930s with their partisan affiliations and patterns of participation relatively undisturbed. By examining the New Deal realignment, we examine our last bridge to the great political changes of the nineteenth century. We examine, too, the roots in individual behavior of continuity and realignment in our own time. And so we return to Boston, a birthplace of realignment theory as it was devised by Key and Lubell, with a mission of reinterpretation. That the political balance changed in the 1930s is no object of dispute. How men and women came to effect that change and what insights those patterns of behavior bring to the larger study of American politics are questions which must be answered. Let us now begin to address them.

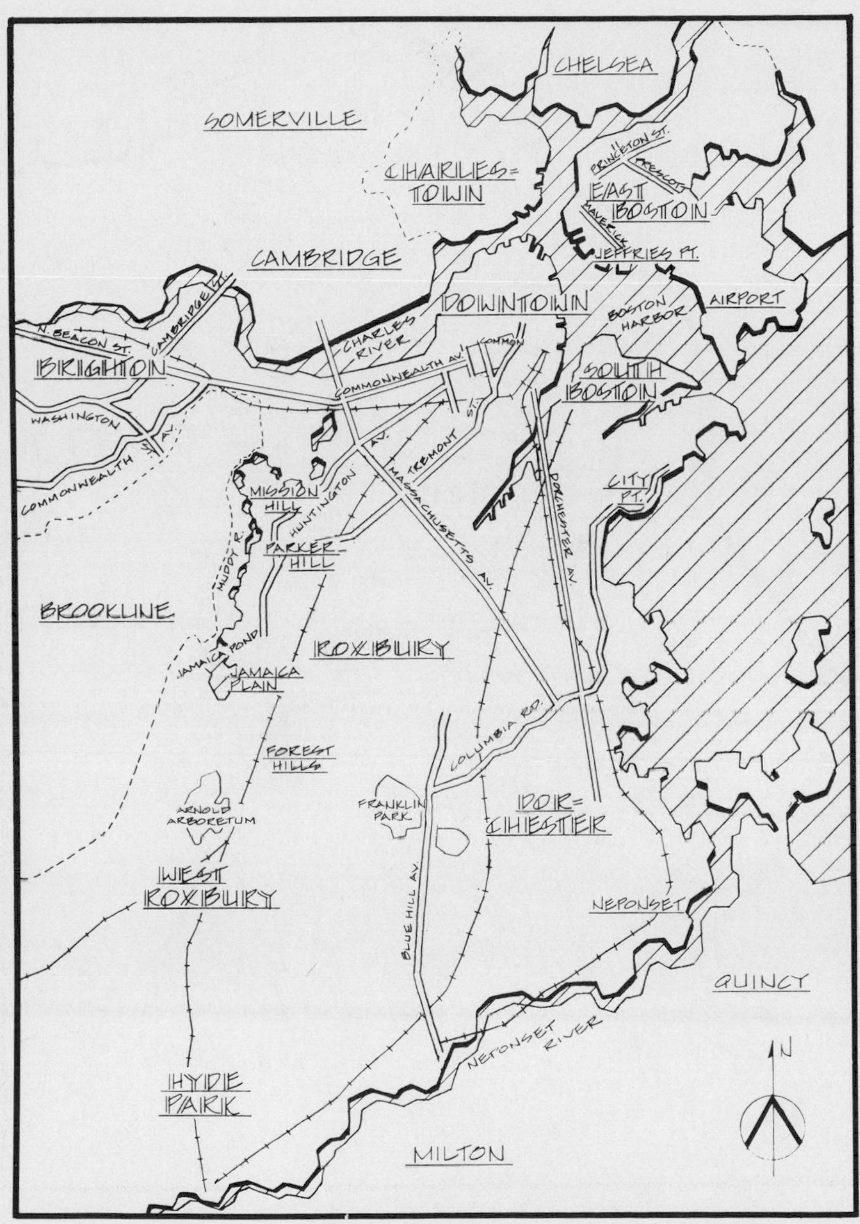

MAP 1 City of Boston

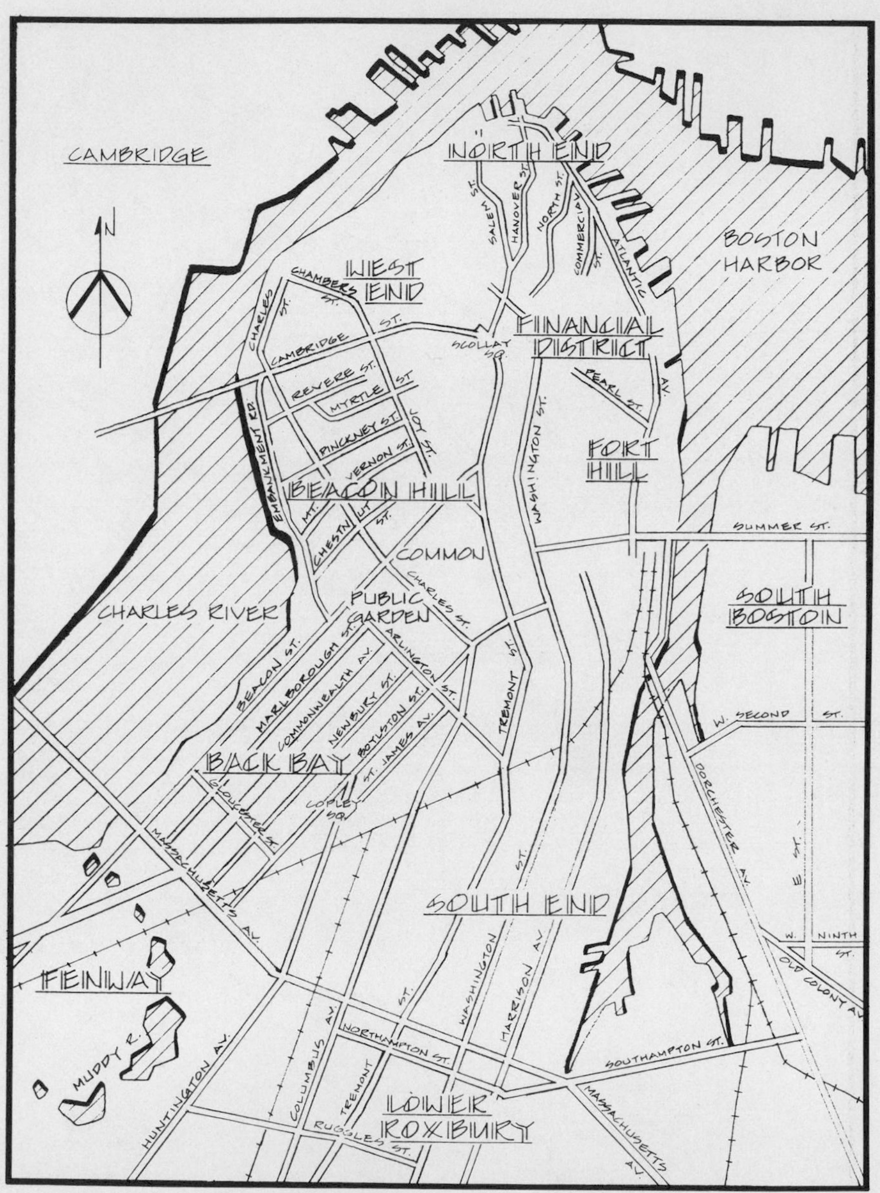

MAP 2 Downtown Boston and Its Neighborhoods

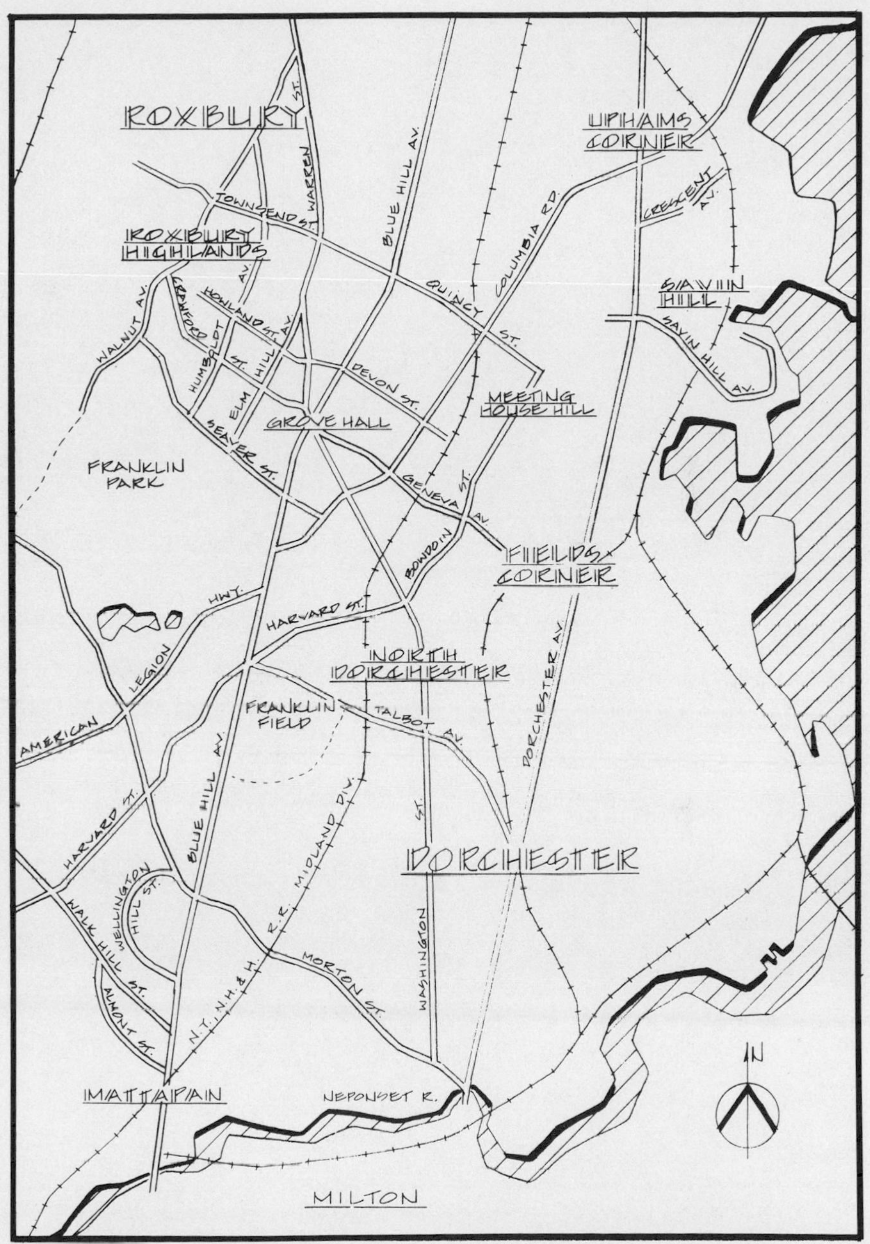

MAP 3 Roxbury and Dorchester

2

The Jews

In the late 1920s and in the 1930s, a transformation of great magnitude revolutionized the political configuration of Boston's Jews. Past studies have emphasized the realignment among Jews from the Republican to the Democratic party, but data from Boston suggest the confluence of other, equally fascinating, events. Perhaps most notably, a community which had consistently voted and registered along sharp class lines became a solid ethnic bloc, voting thoroughly Democratic by 1936 at all socioeconomic levels even as party registration figures continued to reflect past, class-based cleavages.

Further, the timing of that realignment places the most critical election in 1932, with important, even critical, aftershocks in 1936 and 1938. What has often been perceived as the critical election for Jews and for many other ethnic groups—the 1928 candidacy of Al Smith—was, in fact, at least for the Jews of Boston, a deviating election. Jews appear to have voted in 1928 for the person and not for the party: Governor Smith received the support of Jews despite, not because of, the Democratic party whose ticket he headed. Although the 1928 election helped ease the ensuing period of realignment, it was not until they cast their ballots for Roosevelt four years later that Jews began to register in significant numbers as Democrats and to desert the Republican party.

The movement of Jews as a group to the Democratic party was due only partly to the mobilization of new voters; conversion of existing members of the electorate was also crucial to that massive shift in party allegiance. What had occurred in those precincts in the 1930s was a decisive realignment, especially as measured by the votes cast for national office. By 1936 and 1940, Roosevelt was receiving overwhelming support from Boston's Jewish voters. In that realignment partisan registration attachments lagged considerably behind changed voting behavior, recalling the scenario outlined earlier of the relationship between the vote and registration during periods of conversion. Registered Republicans had actually become Democratic voters by 1940. Critical realignment by both mobilization and conversion—and not, as others have suggested, secular realignment—apparently characterized the political transformation of Boston's Jews in this period.

While broad conclusions are rarely justified by the example of one community, Boston's Jews have been the subject of much study over the years, and lessons drawn from their political behavior have often been accorded a more general importance. Ward Fourteen, predominantly Jewish and the center of New England's Jewish population for decades after the 1925 ward redistricting, has had a particularly prominent place in discussions of national Jewish political behavior and the New Deal realignment. The ward, which follows Blue Hill Avenue through North Dorchester and Mattapan, gained distinction for its great concentration of middle-class Jews. "Candidates campaigning for President—from Roosevelt to Truman to Eisenhower to Adlai Stevenson and John F. Kennedy—found it obligatory to stop by the G&G deli on Blue Hill avenue, the center of Jewish political activity in the area."[1] That practical acknowledgment of the importance of the ward has been duplicated in the scholarship of several political scientists. Lawrence Fuchs, in his 1956 book, *The Political Behavior of American Jews,* relies extensively on data obtained from Ward Fourteen in Boston for his analysis. Not only does he regularly feature voting and registration figures from Boston, but, "in order to probe further the salient motivations of Jewish voters in a big city, a systematic sample of the eligible voters in Boston's Ward 14 were interviewed." Drawing on Fuchs's findings, V. O. Key would describe shifts in party registration in that ward between 1928 and 1952 as an important example of the phenomenon of secular realignment described in his 1959 article. Later, in their discussion of the role of Jews in the emergence of the New Deal party system, Ladd and Hadley would similarly cite statistics from Boston.[2]

By 1920, Jews constituted one of the four great immigrant groups of Boston. Census figures for that year indicate that, among the foreign-born white, only the Irish outnumbered Jewish immigrants; nearly as numerous as the Jews were Canadians and Italians. Those four groups of immigrants would continue to be completely dominant and roughly equal in size at least through the censuses of 1930 and 1940. Federal immigration restrictions imposed in the early 1920s—combined with only a trickle of Southern black migrants—had effectively frozen into place the demographic composition of the city for the next generation. In 1920, white immigrants and their children numbered 548,674 persons, or over 73 percent, of the total city population of 748,060. Within ten years, as the population of Boston grew to 781,188, an increase in the size of the second generation nudged the total foreign-stock figure up to 558,626, still almost 72 percent of the city. Finally, by 1940, the reluctance of the United States to accept immigrants between the world wars was manifested in a sharp decline in the number of foreign-stock Bostonians: only 480,284 persons, or 62 percent of a total city population which itself had shrunk to 770,816, were born abroad or born in America to an immigrant parent.[3]

Throughout this period, a number of estimates were made of the size of the Jewish population in Boston. As late as 1875, there were only about 3,000 Jews in the city, most of them of German origin who had immigrated in the middle of the century. Real growth in the size of the Jewish community began in the late 1880s with the onset of immigration from Eastern Europe, so that by 1895 the number of Jews had increased to 20,000. That figure doubled to 40,000 within seven years, and, then, "between 1900 and 1914 they formed the largest racial bloc coming into the state." Jews by 1917 numbered 77,500, making up 10 percent of Boston's total population. That figure continued to rise. By 1927, according to one calculation, there were 90,000 Jews in Boston, over 11 percent of the city's population; a study in 1930 counted 102,000 Jews. Apparently the size of the Boston Jewish community peaked around 1930 and, after that year, began a slow but steady decline. One estimate, which was probably low, suggested that by 1940 the number of Jews in Boston proper had fallen to 91,000, still 12 percent of the entire population of the city.[4]

Reconstructing the geographic distribution of Boston Jews for the period spanning 1920 to 1940 was one of the great challenges of the present study. Many previous works have described the movement of Jews among Boston's neighborhoods only in broad and inexact terms. Even more frustrating, those secondary sources that do claim to detail matters of timing and precise locations differ sharply from each other in their conclusions, and for no period are their analyses more glaringly divergent than the 1920s.

The most significant single issue in this regard is the movement of Jews toward a vast belt of neighborhoods branching off of Blue Hill Avenue and Seaver Street. That area—which reached from Roxbury highlands, or upper Roxbury, in the north, through North Dorchester, and south into Mattapan—had become, by the 1940s, the most important Jewish concentration in the Northeast outside of New York. What scholars do not agree on, however, is the essential matter of when that influx and era of Jewish hegemony began. Jews, according to one account, had begun to move to Roxbury by the 1910s. But, in a recent study of the Boston Jewish community, it is stated that "the Jewish move to the previously Yankee neighorhoods of Roxbury, Dorchester and Mattapan began slowly in the mid-1920s" and that not for another twenty years would Blue Hill Avenue "become the center of Jewish life in Boston." Indeed, there are occasionally serious internal contradictions within single works. One popular scenario, for example, appears to require a process of sudden, even instantaneous, population displacement. An important Boston historian claims that "the relocation of Boston's Jewish community during the first years of the 1930s in Roxbury, Dorchester, and Mattapan displaced Irish residents, exacerbating tensions," while at the same time arguing that by 1936 "the greater part of Boston's Jewish community had settled" in those same neighborhoods. This pattern of widespread confusion and inconsistency over the timing of the Jewish movement thoroughly pervades most historical accounts of the period.[5]

To construct the following account of Jewish population concentrations and shifts, extensive use was made of censuses, lists of residents by street, community studies, and many other surviving documents. All the primary sources consulted were mutually reinforcing and consistent. They together tell a story which is valuable to any examination of Boston's Jewish population, but especially to a voting study which purports to study that population at the precinct level.

The North End was the first neighborhood in Boston to attract Eastern European Jewish immigrants when, in the 1880s, they began arriving in substantial numbers. By 1900, Salem Street had become the main artery of a teeming, congested Jewish village. Soon, however, as thousands of immigrants continued to enter the city each year, Jews formed communities in other sections of Boston as well. A synagogue was established in East Boston in 1892, and by 1900 that area's Jewish population was increasing rapidly. The South End, too, was attracting many Jews during the same period. *City Wilderness,* the 1898 report of the South End House edited by Robert Woods, reported that, while the Irish were still the dominant group in the South End, the number of Jews was growing quickly, and some areas were already "pretty much in the hands of Russian and Polish Jews."[6]

By far the most important Jewish concentration in Boston during this period was the West End. From the late 1890s and for at least the next crucial decade of immigration, it was without rival as the center of the city's Jewish community. A 1902 study by Robert Woods and the South End House, *Americans in Process,* showed the thorough domination by Jews, even at that relatively early point, of the West End's northern half, with the population sprawled around Chambers Street. Elsewhere in that study, estimates suggested that about 14,000 Jews lived in the West End in 1895 and that as many as 20,000 Jews may have been living in the area by 1900. Soon, the 1902 report concluded, the West End would become an entirely Jewish section. Just one year later, Frederick Bushee, in *Ethnic Factors in the Population of Boston,* would neatly summarize the dynamics of the city's Jewish distribution. "The Jews," he observed, "have already taken almost exclusive possession of the northern part of the West End, and in the South End and in East Boston they are becoming numerous.''[7]

While the West End continued to grow in numbers—by 1910, it contained a Jewish population of 30,000—and in importance well into the 1910s, Jews had begun to move to a new district which was even then developing into the largest and best documented community in the history of Boston Jewry, its last urban center before its dispersal to suburbs. The Jewish settlement of Roxbury and northern sections of North Dorchester began to attract attention in 1908, as Eastern European Jews, left homeless by the fire that year in the city of Chelsea, chose to make the short trip southward to reestablish their lives in Boston. Within four years, several thousand Jews lived in the area. Describing the influx from the vantage of the 1910s, Robert Woods and Albert Kennedy of the South End House remarked that ''the Chelsea Fire marked the beginning of an immigration of Russian Jews which has yet to cease.'' From their small area of initial settlement, already it had grown obvious that ''the Jews have extended their colony in every direction'' in Roxbury and adjacent North Dorchester. That section of the city—which had for years, especially in Roxbury, contained a number of assimilated German and English Jews—was quickly distinguished for its great superiority over other Jewish areas in the city in terms of housing and living conditions. Although some of the neighborhoods in North Dorchester attracting the poorer Jews were filled with crowded tenements, the bulk of the expanse of territory in the vicinities of Seaver Street and Blue Hill Avenue soon boasted the respectable three-deckers and even single-family homes of a population rising into the middle class.[8]

Other Jewish concentrations in Boston subsequently began to decline as the more desirable settlements in North Dorchester and Roxbury expanded. By 1920, Italians in the North End had completely displaced the Jews who had once lived there. In other Jewish sections, already bad living conditions deteriorated miserably as the more successful Jews abandoned their old neighborhoods. The City Planning Board reported in 1915 that in East Boston ''the character of the Jewish section has not been kept up; it is rather dirty and unattractive and much in need of repairs, due in part to the slackness and indifference of the occupants who still remain.'' In general, East Boston's Jews ''aspire to better surroundings and the more prosperous families move away.'' A Jewish population in East Boston of about 5,000 people in 1920 had, by the end of the decade, dwindled to barely 1,000. Similarly, in the South End, the flow of incoming Jews slowed and the community there started to move elsewhere as blacks began to enter the area in large numbers. The housing in the South End had grown so poor that this once vital Jewish center was quickly being transformed into a section for only the most desperate

Jews, who would live there only until they could find more permanent housing elsewhere in Boston.[9]

Even the West End Jewish population had ceased growing by the mid-1910s and, by 1920, pressed by encroaching Italians and Poles, it began to fall sharply. A community in 1920 of over 20,000 fell to 8,000 by 1930. In 1938, just 3,080 Jews remained. The West End, the most important Jewish area in Boston for almost two decades, could not be included in this voting study. Careful examination of the names of West End residents on street lists indicates that by 1940 no voting precinct remained in the West End that could be accurately characterized as Jewish.[10]

Old institutions in the West End lingered there long after the vast majority of Jews had left for Dorchester, Roxbury, and Mattapan. As early as the 1910s, though, most subsequent major institutions were established in the newer neighborhoods along Blue Hill Avenue and Seaver Street, indicating that, even by that period, Jews had grown aware that their center of population had shifted dramatically. In 1911, the YMHA, the Young Men's Hebrew Association, moved from the South End to the corner of Warren and Howland Streets in Roxbury. Beth Israel Hospital was established in 1915 and found its first home the following year on Roxbury's Townsend Street, in what in 1916 was considered "Boston's largest Jewish center." When it established district centers in 1918, the Federated Jewish Charities recognized five sections in the city—Roxbury, Dorchester, East Boston, the West End, and the South End—demonstrating the swiftness with which the first two areas had attracted large Jewish populations, real migration having begun but ten years earlier. Hebrew Teachers College was established in 1921 on Crawford Street, again in Roxbury. And, by 1920, there were about twelve synagogues serving the emerging Jewish community in the area.[11]

Indeed, so rapid had been the growth of Jewish neighborhoods in Roxbury and Dorchester that at least one 1921 observer was of the opinion that "Roxbury has about reached its point of saturation" as a potential destination for further Jews. The concentration of Jews in Roxbury highlands and north of Talbot Avenue and Franklin Field in North Dorchester was well established by 1920, although there remained gaps within that territory which Jews had yet to fully infiltrate. In the 1920s, Jews would fill in those remaining areas as well as leapfrog to the southern end of North Dorchester and to Mattapan, creating by the early 1930s a solid stretch of settlement down most of the length of Blue Hill Avenue. That movement further south to Mattapan was anticipated in 1921 by Ben Rosen in his *The Trend of Jewish Population in Boston*. Even in that early year, the "two large Jewish centers" of Roxbury and northern Dorchester were "losing part of their Jewish population: the well-to-do class, who are moving to districts outside of Boston City." Those neighborhoods had by then passed through their period of major growth, "and at all events the Jewish community there will not increase as rapidly or to such an extent as [the southern parts of North] Dorchester [and Mattapan]." Already by 1920, the section just west of Franklin Field, enclosed by Blue Hill Avenue, the American Legion Highway, and Morton Street, was nearly 80 percent Jewish, and Jews were continuing to move into neighboring areas, "Mattapan-way."[12]

The Jewish neighborhoods of North Dorchester and Mattapan included a great swath of territory by the early 1930s—from Quincy Street on the north; to the N.Y., N.H. & H. R.R. Midland Division lines on the east; to the intersection of the railroad lines with Blue Hill Avenue at the Jewish belt's southern extreme; to Almont Street, Walk Hill Street, Harvard Street, Morton Street, American Legion Highway, and Blue Hill Avenue on the west. In upper Roxbury, into parts of which blacks were beginning to move during this period, the solid Jewish settlement as late as 1940 covered the areas bounded by Seaver Street, Walnut Avenue, Crawford Street, Humboldt Avenue, Townsend and Quincy Streets, and Blue Hill Avenue. Precincts were chosen from within these districts, which can be located on map 3.

Francis Russell, an old-stock Protestant who as a boy had lived on Mattapan's Wellington Hill, recalled the steady advance of the Jewish community southward, wave after wave displacing Yankee and Irish neighborhoods alike. Born one decade into the twentieth century, he recalled that "in [his] childhood nobody gave a thought to that new influx a few miles north, although even by then the section near Franklin Field had begun to be called Jewville." But, as time passed, Jewish shops "began to appear along Blue Hill Avenue, starting at Franklin Park, and each year creeping closer to Dorchester [Wellington] Hill. Side street after side street, district after district, became solidly Jewish." The Jewish community of Dorchester and Mattapan "increased yearly like a spreading ripple." Finally, just after the First World War, a home in his own neighborhood was sold to a Jewish family and a "year later half the old families on the Hill had moved away." Speaking from the perspective of the young boy uprooted by mysterious forces rather than of the mature writer recalling the moment years afterward, Russell described those families who had taken over Mattapan's Wellington Hill. "Most of those moving in had been born in Poland, but they had come to America as young men, had learned a Yiddish-inflected English, and though they were not far removed from the ghetto, considered themselves Americans. We considered them Jews." For those Jews, Wellington Hill would become one of the most desirable neighborhoods in the area.[13]

The 1920 census counted about 14,000 Jews in Roxbury and 22,000 Jews in the northern end of North Dorchester. Mattapan and southern sections of

North Dorchester, not as densely settled or as heavily Jewish in 1920 as the two older communities, together contained about 15,000 Jews. By 1930, all three neighborhoods were tightly packed, and their populations remained stable over the next decade. Statistics from 1930 and 1940 suggest that there were in those years about 78,000 Jews in the area. In 1940, there were 16,000 Jews in Roxbury, 29,000 in the northern portions of North Dorchester, and 33,000 in the rest of North Dorchester and in Mattapan. The distribution of Jews among those neighborhoods changed little between the late 1920s and the mid-1940s. By 1930, the net influx into this district was ending, due to, in the words of a 1940 study, "the reduction in immigration, the decreased birth rate, and more lately, the movement of Boston residents to the suburbs"—factors which were affecting all of Boston. Many of those leaving the area were wealthier Jews, moving out to such suburbs as Brookline and Newton, who were replaced by Jews continuing to come from areas like Chelsea and the West End.[14]

Like much of the older Roxbury and northern Dorchester sections, the areas rapidly filling with Jews in the 1920s in southern North Dorchester and Mattapan were generally lower-middle-class communities. The belt of Jewish settlement along Blue Hill Avenue was created by thousands of immigrants—as well as their children—who had achieved genuine upward social mobility since their arrival in America twenty or thirty years earlier. According to a 1940 study, Jewish men, relative to their non-Jewish neighbors, were much more inclined to be engaged in trade, while Jewish women were especially likely "to leave gainful employment to become housewives." Stephan Thernstrom, in *The Other Bostonians,* discovered that in 1909 an astounding 45 percent of Jewish men were engaged "in business for profit." Certainly, he points out, "many of these Jewish 'businessmen' were doubtless mere peddlers with very low incomes. . . . But that the Jews were heavily concentrated in callings that involved risk-taking and developed business skills was nonetheless very significant for the economic future of the group." As he later concludes in his examination of Jewish occupations, "Popular folklore concerning the mobility achievements of the Jews is indeed well founded." An emphasis on education and on other cultural determinants of socioeconomic success thrust Boston's Jews into the middle class with amazing rapidity.[15]

Statistics from the 1940 census attest to the socioeconomic status of the Jewish neighborhoods examined here. The area of lower-middle-class settlement was vast, encompassing all but two of the ten Jewish census tracts. It included the entire district in North Dorchester and Mattapan south of Devon Street (census tracts T-7A, T-7B, T-8A, X-5A, X-5B, and X-6A), and it also included those sections of upper Roxbury which were neither part of the upper-middle-class Jewish district in the streets closest to Franklin Park nor part of the black district slowly expanding outward from its center at Humboldt Avenue and Townsend Street (U-5, U-6A). Table 2.1 presents socioeconomic measures for the ten census tracts which were homogeneously Jewish in the 1930s; although tract U-5 contained a large black population by 1940, only precincts in Jewish sections of the tract were selected. The information in table 2.1 is from the 1940 census, but similar measures from the 1930 census and from other accounts of the area suggest that there were no fundamental changes in the socioeconomic status of each of the tracts during the 1920 and 1930s. By a variety of measures, the eight lower-middle-class tracts exhibited remarkable uniformity. Median gross monthly rents ranged from $42 to $48, about two-thirds of the homes contained mechanical refrigerators, and nearly all of them were centrally heated. The median education of the adult population in these census tracts ranged from 8.3 to 9.7 years of schooling, and between 5.3 and 9.4 percent of the population were professional workers.

Besides these eight lower-middle-class census tracts, there were two others from which precincts were chosen. One was significantly poorer (T-6) and the other was significantly wealthier (U-6B) than most of the Jewish district. Since all ten tracts were contiguous and contained equally high concentrations of Jews, the only salient differences among them were socioeconomic. This

Table 2.1 Socioeconomic Indices for Jewish Neighborhoods in 1940, by Census Tract

Census Tract	% Foreign-Born White	% Naturalized per Foreign-Born	Population per Occupied Dwelling Unit	Median School Years Completed	% Professional Workers	Median Gross Monthly Rent, Dollars	% Mechanical Refrigerator	% Central Heating
T-6	37.0	52	4.13	8.2	4.3	36.09	45	81
T-7A	32.3	64	3.92	9.1	7.7	45.66	68	88
T-7B	37.7	61	4.16	9.3	7.9	43.26	67	95
T-8A	36.7	62	4.24	9.7	8.3	47.65	73	98
U-5*	23.0	64	4.29	9.1	7.5	42.07	61	87
U-6A	34.5	63	4.28	8.8	9.4	44.45	71	93
X-5A	40.3	58	4.37	8.4	6.3	44.87	62	98
X-5B	37.7	58	4.11	8.3	5.4	45.28	60	94
X-6A	37.7	62	4.38	8.9	5.3	47.92	69	99
U-6B	32.3	78	3.68	12.1	12.6	53.60	99	100

Source: United States Department of Commerce, Bureau of the Census, *16th Census of the United States, 1940, Population and Housing—Statistics for Census Tracts—Boston, Mass.* (Washington: United States Government Printing Office, 1942).

*Sections of tract U-5 were heavily occupied by blacks.

pattern of socioeconomic segregation within an ethnically segregated area was significant enough to permit the study of two clusters of precincts in addition to the lower-middle-class cluster.

Tract T-6, the northernmost section of Jewish Dorchester—bounded roughly by Quincy Street, Blue Hill Avenue, Devon Street, and the N.Y., N.H. & H. R.R. Midland Division railroad tracks—was a working-class area. Only 45 percent of the homes in that neighborhood contained mechanical refrigerators and only 81 percent had central heating; the median monthly rent was just above $36. The median level of education was only slightly below that in some of the lower-middle-class Jewish tracts, but very few adults, 4.3 percent of the population, were engaged in professional occupations. Whereas about 61 percent of the foreign-born population in the lower-middle-class neighborhoods was naturalized, only 52 percent of the same group in tract T-6 had become citizens. In the context of its initial settlement by Jews from Chelsea, Francis Russell describes conditions which would persist here. "The Jews," Russell recalls, "first took over the more congested sections [of North Dorchester] near Roxbury, already built up with three-deckers. Because of their poverty, three or four families moved in where one had lived before. . . . Still, Dorchester was an improvement on Chelsea, and those who prospered spread out and moved to better homes in other parts of town." The economic character of this tract, while average for Boston, still placed it noticeably below the other Jewish tracts in this part of the city.[16]

On the other extreme, and treated in this study as an upper-middle-class neighborhood, was tract U-6B. This tract, the sliver of Roxbury highlands just north of Franklin Park, had been, in the latter decades of the nineteenth century, the choicest part of an island of respectable and comfortable Protestants in a sea of working-class Irish. "In ethnic and occupational characteristics," relates Sam Bass Warner, Jr., in *Streetcar Suburbs,* "its population resembled that of the outer suburbs where most of the central and upper segments of the middle class were then building their homes." Although Roxbury highlands encompassed all of what would become the Jewish section of Roxbury, still in the late 1800s "the social status of the land and the size of the houses increased as one approached Franklin Park." Tract U-6B—the neighborhood within Humboldt Avenue, Crawford Street, Warren Street, Blue Hill Avenue, and Seaver Street—maintained its socioeconomic distinctiveness well into the twentieth century, as table 2.1 shows, even as Jews inundated it and all the surrounding districts, replacing former Protestant and Irish Catholic residents. Median monthly rent in the area was $53.60, every home was centrally heated, and 99 percent of the homes had mechanical refrigerators. While the proportion of foreign-born men and women in the population was no lower than that in parts of the lower-middle-class area, fully 78 percent of them in tract U-6B were naturalized. Professional workers made up 12.6 percent of the working population. Most impressive was the median level of education; the average adult in this largely foreign-stock Jewish neighborhood had gone to college. Such indices not only placed this tract much higher on the economic scale than any other Jewish neighborhood but actually made it one of the most select tracts in the entire city.[17]

That Jews in general had been staunch Republicans during the 1920s and had, well before 1940, become Democrats is a belief firmly supported by the literature as well as by the evidence available in Boston. A decisive political realignment transformed the Jewish community, across the country and locally, over the course of those two decades. Their initial Republicanism, many have suggested, developed more out of an antipathy to the vaguely anti-Semitic Irish, who dominated the Democratic party in most major cities, than from any ideological attachment to the Republicans. Also, Jews may have been expressing gratitude to a party that had held the presidency during their years of heaviest immigration. And perhaps Republicans, especially in Irish-controlled Boston, held additional appeal to Jews for their vigorous progressive and reformist wing. Yet that was a partisan allegiance which could not withstand the events of the 1930s. Republican loyalties were shaken by both the popular identification of Herbert Hoover with the Great Depression and the rise of a self-consciously liberal Democratic party under Franklin Roosevelt. Expectations, once confirmed by the policies pursued by the Democratic administration as well as by Roosevelt's strong opposition to Hitler and to Nazism, proved sufficient to reshape the Jewish community into a solid Democratic bloc.[18]

What is particularly stunning in that realignment, however, is its class dimension. Essentially, before 1936, Jews were voting their wallets and pocketbooks at least as much as any ethnic identity. In 1932, when Roosevelt carried working-class Jews by a margin of over four-to-one, he actually lost one of the two upper-middle-class precincts to Hoover and carried the other with just 56 percent of the vote. Yet, beginning in 1936 and continuing to this day, Jews, regardless of their income, have subsumed their supposed class interests and voted instead with a singular degree of ethnic solidarity. Those upper-middle-class precincts that Roosevelt barely won in 1932 he would carry in 1940 with 93 percent of all votes cast, virtually identical to his support that year among working-class and lower-middle-class Jews.

The absence of class divisions in Jewish voting since the New Deal realignment has been extensively documented. Samuel Lubell, remarking on a general pattern of class-based voting after the mid-1930s, notes that the Jews were an important exception. "The highest income areas voting for Roosevelt were Jewish. In Brooklyn he carried streets with $15,000 homes—a comfortable valuation in 1940—and apartment houses with doormen.'' Ladd and Hadley, too, marvel at the extent of Jewish political uniformity in 1936 and 1940, ''a time when most ethnic groups were sharply divided along class lines.'' Jews, concludes Lawrence Fuchs, ''constituted the only ethno-religious group in which differences in Democratic-Republican strength could not be correlated with differences in occupational prestige, amount of income, or education. . . . The poorer Jews, the laborers, the uneducated were no more Democratic than their richer, college-educated coreligionists in business or the professions.'' As Roosevelt implemented the New Deal and war loomed in Europe, Jewish support for the Democrats and their president was solid, transcending all economic cleavages.[19]

That broad-based support lasted for decades after the realignment, probably even to this day, although the degree of support for Democratic candidates has diminished somewhat among all Jews. In his analysis of the 1952 vote for Adlai Stevenson in Boston's Ward Fourteen, Fuchs found that Democratic support actually increased slightly with socioeconomic status. ''By the 1950s,'' report Ladd and Hadley, ''Jews were the most heavily and consistently Democratic of all ethnocultural groups in the United States.'' The Jewish community in the 1980s remains heavily Democratic at all socioeconomic levels.[20]

In light of these and many other attestations to the irrelevance of class or status among Jews in a half-century of voting, probably the least surprising aspect of figure 2.1 are the final two elections, especially the election of 1940, in which Jews voted overwhelmingly for Roosevelt regardless of socioeconomic group. Much more remarkable is the compelling evidence that, prior to that period, Jews split sharply along class lines. Because the rise of public opinion surveys and most studies of political behavior by ethnicity coincided with the formation of the New Deal coalition in the 1930s, there has been little evidence in the literature to challenge retrospective applicability of post–New Deal analysis. Thus it was easy to assume that Jews, who have not voted along class lines since the beginning of such observations, had never voted along class lines. Presumably, Jews had once been staunch Republicans, regardless of class, just as they had uniformly become Democrats by the late 1930s.

That, however, was not an accurate reflection of Jewish political behavior in the years prior to the New Deal realignment, if evidence in Boston can be considered externally valid—and John Allswang's similar findings for Chicago in 1928 and 1932 suggest that Boston was not a unique case.[21] Figure 2.1, which shows the vote for president by socioeconomic class, illustrates the prevalence of class voting among Boston's Jews prior to 1936. So strong were those pre–New Deal class cleavages that they would persist, as figure 2.2 shows, in party registration figures into the 1940s. In the case of Jews in

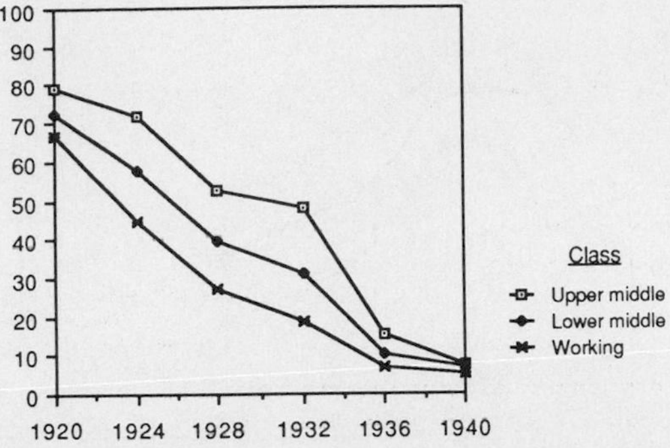

Figure 2.1 Vote in Jewish Precincts for Republican Candidate for President, by Class (as Percent of All Votes Cast)

Boston, party registration appears to have lagged a few years behind actual shifts in party support, as measured by votes cast for president. This, as described in Chapter 1, is evidence of individual voter conversion having effected the realignment. Future Democrats, as will be demonstrated in greater depth below, came in large numbers from former Republican supporters. Thus, although class-based voting ended permanently among Jews with the 1936 presidential election, party registration statistics continued even in 1940 to sharply reflect the vestigial system of class cleavages in party support that had characterized the 1920s and early 1930s.

One peculiarity in figure 2.2 deserves mention. Registration figures indicate that, prior to 1926, working-class Jews were abnormally Democratic. The dip in the graph between 1920 and 1926 is conspicuous because it violates all expectations. It does not correspond to party registration figures for other Jews in that period, to party registration figures for working-class Jews in succeeding years, or even to the vote for president among working-class Jews in 1920 or 1924. What it does suggest is that pressures operated between 1920 and 1924 to incline this group of Jews to register in unusually large numbers as Democrats, pressures which disappeared after 1924 and, even between 1920 and 1924, did not affect decisions made in the voting booth. Probably producing those pressures was the fact that the working-class Jewish precinct was, in the early 1920s, located within a ward that was overwhelmingly Irish and Democratic. Registration, unlike voting, is a public act, and it is likely that poorer Jews were especially susceptible to the lure of satisfying the local political machine. Robert Woods mentioned this tendency in his 1902 study of the West End Jewish population:

> The Democratic leaders have managed . . . to secure a considerable following among the Jews. Were these districts not so overwhelmingly Democratic, the Jews could be kept more closely within the

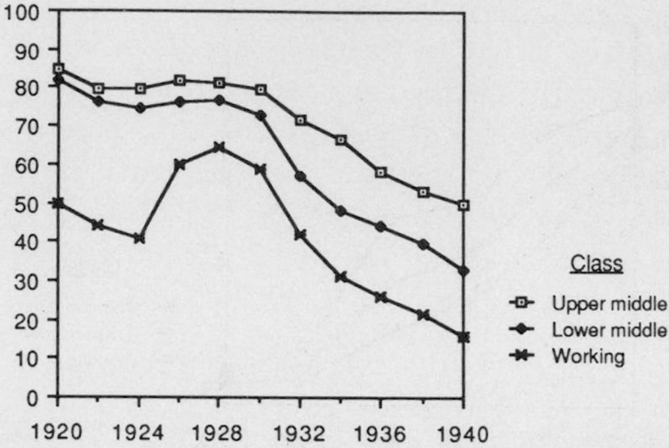

Figure 2.2 Republican Registration in Jewish Precincts, by Class (as Percent of Total Two-party Enrollment)

> Republican fold. As it is, the poorer ones are very likely to be Democrats. They are made to see, in the machine's tangible, lucrative ways, the advantage of supporting the local political powers that be.

In 1925, however, ward lines were redrawn, and the working-class precinct was incorporated into Ward Fourteen, which was dominated by Jewish Republicans. Relieved of the need to conform to the wishes of the Irish Democrats who had controlled their old ward, the number of working-class Jews registered as Republicans soared between 1924 and 1926. A simple change in ward boundaries seems to have permanently eliminated the unusual registration behavior of working-class Jews in the early 1920s and encouraged the open expression of what must surely have been a latent Republicanism.[22]

Jews were, then, realigned on two fundamental levels by the critical elections of the 1930s. They had, as has so frequently been observed, begun to become Democrats, abandoning long-held attachments to the Republican party. Equally important, however, Jews ended what appears to have been an entrenched practice of class-based voting and partisanship. Even in the 1910s, Robert Woods and Albert Kennedy had observed, albeit not on an exclusively political level, a significant amount of class consciousness and differentiation among Boston's Jews.[23] That those cleavages were salient factors in party support through the election of 1932 is evident in figures 2.1 and 2.2 . Even the third-party vote for president in the 1920s was heavily dependent on socioeconomic status. Of the total vote cast, Socialist candidates in 1920 received the support of 24 percent of working-class Jews, 13 percent of the lower middle class, and just 4 percent of the upper middle class. Similarly, in 1924, Robert La Follette, with 43 percent of the vote, actually came within 12 votes of a plurality of the Jewish working class; his support among lower-middle-class Jews was 27 percent and among the upper-middle-class

Jews of Roxbury highlands just 11 percent. Both in terms of minor-party vote and degree of support for the Republican party, Jews, until 1936, had been voting their class interests rather than a common ethnic bond. While the pace of realignment toward the Democrats appears to have been relatively uniform among all three classes—the slopes of the three party registration lines are roughly the same—the fact that the three groups started at different levels would determine the time it would take for each to bring its registration figures into line with its voting. Poorer Jews would register overwhelmingly as Democrats well before richer Jews, although the rate of change for both groups was virtually identical. Indeed, in terms of voting, higher socioeconomic groups actually realigned more sharply than lower groups, since by this measure they had all reached the same level by 1940. The very elections of 1936 and 1940 that split most of the country along socioeconomic lines united the Jews in a single cause which overcame those divisions.

Soon, after presenting party registration figures, I will argue that the two periods most critical to the Jewish realignment were the election of 1932 and the elections of 1936–38. In 1932, Jews began their dramatic transformation into Democrats. It is at that point that party enrollment statistics started reflecting such a shift. Then, in 1936–38, Jews solidified as a cohesive ethnic bloc which voted equally Democratic across all class lines. Implicit in that conclusion is the belief that the vote for president in 1940 was an accurate indicator of partisanship, since Jews continued to maintain the same level of Democratic support in future years, eventually reflecting that allegiance in their votes for state and local offices and in their patterns of party registration. Registration figures for 1940 were, in contrast, poor indices of the depth of support for the Democratic party. Because conversion played such an important role in the creation of Jewish Democrats, there was a striking lag between the point when Jews transferred their allegiances in fact—measured by the act of voting—and the day years later when they would grow to recognize the reality of their conversion and consciously switch party labels. Registered Republicans voted overwhelmingly for Roosevelt in 1936 and 1940. In those elections we can see in retrospect the demise of their attachment to the Republican party and the permanent transfer of their support to the Democrats. While as late as 1940 half of all upper-middle-class Jews who were enrolled in one of the two major parties were registered as Republicans, that identification did not truly reflect the shift that had occurred. By 1940, virtually all Jews, regardless of socioeconomic status, had moved decisively toward the Democratic party. The class cleavages and heavy Republicanism reflected in party enrollment in 1940 were only historical residues of an earlier era. It would take time before those conversions would be translated fully into partisan registration figures.

Table 2.2 presents the vote for president as a fraction of the entire potential electorate. Thus, of all working-class Jews in 1928, 21.9 percent voted for Al Smith, 8.2 percent voted for Herbert Hoover, and 69.9 percent did not vote for either candidate. Over two-thirds of all adult men and women in that group did not participate in the presidential election of 1928.

Interestingly, the vote for president presented in table 2.2 would incline us against viewing the 1932 election, the first of the two realigning periods just described, as critical. Indeed, of the four elections between 1928 and 1940, the 1932 contest is conspicuous at the level of presidential voting as apparently the least important in terms of realignment. The support Roosevelt received in 1932 was virtually identical to that accorded Al Smith in 1928. V. O. Key concluded, of course, on the basis of similar data for a larger population, that "in New England, at least, the Roosevelt revolution of 1932 was in large measure an Al Smith revolution of 1928."[24] What strikes us about 1932 is the continuity from the previous election rather than any critical shift in party support.

Two presidential elections stand out in the table as apparently critical for all three classes of Jews: the elections of 1928 and of 1936. In both those years, the Democratic candidate made gains of a stunning magnitude over the previous election. The 1928 gains were somewhat sharper among poorer Jews and those of 1936 more powerful among richer Jews, but the increases in Democratic support in those two elections were nevertheless tremendous across all class divisions.

It is clear, too, that Jews not only voted in greater and greater numbers for the Democratic candidates, but that they all but abandoned their once heavy support for the Republicans. Thus, among upper-middle-class Jews, between 1924 and 1940 the Republican vote fell a massive 85 percent, from almost one-third of the potential electorate to less than one-twentieth of the same group. Figure 2.3 shows graphically Republican losses and Democratic gains as shares of all adults. Particularly significant is the fact that the Republican vote diminished so precipitously over the period, indicating that a large number of Jews who had voted Republican actually switched party alle-

Table 2.2 Vote in Jewish Precincts for President as Percent of Potential Electorate

	Working Class			Lower Middle Class			Upper Middle Class		
	Dem.	Rep.	Other	Dem.	Rep.	Other	Dem.	Rep.	Other
1920	2.2	15.4	5.5	5.8	27.1	4.7	7.4	34.1	1.7
1924	3.1	10.6	10.2	5.9	22.3	10.5	7.5	31.5	5.0
1928	21.9	8.2		25.9	16.7		24.9	27.7	
1932	24.1	5.6		28.3	12.8		25.0	23.1	
1936	39.8	3.0	0.8	45.9	5.4	0.7	51.3	9.1	0.4
1940	50.7	2.6		55.9	4.2		62.4	4.8	

giances and became Democrats. There was certainly, too, a large amount of increased Democratic strength which came from people who had never voted before and were in this period mobilized to vote for Al Smith and Franklin Roosevelt. What we can see, then, is a pattern of Democratic support coming from mobilization of previous nonvoters as well as conversion of former active Republicans. In general, mobilization seems to have been the primary factor in 1928, while conversion was much more important in 1936.

A similar examination of the vote for offices other than president yields much less information. Because of a number of factors—the presence of popular and strongly entrenched incumbents in many of the races; the fact that some of the contests were unopposed; and the support given to Jewish, "favorite-son" candidates whenever and under whatever party label they ran—it is difficult to discern any constant trend in either the vote for representative in Congress or for state senator. John McCormack, for example, destined to become Speaker of the House in Washington, repre-

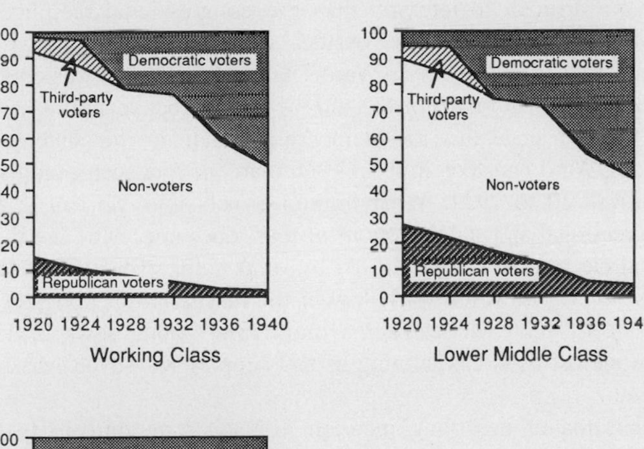

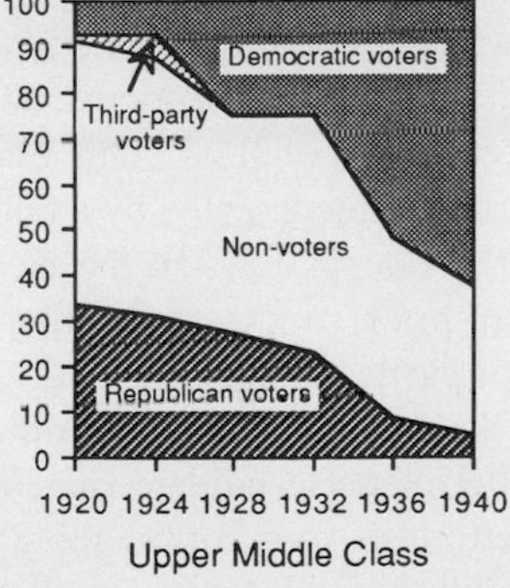

Figure 2.3 Vote in Jewish Precincts for President (as Percent of Potential Electorate)

sented Ward Fourteen and, although a Democrat, handily carried the Republican Jews in his district in 1928. Then, in 1930 and 1932, opposed by a Samuel Abrams and a Bernard Ginsburg, he lost heavily among Jews at the very time they were realigning toward his party. After 1932, McCormack would not again be opposed by a Jewish Republican and he fared well in succeeding elections among Jews. Personal factors, then—McCormack or Republican representative George Holden Tinkham's popularity and the presence or absence of a Jewish candidate—appeared to have been much more important in determining individual outcomes than party labels.

General tendencies, if not strict trends, were, however, discernible in the vote for such lower offices. Among all Jews, Democratic candidates for Congress fared noticeably and uniformly better after 1932 than they had before that election. Without exception, support for Democrats was higher in the later period than it had been in any election between 1920 and 1930. Much of that support came, apparently, from former Republican voters, although, again, mobilization was also important. The vote for state senator is even more difficult to interpret than the congressional race because the contest was unopposed in Ward Fourteen in both 1938 and 1940, and was not only unopposed in Roxbury's Ward Twelve in 1940 but was contested by a Jewish Republican in each of the three elections between 1934 and 1938. At most, we can state that the Democratic candidate for state senate did better among Ward Fourteen Jews in 1936 than had any such candidate in the period from 1920 to 1934. What limited conclusions we can draw, then, from congressional and state elections at least does not contradict the picture of a critical election in 1932 followed by reinforcing critical elections in the late 1930s, as will be described below in the discussion of party registration figures. Indeed, John McCormack's majorities among Jews in 1938 and 1940 were almost as overwhelming as the support Roosevelt was receiving by that time.

One other matter deserving mention is the strong third-party vote for president in 1920 and 1924. While, as mentioned earlier, support for third-party candidates was heavily correlated with socioeconomic status, it was nevertheless important among all three classes of Jews. This phenomenon of minor-party voting has, indeed, been well documented by a number of students of Jewish political behavior and the role of Jews in the New Deal realignment. Ladd and Hadley noted that prior to the realignment Jews "contributed disproportionately to the minor parties of the radical left." And, in his analysis of the Jewish vote in New York, Burner has shown that Jews in 1920 "gave a heavier vote to the jailed Socialist candidate Eugene Debs than to Cox; and in 1924 Robert La Follette also won considerable Jewish support." Many have suggested that this tradition of third-party voting among American Jews is partly responsible for the unusually large number of Jews

Table 2.3 Estimates of Conversion in Jewish Precincts—Vote for President

	Δ Total		Δ Dem. Vote		Rep. Vote	Δ Rep.	% Dem. Gains from Conversion If: All New Dems.		New as Vote	
	Raw	Adj.	Raw	Adj.	Share	Vote	ΔR_p	%	ΔR_p	%
1924–28										
Working class	+6.2	+7.4	+18.8	+19.0	.272	−2.4	−0.5	10	+1.5	21
Lower middle class	+3.9	+5.8	+20.0	+20.3	.393	−5.6	−1.1	22	+1.2	33
Upper middle class	+8.6	+10.8	+17.4	+17.8	.527	−3.8	−1.6	12	+4.1	44
1932–36										
Working class	+13.9	+15.4	+15.7	+16.9	.070	−2.6	−0.3	14	+0.8	20
Lower middle class	+10.9	+13.0	+17.6	+19.0	.104	−7.4	−0.6	36	+0.8	43
Upper middle class	+12.7	+15.1	+26.3	+27.6	.150	−14.0	−1.2	46	+1.1	55

Note: ΔR_p is the predicted change in the Republican vote.

who have traditionally registered as independents. V. O. Key, in his essay on critical elections, documents "a relatively heavy support in 1924 for La Follette in those towns in which Smith was subsequently to find special favor." At the level of voting, it would appear likely that Roosevelt was able to attract to the Democrats the vast majority of former third-party voters. Lawrence Fuchs reports, for example, that "many lifelong Socialists hailed Roosevelt's New Deal and left militant socialism forever." In figure 2.3, then, the third-party vote is placed in the Democratic half of the graph.[25]

While table 2.2 and figure 2.3 both demonstrate that increased Democratic electoral strength came from both former nonvoters and previous Republican supporters, table 2.3 attempts to measure in concrete terms the relative importance of conversion and mobilization in the realignment. Separate calculations are presented for the periods 1924–28 and 1932–36 and for each of the three socioeconomic groups. The underlying goal is to quantify lost Republican support between elections, attributing any genuine fall in support to Democratic conversions.

It is assumed that few Democrats converted to the Republican party in ethnically and socioeconomically homogeneous neighborhoods moving in the opposite direction. Thus the scenario of Jewish Democrats becoming Republicans in an era when virtually all their friends and neighbors were forming Democratic ties is considered highly unlikely. While Democrats, then, could have received new support from mobilization or conversion, Republican gains could have come only from the mobilization of new voters.

For the lower middle class, it is estimated, as shown in table 2.3, that in 1936 actual conversions of Republican voters accounted for between 36 and 43 percent of the increase in Democratic support. To get this estimate, we first calculate the change in the total vote. In 1936, 52.0 percent of the total potential electorate cast a vote for president, while the comparable figure for 1932 was 41.1 percent. There was, then, a raw increase of 10.9 percent in the number of active voters. The actual increase in the number of new voters was higher, however: by 1936, approximately 5 percent of those who had voted in 1932, or 2.1 percent of the potential electorate, had died.[26] Thus, the adjusted figure for the total increase in vote is 13.0 percent—the 10.9 percent raw increase plus the 2.1 percent replacing 1932 voters who had not survived until the next presidential election. Similarly, the Democratic vote between 1932 and 1936 rose from 28.3 to 45.9 percent, a raw gain of 17.6 percent. Again assuming 5 percent mortality over the four years, the adjusted Democratic gain becomes 19.0 percent. Over the same period, the raw Republican vote fell 7.4 percentage points, from 12.8 to 5.4 percent of the potential electorate.

We can now attempt to estimate the contribution of Republican conversions to the total Democratic gain. At this point, two different assumptions are made and corresponding estimates are obtained. The first assumption is that no new voter entering the electorate votes Republican. This case is an extreme version of the argument that new voters are especially attracted to the dominant party; here, we assume that the attraction is perfect. Under this assumption, the only change in the Republican vote—everything else being equal—would come from mortality. Thus, we would expect only that natural processes would remove 5 percent of the 1932 Republican vote of 12.8 percent, for a decline of 0.6 percent in the Republican share of the potential electorate. The difference between the predicted Republican vote loss of 0.6 percent and the raw vote loss of 7.4 percent measures the actual decline in Republican support if that party attracts no new voters. That decline, 6.8 percent of the potential electorate, represents the number of voters who must be accounted for as converts to the Democratic party in 1936. Dividing the 6.8 share of Republican converts by the total gain of 19.0 in the Democratic vote, we conclude that, under this assumption, 36 percent of Democratic gains had to have come from conversion. More than one-third of the increase in Democratic support between 1932 and 1936 came from former Republican voters, even if all new voters are assumed to have voted for Roosevelt.

A slightly higher estimate of conversion is obtained, however, if we assume that new voters cast their vote in the same proportion that the general community split its support for president. For lower-middle-class Jews, then, of all votes cast in 1936, 88.2 percent went to Roosevelt, 10.4 percent went to Alf Landon, and 1.3 percent went to third-party candidates. It is assumed, therefore, that 10.4 percent of all new voters entering the electorate between 1932 and 1936 voted for the Republican candidate. Republican gains from new voters totalled 1.4 percent of the potential electorate—10.4 percent of 13.0 percent, the adjusted increase in the active electorate. Subtracting from this expected gain of 1.4 percent a mortality loss of 0.6 percent in the 1932 Republican base, we predict a net gain of 0.8 percent in the Republican vote. The difference between this net gain and the actual raw loss of 7.4 percent means that a total of 8.2 percent of the potential electorate left the Republican party in the election of 1936. This estimate of Republican losses represents 43 percent of all gains in Democratic support—the 8.2 percent divided by a total adjusted Democratic increase of 19.0 percent—suggesting that converted Republicans accounted for a very substantial amount of Democratic gains.

Conclusions drawn from table 2.3 tend to reinforce the previous discussion of the data presented in table 2.2 and figure 2.3. Especially among the two higher-income groups, conversion of former Republicans is, under both assumptions, fundamental to any understanding of the 1936 shift in party support. Conversion seems less important as an explanation for 1928, but, especially if new voters split as older voters did in their choice for president, voter conversion had real impact that year as well. Working-class Jews apparently were realigned largely from the mobilization of new voters: in 1928 and 1936, only one in five new Democratic votes can be explained by conversion even under the second assumption, that Republicans were able to attract new voters. Although the pattern is less clear, it appears, too, that conversion was a more important factor as socioeconomic status rose. Presumably, since richer voters were already more mobilized and more Republican in the 1920s than poorer voters, many more of that large pool of active voters had to switch sides to effect a large partisan change. In a less mobilized population, there would have been many more nonvoters from which the Democratic party could have found support, thus not necessitating the degree of conversion necessary for a similar realignment in a highly mobilized community.

If we look now at table 2.4, which details party registration figures by class and by gender, two important additions to the voting-based discussion merit attention. First, the 1928 "realignment" was more apparent than real. There was no critical election among Jews in 1928. Rather, the vote for Al Smith represented a deviating election which, only four years later, with Roosevelt's candidacy, would be translated into a genuine critical election. And, second, it appears that conversion of former non-Democrats was a much more important explanation of the realignment among men than among women; at the same time, mobilization of new voters was of greater importance to the shift among women. It is worth noting that, as might be expected, conversion seems to have been relatively more important not only among men but also among the higher-status groups. Those Jews, then, who as Republicans were already highly mobilized in the 1920s, logically contributed a disproportionate share of converts to the Democratic party in the 1930s.

Table 2.4 Party Registration Figures in Jewish Precincts as Percent of Total Potential Electorate

	Working Class Men				Working Class Women			
	All Reg.	Dem.	Rep.	Ind.	All Reg.	Dem.	Rep.	Ind.
1920	41.7	10.3	9.5	21.9	3.2	0.1	0.8	2.3
1922	39.0	8.0	5.9	25.1	8.9	1.1	1.2	6.6
1924	39.2	13.6	9.4	16.2	8.7	1.9	1.1	5.7
1926	41.8	14.0	18.0	9.8	11.8	1.8	5.8	4.2
1928	47.3	12.5	20.4	14.4	15.3	3.2	7.5	4.6
1930	46.1	13.7	17.3	15.1	15.6	3.2	6.7	5.7
1932*	52.3	21.0	14.5	16.8	21.6	7.6	6.2	7.8
1934	53.9	29.1	13.2	11.6	24.6	13.4	5.9	5.3
1936	53.8	28.3	9.5	16.1	25.8	13.3	5.2	7.2
1938	57.8	32.7	8.5	16.5	31.6	15.5	4.6	11.5
1940	59.1	37.1	7.1	14.9	41.7	21.4	4.0	16.3
	Lower Middle Class Men				Lower Middle Class Women			
	All Reg.	Dem.	Rep.	Ind.	All Reg.	Dem.	Rep.	Ind.
1920	58.4	8.0	33.0	17.3	13.4	0.3	4.3	8.8
1922	56.8	10.3	33.7	12.8	26.9	3.3	10.7	12.9
1924	54.2	12.1	32.9	9.2	25.2	3.7	13.9	7.6
1926	56.0	11.6	34.4	10.0	28.1	4.1	16.4	7.6
1928	60.0	11.0	33.3	15.6	30.0	4.2	17.5	8.3
1930	58.2	12.9	30.4	14.9	29.5	4.6	15.8	9.2
1932*	61.8	21.3	25.6	14.9	33.2	10.2	15.7	7.3
1934	62.5	27.6	23.1	11.8	35.4	13.1	14.2	8.0
1936	63.9	28.8	20.3	14.9	39.1	14.7	14.0	10.3
1938	64.6	31.9	18.7	14.0	41.9	17.5	13.4	11.0
1940	67.4	35.4	16.2	15.8	48.6	21.7	11.6	15.3
	Upper Middle Class Men				Upper Middle Class Women			
	All Reg.	Dem.	Rep.	Ind.	All Reg.	Dem.	Rep.	Ind.
1920	70.2	7.8	43.1	19.3	14.3	0.9	5.0	8.3
1922	69.9	11.5	46.2	12.2	33.9	3.7	13.8	16.4
1924	66.6	10.3	36.2	20.0	33.2	3.3	16.2	13.6
1926	66.9	11.0	44.1	11.7	35.0	3.7	21.1	10.2
1928	70.6	10.0	42.1	18.6	30.9	4.3	20.5	6.1
1930	66.7	9.2	35.8	21.7	31.9	4.3	16.2	11.4
1932*	70.8	15.4	37.8	17.5	41.3	8.8	23.6	9.0
1934	69.1	19.7	36.0	13.4	45.0	11.0	25.1	8.9
1936	71.4	22.2	29.3	19.9	49.2	14.3	21.7	13.2
1938	72.7	26.7	29.1	16.9	53.7	16.5	19.9	17.3
1940	72.9	28.2	27.8	16.8	56.1	18.8	19.1	18.1

*The 1932 figures are estimates, based on Ward Fourteen totals (1930, 1932, 1934).

While, as V. O. Key long ago argued, the 1928 vote for Al Smith in New England may have been a precursor to Roosevelt's election in 1932, the evidence presented in table 2.4 casts serious doubt on the proposition that 1928 was a critical or realigning election for these voters. Many have suggested that, in a city such as Boston, Al Smith's candidacy was the primary force behind the New Deal realignment. Those conclusions and that general perception have relied almost totally on analysis of the vote cast for president. And, as the discussion of the Jewish presidential vote reveals, on that basis it is tempting to see in the 1928 election an event of critical proportions. Certainly Key, in his "A Theory of Critical Elections," bases his conclusion that 1928 was a realigning election on an analysis of presidential elections. Burner, too, although he makes the statement without elaboration that "Jews in the nation at large . . . remained Republican until 1932," oddly presents as his only evidence for realignment the stunning Jewish majorities for Al Smith in Chicago and New York. Other apparent proponents of the concept of a 1928 realignment include Kristi Andersen, who, like Key, finds it "clear that the key Democratic advantage [in Chicago's foreign-stock wards] was gained in the 1928 election," and James Sundquist.[27]

For Boston's Jews, however, the election of 1928 had no impact on party registration figures; there were no substantial accretions to the ranks of Democrats between 1926 and 1930. The vote for Al Smith, which, standing by itself, has long been perceived as signaling a realignment, was a deviating election. That characterization results ineluctably when the election is viewed in the context of its effect on party enrollment, as in table 2.4. Erbring et al., in their aggregate national study, conclude that for "new ethnics" the critical period of realignment was 1936–38. Not only do they join Key and a generation of other scholars in arguing that no realignment occurred in 1932, but they go on to dispute the belief that 1928 was a critical election. "There is no evidence," they state, "that new ethnic partisanship was at all affected by the intervening presidential elections—including the candidacy of a Catholic son of Irish parents in the person of Al Smith in 1928."[28]

What occurred in 1928 was instead merely a testament to the popularity among Jews of Al Smith. The former governor of New York was not only fairly liberal and friendly to Jewish interests, but he was a victim along with Jews of religious discrimination and bigotry. Thus, in 1928, Jews voted for Smith but without wavering in their commitment to the Republican party—although, of course, their Democratic vote that year might have made them more susceptible to realignment in the future. As the *Boston Herald* argued after Smith had succeeded in attracting the support of newer ethnic groups: "It is inevitable that, with the influences of 1928 at work, a great many persons who have been Republican, and who will be Republican, should have gone for a little outing behind the Democratic donkey. But the holiday will be short, the picknickers will return for their regular home fare, and Massachusetts will stand where she has stood always.''[29]

The *Herald,* from the perspective of 1928, was absolutely correct, at least as it applied to Boston's Jews. Although party registration may not immediately reflect the degree to which a group of voters has switched parties, it can at the very least be expected to indicate when a shift has begun to occur. Even in the very earliest stages of realignment, an initial handful of voters would be expected to change parties and new voters entering the electorate would likewise be expected to register in the direction of the new dominant party. Yet in 1928 absolutely no change occurred in the delicate balance of party enrollments. Republicans went into the polling booth to vote for Al Smith and, five minutes later, from that booth out walked the same Republicans. Had not a stock market crashed, a Great Depression begun, and an attractive candidate arisen to transform the Democratic party into a force for liberal change, Jews would have remained unshaken in their commitment to Republicanism. But extraordinary events obscured the deviation of 1928 and transformed it into a foreshadowing of the realignment which was to come.

As the party registration figures in table 2.4 demonstrate, the realignment occurred in two stages. A critical election in 1932 was followed by reinforcing elections in the period 1936–38. In general, men were largely converted and women were largely mobilized. Among working-class Jews, for example, the number of registered men rose from 46.1 percent of the potential electorate in 1930 to 59.1 percent in 1940, a gain of 13.0 points and a 28 percent increase over the 1930 figure. Women, on the other hand, were registered in 1940 at a level fully 167 percent higher than they had been just ten years earlier. In that same period, Republican registration fell 10.2 percentage points among men and 2.7 points among women. Even among this most undermobilized group of Jewish men, there were nearly as many lost Republicans as there were total new voters over the decade. Women, on the other hand, experienced tremendous mobilization of new voters. While many of the new Democratic men apparently came from the ranks of registered voters who had previously been either unenrolled or enrolled as Republicans, the bulk of such gains among women can be explained by accretions to the active electorate. Among both groups, the periods 1930–34 and 1934–40 frame the moments of greatest Democratic gains. It would appear, then, that the elections of 1932 and 1936–38 possessed genuine realigning force.

A similar analysis could apply almost as well to lower-middle-class and upper-middle-class Jews. The elections of 1932 and 1936–38 were critical for both groups and for both sexes within each group. And, among the lower middle class, conversion of existing non-Democrats is essential to understanding the realignment among men, while mobilization is much more crucial to the process among women. The only exception to these general observations concerns the 1932 realignment for the richest group of Jewish men. Between 1930 and 1934, Republican registration actually rose among upper-middle-class men. The simultaneous doubling of Democratic support, then, over this period must be attributed primarily to either mobilization of new voters or attraction of former unenrolled registrants to the Democratic party. A comparable phenomenon occurred at the same time among upper-middle-class women who, like the men within their own group and like other Jewish women in general, moved toward the Democratic party in this period through a process of mobilization. The striking thing about this particular movement, however—the 1932 movement of the richest women—was that Republicans actually out-mobilized Democrats over the four-year period. While Democratic registration increased 150 percent between 1930 and 1934, Republicans lost no ground but actually gained the support of an additional 8.9 percent of the potential electorate. Overall, even with the earlier caveat concerning the absence of conversion in 1932 among upper-status Jewish men, it seems safe to say that realignment occurred at the same rate between sexes, with critical elections in 1932 and 1936–38. The individual mechanics of the realignment appear, though, to have been different—men largely converting and women mobilizing.

Table 2.5 is an attempt to measure the contribution of conversion to increased Democratic support, using registration data in a fashion similar to the earlier use of presidential voting figures in table 2.3. All the information refers only to lower-middle-class Jews, who made up the bulk of the Jewish population in Boston and fall in income and status between the other two groups that have been examined. Separate figures are presented for men and women. Also, not only are the two earlier assumptions concerning the partisanship of new voters continued here, but three separate cases are considered.

In the first case, it is assumed that any Republican registrants dropping their party ties immediately become Democrats; former Republicans, in this extreme case, cannot simply drop their party enrollment and become independent registered voters. Calculations under this assumption are identical to those made earlier for the presidential vote. Registrants unenrolled in either party are ignored, and the change in Republican registration—under the assumptions that new registrants become Democrats and that new registrants split as the general population had split in the vote for president—is compared to the change in Democratic registration. The size of the Republican drop compared to the size of the Democratic gain yields an estimate of conversion of former Republican registrants.

Skipping for a moment the second case, we find represented in the third case an opposite extreme to the first case's assumptions. This third case supposes that Democratic gains from the existing electorate come not from

Table 2.5 Estimates of Conversion in Lower-Middle-Class Jewish Precincts, Party Registration Figures

Case I. All former Republican registrants becoming Democrats

	Δ Total		Δ Dem. Reg.		Rep. Vote Share	Δ Rep. Reg.	% Dem. Gains from Conversion If: All New Dems.		New as Vote	
	Raw	Adj.	Raw	Adj.			ΔR_p	%	ΔR_p	%
Men										
1930–34	+4.3	+7.2	+14.7	+15.3	.311	−7.3	−1.5	38	+0.7	52
1934–40	+4.9	+9.6	+7.8	+9.9	.104	−6.9	−1.7	53	−0.7	63
Women										
1930–34	+5.9	+7.4	+8.5	+8.7	.311	−1.6	−0.8	9	+1.5	36
1934–40	+13.2	+15.9	+8.6	+9.6	.104	−2.6	−1.1	16	+0.6	33

Case II. Democratic gains from former non-Democratic registrants

	Δ Total		Δ Dem. Reg.		Rep. Vote Share	Δ R+I Reg.	% Dem. Gains from Conversion If: All New Dems.		New as Vote	
	Raw	Adj.	Raw	Adj.			$\Delta(R+I)_p$	%	$\Delta(R+I)_p$	%
Men										
1930–34	+4.3	+7.2	+14.7	+15.3	.311	−10.4	−2.3	53	−0.1	67
1934–40	+4.9	+9.6	+7.8	+9.9	.104	−2.9	−2.6	3	−1.6	13
Women										
1930–34	+5.9	+7.4	+8.5	+8.7	.311	−2.8	−1.3	17	+1.0	44
1934–40	+13.2	+15.9	+8.6	+9.6	.104	+4.7	−1.7	0	0.0	0

Case III. All former Republican registrants becoming Independents

	Δ Dem. Reg.		Initial Rep. Reg.	Expected Rep. Reg.	Final R+I Reg.	% Dem. Gains from Conversion If: All New Dems.		New as Vote	
	Raw	Adj.				Diff.	%	Adj.	%
Men									
1930–34	+14.7	+15.3	30.4	28.9	34.9	+6.0	0	+2.2	0
1934–40	+7.8	+9.9	23.1	21.4	32.0	+10.6	0	+1.0	0
Women									
1930–34	+8.5	+8.7	15.8	15.0	22.2	+7.2	0	+2.3	0
1934–40	+8.6	+9.6	14.2	13.1	26.9	+13.8	0	+1.7	0

Republicans but from independents. Any Republican losses in registration must, then, be accommodated within the number of new unenrolled voters. Between 1930 and 1934, for example, the number of men registered as Democrats rose from 12.9 to 27.6 percent of the potential electorate—a raw gain of 14.7 percent, which, once adjusted for mortality, yields a true Democratic gain of 15.3 percent. The level of Republican registration in 1930 was 30.4 percent; four years later, mortality would lower that figure to a predicted registration of 28.9 percent of the total electorate. But, in that year, 1934, the combined total of Republican and independent registrants was 34.9 percent. There is then, a difference, of 6.0 percent between the number of 1930 Republicans who would need to be accommodated in 1934 and the number of independent and Republican spaces available to accommodate them. Assuming no new voters register as Republicans, there is a gain in available Republican spaces of 6.0 percent and thus no Republicans need have been converted in that period. If new registrants enter split between the parties, then a gain of 2.2 percent (the adjusted total increase in registration multiplied by the Republican share of all votes cast for president in 1932) would be expected in Republican ranks, still less than the actual 6.0 percent increase. Even in this case, then, mobilization could have accounted for all of the Democratic increase.

Falling between these two extreme assumptions is the second case, which is more a reflection of reality than a hypothesis. This case is an actual measure of Democratic gains in registration from former non-Democratic registrants. Calculations are identical to those made in the first case, except that here all non-Democrats are used instead of just Republicans. The change in non-Democratic registrant strength is measured by summing Republican and independent registrants and using the change in that sum between years. What this case gives us, then, is a true measure of the importance to Democratic gains of "conversion" of previously non-Democratic members of the active electorate.

Looking at these three cases for lower-middle-class men and women, we find some support for our earlier conclusions. In 1932, it does appear that conversion was much more important to the realignment among men than among women. The second case, for example, indicates that between one-half and two-thirds of all gains in Democratic support came from conversion within the active electorate. It is likely, as the first case demonstrates, that much of that gain came from Republican registrants, although the third case proves that the gain could equally have come from the ranks of independents. It is significant, however, that Republicans and independents together contributed so heavily to the Democratic gain among men in 1932, showing that the mobilization of new voters could at best have accounted for a minority of increased Democratic registration. Women over the same period appear to have experienced significantly greater mobilization, although conversion of existing registrants was of at least moderate, and perhaps great, importance.

In 1936–38, the mobilization of new voters into the active electorate could have completely accounted for gains in Democratic registration among women. As the second case shows, the increase in unenrolled registrants more than offsets the loss of Republicans, so that the entire increase in Democratic support could have come from outside of the electorate. Even assuming, as in the first case, that all lost Republicans register as Democrats, mobilization is still the primary explanation of this realignment. Almost all of the Democratic gains made by men in 1936–38 could also have been due to the mobilization of new voters. The second case proves that no more than 13 percent of the increase in Democratic support came from within the active electorate. While the first case does give very high estimates of conversion on the assumption that declines in Republican registration represent Democratic gains, it appears that virtually all of those lost Republicans could have been easily absorbed by the increased number of independent registrants. Conversion, then, appears to be correlated most strongly with the 1932 realignment and with men. It is in 1932 that conversion is more important among both men and women, and in both 1932 and 1936–38 men are more likely to have converted than women.

Thus the Jewish community of Boston, while acting in accordance with expectations drawn from studies of realignment and American Jewish political behavior, has also provided some intriguing additions to that body of scholarship. Comparisons of the presidential vote with registration statistics yield the startling result that 1928 was—even in Boston and even among at least one group of new ethnic voters—a deviating election. The critical elections for Jews came not in 1928, but in 1932 and 1936–38. By 1940, support for Roosevelt was so overwhelming that in one precinct he received an incredible 1,174 votes to just 28 for Wendell Willkie. There was no secular realignment in this community, as Key has argued. Rather, it just took time for registration figures to catch up to a realignment which by the late 1930s had already occurred.

One reason there was that lag between registration figures and voting was the importance of conversion to the realignment of Boston's Jews. Between 1932 and 1936, the vote for Roosevelt among lower-middle-class Jews increased 17.6 percentage points as a share of the potential electorate, while the number of Democratic registrants increased just 6.0 percent. Nearly two-thirds of the new support Roosevelt was receiving in 1936 thus came from Republican and independent registrants who had not yet translated their Democratic voting into formal party enrollment. Most of these voters were converts-in-process, who only by the late 1940s and early 1950s would register as the Democrats they had genuinely become by 1940.

Conversion of existing members of the electorate was an important phenomenon among Jews in the 1930s. It was, however, most significant in the early years of realignment and most evident among men. Women and the latter half of the 1930s were characterized much more strongly by the mobilization of new voters into the active electorate. Both processes—conversion and mobilization—are, however, fundamental to a complete understanding of the realignment of the Jewish community in the 1930s.

Finally, it should be recalled that much more occurred in the 1930s than the transformation of a Republican group into a Democratic bloc. That, of course, did occur. What was, however, just as significant and just as dramatic was the demise of class politics in the Jewish community. In Boston, a contiguous, ethnically homogeneous area was divided sharply in the 1920s along class lines. Those cleavages were not only still apparent in the early stages of the realignment, but they persisted as vestiges even beyond the 1930s in the form of partisan registration figures. Thus, although by 1940 upper-middle-class Jews had already converted en masse to the Democratic party, as measured by their vote for president, the staunch Republicanism and class divisions which had characterized the system prior to the New Deal continued to be reflected in the lagging indicator and historical residue of party registration figures.

It is in this class dimension that the two stages of the realignment can perhaps be best comprehended. In 1932, all Jews, regardless of class, began to move toward the Democratic party in terms of registration as well as votes. The movement was, however, erratic and not always unidirectional. As mentioned earlier, for example, Republicans between 1930 and 1934 actually out-mobilized Democrats among upper-middle-class women. Then, by 1936–38, previous Democratic gains were consolidated and the flow toward the Democratic party among all Jews suddenly became steady and strong. In that period, measured by the vote cast for national offices, lingering attachments to the Republican party collapsed. Of course it would take more time for that conversion to translate fully into party registration figures. But that fact made the conversion no less real—there was no longer any hesitation in the shift toward the Democrats. By the late 1930s, all Jews had united in a joint political cause and spoke in a single voice. The party ties that had begun to fray in 1932 were finally severed by 1938, as the members of Boston's Jewish community made the unprecedented discovery that, politically, their self-interests had come to coincide with their common interest.

3

The Italians

There was no partisan realignment among Bostonians of Italian heritage. Unlike Jews or blacks, Italians in Boston had been Democratic well before the 1930s. In 1920, the group's "peak" year of Republican strength in the two decades studied, Democrats accounted for 83 percent of all registered voters enrolled in one of the two major parties. Although short-term factors occasionally affected electoral decisions—in 1940 little less than in 1920—the Democratic vote remained, on the whole, solid throughout the period. Democratic candidates for Congress and for the state senate in 1924 both received about 90 percent of the total Italian vote cast that year. It did not take an Al Smith or a Franklin Roosevelt to convince Boston's politically active Italians to register and vote overwhelmingly Democratic.

What did occur after 1928, however, was a tremendous mobilization of new voters on behalf of the Democratic party. In East Boston, twice as many men and three times as many women were registered in 1940 as had been in 1924. The growth of the active electorate was even more dramatic in the North End, the poorer of the two lower-class communities. Between 1924 and 1940, the level of political participation in the North End tripled among men and multiplied by a factor of eight among women. Although there was no realignment within the Italian community, the mobilization of new Italian voters would have a profound impact on the aggregate realignment occurring at that time in the city, the state, and the nation.

Previous studies have suggested that, in some places outside of Boston, there were Italians who had indeed realigned between 1928 and 1936, shifting in those instances from traditional Republican allegiances to the Democratic party. John Allswang documents just such a shift in Chicago. In 1928, of those Chicago Italians registered in one of the two major parties, only 15 percent considered themselves Democrats. Even so, in that year Al Smith received the support of most of Chicago's Italian community. An erosion of identification with the Democratic party, which had been occurring among that group during the 1920s, was finally reversed, Allswang claims, in 1930.[1]

Samuel Lubell similarly notes that, with the 1928 candidacy of Al Smith, "throughout New England, whole voting elements such as the French-Canadians and Italo-Americans were swung out of the Republican party never to return." He offers as an example the case of Rhode Island's transformation, which culminated in the "bloodless revolution" of 1934. Since the nineteenth century, Rhode Island's Irish and Yankees had been engaged in a constant struggle for control of the state's political machinery. In the middle and holding the balance of power were the Italians, an increasingly large and important element. Beginning gradually after the First World War but accelerating after 1928, once-Republican Italians began to move to the Democratic party. That movement was responsible, Lubell argues, for the ultimate success of the Irish and the Democrats in gaining control of the state government by the mid-1930s.[2]

Perhaps nowhere outside of Dublin, however, did the Irish more thoroughly dominate politics than in a city just north of Providence. Only by considering the complex relationship in Boston between the city's Irish and Italians can the early strength of the Democratic party among Boston's Italians be placed in its proper context.

By 1920, the Irish had been in Boston for three or four generations. While they still clashed with the Yankees, who continued to control the city's social and economic life even as the Irish had assumed dominance in city politics, the two groups shared a certain hostility toward the new immigrants from southern and eastern Europe. The sentiment was rarely expressed, but—at least in opposition to the invading hordes of Italians and Jews—the Yankees and Irish grudgingly recognized their common roots in the British Isles. A 1930 volume reflecting on the city's tercentenary remarked that "Boston remains the most British, and particularly the most Irish, among the large American cities." Especially notable in that comment is the equation of Irish and British, striking at a time when discrimination against the Irish by the Yankees was still so pervasive. John Stack contends, then, that the insularity of Boston's Italian community in the 1920s and 1930s was in part a response to both "Irish political discrimination and Brahmin-Yankee socioeconomic prejudice."[3]

Yet, bonds between the Irish and the new immigrants did exist. Both groups remained outside the culture and life of Protestant America. The divide between Yankee and Irish in Boston had historically been a sharp one and remained so during this period. With the new Italian immigrants, the Irish shared a common religion and were victimized by a common bigotry. So the Irish recognized in the prejudice against the newer immigrants the same forces which had been arrayed against them for almost a century. Italians, moreover, surely sympathized with a certain Irish hostility toward the Jewish community. The two, poor, Catholic groups, after all, faced not only an entrenched Yankee establishment but an immigrant-stock community with an alien culture swiftly attaining middle-class status. As Jews in Boston continued to improve their material and social situation, the Irish and the Italians realized with some bitterness the difficulties they themselves were experiencing. But all immigrants, if especially the Italians, must have seemed to the Irish promising political allies in the fight against the exclusionary, Yankee-dominated system. Thus the Irish helped lead the opposition to legislation designed to curtail immigration as well as to quotas restricting the number of black and Jewish students at Harvard.[4] The period was shaped by a great paradox: the same recent immigrants who would be religious and political allies of the Irish in opposition to the Yankee establishment would also, in their very foreignness, dramatically attest to and affirm the Americanism of the Irish.

That ambivalence with which the Irish beheld the Italians, that desperate belief in superiority clouded by nagging doubt, shaped relations between the two groups in the 1920s and 1930s. As they came into contact, an early paternalism often degenerated into the bitter competition of equals. Soon after arriving in Boston, for example, the Italians tired of the local organization of the Roman Catholic church, which was completely controlled by the Irish. They proceeded, then, to form their own "national" churches. Such churches—St. Leonard's and Sacred Heart in the North End, St. Lazarus and Our Lady of Mount Carmel in East Boston—were distinct from the geographically centered parish churches and existed specifically to serve Italians in the area.[5]

Economic factors, too, contributed to a grinding tension between the two groups. Throughout these years, the Italians shared with Irish immigrants particularly miserable living conditions and little hope of socioeconomic advancement in their lifetimes. Stephan Thernstrom recalls that "it was widely believed at the time that the new immigrants were an inferior breed, and were far less likely to become assimilated into the American mainstream than their predecessors." He finds, however, that such a generalization was untrue, that the new immigrants from southern and eastern Europe, including the Jews and the Italians, did not share common patterns of socioeconomic mobility which distinguished them from such old immigrant groups as the British and the Irish. "What was thought to be the old-immigrant pattern applied to the British but not to the Irish," finds Thernstrom; "what was taken to be the new-immigrant pattern applied to the Italians but not to the East Europeans." Further, he adds, "these parallels between the Italians and the Irish and between the British and the East Europeans apply not only to the initial occupational distribution of these groups but to the pace of their subsequent occupational advance as well." The Irish and the Italians were "drastically overrepresented" in the lowest-status jobs and a "skidding syndrome'' ensured that succeeding generations of those groups would fare little better. A variety of explanations were given for this situation. Among them were an agrarian background which supposedly encouraged short-term consumption over long-term goals like education, thrift, and development of a career. John Stack suggests that these problems were compounded by the Italian reliance on neighborhood and family ties, and the inability of those institutions to engender educational or socioeconomic mobility. Concentrated at the bottom of Boston's socioeconomic ladder, the Italians and the Irish were, of all the city's white ethnic groups, struck most severely by the Great Depression.[6]

Circumstances helped to bring the city's Irish and Italians into close and constant physical contact. The two neighborhoods that by 1920 were home to most of the city's Italians—the North End and East Boston—had only a few decades earlier been two of the most Irish sections in the city. In assuming dominance over the North End and over large sections of East Boston, the Italians had not only directly displaced Irish, but they were daily confronting Irish institutions still operating in those areas as well as the fact of a continued Irish presence in nearby Charlestown. Every Sunday, streams of Irish Catholics from Charlestown would pour into the city to worship at St. Mary's, a mission church in the North End.[7]

The North End is the oldest residential area in Boston. It is a well-defined area at the northern tip of Boston's peninsula, on the waterfront and at the edge of the city's financial district; it is identified on map 2. Settled by early colonial settlers, it remained a Yankee neighborhood until the middle of the nineteenth century. At that time, the Irish immigrants arriving in Boston began to make their homes there. The North End, within twenty-five years, was almost solidly Irish. After two centuries as a section of Boston attractive to old-stock Yankee residents, the North End had evolved into the single largest concentration of foreigners in the city. Soon, however, the Irish were themselves displaced by newer waves of immigration. By 1895, the area contained 7,700 Italians, 6,200 Jews, and only 6,800 Irish. Another transition had begun, and within a generation, Italians, and especially southern Italians, completely dominated the North End.[8]

One estimate placed the Italian population in the North End at 14,000 by the turn of the century—representing all but 4,000 of the Italians in the city and fully half of the entire North End population. In *Americans in Process,* written in 1902, Robert Woods stated his belief that soon the North End would be an Italian stronghold. Already by that year other groups in the neighborhood had begun to leave. ''When the North End reached the point of human saturation, the less persistent material—that is, the Jews and the Irish—found its way to neighboring places, leaving the Italians in possession.'' Frederick Bushee referred to the area in 1903 as principally an Italian quarter, although it still contained at that time large numbers of Jews and Irish. It was a neighborhood packed with tenements, where, as Bushee wrote, ''the Italians live in a more crowded manner than any other people in the city.'' The number of Italians in the North End continued to soar, reaching almost 30,000 by 1910. On the eve of World War I, Italians finally constituted almost all of the North End's population. The 27,000 Italians in the area in 1920 represented over 90 percent of a total population in the North End of 29,000 and a large, if shrinking, share of the 80,000 Italians then living in Boston. Hanover Street ran through a compact village of Avellinese, while North Street was in the heart of a thoroughly Sicilian neighborhood. By the early 1920s the population of the North End had begun a gradual decline, as residents left the congested section for the West End and East Boston. About 21,000 people, virtually all of them Italian, still lived in the North End in 1930. The same area in 1940 contained fewer than 18,000 inhabitants. Between those years, the total number of persons in the city of Italian stock rose above 90,000.[9]

Absorbing a steadily increasing share of Boston's Italian-stock population throughout the period was East Boston. Unlike the West End, which was also attracting thousands of Italians, the community in East Boston had emerged by 1920 as an important and highly homogeneous center of Italian population. By the late nineteenth century, in a pattern paralleling events in the North End, Irish immigrants had displaced most of the Yankees living in East Boston. Then, beginning in the 1890s, Italians and Jews began to enter certain sections of East Boston, spurring an exodus of Irish.[10]

By the 1910s, Robert Woods and Albert Kennedy, in *The Zone of Emergence,* described an Italian community of more than 10,000 people centered around Cottage, Sumner, Havre, and Decatur Streets in the southern section of East Boston. That colony, they wrote, had begun forming in the mid-1890s, but had experienced the bulk of its growth only since 1904. Most of the Italians moving to East Boston had come from the North End. Although the new area was nearly as poor as the North End, it was less congested and contained a greater number of second-generation Italians. The City Planning Board, in a 1915 study of East Boston, discussed the Italian presence:

> Attracted by the low rentals, pleasant open spaces and sunny gardens on Jeffries Hill, the Italians began ten years ago to cross from the North End and to buy or build with a view to establishing permanent homes in East Boston. They have increased greatly in numbers and now form an important factor in the community, where they bid fair to spread over much more of the territory in the future. They have found cheap land and agreeable living conditions and appear to be contented to make their homes permanent, and they seem to thrive even in the more crowded sections. . . .

> Italians have replaced the Jews at Jeffries Point, with a center at Cottage and Maverick streets. They have spread into Chelsea street nearby and are building out into the newly-filled marsh areas.

By 1920, there were virtually no Jews left in the area south of Marion Street. They, like the Irish, had largely left, and their former neighborhoods had been taken over by a growing Italian population. Ward Two—the entire section south of Prescott and Princeton Streets, shown in map 1—contained, in 1920, almost 21,000 first- and second-generation Italians. With a comparable population of 23,000 a decade later, that area had by 1930 surpassed the North End as the largest concentration of Italians in Boston. One thousand more persons of Italian heritage were living there in 1940; by the 1930s, then, a large, established Italian community was massed in the southwestern corner of East Boston.[11]

As Italians came, by force of numbers, to dominate the North End and large sections of East Boston, they encountered an entrenched Irish political network. By the turn of the century, ironically just as their Irish population bases began to crumble, John F. "Honey Fitz" Fitzgerald had gained control of the North End, while Patrick "P. J." Kennedy was ward boss in East Boston. Only much later would the power and achievements of the two men be overshadowed by a future grandson.[12]

The ambivalent relationship between Irish and Italians in this period was translated into the political sphere. Italians defined their political preferences in relation to a Democratic party run by the Irish. Thus J. Joseph Huthmacher contends that "the Republicans won the bulk of the New Immigrant vote in the early years" because of dissatisfaction with Irish politicians. "Irish Democrats, having just recently won for themselves the fruits of political success on the local level, were generally loathe to share them with later arrivals." Resented by the newer immigrants, the Irish and the Democratic party were rejected by many Italians in favor of the Republicans, who were perceived as the party of a strong economy. In some areas, certainly, Irish ward bosses, by dispensing favors, "accommodated the newer immigrant elements and secured their allegiance" to the Democratic party, at least in local elections. But, overall, there was initially a general inclination among Boston's Italians to vote Republican. Serino, contending that aversion to Irish Democrats motivated Italians to become Republicans for years after they had first begun voting, argues:

> The abusive treatment which Italian immigrants and their children underwent at the hands of their Irish neighbors in the North End and East Boston was to evoke feelings of resentment which lingered long after the original motives for these difficulties had disappeared. The repercussions of this mutual dislike were felt throughout both periods. It can be presumed that many Italians selected the Republican Party only because it represented the party in opposition to the Irish-Democrats.

Contemporaries at the turn of the century confirmed in their observations the tendency of Italians to vote for the Republican party.[13]

Even then, however, it was clear that those ties had begun to erode seriously and that the Democrats were having increasing success in attracting Italian support. "The Irish," noted Robert Woods in 1902, "have made great efforts to win the Italians to the Democratic party. They are co-religionists, and they can love each other for their common enmity to the Jew." By the early 1910s, the vast majority of Italians in Boston had become Democrats. They had shifted sides partly because they began to identify with the Irish and partly because of the pressures exerted by machine politics. Compared to the Jews, who boasted of their independence from party machines and refused to follow anyone's advice on how to vote, the Italians seem to have cooperated more with the wishes of the local Democratic hierarchy. They "are much more docile," according to Woods's 1902 account. West End Democratic leaders welcomed the exodus of Jews from that area to Roxbury and Dorchester because "they were somewhat more troublesome to deal with than were the Italians." As Woods commented, the Italians "make good political workers. They organize effectively, and are quite disinterested." Whether because of inducements provided by Irish Democratic politicians, a basic unfamiliarity with the political system, or an alienation from the business of politics as it was conducted in Boston, most Italians either absented themselves from the active electorate or came to accept the leadership of the local Democratic party and its Irish bosses.[14]

Table 3.1 presents registration figures for Italian men and women in Boston between 1920 and 1940. Again, as in Chapter 2, all numbers are expressed as fractions of the total potential electorate. Thus, for example, of all adult men living in the North End, only one in five was registered to vote in 1926. Throughout the period, Democrats enjoyed an overwhelming advantage in party enrollees. As mentioned earlier, in 1920—the best year for Republican registrants—83 percent of all voters identifying with one of the major parties considered themselves Democrats. By 1940, that figure had climbed above 95 percent. At least by this measure, there is no evidence of any realignment in the twenty years.

What did occur, however, was a tremendous mobilization of new voters. The number of people registered to vote soared during this era. Although the Democrats made immense gains, virtually all of those increases in support resulted from former nonvoters entering the active electorate. There is no basis for believing that conversion of Republicans was a significant factor in what was almost exclusively a massive Democratic mobilization. In three of the four groups of Italians, the number of Republican registrants actually increased between 1920 and 1940. And, among East Boston men, the fourth group, the decrease in Republican enrollees—2.2 percent—represented only

Table 3.1 Party Registration Figures in Italian Precincts as Percent of Total Potential Electorate

	East Boston Men				East Boston Women			
	All Reg.	Dem.	Rep.	Ind.	All Reg.	Dem.	Rep.	Ind.
1920	26.9	17.8	4.4	4.7	5.1	3.6	0.2	1.3
1922	27.8	22.3	3.7	1.8	11.0	8.8	0.9	1.4
1924	29.8	21.9	4.2	3.7	14.1	10.7	0.9	2.4
1926	25.1	19.0	3.4	2.8	12.1	8.8	0.7	2.6
1928	34.1	24.6	3.4	6.2	15.3	11.2	0.8	3.3
1930	38.9	27.1	3.3	8.5	18.9	14.0	0.5	4.4
1932*	46.3				25.0			
1934	51.1	45.5	2.9	2.8	30.5	22.6	0.8	7.0
1936	54.3	44.9	2.6	6.8	32.8	31.3	1.1	0.4
1938	58.1	50.4	2.0	5.7	38.8	37.2	1.2	0.5
1940	62.3	54.3	2.2	5.7	42.2	36.2	1.1	4.8
	North End Men				North End Women			
	All Reg.	Dem.	Rep.	Ind.	All Reg.	Dem.	Rep.	Ind.
1920	15.4	10.9	1.8	2.6	0.7	0.4	0.0	0.3
1922	19.2	13.4	2.0	3.8	5.2	4.0	0.3	0.9
1924	18.4	14.2	1.9	2.2	4.8	3.8	0.4	0.6
1926	20.0	14.6	2.0	3.3	6.9	5.3	0.3	1.3
1928	26.4	16.2	2.0	8.2	7.4	5.2	0.4	1.8
1930	31.7	20.1	1.8	9.8	9.7	6.3	0.6	2.8
1932*	36.7				10.2			
1934	47.3	33.4	1.9	12.0	20.6	16.4	0.8	3.4
1936	51.0	44.1	2.3	4.6	27.8	23.8	0.9	3.1
1938	54.4	49.7	2.4	2.3	31.3	27.6	0.8	2.9
1940	57.2	40.2	2.2	14.9	37.7	30.6	1.2	5.9

*Party enrollment figures are not available for 1932.

a minute fraction of the Democratic increase of 36.5 percent of the electorate. No evidence exists, then, for supposing that Republican conversions were of any importance in the expansion of the Italian Democratic majority in patterns of party registration.

Mobilization of new voters must similarly account for the great gains at the ballot box made by Democratic candidates in this period. As table 3.2—the Italian vote for president, representative in Congress, and state senator—shows, accretions to Democratic totals were substantially greater than any Republican losses. In East Boston, for example, the Democratic vote for state senator increased 17.3 points between 1924 and 1932, while the Republican

Table 3.2 Vote in Italian Precincts for President, Representative in Congress, and Senator in General Court as Percent of Potential Electorate

	East Boston President			East Boston Congressman		East Boston State Senator	
	Dem.	Rep.	Other	Dem.	Rep.	Dem.	Rep.
1920	5.9	8.0	1.0	5.6	9.5	6.9	6.4
1922				11.6	2.5	10.0	3.4
1924	6.9	5.3	3.8	15.6	1.9	12.7	1.8
1926						10.0	2.7
1928	23.9	1.9		20.7	1.9	19.7	1.9
1930				20.7	1.3	19.7	1.1
1932	27.4	1.6		29.1	1.3	30.0	1.8
1934						28.7	1.6
1936	34.8	3.9	2.3	31.9	4.6	33.0	4.6
1938							
1940	29.7	17.5		36.4	7.2	33.5	7.9
	North End President			North End Congressman		North End State Senator	
	Dem.	Rep.	Other	Dem.	Rep.	Dem.	Rep.
1920	2.4	6.1	0.2	2.8	5.7	4.7	2.9
1922				7.5	1.1	5.9	2.3
1924	4.5	4.1	2.0	10.0	0.9	6.8	1.2
1926						6.5	3.3
1928	20.7	1.2		19.3	1.3	19.2	1.1
1930				15.5	1.3	15.4	0.8
1932	23.2	1.7		23.3	1.2	22.5	0.9
1934						27.1	1.3
1936	33.9	4.1	1.4	29.4	4.9	33.7	3.2
1938							
1940	23.4	22.4		32.6	7.5	29.3	9.1

vote remained unchanged. A similar phenomenon occurred in the North End: between 1924 and 1936, when the Republican candidates for president were supported by identical numbers of potential voters, the level of Democratic support rose 29.4 percentage points. It seems logical to conclude that virtually the entire Democratic gain in electoral support was made up of persons newly mobilized to vote.

Surely, despite an overall pattern very similar to registration figures, actual voting decisions did fluctuate in ways that would seem to contradict earlier conclusions. It has often been argued, for example, that men and women like those living in these precincts had been steadily deserting the Republican party during the 1920s until they finally became Democrats with their votes for Al Smith in 1928. In 1920, after all, Warren G. Harding, a Republican, carried Boston's two Italian communities with comfortable margins. Four years later, Democrat John W. Davis would win those communities, but only with a narrow plurality. Looking at the votes for president between 1920 and 1928—a Republican majority, then a close Democratic plurality, then an overwhelming vote for Al Smith—one is tempted to see a realignment toward the Democratic party over the course of the decade. Governor Smith did, of course, enjoy enormous popularity among Boston's Italians. The issues which his campaign symbolized—his Catholicism, his immigrant background, his familiarity with the big cities—were issues which had particularly strong appeal to Italians, who saw in the candidacy of Al Smith a test of their own eventual acceptance by other Americans. Consequently, Italians turned out in unprecedented numbers to vote for Smith in 1928. In the North End, turnout more than doubled between 1924 and 1928, while in East Boston it rose 60 percent. The belief that generations of Republican dominance, especially among immigrant groups like the Italians, finally ended in 1928 is one held not unreasonably by a number of important scholars who have relied primarily on voting statistics.[15]

Indeed, many have suggested not only that this election signaled the end of an era, but that the mobilization in 1928 on behalf of Al Smith was largely due to women finally beginning to exercise their franchise. It is in this sense that Lubell claims that "the outpouring of women lifted the number of voters" in Boston by 44 percent over the 1924 presidential election. "Smith," he argues, "made women's suffrage a reality for the urban poor." David Burner concurs in that observation. He states that "part of the explanation for Smith's strength in the immigrant cities . . . was an apparent rise in voting among Roman Catholic women." Examining Italian census tracts in Boston to support that argument, Burner concludes that, presumably between 1924 and 1928, "female registration rose by twenty-nine per cent" in precincts he identified as Italian. Andersen cites that figure to buttress her contention that "immigrant women, . . . who had received the franchise in 1920 but had failed to vote then or in 1924, suddenly turned out in 1928 to support Smith."[16]

Evidence from Boston suggests, however, that the Italians in that city were not gradually realigned in the 1920s. Further, the important mobilization that did occur did not reach its climax with the candidacy of Smith in 1928. And, most interestingly, it is clear that the bulk of new voters attracted to Smith that year were men; the mobilization of large numbers of women in these neighborhoods did not take place until the 1930s.

The basic fallacy in seeing in the Italian vote for Harding evidence of Republican support is to view that vote, and subsequent presidential votes, in isolation. It is of compelling importance to examine other variables such as party registration and votes for lower offices. What those measures suggest is a fundamental commitment to the Democratic party by Boston's Italians that was already established by 1920. The Republican votes in 1920 for national offices were apparently deviating votes. Italians, along with many other Americans, had grown disillusioned with Woodrow Wilson and his party. A long and bloody war had resulted in a world neither safer nor more hospitable to democracy. In 1920, Italians repudiated the national Democratic leadership and opted for Harding-style "normalcy." That deviancy filtered down to the vote for congressman and even the vote for state senator, exaggerating Republican support for both offices. While Italians did not enthusiastically endorse the national party ticket in 1924, they at least voted overwhelmingly Democratic in both the congressional and state senatorial races. Throughout those years, their commitment to the Democrats in terms of party registration was solid, immune to short-term influences.

Corroborating this understanding of the presidential votes in the 1920s as being only a poor reflection of underlying party affiliations are the elections which came before and after that period. Burner, whose analysis of the Italian vote appears at least roughly accurate, estimates that in 1916 Wilson received 67 percent of the Italian vote in Boston. If that is true, it makes little sense to view support for Harding in 1920 as a true indicator of Republican strength in the community. What it does show is enormous fluctuation in the Italian vote for president. Similarly, long after the consolidation of whatever realignment supposedly transformed them into loyal Democrats, Italians were again voting in large numbers for Republican candidates for national office. Franklin Roosevelt had alienated many Italians by characterizing Italy's invasion of France as a "stab in the back." As a result, in 1940, Wendell Willkie fared better in East Boston and in the North End than had any Republican candidate since 1920.[17] Table 3.2 shows the depth of resentment against the Democratic party, as Republican votes rose sharply even for congressional and local elections.

The pattern of strong support for Wilson in 1916, followed by a Harding victory in 1920 and only tepid backing for Davis in 1924, and finally culminating in Democratic landslides in 1928 and 1932, characterized New York as much as Boston.[18] Whether the Italian communities of New York or any other city also exhibited strong attachments to the Democratic party as early as 1920 deserves future investigation. But that the underlying loyalties of Boston's Italians were Democratic throughout the 1920s and 1930s is clear, and that fact is hardly refuted by temporary forces operating in elections at both ends of the period. Attesting to the lack of any realignment in the North End or East Boston during these decades was the massive Democratic edge among party registrants, as shown in table 3.1, and the support, seen in table 3.2, enjoyed by Democratic candidates for Congress and for the state senate. Both sets of statistics indicate a basic identification with the Democratic party sturdy and in place throughout these years.

From table 3.1, some interesting conclusions can be drawn for the nature of the Italian mobilization in the 1920s and 1930s. It is obvious, first, that the election of 1932—rather than that of 1928—was at the center of the single greatest surge in mobilization of new registered voters.[19] Between 1930 and 1934, striking gains were made within each group in attracting members of the potential electorate to active political participation. There were, to be sure, important increases as well between 1926 and 1930 and between 1934 and 1940, depending on the particular set of Italians examined. Those increases, however, were generally not as large as those over 1932, and only the 1932 gains were tremendous across all divisions, among both women and men in both the North End and East Boston.

Curiously, those comparative increases in registration did not show up in the votes for president in 1928 and 1932. Table 3.2 shows only a moderate gain in support for Roosevelt in 1932 over the 1928 vote for Al Smith. What apparently happened was that almost everyone registered to vote in 1928 did so, while in 1932, when the number of registered voters was rising sharply, many registered voters did not exercise their franchise. Even though greater permanent gains in mobilizing new registrants were made in the 1932 election, Al Smith as a candidate was much more successful than Roosevelt in attracting those new voters to the polls.

The comparison between 1928 and 1932 becomes even more interesting upon realizing that not only did the total number of registrants increase more sharply in 1932 (as measured by differences in registration patterns between 1930 and 1934) than they had in 1928, but so did the number of registered Democrats. That is, between 1926 and 1930, many of those newly registered to vote did not enroll in either party. Between 1930 and 1934, in contrast, the increase in Democratic identifiers kept pace with, and sometimes even outstripped, gains in total enrollment. In 1928, then, a large number of new registrants entered the active electorate as independents yet turned out in record percentages to vote Democratic. Four years later, more people registered to vote and the vast majority of them assumed Democratic identification, but the fraction of them actually casting votes in support of Democratic candidates fell sharply from 1928 levels. It is, admittedly, a paradox. All that can be said is that the mobilization of new voters in these precincts—viewed in terms of voting as well as registration figures—occurred in at least two stages, and that the election of 1928 represented an initial, not the final, stage in the mobilization of Boston's Italians.

One last point raised by table 3.1 is worthy of discussion and indeed may yield the most fascinating insight into the politicization of this community. Contrary to accounts mentioned earlier suggesting that immigrant women were largely responsible for the 1928 mobilization on behalf of Al Smith, such a scenario cannot accurately describe the electoral behavior examined in this chapter. That fact is particularly interesting since much of the empirical evidence supporting the notion of a huge surge in the women's vote in 1928 was drawn from Italian precincts in Boston. In truth, as table 3.1 shows, the peak period of mobilization among women coincided with the elections of 1932 and 1936. Men, on the other hand, were mobilized earlier, primarily around the elections of 1928 and 1932. Between 1926 and 1930—the years before and after the supposed surge by women to Al Smith—registration increased 6.8 points among women in East Boston and just 2.8 points in the North End. Over the same period, men made gains in registration of 13.8 percent of the potential male electorate in East Boston and 11.7 percent in the North End.

In addition, there was at this time an imbalance in the number of men and women in Boston's Italian community. A number of sources have noted that an unusually high percentage of the Italian immigration consisted of young men who had come to the United States for economic reasons.[20] As late as 1928, 53.4 percent of the Italians in East Boston and 58.4 percent of those in the North End were men. Even if the same fraction of men and women had been mobilized on behalf of Smith that year, the contribution of male registrants to the total gain would have been greater simply because a significant majority of the potential electorate was male. Men, however, were mobilized with an intensity unmatched by women in 1928. As fractions of their respective potential electorates, more than twice as many new men voters as new women voters in East Boston were mobilized in 1928. In the North End, four times as many men as women were mobilized that year. And compounding those ratios was the basic fact that there were many more men than women in the population. Thus, in terms of absolute number of votes, the increased support among men represented an even larger number of actual new voters.

The mobilization of Democrats in 1928 was, then, the result of a heavily male-based mobilization. Women did not begin to mobilize in comparable numbers until 1932, as table 3.1 illustrates. Apparently, Al Smith's base of support was among newly registered men and not, as previously thought, among women in those neighborhoods. Men experienced their largest gains in mobilization between 1926 and 1934, in reaction probably to the campaigns of Al Smith and Franklin Roosevelt and the intervening onset of the Depression. Women, on the other hand, were mobilized somewhat later.

Throughout the 1930s new women continued to register to vote in substantial numbers even after the pace of mobilization had slowed among men. The emotional hurdles to the exercise of the ballot among Italian women seem to have taken some time to overcome. Perhaps the candidacy of Al Smith helped to prepare women for later registration and voting, but it was not until the Roosevelt elections of the 1930s that they actually began to act.

V. O. Key, Jr., in his analysis of presidential elections, remarked that in 1928 in New England "a sharp and durable realignment . . . occurred within the electorate, a fact reflective of the activation by the Democratic candidate of low-income, Catholic, urban voters of recent immigrant stock."[21] No group better fits that description than the one we have just examined: Boston was and remains the urban center of the region, and at that time the only significant new immigrant group of Catholic voters was the Italians. Still, it is important to recognize that Italians in Boston were not realigned at any point in the 1920s or 1930s, even as they were surely "activated" in great numbers. Although the community was unwavering in its underlying commitment to the Democratic party, it did make large numerical gains in active electoral support through the mobilization of new voters.

A version—substantially condensed in time—of Key's notion of secular realignment had taken place in the North End and East Boston. While Key's perspective was one of long-term, gradual change, his description of the mechanism of that change was particularly apt for the situation of Italians in New England. "A plausible hypothesis," he wrote, "would be that the major shifts in partisan balance over the history of the party system have been in considerable measure the product of cumulative secular changes, changes that reflected both relative increases in the numbers of some sectors of the population and declines in others as well as the gradual growth in political consciousness and solidarity of the swelling population categories." The central word for Key in that description of secular realignment was probably "gradual." There was, though, nothing gradual about the mobilization of Italians in Boston. It was massive and sharp and durable, and even if it did not effect a realignment within the Italian community, the addition of these large numbers of new voters to the total electorate did contribute to the city's aggregate realignment toward the Democratic party. Samuel Lubell knew the consequences of Italian political activity: "By 1915, one of every five babies born in Rhode Island was Italo-American. In 1938, the state legislature declared Columbus Day a legal holiday, less in tribute to Columbus' discovery of America than to its discovery that every fifth voter in the state was Italo-American." Many of Boston's Italians had, by the end of the 1930s, mobilized to vote. As a group, they had grown just slightly more Democratic between 1920 and 1940. But in that time the size of their active electorate had exploded, and the Italian vote, in terms of absolute numbers, had become a serious factor in local and state politics. In 1936, Columbus Day was made an official state holiday by the General Court of the Commonwealth of Massachusetts.[22]

4

The Blacks

The story of the New Deal realignment in Boston's black community is the story of a gender gap. By any measure of voting, that community was mobilized and decisively realigned between 1932 and 1936. From registration figures, however, we find among black men only a pattern of slow, secular realignment beginning in 1928 and continuing for a decade. At no point is there an acceleration or deceleration of movement toward the Democratic party. Had men alone exercised the franchise, the realignment would have been gradual, taking shape surely but slowly in the years following Al Smith's candidacy. That a realignment occurred in the mid-1930s strong enough to suddenly destroy group party attachments rooted in the Civil War witnesses to the power of the female vote. Black women, unlike black men, did not realign gradually. Rather, they mobilized in a large surge in 1936. At this time we can only guess at what the forces behind that mobilization were, but its impact was tremendous. In timing and force, that realignment was so great as to finally characterize the entire community, ironically obscuring the role of paramount importance played by women.

Years before, there had been a much less serious threat to the staunch Republican ties of Boston's black community, one which was defused within the party and, presumably, within the active electorate. At the beginning of the twentieth century, blacks in Boston were critical of their national party's leaders. John Daniels, in his 1914 account of the city's black community, *In Freedom's Birthplace*, vividly describes the "hostile sentiment" of the period, which was directed principally toward President Theodore Roosevelt and William Howard Taft, his heir apparent. The event which ignited the wave of criticism was Roosevelt's 1904 dismissal of part of a black regiment "for the alleged 'shooting-up' of the town of Brownsville, Texas. . . . Taft, who as Secretary of War carried out the obnoxious Brownsville order, was blamed along with his chief." Exacerbating the delicate situation was the pervasive belief among blacks that Roosevelt was abandoning their interests in an effort to achieve reconciliation with Southern whites.[1]

Black Bostonians, as the contest for the presidency approached, organized a mass meeting in Boston's Faneuil Hall in the spring of 1908. Their objective was to block the selection of Taft as the Republican nominee. Not only had Taft reportedly referred to blacks as "political children, not having the mental stature of manhood," but—and perhaps even more important—he was viewed as "Roosevelt's candidate," and it was widely feared that he would "carry out the latter's policies," including those inimical to the black community. Efforts to block Taft's nomination failed, though, and in November he received overwhelming support from the nation's blacks in his race against William Jennings Bryan.[2]

As Daniels relates from his 1914 vantage, Taft's nomination did, in fact, prompt some of the more radical black "agitators"—including William Munroe Trotter, editor of the Boston *Guardian*—to go "to the extreme of advising the Negroes to vote for Bryan, the Democratic nominee. To the great mass of the Negroes, however, this, of course, appeared like jumping from the frying-pan into the fire." Loyalty to the Republican party was too deeply ingrained. "So strong is the influence of tradition in the Negro's party allegiance . . . and so unpromising any alternative political alignment which has thus far presented itself," observes Daniels, "that the actual proportion of this race in Boston who in national elections vote otherwise than as Republicans, is slight." For blacks and chronicler Daniels alike, the idea of blacks "turn[ing] their ballots against that party to which they are indebted for the franchise itself" was a notion bordering on sheer ludicrousness.[3] And yet, within barely two decades, blacks, at least as a group, decisively severed their links with the Republican party and became Democrats, as the mobilization of new voters overwhelmed the prior Republican advantage. "Jumping into the fire" had become, in Boston as elsewhere, an attractive political option by the 1930s, as blacks who had previously been apathetic suddenly began to mobilize to vote.

Various accounts of the period confirm that realignment nationally. Ladd and Hadley cite studies of Chicago and Cincinnati in support of their contention that blacks, for the last time, "apparently remained decisively Republican in the 1932 Presidential election." After that year, blacks across the country moved into the Democratic party. "[Franklin] Roosevelt took about 70 percent of the black vote in both 1936 and in 1940," report Ladd and Hadley, "at least doubling his 1932 proportion." Blacks, it is argued, realigned in 1936 for pragmatic, economic reasons; they were benefiting in concrete ways from President Roosevelt's programs. Such a massive shift in party support occurred, argue Ladd and Hadley, even though many blacks continued to identify with the Republican party. As late as 1940, "blacks were roughly evenly divided in self-described party loyalties." What Ladd and Hadley suggest, then, is that conversion was essential to the realignment among blacks, that Roosevelt was attracting the votes of many Republicans who only later would bring their partisan identification in line with their new loyalties.[4]

In his examination of voting in New York and Chicago, David Burner offers examples of different realignments in two black communities. As Ladd and Hadley suggest, Burner finds that blacks in Chicago were still fiercely Republican in 1932, giving 70 percent of their vote to Herbert Hoover. New York blacks, in contrast, appear to have already realigned that year in favor of the Democratic party. Whereas in 1928 Hoover received 59 percent of the two-party vote, his share four years later was only 42 percent. Roosevelt apparently captured the loyalty of blacks in New York as early as 1932. Part of Roosevelt's and Al Smith's success in New York—for, though not attaining a majority, Smith, a Democrat, did remarkably well among blacks—was the fact that they were both highly popular New York governors and thus had special appeal to voters in that state.[5]

As a general rule, though, it is believed that the year of realignment among American blacks was 1936. Samuel Lubell points out that, while a majority of blacks voted Republican in 1932, by 1936 "in many cities two out of every three Negro voters were for Roosevelt." Older blacks, reports Lubell, were appalled by the shift in party allegiance. They rued their community's betrayal of the party of Lincoln: "Our people are selling their birthrights for a mess of pottage."[6]

Kristi Andersen, in *The Creation of a Democratic Majority,* goes beyond simply placing the realignment of blacks in 1936 to actually discussing the electoral mechanics of that realignment. In her study of Chicago at the ward level, she confirms the overwhelming support for Hoover in 1932 revealed by Ladd, Hadley, and Burner. Between 1932 and 1936, further, the fraction of the two-party vote received by Roosevelt doubled from 24 percent to 48 percent. But especially interesting is Andersen's assessment of that realignment in terms of the full potential electorate:

> A notable change took place between 1932 and 1936 in which Democrats more than doubled their share of the electorate, from 16 percent to 34 percent, and the Republicans' portion declined from 52 percent to 37 percent. This appears on the surface, at least, to be an instance of real change in preferences on the part of individual voters. The turnout rates in these two presidential elections were nearly identical. . . . [T]he magnitude of the change implies a good deal of individual change—something not found in either the native or ethnic white neighborhoods.

This passage is significant as the only substantial instance of voter conversion discovered by Andersen in her study of Chicago—and is for that reason cited by Sundquist in support of his own conversion scenario. Realignment among every other ethnic group Andersen examines appears to be explained largely by mobilization of new voters.[7]

Most scholars, in fact, seem convinced that conversion, rather than voter mobilization, was fundamental to the realignment among blacks. Not only Andersen, but Ladd and Hadley as well, subscribe to that belief. Further support for the position is provided by Erbring et al., who, along with Sundquist, suggest that the realignment among blacks became noticeable as early as 1934.[8] "While there is some evidence of 'recruitment' in 1936, much of partisan change must . . . be attributed to 'conversion,' " argue Erbring et al. "Black voters really did desert the GOP."[9] They attribute Democratic gains among blacks to economic issues, and they are convinced that conversion within the active electorate accounted for much of those gains. As the same scholars mention in another article, black turnout "remains dramatically below everyone else's throughout the entire period"; there was no dramatic mobilization of new voters.[10]

Among those who have considered the issue, then, there appears to be a consensus that blacks were realigned at least by 1936, and that the realignment was a classic example of voter conversion. Indeed, even Kristi Andersen, the foremost proponent of the mobilization argument, finds conversion in her study of Chicago's black population. Connected to this conversion scenario is the assertion that blacks turned out in very low numbers, that the fraction of the black potential electorate actually voting was well below that of most, if not all, other ethnic groups.

There is no evidence from Boston's black precincts to support such conclusions. Turnout among the city's blacks was never remarkably low and it rose steeply after 1932. While black Bostonians were indeed realigned in 1936, or perhaps even 1934, that realignment represented largely a mobilization of new voters, especially of women. It was that mobilization, not a large-scale conversion of former Republicans, that fueled the development of a Democratic majority in the black community in Boston.

Between 1920 and 1940, Boston's small black population was concentrated in an area straddling the upper South End and lower Roxbury. In addition, there was by 1940 a growing black presence in upper Roxbury, beginning to displace the Jewish community which had been there for years. That latter area, in Roxbury highlands, can be located on map 3. Its center was the point where Humboldt Avenue meets Townsend Street; from there blacks had consolidated a neighborhood that stretched three blocks in every direction except southeast. The much larger black district, though, and that from which precincts were chosen for this study, was located several blocks to the north, in lower Roxbury and the upper parts of the South End. By 1940, blacks dominated the area bordered by Ruggles Street, Washington Street, Northampton Street, and Columbus Avenue, as well as, for several more blocks closer to downtown Boston, the area just south of the nearby railroad lines and north of Columbus Avenue. Those neighborhoods are shown on map 2.

As Stephan Thernstrom notes with wry understatement, there was no population explosion in Boston's black community in the period under study. "Boston was somewhat distinctive in attracting less than its share of Negro newcomers during the Great Migration of World War I and its aftermath," he writes. "The Boston Negro population grew by only half between 1910 and 1930, while Detroit was registering gains of 1900 percent, Cleveland 800 percent, Chicago 430 percent, New York 250 percent, and Philadelphia 160 percent." In 1920, there were 16,350 blacks in Boston; by 1940, there were 23,679. Against a static total city population, this represented a rise to 3.1 percent of Boston's population from 2.2 percent twenty years earlier. At a time when other Northern cities' black populations were rapidly expanding, Boston's grew by only 45 percent over two decades.[11] Although this fact might limit generalizing from findings in Boston to the rest of the country, the relative stability of the city's black community does offer assurance that demographic changes did not entirely eclipse more subtle political changes. Had Boston's black community of 1920 become only a minor fragment of a vastly larger community twenty years later, any discussion of electoral mechanics would be overshadowed by the effect of newcomers to the potential electorate. While the potential electorate in these precincts did expand in the 1920s and 1930s, its base remained intact, permitting us to view with some accuracy the political change that occurred in the black electorate in that period.

Various authorities confirm the tremendous concentration of blacks in Boston's upper South End and lower Roxbury, a concentration in place by the 1910s and persisting for decades after 1940. Long established in the West End, the center of Boston's black population had begun to shift first to the lower—not upper—South End by the end of the nineteenth century. Southern migrants, especially, had constituted a significant presence in the lower South End since Reconstruction.[12] More general movement to the South End began in the 1890s. The influx was apparently led by the more respectable leaders of black society, eager to escape the squalor of the West End and the back of Beacon Hill. Attracted by the spacious town houses built in the early years of the century for upper-class whites who never came but instead flocked to the Back Bay, these respectable blacks formed the nucleus of the South End's emerging black community. They came first to the lower South End, but spread quickly away from town. As the older black communities of the West End and the lower South End deteriorated, the city's blacks moved in a huge exodus to the upper South End and lower Roxbury. Frederick Bushee, writing in 1903, observed: "The Negroes have been living in the West End and in the South End almost exclusively for many years, but now a new section near the Roxbury line is becoming the most popular of all."[13]

Ten years later, John Daniels referred to that "new section" as "the principal Negro center of Greater Boston." The blocks "from Camden to Hammond Street," noted another settlement house worker in the 1910s, "has been entirely surrendered by the Irish to the Negroes who began to settle thereabouts some twenty years ago." By 1914, according to Daniels, "5000 Negroes, or 40 per cent of the entire Negro population of Boston proper," lived in the area bounded by Northampton, Ruggles, Washington, and Tremont Streets in lower Roxbury and the upper South End. Still, within that area, blacks constituted only about one-third of the whole population; Irish, Yankees, and Jews made up the remainder. "But to-day [in 1914] the Negro population is rapidly increasing from without, and promises to be, for some years at least, the largest racial element." Daniels was prescient. Although, at the time, this area was "far from being a solid Negro quarter," it quickly developed into such a neighborhood, as later census figures and other sources confirm.[14]

Throughout this period, Boston's blacks continued to be confined to unskilled, menial jobs. Data reported for census tract R-1 yield some insight into the lives of the black men and women studied in this chapter. That census tract covered much of the black district in lower Roxbury and the upper South End. In 1930, 5,481 blacks were counted in the census tract, 80 percent of a total population of 6,860. The average housing unit in tract R-1 rented for about $25 a month in 1930, at least $10 below the citywide average—and that figure of $25 probably represented housing of even lesser value, since patterns of residential segregation limited housing options for black families and often forced them to pay unusually high rents. Only 26 percent of the families in this census tract owned a radio set in 1930, compared to 56 percent of all of Boston's families. By other measures, too, the area from which precincts were chosen was relatively poor. Its homes were crowded and often dilapidated, and secure, well-paying jobs were rare. As Thernstrom writes, "There was virtually no improvement in the occupational position of black men in Boston between the late nineteenth century and the beginning of World War II."[15]

The task of selecting black precincts was obviously a delicate and complex one, since the great concentration of blacks was, even in the early 1920s, still diluted by the presence of many other ethnic groups. Fortunately, many streets in this area were labeled in accounts from the 1910s as solidly black, solidly white, or mixed. That information was combined with block data from the 1940 census, and precincts were chosen in the areas of greatest black concentration within the larger district of the upper South End and lower Roxbury.[16]

Like many others across the country, blacks in Boston were realigned permanently by 1936. In that year, Roosevelt received 68 percent of the two-party vote, a substantial gain from his 46 percent share four years earlier. Support in the black community for Democratic candidates for Congress and the state senate also increased markedly in that period.

Far more interesting for present purposes, however, is the nature of that increase at the level of the individual voter, especially the question of whether it arose from the conversion of former Republicans or the mobilization of new voters. One way of measuring this is to look at the level of support for Republican candidates as a percentage of the total potential electorate. It is assumed that if the same number of people, as a proportion of the potential electorate, are voting Republican from one year to the next, then the Republican party has not lost supporters to the Democrats. In that case, it is unlikely that much of the Democratic gains could come from conversions. And, as table 4.1 shows, the Republican vote for president—examined as a fraction of the total potential electorate—actually rose slightly between 1932 and 1936, and again between 1936 and 1940, although it had fallen from higher, 1920s levels. Hoover received the votes of 14.1 percent of the potential electorate in 1932, Alf Landon received 14.7 percent in 1936, and Wendell Willkie received 15.8 percent in 1940. There is, then, at least if it is assumed that we are dealing with the same Republicans throughout the period, no loss of Republican support for that party's presidential candidate. Similar trends are visible in elections to Congress and the state senate.[17]

Table 4.1 Vote in Black Precincts for President, Representative in Congress, and Senator in General Court as Percent of Potential Electorate

	President			Congressman		State Senator	
	Dem.	Rep.	Other	Dem.	Rep.	Dem.	Rep.
1920	2.9	26.9	0.7	3.5	27.3	4.5	24.4
1922				4.3	15.8	5.8	13.5
1924	4.2	22.8	1.8	4.5	21.5	5.7	14.5
1926						3.8	10.6
1928	9.2	19.7		4.1	24.3	7.0	18.5
1930				4.2	16.3		
1932	12.1	14.1		5.9	20.3	8.2	17.6
1934						16.6	12.1
1936	30.9	14.7	0.5	15.4	26.2	21.0	15.5
1938				13.0	27.8	20.8	15.9
1940	36.5	15.8		17.7	27.6	24.0	16.5

While Republicans were successfully maintaining their base of support in the potential electorate, Democrats benefited from massive mobilization. Between 1932 and 1940, Roosevelt's vote as a percentage of the potential electorate grew threefold, from 12.1 percent in 1932 to 36.5 percent in 1940. The bulk of that gain occurred between 1932 and 1936—in that time, the Democratic share increased a full 150 percent, to 30.9 percent of the potential electorate. The huge increase in the number of Democratic voters, combined with a stable number of Republicans, clearly indicates that the mobilization of former nonvoters into the Democratic party played the central role in realigning Boston's black community.

A nearly identical increase in Democratic support occurred in the congressional and state senatorial races. For Congress—against George Holden Tinkham, a firmly entrenched Republican incumbent who actually increased his share of the black potential electorate throughout the 1930s—the Democratic vote rose from 5.9 percent of the potential electorate in 1932 to 15.4 percent in 1936. A similar increase, also in excess of 150 percent, occurred in the Democratic share for state senator, from 8.2 percent in 1932 to 21.0 percent in 1936.

Although all three levels of voting reflected sizable Democratic gains in the potential electorate, there are differences among them worth noting. The uniform 150 percent rise in the Democratic votes between 1932 and 1936 obscures the fact that absolute increases were not identical. Thus, the Democratic vote for Congress increased by 9.5 points from its 1932 base of 5.9 percent, a gain identical in relative, but not absolute, terms with the 18.8 point increase in the presidential vote, which began in 1932 from a base of 12.1 percent. It appears that, while lower offices were gaining Democratic support proportionally at the same rate as Roosevelt, their gains in terms of absolute numbers of voters were not as large. Blacks were not voting for Democrats at lower levels as strongly as they were voting for a Democratic president. But, of course, levels of support in these precincts had always been less for lower offices, and the Democratic vote for local candidates was, indeed, increasing at a clip at least as fast as the increase at the presidential level.

It would seem, then, that the mobilization of new voters accounted for most, if not all, of the Democratic gains between 1932 and 1936, the period of feverish realignment in voting in Boston's black community. In that period, Republicans maintained a constant level of support within the potential electorate—actually gaining voters at the presidential and congressional levels, while losing a few voters in the much more erratic state senatorial races. The Democrats, on the other hand, received two and one-half times as many votes in 1936 as they had received just four years before. Mobilization, not conversion, can conceivably account for virtually all that gain.

Table 4.2 is an attempt, like that in Chapter 2, to measure the actual amount of conversion under two different assumptions. If it is assumed that all new voters voted for Democrats—a notion which, while extreme, does place an upper limit on mobilization—then conversion is unnecessary as an explanation at either the presidential or congressional level. There are enough new voters to cover the change. The massive increases in Democratic support for those offices were the result, under this assumption, of pure mobilization. Again, the vote for state senate is not as useful a measure, the Republican share especially having fluctuated much more than for the other two offices throughout the 1920s and 1930s.

In the second case for which conversion is measured, we assume that entering voters split their party vote in the same manner as the rest of the electorate. That would mean that the presidential two-party share of 1936 (not included is the third-party vote that year, 1.2 percent), 66.9 percent Democratic and 31.9 percent Republican, reflected the composition of new as well as existing voters. This, then, is our upper limit for conversion, the assumption that Republicans were able to mobilize an important share of new voters. Under this assumption, Republican conversion explains 37 percent of the rise in the Democratic vote for Congress and accounts for 28 percent of Roosevelt's increased support. On the whole, however, mobilization appears to be the principal factor behind the increase in Democratic electoral support among blacks in 1936.

That large rise in Democratic support coupled with a stable Republican base is duplicated in party registration figures. In contrast to conclusions reached by students of blacks in other cities, blacks in Boston were as active politically as most other ethnic groups. "As to the proportion of those [Negroes] who actually go to the polls and vote," according to Daniels, in his 1914 study of Boston's black community, "it may be said that this appears to be not far below the corresponding proportion in the case of the white population, and that in a similar way it varies greatly from time to time and

Table 4.2 Estimates of Conversion in Black Precincts—Vote for President, Representative in Congress, and Senator in General Court, 1932–1936

	△ Total		△ Dem. Vote		Rep. Vote	△ Rep.	% Dem. Gains from Conversion If: All New Dems.		New as Vote	
Office	Raw	Adj.	Raw	Adj.	Share	Vote	ΔR_p	%	ΔR_p	%
President	+19.9	+21.2	+18.8	+19.4	.319	+0.6	−0.7	0	+6.1	28
Congressman	+15.4	+16.7	+9.5	+9.8	.630	+5.9	−1.0	0	+9.5	37
State senator	+10.7	+12.0	+12.8	+13.2	.425	−2.1	−0.9	9	+4.2	48

Note: ΔR_p is the predicted change in the Republican vote.

in accordance with the occasion.''[18] The number of men registered to vote as a fraction of all adult men was 38.3 percent in 1920, hovered at or just below 40 percent until after 1932, and then rose to 58.2 percent by 1940. Women, too, having just been extended the franchise in 1920, recorded registration rates at or slightly above 30 percent in the late 1920s and early 1930s, which soared to 54.7 percent by 1940. Thus, political participation among all blacks appears to have been moderate in the earlier part of this period, reaching significantly higher levels by the mid-1930s. The size of the total active electorate rose from 34.8 percent to 48.6 percent between 1932 and 1936, by far the sharpest four-year gain in the period among Boston's blacks.

What is particularly exciting in evaluating the mechanics of the realignment is the breakdown of registration figures by gender. Men—perhaps surprisingly, considering the apparent sharpness of the realignment among all blacks in 1936—had been gradually mobilizing since 1928. Both in terms of total registered voters and registered Democrats, gains on the average of 5 percent were made every two years between 1928 and 1936. As table 4.3 shows, total registration among men as a fraction of the potential electorate increased over the eight years from 34.8 percent to 53.1 percent, while registered Democrats increased from 5.2 percent to 24.4 percent. At the same time, Republican registration fell 5.2 percent and the number of unenrolled rose 4.3 percent. There was no sharp partisan change in 1936, as might be expected from the voting figures. Rather, there was a slow drift among men toward the Democratic party corresponding to a gradual rise in the number of registered voters.

Table 4.3 Party Registration Figures in Black Precincts as Percent of Total Potential Electorate

	Men				Women			
	All Reg.	Dem.	Rep.	Ind.	All Reg.	Dem.	Rep.	Ind.
1920	38.3	7.9	18.9	11.6	10.8	0.6	5.8	4.4
1922	40.0	7.5	16.2	16.3	23.6	2.6	5.9	15.1
1924	40.8	9.3	20.5	10.9	25.5	3.9	12.1	9.5
1926	35.8	5.5	18.1	12.2	25.6	2.4	11.7	11.5
1928	34.8	5.2	20.3	9.3	29.5	3.1	15.3	11.1
1930	41.1	10.7	16.2	14.1	36.1	10.7	14.1	11.3
1932*	39.2				30.6			
1934	45.9	20.4	14.8	10.8	35.9	12.6	11.9	11.4
1936	53.1	24.4	15.1	13.6	44.5	19.7	11.6	13.2
1938	52.2	24.4	12.2	15.5	47.8	20.6	12.3	14.8
1940	58.2	26.8	12.5	18.9	54.7	23.6	13.4	17.7

*Party enrollment figures are not available for 1932.

Women, in contrast, mobilized to vote and registered as Democrats largely in one surge at the time of the 1936 election. Between 1934 and 1938, total registration among black women increased from 35.9 percent to 47.8 percent, as table 4.3 shows. In the same period, Democratic registrants increased from 12.6 percent to 20.6 percent of the female potential electorate, as the number of Republicans and unenrolled were also rising. The only other sudden rise in the share of registered Democrats occurred between 1928 and 1930, for reasons undetermined. That earlier gain, however, may well have been due to local conditions. Indeed, overall registration in 1930 surpassed comparable figures for the presidential election years of 1928 and 1932, suggesting that unusual and temporary factors caused the 1930 increase in Democratic registration. Unlike black men, then, black women were permanently mobilized with a rush, and in that manner became Democrats, in 1936.

As is shown in table 4.4, the amount of conversion suggested by registration figures for black men and women can be estimated under assumptions similar to those made in evaluating the presidential vote. These calculations, again, are identical to those used in Chapter 2 for estimating the extent of Jewish conversions. In one column, it is assumed that all new registrants become Democrats; in the other column, it is assumed that new registrants divide in the same manner as the presidential vote of the whole black community.

In addition to those two scenarios, three cross-cutting assumptions are made to reflect the presence of a large pool of registrants who enroll as neither Republican nor Democrat. The first case assumes that any decline in Republican support reflects a loss of those Republicans directly to the Democrats; that is, no lost Republican simply drops his party affiliation and becomes independent. The second case measures the amount of Democratic conversions from all non-Democratic registrants, combining Republicans and the unenrolled as potential converts. The third case accounts for the amount of conversion necessary if the maximum number of lost Republicans simply drop party affiliation and become unenrolled, and the Democratic gain thus arises from others among the unenrolled adopting a party affiliation.

Application of this potpourri of assumptions to the registration data for black men yields a number of conflicting conclusions. If it is assumed, as in the first case, that registrants dropping their Republican affiliation immediately became Democrats, then conversion was very significant both in the longer period of 1928–36 and the more compact period surrounding 1936. The gradual growth in the number of Democratic registrants between 1928 and 1936 came, to some extent, probably, from within the active electorate. Electoral mechanics are less clear for 1936. In both periods, especially once

Table 4.4 Estimates of Conversion in Black Precincts, Party Registration Figures

Case I. All former Republican registrants becoming Democrats

	△ Total		△ Dem. Reg.		Rep. Vote Share	△ Rep. Reg.	% Dem. Gains from Conversion If: All New Dems.		New as Vote	
	Raw	Adj.	Raw	Adj.			$\triangle R_p$	%	$\triangle R_p$	%
Men										
1928–36	+18.3	+21.8	+19.2	+19.7	.319	−5.2	−2.0	16	+5.0	52
1934–38	+6.3	+8.6	+4.0	+5.0	.319	−2.6	−0.7	38	+2.0	92
Women										
1928–30	+6.6	+7.3	+7.6	+7.7	.538	−1.2	−0.4	10	+3.5	61
1934–38	+11.9	+13.7	+8.0	+8.6	.319	+0.4	−0.6	0	+3.8	40

Case II. Democratic gains from former non-Democratic registrants

	△ Total		△ Dem. Reg.		Rep. Vote Share	△ R+I Reg.	% Dem. Gains from Conversion If: All New Dems.		New as Vote	
	Raw	Adj.	Raw	Adj.			$\triangle(R+I)_p$	%	$\triangle(R+I)_p$	%
Men										
1928–36	+18.3	+21.8	+19.2	+19.7	.319	−0.9	−3.0	0	+4.0	25
1934–38	+6.3	+8.6	+4.0	+5.0	.319	+2.1	−1.3	0	+1.4	0
Women										
1928–30	+6.6	+7.3	+7.6	+7.7	.538	−1.0	−0.7	4	+3.2	55
1934–38	+11.9	+13.7	+8.0	+8.6	.319	+3.8	−1.2	0	+3.2	0

Case III. All former Republican registrants becoming Independents

	△ Dem. Reg.		Initial Rep. Reg.	Expected Rep. Reg.	Final R+I Reg.	% Dem. Gains from Conversion If: All New Dems.		New as Vote	
	Raw	Adj.				Diff.	%	Adj.	%
Men									
1928–36	+19.2	+19.7	20.3	18.3	28.6	+10.3	0	+7.0	0
1934–38	+4.0	+5.0	14.8	14.1	27.7	+13.6	0	+2.7	0
Women									
1928–30	+7.6	+7.7	15.3	14.9	25.4	+10.5	0	+3.9	0
1934–38	+8.0	+8.6	11.9	11.3	27.1	+15.8	0	+4.4	0

the pool of unenrolled voters is included, mobilization, too, appears to have been a very important factor.

For women, mobilization has great explanatory power for the 1936 realignment, accounting completely for the Democratic gains in all but the most extreme of the six cases. Indeed, it seems much safer to endorse mobilization and rule out conversion among women in 1936 than among men. Clearly, the odd movement of women toward the Democrats in 1930, mentioned earlier, depended more heavily on the conversion of existing voters than did the definitive realignment of 1936; perhaps as much as half of the Democratic gain in 1930 came from existing non-Democratic registrants. There was, though, no realignment in 1930, as the term is conventionally understood. The gains made by women in that year were probably due to local factors, and, more important, they were temporary. In 1936, the year of the great, enduring black shift toward the Democrats, women acted in one great wave of mobilization.

The realignment of blacks in Boston, then, so vivid and sharp in the 1936 elections, was accompanied by a commensurate rise in the number of Democratic identifiers among registrants. Between 1928 and 1936, the Democratic vote for president as a fraction of the potential electorate increased 21.7 percent, while the corresponding increase in Democratic registrants was 17.8 percent. By 1938, Democrats outnumbered Republicans by almost two-to-one on registration rolls. It is reasonable to conclude that, in Boston at least, the vast majority of those voting for Roosevelt and for other Democratic candidates in the mid-1930s were people who had recently registered and enrolled as Democrats. There was no large time-lag between the registration and voting statistics, suggesting that very little of Roosevelt's support was coming from converted Republicans. Rather, as a comparative examination of tables 4.1 and 4.3 indicates, registered Republicans continued to vote Republican. The bulk of Democratic votes was probably coming from newly registered Democrats as well as from registrants enrolled in neither party.

Even more specifically, it appears that the realignment of 1936 was due primarily to the mobilization of new women voters. Black men, largely through mobilization but also through conversion, had been gradually shifting toward the Democratic party over the course of a decade. The shift in 1936 among black men was no more emphatic than it had been at any other point in that period. Indeed, that slow and constant rise in the number of male Democratic registrants appears to have helped produce the concurrent, gradual increase in support for Democratic candidates that began with the candidacy of Al Smith in 1928. Against that backdrop of black men steadily moving toward the Democratic party throughout the late 1920s and the 1930s suddenly came the decisive realignment of 1936. In that year, black women surged toward the Democrats in unprecedented numbers; black men merely continued their long-term, gradual movement in that direction. The unmistakable conclusion, then, is that the realignment in Boston's black community, while dependent on past trends among men, was the immediate result of the decisions of women of voting age. What we can too easily consider a black realignment in 1936 was instead a realignment of black women. So successfully were they mobilized as Democrats and so sharply did they realign existing political forces that the decisions of those Boston women in 1936 would be long misread as a realignment of the entire black community.

5

The Yankees

It was by the 1920s and 1930s a group small in numbers but still possessing immeasurable influence and mystique. They were the Yankees. The Brahmins. They were, without resort to hyperbole, a city personified, the Proper Bostonians. An illustrious tradition of political leadership has for centuries characterized and, indeed, helped define Boston's Yankee elite, the men and women of Anglo-Saxon Protestant stock many of whose forebears had helped found the infant Massachusetts Bay Colony. When the Republican National Convention convened in Chicago in 1920, the prominence in state and national affairs of several socially correct Bostonians occasioned little excitement. Henry Cabot Lodge, who had served in the United States Senate since 1893 and had arguably long been the most powerful member of that body, was in the midst of waging a national campaign against the League of Nations, a campaign which he did in fact ultimately win. The speaker of the United States House of Representatives in 1920, Congressman Frederick Gillett, was, too, a well-bred son of Massachusetts. And just beginning his second and final term as governor was Calvin Coolidge, whose national stature had increased enormously with his handling of the Boston police strike the preceding year. All three men were, by virtue of their ancestry and their place in society, true Brahmins.[1]

At the Republican convention, as he rose to nominate Coolidge for vice-president on the ticket headed by Warren G. Harding, a member of the Oregon delegation paid homage to the Bostonian's heritage. He rose to speak and, recognized by Lodge—keynote speaker and permanent chairman of the convention—"took the Convention by storm." First, he noted, he had come to Chicago with explicit instructions from the electors of Oregon to place Lodge's name in nomination for the vice-presidency, but the "senior Senator from Massachusetts, . . . [t]his distinguished statesman," had asked that he refrain from doing so. As a result, he now wished to nominate "another citizen of Massachusetts who has been much in the public eye during the past year." His ensuing brief remarks, emphasizing history and family, captured an important facet of the Boston Brahmin's conception of himself and his environment. "In this tercentenary year of the landing at Plymouth," he observed, "it is peculiarly fitting that we put on our National ticket a gentleman of New England birth and ancestry, whose public career exemplifies those principles of liberty under law which his forefathers brought across the Atlantic." With that rhetorical flourish, surely more serious than sarcastic, Governor Coolidge's name was placed before the convention. In three years this "gentleman of New England birth and ancestry" would, upon Harding's death, become president of the United States of America.[2]

Throughout the 1920s and 1930s, and as true in the decades before as in the decades to follow, old-stock Yankees with firm roots in the tradition and heritage of the Boston community practiced and succeeded admirably in the field of public service. Coolidge ran for and won election to the presidency in 1924. In the same year Alvan T. Fuller was chosen governor of Massachusetts and Frederick Gillett was elected to the Senate seat formerly held by David I. Walsh, an Irish Catholic and the state's first Democratic senator since the Civil War. Then, in November, Henry Cabot Lodge died, two years after having been reelected to his sixth consecutive term as senator. His seat was assumed by yet another solid Republican and Brahmin, William M. Butler, who proceeded to lose it to Walsh in the 1926 election. Charles Francis Adams—"patriarch of all present-day Adamses," wrote Cleveland Amory, "he is, in a City of First Families, Boston's acknowledged First Citizen"—was appointed secretary of the navy by President Hoover in 1929. In 1930, having served one term in the Senate, Gillett retired. His seat in Washington was then captured by a Democrat, albeit one with an impeccable old-stock Yankee ancestry, Marcus A. Coolidge. Finally, six years later, the Massachusetts Republican party and his family regained their place in Washington when Henry Cabot Lodge, Jr., was elected to the Senate. When, in 1938, Leverett Saltonstall, Speaker of the Massachusetts House of Representatives, won election to his first term as governor, the Brahmins of Boston showed no signs of disengagement from affairs of state. The decade ended, after all, with a Cabot Lodge in the Senate and a Saltonstall in the State House. Little had changed since 1920 in terms of the political involvement of the Yankee elite or the mutual affection between them and the Massachusetts electorate.[3]

In those same two decades, however, the context in which political battles were waged had changed tremendously. A state which in 1920 had been predictably Republican had become fiercely competitive by 1940. Realignments had transformed the political composition of Massachusetts while creating a Democratic majority nationally.

Of the five Boston groups studied in this work, only the Yankees remained steadfast in their Republicanism. The privileged old-stock elite residing on Beacon Hill and in the Back Bay barely wavered in their loyalty to the party throughout the years of its demise locally and nationally. In 1920, of all men and women registered to vote and enrolled in one of the two major parties, 93 percent were Republicans. By 1940, still 84 percent of the Yankee electorate was Republican. Conversely, the number of Democrats in the Yankee population more than doubled, from 7 percent to 16 percent of the population. There was less of a slow drift toward the Democratic party than a small, sudden lurch in 1932. One is struck, however, not by the relatively meager movement toward the Democrats but by the continued solid support for the Republicans. That constancy is reflected not only in registration figures but in the votes for state and national officials.

Certainly at least as interesting as the decisions made by voters, though, were those made by their friends, neighbors, and relatives who remained outside the active electorate. In what is one of the more paradoxical findings of this study, Boston's Brahmins and the only slightly less distinguished Yankees living in their midst—the group which was by all measures the best educated, the wealthiest, and the most privileged in the city; the group residing in the single area of the city which was made up of virtually all native-born Americans; the group from which came many if not most of the state's political leaders—to a large extent abdicated their franchise.[4] The city's Yankee elite did not participate in the mobilization surge which affected the rest of the population.

Indeed, those Yankees apparently experienced a slight political demobilization coinciding with the realignment of the early 1930s. Whereas participation rates increased substantially for all those groups supporting the Democratic party, they fell among these Republican adherents, probably demoralized by their party's new minority status. The Yankees, who had already lost their influence in a city dominated since the turn of the century by Irish Democrats, now were greatly weakened at the state and federal levels. In 1920, only Boston's Irish and middle-class Jews were registered to vote in larger numbers than the men of the Back Bay and Beacon Hill. By 1940, Yankee voter activity had declined mildly in absolute terms, but much more sharply on a relative basis; these scions of Boston society had been surpassed by every other group measurable in the city. No other group—whether black or white, middle-class or poor, native-born or foreign-born—exhibited such profound political apathy.

The roots of this mass Yankee withdrawal from politics can be traced to the influx of Irish immigrants into Boston which began in the 1840s. Prior to that period, Boston and Massachusetts had retained for two centuries a remarkable degree of ethnic homogeneity. Since the foundings of Plymouth in 1620 and Boston in 1630, English settlers and their descendants represented the vast majority of the area's population. That long-established fact was sharply and permanently altered by the arrival of Irish immigrants escaping the mid-nineteenth century famine in their own country. Boston and its Anglo-Saxon citizenry were unprepared for and traumatized by the invasion. As the immigrants huddled into once-genteel neighborhoods, shock swiftly degenerated into revulsion and discrimination. The Irish were not welcome in Boston.[5]

Their arrival, though, forced the city's Yankees to evolve a clear conception of themselves and their English heritage, a self-definition which had become important because of the contrast with obvious outsiders. Thus the Brahmins, descendants of the earliest settlers of the Puritan colony who had since achieved great success in commerce or manufacturing, recognized the common bond that they shared with the less privileged Yankees. Together the two groups of old-stock Yankees had built the city and the state and happily co-existed in its political and social systems; now, in common, they faced an intruder. Beyond that simple recognition of Anglo-Saxon solidarity, though, the coming of the Irish inculcated the city's most privileged Yankee class with a deep sense of its own existence and identity. "It was in reaction to these untouchable newcomers that the tradition of Boston *hauteur* came into being, the proper Bostonian, the myth of the Brahmin." Accompanying this growing self-awareness, the city's Yankee elite developed an enormous affection for Britain and all things British. Boston, the seat of the American Revolution, was now engulfed by Anglophilia.[6]

While the sheer presence of the Irish was profoundly unsettling to Boston's native-stock citizens, even more disturbing was the prospect of these immigrant peasants assuming control over city politics, a situation little ameliorated by the increasingly active supervisory role assumed by the still-Republican Yankee state legislature over the city government. Hugh O'Brien in 1884 became the first Irish mayor of Boston. Although O'Brien was eager to accommodate the Yankee community, the elections of John F. Fitzgerald in 1905 and James Michael Curley in 1913 signalled the ascendancy of a more bitter and class-conscious type of politician. "Corroded with hatred of the Beacon Hill Brahmins," Curley, once in power, avenged himself by neglecting the downtown Yankee neighborhoods, leaving the area "to wallow in its Puritan self-righteousness." By the 1930s Yankee political power had long since dissipated in Boston, even as the Yankees continued to control the city's economic and cultural life. The reformist Good Government Association, a group formed to check the abuses of the Irish Democratic administrations, had disbanded by 1933, also the last year a Yankee would be a serious contender in the mayoral election. "The control of the municipal government," noted the 1930 chronicler of Boston's tercentenary celebration, "has passed out of the hands of the Colonial Americans." Having lost control, the Yankee elite apparently lost interest in what had, at least locally, become a losing and futile cause.[7]

And, yet, even as the Irish threatened to overrun the city and represented an increasingly potent political challenge, the Brahmins did not vacate their Boston homes and escape en masse to the city's suburbs. Instead they congregated in what were, at least by the end of the nineteenth century, the two exclusive neighborhoods still remaining in Boston, the Back Bay and Beacon Hill, both of which can be found on map 2. Thus Charles H. Trout, explaining that some Yankees left the inner city in response to the waves of immigrants, does note that "a substantial number of First Families . . . took refuge in the commodious town houses of the Back Bay where they looked on despairingly at the inundation." Francis Russell speaks, too, of the Brahmin response, commenting that "the Yankee epigoni, appalled by the Celtic locust-swarm, withdrew to the Beacon Hill-Back Bay redoubt. Unlike their Tory predecessors, they did not quit the fort." Although other areas of Boston—West Roxbury, Hyde Park, the Fenway, southern Dorchester, Jamaica Plain, Brighton—attracted many working- and middle-class Yankees well into the twentieth century, they had by the 1920s and 1930s also attracted other ethnic groups, especially large numbers of successful Irish. Only Beacon Hill and the Back Bay retained their ethnic homogeneity into this period, maintaining even through the Depression their distinctiveness as the city's only upper-class sections and its only remaining Yankee enclaves. "The well-to-do old Americans," as one 1930 observer so aptly and pithily described them, yet "cling precariously to Beacon Hill and the Back Bay."[8]

Beacon Hill is the older of the two neighborhoods. Its tenure as a wealthy enclave reaches back across the history of the nation to the late 1790s. At that time the Mount Vernon Proprietors formed a commercial syndicate to develop, in the shadow of the just-completed new Massachusetts State House, the pastures on the southern slopes of the steep hills into desirable residential property. Their venture was a historic success. Their legacy, a handsome neighborhood of early nineteenth century red-brick town houses often termed "more London than London," stands as one of the city's most tangible links to its venerated past.[9]

Some decades passed before the noxious waters of the nearby Back Bay were filled and a residential district arose on the "made land." By the early 1860s, however, the first substantial brownstone houses had been built on the lots nearest to the Public Garden. Swiftly, the Back Bay became the most desirable area in the city. "Of all the residential quarters in Boston," remarks Walter Firey in his 1947 book, *Land Use in Central Boston,* "the Back Bay has been generally known as the fashionable district *par excellence*. At one time it was the home of nearly one-half the *Social Registerites* in [Greater]

Boston.'' Until past the turn of the century, upper-class families moved to the Back Bay and constructed on its wide and elegant streets handsome town houses.[10]

Geography and deliberate decisions established clear physical boundaries to both the Back Bay and Beacon Hill. As a result, both areas, although located in central Boston, were effectively isolated from the rest of the city; they could develop and flourish in isolation, physically adjacent to the poorest areas in the city, yet lacking any contact with those same areas. ''The belt immediately about the business section, hemming it in,'' remarked Woods and Kennedy, ''is given over to a circle of poor and crowded neighborhoods broken in one place by a downtown residential quarter illustrating wealth and social power.''[11] A sense of security and community could pervade these Brahmin districts, held tightly together by the same forces which kept them apart and aloof.

The Back Bay was surrounded by the Charles River, the Muddy River, railroad tracks, and the Public Garden. It resembled a rectangle, a too-perfect series of parallel and perpendicular streets dropped in the middle of the tangled web that is the rest of Boston. As Walter Muir Whitehill describes the ''splendid isolation'' of the Back Bay, he talks of the railway lines which ''created a dreary kind of no man's land,'' firmly dividing the Back Bay from the otherwise adjacent South End. The central street in the Back Bay was Commonwealth Avenue. On one side, toward the Charles River, lay Beacon and Marlborough Streets, on its other side were Newbury and Boylston Streets, and intersecting the five main streets were several cross streets running westward from the Public Garden in neat alphabetical order. The most impeccable addresses in the Back Bay were the water side of Beacon Street and the sunny side of Commonwealth Avenue. Certainly, however, few ever doubted the prestige of living on even the ''wrong'' sides of Commonwealth Avenue and Beacon Street or on Marlborough Street. Fully two hundred feet wide with a park—or ''mall''—down its entire length, Commonwealth Avenue, especially, evoked images of great French boulevards. Or, perhaps, it is more appropriate to recall the vision of the late George Apley, a fictional character created by John P. Marquand, who, upon his arrival in Paris expressed his astonishment when he first saw the Champs Elysées. ''It is surprising,'' he wrote, ''how very much it is like Commonwealth Avenue.''[12]

Beacon Hill, too, was carefully planned to limit access from outside the neighborhood. Its boundaries on three sides were natural: the Charles River on the west, Boston Common to the south, and the State House just past Joy Street on the east. The one physical boundary which had to be artificially created was what one author has termed the ''Pinckney St. Wall'' and what another has called simply ''the border-line between wealth and poverty.''

From the time of the original development of a large, upper-class Yankee community on Beacon Hill, it was decided to limit the district to the south slope of the Hill. On Beacon Hill's back side and extending across Cambridge Street to the North End was Boston's West End, by the 1920s and 1930s a poor immigrant community crowded with tenements and transient housing. "No sharper contrast in physical appearance, economic well-being, or social prestige could be imagined," argued Firey in 1947, "than exists between Beacon Hill proper—occupying the south slope—and the West End." And "this social dichotomy between two directly contiguous neighborhoods has prevailed since the original development of the Hill." Streets were laid out, then, with the specific intention of excluding traffic and persons from the north slope. Pinckney Street became the northern boundary of this self-contained network of streets. To its south and roughly parallel to one another were Mount Vernon, Chestnut, and Beacon Streets. All three have enjoyed enormous popularity, as well as, of course, Louisburg Square, a group of town houses between Mount Vernon and Pinckney Streets arranged around an oval park owned jointly by each of the abutting homeowners. On Chestnut Street, "full of memories of that time when Boston was the Mecca for every literary aspirant, every admirer of genius," lived, at least in the first half of this century, many of the Hill's wealthiest families. And it was Henry James who called Mount Vernon Street "the happiest street-scene the country could show." But Beacon Street, overlooking Boston Common, was probably the street which has been consistently the most desirable of all. "The sunny street that holds the sifted few" was the appellation bestowed upon it by no less a man than Oliver Wendell Holmes.[13]

In the latter decades of the nineteenth century, the development of the grand Back Bay drew Brahmins from virtually all areas of the city. Firey notes that the area soon became "the truly aristocratic section of Boston." By 1910 "hundreds of Boston's most exclusive families made it their home, and most of the city's finest churches, schools, libraries, and other cultural institutions were located there. No other neighborhood either within the city or in its environs could claim equal distinction." Only Beacon Hill survived the challenge, and even it was severely weakened by the movement of population to the Back Bay. Compared to its past prestige, Beacon Hill had by the turn of the century fallen into relative disfavor, as "many old Hill families, attracted by the magnificence and prestige of the new lands, abandoned their historic neighborhood and settled in the Back Bay." Rooming houses, stores, and clubs began to infiltrate a deteriorating Beacon Hill. Still, in 1898 Robert A. Woods could observe that "many of the old families have always remained" on Beacon Hill, even if it was in the Back Bay "where the city's wealth and fashion have made their home."[14]

It was only in the 1910s, just as the Back Bay had reached its zenith, that Beacon Hill was able to reverse the decline of the previous years and slowly begin a resurgence in popularity. Spurred by the activity of two residents in the area, after the turn of the century the neglected town houses were slowly, one by one, renovated. Gradually Beacon Hill's former prestige and reputation began to return as the Yankee aristocracy reclaimed their historic homes. Accompanying this revival was the new popularity of the recently developed land between Charles Street and the Charles River, which had once been filled largely with stables and small workshops. Improvement of the area was effected by the creation of the Charles River Basin and the Embankment, where once there had been unsightly mud flats. ''After 1910, when the Embankment was officially opened,'' observes J. Ross McKeever, ''wooden shacks were condemned by the City, stables were torn down, and blocks of new houses and four and five-story apartments were erected in harmony with the architectural spirit of the older sections of the Hill.'' The area now attracted the same types of families long associated with Beacon Hill itself. On Brimmer Street, an older street in the heart of the new district, ''the houses,'' to the memory of Helen Howe, ''breathe . . . an air of comfort and conformity.'' The Hill's restored and enhanced prestige, as well as the popularity of the new western district on the Charles, continued unabated into the 1930s. Beacon Hill, still a ''single family district,'' remarked McKeever in 1935, ''has preserved its character almost intact . . . since its first development.''[15]

In that same period, however, the Back Bay went into decline. Driven out by prohibitively high property taxes and an increasing scarcity of cheap domestic servants, a large number of families began to desert the Back Bay. They were attracted to the suburbs, which were lately made accessible by the advent of the automobile. The *Back Bay Ledger and Beacon Hill Times,* in a 1940 editorial, commented on the change: ''Commonwealth avenue is a beautiful street in many ways; but it looks like a deserted village in many block lengths, where house after house has been boarded up, and the one time residents gone.'' Some homes were converted into expensive apartments or offices; others remained vacant, ''hollow shells of former mansions'' waiting for a suitable buyer. Although he was specifically thinking of his son's decision to leave Boston for New York, George Apley's thoughts could well have had a more general meaning when (as we are told by John Marquand) he wrote:

> The house was very quiet. Outside the fronts of Beacon Street, the brick walks and the asphalt shone emptily beneath those new glaring street lights that illuminate our front rooms and disturb our slumber. For one of the first times I can remember it seemed to me that Beacon

> Street was a trifle sad in its emptiness. It was as though something had left it. It was like that street in Ecclesiastes "when the sound of the grinding is low."

Meanwhile, especially after the 1910s, retail stores and financial offices began to encroach on Newbury Street and Boylston Street residences, and both streets quickly lost whatever retentive strength they had once possessed. "Though still surpassing in numbers [of elite Yankee families] any other neighborhood," the Back Bay, notes Firey in the 1940s, "has undergone a steady invasion of apartment buildings, rooming houses, and business establishments which are destroying its aristocratic character." Those Brahmins remaining into the 1940s, of whom there were still many, lived on Beacon Street, Marlborough Street, and Commonwealth Avenue, as well as on the several cross streets.[16]

Table 5.1 details one crucial measure of the popularity of Beacon Hill and the Back Bay over time. The table, containing the number of families listed in the Boston *Social Register* and the location of their residences, reveals both the increased prestige of Beacon Hill between the World Wars and the simultaneous sharp decline in the Back Bay. As a directory which confines itself to the most distinguished of the old-stock Yankee families, the Boston *Social Register* is useful in tracing the society leaders of the elite Yankee cohort as well as, presumably, other, unlisted, members of that cohort.[17]

By 1940, still, despite the two-decade-old movement out of the Back Bay by Brahmins, both Beacon Hill and the Back Bay retained their distinctiveness as neighborhoods of wealth and family. A 1937 report for the Works Progress Administration could describe Beacon Hill as "a conservative residential section" and note, too, that " 'The Three Streets' of Boston"—the Back Bay's Commonwealth Avenue, Marlborough Street, and Beacon Street—were still "impeccable residential addresses in their lower numbers." Elite Yankees continued to dominate life in the two districts throughout the

Table 5.1 Boston Families in *Social Register,* by Residential District

District	1894	1905	1914	1929	1943
Within Boston					
Beacon Hill	280	242	279	362	335
Back Bay	867	1166	1102	880	556
Other	372	227	178	122	71
Suburbs	403	807	1049	1345	1993
Totals	1922	2442	2608	2709	2955

Source: *Social Register: Boston,* as tabulated in Walter Firey, *Land Use in Central Boston* (Cambridge: Harvard University Press, 1947), p. 115.

1920s and 1930s. Thus, as a percentage of all homes in each of the two neighborhoods, while 23 percent of Beacon Hill families were upper-class Yankees listed in the 1943 *Social Register,* at that late date such families continued to account for 22 percent of the Back Bay. The numbers had admittedly declined steeply since 1929—when 36 percent of Beacon Hill and 58 percent of Back Bay families were in the *Register*—but even in 1943 they represented substantial segments of the two populations, and were as important numerically in the Back Bay as on Beacon Hill.[18]

Perhaps the best indicator of the high degree of homogeneity that persisted on Beacon Hill and the Back Bay until at least 1940 is the objective information provided by the 1930 and 1940 censuses. Fortunately, census tracts for those censuses coincide quite closely with the boundaries of the two Brahmin neighborhoods. Thus census tract K-2 approximates Beacon Hill, containing all of the south slope between the Charles River and the State House; it, however, goes just north of Pinckney Street to Revere and Myrtle Streets, thus including a sliver of the heavily immigrant north slope. Similarly, census tracts K-3 and K-5 are drawn fairly snugly to the boundaries of the Back Bay. Tract K-5 embraces the southerly side of Marlborough Street and almost all of Commonwealth Avenue, but then continues southward to encompass both Newbury and Boylston Streets as well as part of St. James Avenue. Indeed, tract K-3 is the only tract which falls wholly within the bounds of either of the two prestigious Yankee neighborhoods. Running the length of the Back Bay from Arlington Street to Massachusetts Avenue, tract K-3 includes Beacon Street, the sunny side of Marlborough Street, and two blocks of Commonwealth Avenue.

While all three census tracts will be examined, special attention will be accorded tract K-3. Not only should tract K-3 be the purest of the tracts, both ethnically and socioeconomically, but its characteristics can reasonably be considered applicable to the most desirable sections of the other two tracts. Also, especially since only a small part of Beacon Hill's tract K-2 includes nonelite areas, it should become immediately obvious if, by 1930 or 1940, tract K-3—and thus, by extension, the Back Bay—had declined so severely that it no longer stood comparison to Beacon Hill. Walter Firey, in his 1947 study, implies that by then such a case could indeed have been true. What might be possible, however, is that Firey, in his exhaustive effort to examine the two neighborhoods and contrast the obvious stability of Beacon Hill with the erosion of the Back Bay aristocracy, gives so strong an impression of the differing dynamics of the two areas that he overwhelms the simple fact that the Back Bay, even in 1940, remained as Brahmin as Beacon Hill.[19]

In 1920 the total population of Beacon Hill was 5,897; it fell to 4,486 by 1930 and then rose slightly to 4,613 in the 1940 census. The Back Bay, too, experienced a loss of residents in the 1920s, declining from 9,511 in 1920 to 7,814 a decade later. By 1940, there were 8,928 persons living in the Back Bay. Census tract K-3 is the only one of the three census tracts which was more populous in 1940 than it had been in 1920. Sharp losses in the 1920s obviated whatever subsequent gains were made in tracts K-2 and K-5.[20]

One of the most striking aspects of the Beacon Hill and Back Bay population of this period was the overwhelming preponderance of women. In 1930, in a total population of 12,300, there were 8,612 women and 3,688 men; in 1940, there were 8,826 women and 4,715 men. For every man, there were 2.3 women in 1930 and 1.9 women in 1940. Part of this imbalance was due to a substantial number of clerical workers as well as other young adults, male and female, living in apartments in the two neighborhoods.[21] But factors characteristic of upper-class Yankee households accounted for the bulk of the excess of women over men: a large number of elite Yankee women who had never married and an even larger number of foreign-born domestic servants.

To estimate the number of single Brahmin women living in the Back Bay and on Beacon Hill is not easy. Probably the best figures are those from the 1930 census. In 1930, the number of young, nonelite adults living in the area was still quite low. Indeed, as mentioned above, nearly half of all households were in 1929 listed in the *Social Register,* indicating the presence of an overwhelmingly upper-class Yankee population on the eve of the Depression. Additionally, only in the 1930 census is information available at the level of the census tract regarding marital status and the nativity of parents. Students of the Back Bay and Beacon Hill in this and earlier periods have long noted the presence of a sizable, unmarried female population, of what Helen Howe has referred to as ''the spectacle of a maiden life laid down on the altar of a father's memory.'' Firey, for example, while regretting that ''there are unfortunately no statistical data available on the marital status of the upper class population of Beacon Hill,'' does offer ''the commonplace observation . . . that 'half the aristocratic old maids in Boston live here.' Spinsterhood,'' he adds, ''is a phenomenon that typifies upper class Yankee stock in a good many New England communities.'' Partial explanation of this tendency lies in the fact that while elite men could marry downward without jeopardizing their social status, elite women could not. As a result, many of these women never married.[22]

In the demographic group which comes closest to approximating the Brahmin population—native white persons of native parentage fifteen years of age or over living on Beacon Hill or in the Back Bay—there were twice as many single women as there were single men. Married couples accounted for 37 percent of this population: of 6,022 persons, there were about 1,100 married men and 1,100 married women. Widows and widowers, 571 women and 118 men, formed another 11 percent of the population; divorced persons and those whose status was unknown amounted to just 1 percent. Fully half of the teenage and adult elite Yankee population, therefore, was made up of persons who had never married, 1,078 men and 1,951 women. Many of those, undoubtedly, were too young to marry or were still in school. It seems fair, then, to say that there were as many as 2,200 or 2,300 unmarried and widowed Brahmin women, or at least 1,300 more than the similar group of Brahmin men.

On the opposite end of the social spectrum, but in one of fate's great ironies perhaps the single most definitive indicator of the presence and size of the Yankee elite population, was the overwhelmingly Irish and female domestic servant class. "One could almost be certain," remarks Dennis P. Ryan, "that wherever upper-class Yankees were dining on codfish or scrod, it was being served by steady, dependable, female Irish hands." In 1930, when 8,199 women above the age of fourteen lived on Beacon Hill and in the Back Bay, the census counted 3,301 women engaged in "domestic and personal service." A decade later, the next census would find 1,831 "domestic service workers" in a total female population, age fourteen and over, of 8,574. Fully 40 percent of all women living in the two neighborhoods in 1930 were domestic servants; in 1940, Yankee households having been decimated in the interim by the Depression and by movement out of the city, 21 percent of the female population were still employed as servants to upper-class homes. Indeed, in both years, one out of every five domestic servants in the city lived in the two Yankee neighborhoods. And, despite the sharp drop in the number of servants in the Back Bay and on Beacon Hill in this period, an even sharper drop in the rest of the city resulted in an increasing concentration of Boston's domestic servants in those two neighborhoods by 1940.[23]

Examination of the Back Bay's census tract K-3 illustrates well the demographic characteristics of this servant population. In 1930 there were 2,558 women in tract K-3 who were at least fifteen years of age. Of those, 1,698 were gainfully employed and 1,433 were employed as domestic servants. An incredible 84 percent of the working population and 56 percent of the total female population over the age of fifteen were engaged in domestic service, presumably to wealthy Yankee households. This was, it should be stressed, an overwhelmingly female phenomenon. As a percentage of gainfully employed adults, tract K-3 ranked first in the city for men as well as for women in terms of numbers engaged in domestic or personal service. Still, there were, in addition to the 1,433 female domestic servants, just 79 men similarly employed—representing a mere 5 percent of the total servant population.

It appears, further, that these female servants were virtually all single and foreign-born, the vast majority of them of Irish or other northern European heritage. In a population of 1,353 foreign-born white women, 1,219 were single and 73 were married. Over 90 percent of foreign-born women in tract K-3 had never married, the highest figure of any of the city's census tracts. The comparable statistic for all of Boston's foreign-born white women, in fact, was 20 percent. Whereas eight of ten such women citywide had married, only one in ten in tract K-3 had done so. The Back Bay's foreign-born female population was also peculiar in that there was no significant population of native-born persons of a foreign-born parent. In the city, for example, 31 percent of all white women in 1930 were foreign-born and another 44 percent were born in the United States to immigrants. In census tract K-3, however, the number of foreign-born women, 51 percent, was the highest of any tract in Boston but the number of second-generation women, 8 percent, was the lowest. The juxtaposition of the two figures is stunning. While citywide there were 1.43 second-generation women for each foreign-born woman, in tract K-3 there were only 0.15. Those immigrant women living in the Back Bay and on Beacon Hill were surely not in those neighborhoods to raise families. Finally, it is clear that these women had come in unusually large numbers from Ireland, and, in lesser numbers, from the United Kingdom, Scandinavia, France, and Canada. Thus, of all foreign-born white women, 58 percent were Irish. Of everyone in tract K-3, both male and female, who had been born in Ireland—a total of 797—all but eleven were women: 99 percent of the Irish-born population was female. With a female population whose foreign-born component, at 58 percent, was nearly three times as Irish as the city, the most exclusive Brahmin census tract in the city contained more women born in Ireland than any other census tract in Boston.

How, then, one may fairly ask, can an area whose women were second to none in the city in terms of numbers foreign-born and numbers born in Ireland and numbers engaged in domestic service be considered a homogeneously wealthy and Yankee district? The answer becomes apparent from further investigation. That the Yankees of Beacon Hill and the Back Bay were wealthy is beyond dispute. In 1930, of 910 owned homes in the three census tracts, 711, or 78 percent of the total, were valued in the highest census category, $20,000 and over, representing one-third of all such homes in Boston. Half of all rented homes on Beacon Hill and in the Back Bay—707 units of a total 1,415—cost in excess of $100 a month, again representing one-third of all such rental units in Boston. Indeed, of those units renting for the highest price, $200 or more a month, there were 295 in the two Yankee neighborhoods, accounting for fully two-thirds of the most expensive rental housing in Boston. Citywide, the median home was valued at $7,500 and rented for about $37 a month. While there was occurring in this period a transition away from traditional one-family occupancy of town houses in the Back Bay, in 1930 only two census tracts in the city contained a greater proportion of single-family homes than tract K-3, in which 90 percent of all structures were occupied by one family. The occupations that men in this district pursued were, too, among the most prestigious and lucrative. Of all men gainfully employed in census tract K-3, 15 percent in 1930 were engaged in banking and brokerage; 7 percent were engaged in insurance and real estate; and 33 percent were engaged in ''other professional and semiprofessional service,'' which must by default include such fields as law, medicine, and academe. The proportions of men in each of those ''industry groups''—banking, insurance, and professions—were higher in tract K-3 than in any other tract in Boston.

These families were, however, distinguished for more than their wealth. They were, just as clearly, of thoroughly Yankee stock. According to the 1930 census, 981 men lived in tract K-3. Of those, just 113 were foreign-born, 12 percent of the total and the lowest number for any tract in the city. An additional 104 men were native-born to immigrant parents, at 11 percent second-lowest of all census tracts. The bulk of the male population, 764 persons and 78 percent, were native-born to native parents, the highest such figure in Boston. In a city in which barely one in four men could claim a set of American-born parents, more than three in four could make such a claim in the Back Bay.

Beacon Hill and the Back Bay, then, were in 1930 composed of a dominant Yankee class and a largely Irish-born female servant class. Few lived outside the sphere of the Yankee household. For both men and women, the number of second-generation persons was negligible, placing tract K-3 second-lowest for men and lowest for women of all tracts in Boston. The number of foreign-born persons was one of the most striking features of tract K-3, which at once contained the greatest number of foreign-born women and the fewest number of foreign-born men in the city. Virtually all the women born abroad, and probably some of the foreign-born men, were servants. Making up the remainder of the population were Yankees, the subjects of this chapter. It has already been noted that 78 percent of the male population, the highest proportion in Boston, was of native stock. Equally significant is the fact that fully 42 percent of the female population was born to American-born parents, making it, despite the enormous number of foreign-born servants, the eighth most native census tract in a city of 128 tracts. As should be expected, 81 percent of all white heads of households in tract K-3 were in 1930 of native stock, again the highest proportion in Boston. Even those relatively few men not born in the United States to native-born parents did not dilute the highly Yankee nature of Beacon Hill and the Back Bay. While the women in tract K-3 were among the most Irish in the city, the men in the same area were the most British. Of all foreign-born white men, 70 percent were born in the United Kingdom or Canada; only 34 men in a total population of 981 were born overseas in non-English-speaking countries.

By 1940, the basic facts of ethnicity and socioeconomic status had been modified but hardly overturned. The elite movement out of Beacon Hill and especially the Back Bay had continued and apparently accelerated in the 1930s. Many young couples and clerical workers made homes in apartments carved out of former town houses. Still the underlying character of the population remained relatively stable. Old Brahmin families continued to dominate life in the two districts. Of all residential structures in tract K-3, two-thirds, or 408 of 615, continued to be devoted to one-family, and thus presumably to elite Yankee, occupancy. Only six other census tracts in Boston, including the Back Bay's other tract, K-5, contained a larger fraction of single-family dwellings; tract K-2, on Beacon Hill, was not among them. And, importantly, much of the Yankee movement out of the Back Bay was not accompanied by a correspondingly large in-migration and dilution of the population. The 1940 census reported that 31 percent of all dwelling units in tract K-3 were vacant, the second-highest proportion in Boston and five times the city average. A large number of elite Yankee families either could not or would not find a suitable buyer for their deserted homes in the 1930s.

The Great Depression had by 1940 caused a serious deflation in property values, but the effect in the rest of the city had been even more severe than in the two Yankee neighborhoods. In 1930, 78 percent of all owner-occupied homes in the Back Bay and on Beacon Hill had been worth at least $20,000. By 1940, only 218 of 674 homes, or 32 percent, remained in that category—but now those 218 homes represented three-fifths of all such homes in Boston. The homes with the city's highest average value were in tract K-3; second was Beacon Hill's tract K-2. Positions of the two tracts were reversed in calculations of median value. In both cases, tract K-5 was ranked third. There were in all 550 homes in the Brahmin areas worth $10,000 or over, accounting for 82 percent of all homes on Beacon Hill and in the Back Bay and one-third of all Boston homes valued in excess of $10,000. Citywide, the median home was now worth less than $4,000. Similarly, by 1940, only 207 of 3,269 occupied rental units in the two districts cost $200 or more a month, but those 207 units represented 80 percent of the most costly rental property in the entire city. The number of units on Beacon Hill and in the Back Bay renting for $75 or more a month was 1,276, or 39 percent of all tenant-occupied dwellings in the Yankee areas and fully 43 percent of all units in the

City of Boston costing that amount of money. The city median monthly rental had declined since 1930 to $28. While the Depression and the exodus of Brahmins had contributed to declining property values in the two elite areas, those homes had retained and actually increased their position of vast superiority, in terms of valuation, to the rest of the city. As indices of wealth, housing prices suggest that the Back Bay and Beacon Hill suffered no relative decline during the 1930s.

So, too, the composition of the female population in 1940 shows that a great decline in the number of domestic servants had occurred since the last decennial census, but that the decline, as previously indicated, was even sharper in the rest of Boston than on Beacon Hill and in the Back Bay. While in 1930 more than half of all women in census tract K-3 had been foreign-born, a city high, by 1940 only 32 percent of the tract's women were immigrants—a proportion still above the city average, but far from the highest in the city. The foreign-born population remained heavily Irish and northern European, but slightly less so than in the previous census, evidence of a minor influx into the Yankee neighborhoods of foreign-born individuals who were not servants. In 1940, women born in Ireland still, however, represented just under half, or 47 percent, of all immigrant women living in the census tract most representative of the Back Bay and Beacon Hill. And the Irish population in those areas remained almost entirely female, a statistic confirming the theory that virtually all Irish found in these Yankee neighborhoods were still in 1940 single servants living in Brahmin households: of 430 persons in tract K-3 born in Ireland, 413, or 96 percent, were women. Domestic servants in that tract continued to account for 51 percent of all employed women—highest of any of the wealthier census tracts in the city—and 28 percent of the total adult female population.

Nonelite elements had obviously entered the Back Bay, and, to a lesser extent, Beacon Hill, since 1930. While the number of residential structures, for example, had remained fairly stable over the decade, the conversion of single-family town houses into apartments and fashionable lodging houses had caused a near doubling in the number of inhabitable dwelling units. Vacancy rates and a dwindling number of domestic servants attested further to the gradual displacement of upper-class Yankees.

Yet in 1940 the population retained still its outstanding characteristics of ethnic and socioeconomic homogeneity which, while having surely diminished some since 1930, were hardly less salient. The male population of Beacon Hill and the Back Bay contained even fewer foreign-born individuals in 1940 than it had in 1930—only 162 men in, or 11 percent of, a total population of 1,449 were immigrants—making tract K-3 the most native-stock census tract in the city, save one. While for 1940 statistics are not available at the level of the census tract regarding the parentage of native-born men, it is again true that the foreign-born reflected a substantial British and Canadian contingent, at 46 percent of the total further reinforcing the Yankee nature of tract K-3. The men in these areas were, too, easily the best-educated in Boston. Indeed, in order of median school years completed, the men of tracts K-3, K-2, and K-5 ranked one, two, and three in the city. The median education attained by the male population in tract K-3 was 15.8 years; it was 13.0 in tract K-2 and 12.9 in tract K-5. Citywide, the male median was 8.8 years. Even the women in these three census tracts were, despite the large number of less-educated foreign-born servants, among the most schooled in Boston, with tracts K-2 and K-3 sharing the distinction of containing the city's best-educated females, the women in them having completed a median 12.4 years of formal schooling. Finally, occupationally, although the census categories had been drastically revised, little had changed substantively since the 1920s. In 1940, in census tract K-3, more than half of the working adult male population held obvious positions of leadership. Of 989 men, 248 were professional workers, at 25 percent the highest proportion in Boston, and another 260, or 26 percent, were proprietors, managers, and officials, a number exceeded only by the Jewish tract U-6B discussed in Chapter 2. There were only 5 male laborers in the population, or 0.5 percent of all working men, fewer than any other census tract in the city.[24]

The 1930 census, combined with the Boston *Social Register,* gives powerful support to the argument that, at least until that year, the Back Bay remained with Beacon Hill as an aristocratic Yankee neighborhood. From 1920 to 1930 there can be little ground for questioning the homogeneity of the district. As Walter Firey and many other observers have pointed out, though, the 1930s witnessed an important transition in the composition of these neighborhoods, especially of the Back Bay. Firey, in fact, contrasts the stable social complexion of Beacon Hill with the Back Bay's decline. Still, at least in 1940, even after years of deterioration, the Back Bay retained the prestigious families, ethnic composition, and single-family town houses that had characterized both neighborhoods in preceding decades and would continue to characterize Beacon Hill in future years. There is no evidence, either in census data or information from the *Social Register,* to contradict the notion that the Back Bay retained throughout the 1930s its shared position with Beacon Hill as one of Boston's two socially preeminent neighborhoods. In fact, as late as 1940, the census consistently indicated that, if any comparison had validity, the Back Bay's tract K-3 was superior across the spectrum of ethnic and socioeconomic characteristics to Beacon Hill and tract K-2.

For the purposes of this study, then, Yankee precincts have been selected to encompass both Beacon Hill and the Back Bay. The specific precincts chosen for the period are listed in Appendix 2. It should be noted that, reflecting the demographic shifts which were occurring, after the early 1920s only those Back Bay precincts in the most desirable residential sections of the Back Bay—effectively covering Beacon Street, Marlborough Street, and the sunny side of Commonwealth Avenue, as well as all cross streets between Arlington and Gloucester Streets inclusive—were studied. Those streets, as well as the south slope of Beacon Hill and the area west of Charles Street, form the basis for this examination of elite Yankee voting in Boston.

An important basic assumption is that domestic servants, who composed much of the female population in these years, did not vote in appreciable numbers. It is, ultimately, an assumption impossible to prove without recourse to lists of registered voters in each of the precincts, but such lists, regrettably, no longer exist. However, it is clear that the domestic servant population possessed a number of characteristics any one of which would have discouraged active political participation. They were, first, largely foreign-born. There is no evidence that servants were drawn from even the second generation of immigrants; as will be remembered, the women in tract K-3 were notable in 1930 for simultaneously containing more foreign-born than any other tract in the city and the smallest number of native-born individuals born to foreign parents. Not only were they foreign-born, they were also female, single, and, as Oscar Handlin suggests, usually quite young. Ryan, in fact, argues that Irish women "turned to domestic service" precisely "because so many of them had immigrated while still single, and because they could speak English." The Irish servant was, he notes further, "usually required to live in" and naturally expected "to leave her adopted home at the time of her marriage." Samuel Eliot Morison, recalling his own home on Brimmer Street, mentions that "the cook, the waitress and the chambermaid were always Irish Catholics. Irish born they mostly were, too; girls of character, whom we loved and they us, although they generally stayed only long enough to find a Boston Irish husband." Alone in the neighborhood or perhaps even in the country, these women lacked familial support in gaining citizenship and then entering an unfamiliar political process. Even their Yankee employers set a poor example. Rather than inculcating in their servants the responsibility of all Americans, new and old, to vote, the Yankees, as statistics below will show, tended toward an astounding political apathy. Compounding all these difficulties is the probability that most of the domestic servants on Beacon Hill and in the Back Bay were not permanent residents of the neighborhoods but rather transient help. Without a stable address or home, it seems likely that the act of registering and voting was made even more difficult. Nevertheless, even this assumption—that the servants at no point constituted an important share of the active electorate—will be scrutinized in the examination of voting and registration data below.

Fortunately, it is possible to isolate the men, a population in which domestic servants were a minor factor, and compare their actions with the women, whose voting and registration data would have been much more affected by a politically active servant class.[25]

Northern Protestants in general, and wealthy Northeastern Yankees in particular, have long served as a classic control group in American electoral studies. Their historic allegiance to the Republican party since its formation in the middle of the nineteenth century has been a basic truth to students of American voting patterns from the inception of the science. Roots of the Republican sentiment can be traced back both to the Civil War and to the reaction against unfamiliar immigrants in the Northern cities, who were often mobilized by and subsequently identified with Democratic political machines. Well into the twentieth century, the Republican party continued to serve as the main political conduit for Northern Yankees, echoing, with varying stress, their own peculiar blend of Progressivism and support for the interests of business. Even the upheaval of the Great Depression and the ensuing New Deal realignment did not affect the commitment of Yankees to Republicanism. The traumatic decade of the 1930s perhaps only intensified the tenacity with which Yankee voters, at least for many years more, clung to what had suddenly become the minority party.

In elite groups such as Boston's Brahmins were found two major characteristics the confluence of which gave strength and durability to these Republican ties. The first of those characteristics related to ethnic and regional loyalties. From the birth of the Republican party in the Civil War to its reconsolidation in the upheaval of 1896, the main political lines of division were between the industrialized North and the agrarian South—and, in the North, between Protestant and Catholic, native and immigrant. Thus Francis Russell describes his own boyhood community, "a fairly typical American-Protestant lower-middle-class settlement" in early twentieth-century Boston: "Politically it voted straight Republican, partly for the myth's sake, partly because of the Irish-Democrats." As old-stock New Englanders, most wealthy Yankees in Boston identified naturally with the Republicans. This identification was strengthened by a second characteristic, economic cleavage between the parties, an undercurrent in the old political system that became a paramount issue with the remaking of the party system in the New Deal era. Ronald Story argues that already by 1865 (a date, incidentally, which some other scholars believe three decades too early) Republicanism in Boston "was almost the sole political vehicle of the upper class" and that "such Republican unity and strength was a fact of Brahmin life for the rest of the century." Maybe class divisions had been that strong at so early a date; it is certainly not an inconceivable proposition. Yet not until the 1930s did such cleavages become a central characteristic of the party system. ''The appeal of the New Deal was,'' as Campbell, Converse, Miller, and Stokes write in *The American Voter,* ''strongly economic in character. . . . [I]t can be said with assurance that the economic and class distinctions between the two parties increased during this period.'' Perhaps Lubell, ever lucid, put best the mutually reinforcing roles of ethnicity and class in shaping party allegiances, even on the eve of the realignment. ''Throughout the industrialized East,'' he observed, ''the make-up of society was such that Protestantism coincided largely with the Republican party, with millowners and financiers, with the snobbish members of exclusive clubs—in short, with the upper class.''[26]

And those individuals developed no great affection for the Democratic party even as a new party system emerged. As Ladd and Hadley remark, ''Northeastern white Protestant backing for the GOP showed remarkable continuity into the 1930s.'' Nie, Verba, and Petrocik note that white northern ''upper status Protestants'' had been, at least prior to 1960, ''as traditionally Republican as white southerners had been Democratic.'' So, logically, Trout finds that in Boston, ''of the major ethnic groups, only Back Bay Yankees held absolutely steady from 1932 to 1940, and they, of course, continued to oppose the President.'' Harold F. Gosnell attested to the persistence of Yankee Republicanism in Chicago. ''The only sections of the city that seemed to resist the charms of Roosevelt's personality and the assaults of the Democratic machine were,'' he observed in 1937, ''those units which were inhabited largely by native white Protestants of native parentage who were comfortably well off, owned their own homes, and who read regularly the *Chicago Tribune* and the *Chicago Daily News.*'' In Chicago and Boston as elsewhere across the North, the Republican party in the 1930s only reinforced its traditional strengths among ''the men of wealth, the scions of older Protestant families, [and] the women with money and leisure.''[27]

Al Smith's candidacy in 1928, while attracting widespread support from Jews and Catholics, was anathema to most Yankees. Indeed, Walter Dean Burnham argues that there was in that year a ''Hoover surge'' among the nation's native-stock Protestants as powerful as the counter mobilization by newer immigrant groups on behalf of Al Smith. ''Generally,'' Lubell observes, ''American elections blur social divisions. But in 1928, economic, racial, religious and cultural differences all sharpened the cleavage.'' Addressing M. A. DeWolfe Howe, who was a respected writer and scholar, another Boston Yankee expressed his fear that the Catholic church ''would burn you and me at the stake tomorrow, if it could, to save our souls. The whole of South America,'' this gentleman pointed out, ''is the living witness of what we shall be taking a step towards, if we elect Al. Smith.'' Ethnic blocs rarely behave as monoliths, however. There were important Yankees in Boston as well as in other cities—including Howe himself—who supported Smith with unusual enthusiasm and vigor. Indeed, some prominent Brahmins defied social pressure throughout this period and, in the spirit of those Mugwumps who had supported Grover Cleveland, were regularly considered independents or even, at least at the state and national levels, Democrats. Some of those backing Smith sympathized with him in his fight against bigotry or in his opposition to Prohibition, while others saw in Smith a great liberal, heir to the Progressive tradition. Those individuals remained, however, heretical exceptions. To most Yankees, Al Smith, a foreign-stock Catholic, embodied all that threatened the world they had built. The wealthy Yankees of the North similarly accorded Roosevelt little more than perfunctory and short-lived tolerance when he ushered in a new political order. From their perspective, "especially after the tempestuous term of Governor James Michael Curley had expired," observes Trout in his study of Boston, "Yankees found it hard to resist the conclusion that Irish politicians, in league with Franklin Delano Roosevelt, had made economic catastrophe far worse." In most national studies, 1936 is offered as the year in which class divisions had hardened into a defining aspect of the New Deal party system. While animosity along socioeconomic lines was relatively absent in the passionless election of 1932, by 1936 "wealth and privilege," according to Allswang as well as many others, "were quite strongly united against the New Deal." President Roosevelt, according to Lubell, had by 1940 "welded the upper class" into solid opposition. For many years more the Republican party could depend on this class's continued fierce loyalty.[28]

Most of this conventional understanding seems relevant to findings drawn from Boston. The men and women living on Beacon Hill and in the Back Bay in the 1920s and 1930s were indeed staunch Republicans hardly swayed by the turbulent events associated with the New Deal realignment. Unlike the city's blacks and Jews, who had also been solidly Republican in the 1920s, the Yankees, in their attachment to the party, survived the following decade undisturbed. They were, in fact, bystanders, effectively watching the realignment without affecting it. Neither their partisan makeup nor their level of political participation changed substantially over the period. While perhaps they were indifferent to the great political upheaval of the 1930s, it would appear more likely that Boston's Yankee elite simply became overwhelmed by their own powerlessness and their sudden inability to shape events.

For the most interesting fact revealed by registration and voting statistics in these two neighborhoods is the lack of growth in the size of the active electorate. Unique among all groups studied in the City of Boston, the Yankees of Beacon Hill and the Back Bay did not respond to the events of the 1930s with increased turnout and participation. They were, in fact, registering and voting in smaller numbers in the 1930s than they had in the 1920s. A real, if gradual, demobilization occurred in this Republican stronghold simultaneous with the New Deal realignment.

Table 5.2 presents the Yankee vote for president, congressman, and state senator. Throughout the period studied, Republican candidates consistently received the support of the Yankees of Beacon Hill and the Back Bay. There seems, too, to have been a pattern of a greater Republican vote the more local the office. M. A. DeWolfe Howe "always," recalled his daughter, "voted for the Democratic candidate in national, although rarely in city elections"[29]—and he, apparently, was not alone. Republican candidates for president received, with one exception, between 75 and 82 percent of the vote cast in the six elections between 1920 and 1940. Thus Willkie in 1940 was supported by 78.3 percent of the active electorate, barely less than Harding's level of 82.0 percent recorded two decades earlier. In elections for representative in Congress and for senator in General Court, by comparison, Republican candidates, again with one exception, uniformly surpassed the 82 percent threshold throughout the 1920s and 1930s, with some individuals receiving more than 90 percent of the vote cast. It was, to be sure, never more than a small minority of the active electorate, but the number of Democratic voters for president was generally about 50 percent greater than the number of those supporting Democratic candidates for lower offices.

On a relative basis, then, national Democratic candidates were considerably more appealing to upper-class Yankee voters than more local ones. The phenomenon was not specific to any particular candidate. It applied as

Table 5.2 Vote in Yankee Precincts for President, Representative in Congress, and Senator in General Court as Percent of Potential Electorate

	President			Congressman		State Senator	
	Dem.	Rep.	Other	Dem.	Rep.	Dem.	Rep.
1920	6.1	30.2	0.6	4.0	31.7	3.2	32.1
1922				2.8	26.3	2.7	25.9
1924	5.5	32.9	1.9	4.2	33.8	3.7	31.3
1926						3.4	27.0
1928	14.7	35.9		9.8	38.7	9.7	38.9
1930				5.3	28.0	3.9	29.3
1932	10.1	36.9		6.5	39.6	6.8	38.8
1934						7.0	35.5
1936	11.2	38.7	1.5	6.3	43.5	7.6	41.1
1938				6.3	41.1	6.9	40.1
1940	11.8	42.5		9.0	43.2		

accurately to the rather mediocre James Cox and John W. Davis as to the more charismatic Al Smith and Franklin Roosevelt. Apparently, there were pressures operating beneath the national level which caused many who voted for a Democratic president to split their tickets and back Republicans for Congress and for the state senate; that, at least, seems to be more logical than the alternate scenario which would require Democrats to have voted straight tickets and Republicans to have spurned Harding for Cox in the midst of a Harding landslide. Why Yankees, even those voting for a Democratic president, would have avoided local Democratic candidates is not hard to understand. Local Democratic politics, at first in Boston but by the 1920s increasingly statewide, was dominated by Irish Catholics. Whereas the candidate for president was selected by a Democratic party still heavily influenced by supposedly public-spirited Protestant elements, those running for lower offices were, in the eyes of Boston's Yankees, agents of corruption and sworn enemies of the old-stock elite. That local Democratic candidates received so little support, especially compared to national candidates, would appear to be prima-facie evidence that the active electorate in these precincts was, throughout this period, thoroughly Yankee. Had Irish domestic servants been voting in considerable numbers and as Democrats, it would seem likely that they would have supported local Irish Catholics. Since the local party received such negligible support on Beacon Hill and the Back Bay, however, it seems apparent that few domestic servants voted. Or, if they did vote, they simply echoed the partisan decisions dictated by the Yankee heads of their households and voted Republican. Either way, a deep-rooted Republicanism accurately characterized Boston's Brahmin population, a Republicanism even firmer in local elections than in national elections.

At all levels, though, the election of 1928 is notable both because of the tremendous interest it generated and the mild shift toward the Democratic party it foreshadowed. There is more happening in 1928 than simply a "Hoover surge," although that characterization does explain much. Turnout in that year reached a new high. For the first time in history, a majority of men and women in the Yankee precincts voted in the state and federal elections. That is particularly significant, since so much of the adult population was, most probably, effectively disenfranchised. According to the 1930 census, 44 percent of adults in census tract K-3 and 31 percent of adults in the three tracts covering Beacon Hill and the Back Bay were domestic servants, largely foreign-born, single, and female. What makes the mobilization of 1928 so interesting is that it benefited both political parties. More persons voted Republican in that year than in any previous election studied, and more Democratic votes were cast than in any election before or since. Between 1924 and 1928, the number of Democratic voters more than doubled. Fully

14.7 percent of the adult population, and 29.1 percent of those voting, supported Al Smith; Democratic candidates for the two lesser offices received the backing of just under 10 percent of the potential electorate. Compared to low-single-digit showings in prior elections, these were significant results. They were, importantly, results and trends which were equally evident in all political contests that year. Once having made inroads into the Yankee neighborhoods, the Democratic party enjoyed a higher plateau of support in the 1930s than it had prior to the 1928 elections.

Two explanations for the 1928 voting seem possible, and neither precludes the other. One is a function of the local demographic environment, while the other is a more general, issue-oriented explanation. It is possible, first, to argue that the 1928 evidence suggests that domestic servants were not wholly politically inactive. The large vote for Al Smith and for other Democrats could be viewed as a distortion of the normal Yankee vote caused by an outpouring of enthusiastic Irish Catholics, mobilizing in that year in support of Smith's candidacy. Presumably, once mobilized, these servants maintained their registration and continued to vote through ensuing elections, explaining the increased number of persons voting Democratic in the years after Al Smith's candidacy. Thus, while in 1920 and 1924 just 6 percent of the active electorate voted for the Democratic candidate for president, between 10 and 12 percent supported Roosevelt in his first three elections. That edge, achieved somehow in the late 1920s and early 1930s, could, then, be attributed largely, or even solely, to a suddenly activated servant class.

There are, however, important problems with dismissing the Democratic votes as mere Irish residue. Much more likely, it seems, is the argument that domestic servants were no more apt to vote in the 1930s than they had been in the previous decade and that the Democratic advances were, therefore, evidence of genuine Yankee change. There were, after all, proportionately twice as many servants in the 1920s as there would be in the 1930s. To explain the new Democratic support on the basis of these servants necessitates the difficult task of suggesting that the number of servant voters was increasing sharply, accelerating even as the total number of servants was falling precipitously. The election of 1928 might well have captured the interest of some of these Irish women, but it is unlikely that a failed candidacy could have so utterly transformed an apathetic servant class into one permanently politicized.

More persuasive, certainly, is the additional evidence provided in table 5.3, which displays registration figures for men and for women. Had 1928 been the pivotal election in mobilizing the female servants, it would have been characterized by a large increase in the number of women registered to vote. Yet, between 1926 and 1930, the number of female registrants rose by an increment of only 5.6 percent of the total female population, from 28.9 to

Table 5.3 Party Registration Figures in Yankee Precincts as Percent of Total Potential Electorate

	Men				Women			
	All Reg.	Dem.	Rep.	Ind.	All Reg.	Dem.	Rep.	Ind.
1920	56.5	3.0	34.5	19.0	15.1	0.1	5.4	9.6
1922	56.8	3.2	34.3	19.3	24.8	0.5	7.3	17.0
1924	56.3	3.2	38.6	14.5	27.3	0.9	13.7	12.7
1926	52.8	3.7	34.7	14.4	28.9	1.1	13.4	14.5
1928	56.2	3.9	40.4	11.9	37.5	1.9	19.9	15.6
1930	59.4	3.7	36.6	19.2	34.5	1.7	17.9	15.0
1932*	52.1	4.9	34.3	12.9	35.8	2.8	17.5	15.6
1934	50.7	7.3	31.7	11.6	39.7	4.6	17.7	17.4
1936	55.5	5.7	32.9	16.9	41.8	4.6	21.0	16.2
1938	52.3	5.6	31.5	15.3	40.7	4.5	19.8	16.4
1940	52.0	5.4	27.4	19.2	43.2	3.5	18.1	21.6

*The 1932 figures are estimates, based on Ward Five totals (1930, 1932, 1934).

34.5. And virtually all of that gain was made by the Republican party. Servants, perhaps even those registering specifically to vote for Al Smith, might have felt a real pressure in the Back Bay and on Beacon Hill to publicly register as Republicans. Still, an increase in Republican registrants does support with at least as much force the notion that Yankee women, not their servants, had entered the active electorate. It is significant, too, that the number of male registrants rose by 6.6 points between 1926 and 1930, from 52.8 to 59.4 percent of the potential electorate. Since men entered the active electorate over the 1928 election in numbers greater than women, and since few men were servants, probably servants did not lead the movement to Al Smith or nudge these precincts toward the Democratic party in ensuing years.

There was, apparently, a very small-scale version of the New Deal realignment within the ranks of Boston's Brahmin elite. It was foreshadowed—much as in the Jewish and Italian communities—by an unusually strong Democratic vote in 1928. Part of the vote for Smith and other Democrats, of course, may well have been cast by Irish servants, but their participation, if it did occur, was likely a one-time event: there was little vestige of such a servant vote in the relevant 1930 registration figures. Much more important was the support suddenly accorded Smith by Yankees. ''Anti-Prohibition sentiment in G.O.P. ranks, and the response of some old-stock people to Smith's appeal as a cultural liberal,'' Huthmacher writes, ''accounted in part for the increased Democratic percentage of the vote in certain Republican strongholds.'' Robert K. Massey speaks, too, of ''some of the more wealthy citizens who had voted for Smith because of his opposition to legalized temperance.'' Indeed, Massey notes, the unusually high degree of support which Smith enjoyed in Beacon Hill and the Back Bay in 1928 was paralleled by similar strength in the affluent suburbs of Brookline and Newton. In 1928, then, even as their neighbors were mobilizing to defeat Smith and his Catholic hordes by electing Herbert Hoover, a significant minority of Yankees deviated both from their cohort and from their own past Republican tendencies and cast protest votes for the Democratic party. It was an election of unusual intensity, which excited partisans on both sides of the divide.[30]

What had been a one-time political statement, though, was transformed by the 1932 election into genuine partisan conversion. The election of 1928 created no new Democrats. Between 1926 and 1930, female Democratic registrants increased from 1.1 to 1.7 percent of the potential electorate, while men remained static at 3.7 percent. Al Smith had no lasting impact on registration figures. Not until 1932 was the electorate permanently transformed. The number of men registered in the Democratic party doubled to 7.3 percent by 1934. Women Democrats rose to 4.6 percent. Prior to the election of Roosevelt in 1932, the number of male Democrats fluctuated between 3.0 and 3.9 percent; after his election, the comparable figure was 5.4 and 7.3 percent. Women were transformed as well. While before 1932 no more than 1.9 percent of the female population identified with the Democratic party, after that year between 3.5 and 4.6 percent did so.

The miniature surge in Democratic support must, naturally, be kept in proper perspective. It was, after all, merely an appendix to the story of a group's generally unwavering fidelity to the Republican party. Still, some Yankee Democrats were created, energized by the events which on a much larger scale would be termed the New Deal realignment. That men moved in 1932 simultaneously with women reinforces the notion that the permanent Democratic shift in the Back Bay and Beacon Hill could not have been the result of the mobilization of Irish servants. That mobilization would, first, have been most likely to occur in 1928. And second, and much more powerful, is the fact that men shifted as much as the women. Had the movement toward the Democrats in the 1930s—visible in tables 5.2 and 5.3—reflected only servants, only the registration figures of women would have been affected. Since men converted and since those men were Yankees, it is logical to assume that the women converting were Yankees as well. Finally, the sharpness of Democratic movement, as reflected in the registration figures surrounding 1932 as well as in the immediately preceding and anticipatory election of 1928, argues against any primary explanation that the new Democrats were the clerical workers, some of whom were not Yankees, who were infiltrating the neighborhoods during the Depression. Such an explanation could account for a gradual, secular realignment, but not for the sudden shift apparent from all available data.

There was in 1932, then, a movement of measurable but not substantial dimensions toward the Democratic party. It was a movement characterizing both men and women, and obvious from election and registration data. Although Roosevelt and other Democrats in the 1930s fared slightly poorer than had Smith in 1928, it was only in the early 1930s that the Democratic party gained permanent new members in Boston's Yankee neighborhoods. Howe, hospitalized at the time, wired Roosevelt on his election in 1932: "Am acutely conscious of a new spirit in America. I believe this to be your own spirit. The true democrat of the old order who has always known the new order to be a vital part of it seems coming into his own." His optimism and enthusiasm, although those of a lifelong Democrat, were apparently shared initially by some other Yankees. One friend, who would soon be much more disillusioned than the letter indicates, wrote to Howe in March 1933 and detailed proper Boston's first reaction to Roosevelt:

> You will be interested to hear what are the principal subjects of discussion, for in Boston we never talk of more than one or two things at the same time. I think the chief feature has been the new President and the way he has taken hold, and the way people feel about it would have gratified your loyal democratic heart. Even the most benighted Republicans and the most hardened cynics admit that he has done a first rate job to date. He has been simple, clear, politically wise and extraordinarily courageous, has forced, through Congress, an economic programme which involves cutting the benefits of the Veterans to a reasonable measure, the legalization of beer, and is to be followed by bills dealing with the woes of the farmers, unemployment, etc. Better yet, he has done the whole thing with a good nature and human touch, which has made everybody like, as well as respect him. . . . Moreover, he has done a lot of gracious little things which help out. Such, for example, as calling on Justice Holmes on his birthday. . . . Indeed, he seems to keep in well with the Liberals while giving them very little, for his administration so far has leaned in all essentials toward the right.

While not as popular as Smith and little less feared among most of the city's Yankee elite—who, despite momentary lapses, largely considered him a radical and a scoundrel—Roosevelt and the events of the time did inspire a small group to give their backing during the ensuing decade to the Democrats.[31]

A fact already noted but deserving of repetition is the tight congruity between the political decisions of men and women in this period. The subtle shift toward the Democrats, for example, occurred in 1932 among both groups. Yankee women were, unlike most other women in the city, politically sophisticated and experienced by that time. Their participation rates did not rise appreciably in the 1930s. Rather, women on Beacon Hill and the Back Bay were largely mobilized within less than a decade of acquiring the franchise. In fact, the early suffrage movement was to a large extent motivated by the notion that respectable, old-stock Protestant women needed the ballot to counteract the pernicious political decisions made by ignorant male immigrants. And, to a large extent, that intent of the Nineteenth Amendment achieved initial success. In cities and towns across the country, registered women voters in the 1920s tended to be more Republican than comparable groups of men; wealthier, native-born women, clearly, were voting in numbers disproportionately larger than those for foreign-stock women.[32] Once adjusted to reflect the number of servants in the population, the number of women registered to vote by 1928 appears to have equalled and even exceeded the number of men as fractions of their respective cohorts. Those Yankee women, while participating in the slight Democratic shift of 1932, shared, too, with the men of the area an overwhelmingly Republican preference throughout the two decades. Of those registering in one of the two parties, well over 90 percent of both men and women selected the Republicans in the early 1920s and nearly 84 percent of both groups were still Republican in 1940. The consistent parallel movement of men and women and their nearly identical partisan compositions reinforce earlier assumptions that Irish servants did not compose an important segment of the female active electorate.

That proposition is used as the basis for table 5.4 and figure 5.1, both of which show changes in the size of the active electorate over time. What distinguishes table 5.4 from table 5.3 is a revision of the size of the potential electorate. In table 5.3, registration figures are presented as fractions of all adults in the precincts studied. If, however, domestic servants did not vote, their numbers can be safely excluded from the number of total adults composing the potential electorate. As the size of the servant population falls over time, one would expect a commensurate increase in the size of the active electorate when expressed as a percentage of all adults. Table 5.4, by accounting for servants in the population, attempts to measure the Yankee voter activity in the 1920s and 1930s.

To construct table 5.4, raw participation levels, the number of registrants as a fraction of the total population, were drawn from table 5.3. Next, estimates were made of the size of the true potential electorate by subtracting from the total adult population all domestic servants. For the number of domestic servants, the three census tracts covering the Back Bay and Beacon Hill were consulted. In 1930, 7.8 percent of all men and 40.3 percent of all women were

Table 5.4 Registration Figures in Yankee Precincts as Percent of Nonservant Potential Electorate

	Men				Women			
	Raw Reg.	Domestic Servants	Non-Servants	Adj. Reg.	Raw Reg.	Domestic Servants	Non-Servants	Adj. Reg.
1920	56.5	7.8	92.2	61.3	15.1	40.3	59.7	25.3
1922	56.8	7.8	92.2	61.6	24.8	40.3	59.7	41.5
1924	56.3	7.8	92.2	61.1	27.3	40.3	59.7	45.7
1926	52.8	7.8	92.2	57.3	28.9	40.3	59.7	48.4
1928	56.2	7.8	92.2	61.0	37.5	40.3	59.7	62.8
1930	59.4	7.8	92.2	64.4	34.5	40.3	59.7	57.8
1932	52.1	6.7	93.3	55.8	35.8	36.5	63.5	56.4
1934	50.7	5.7	94.3	53.8	39.7	32.7	67.3	59.0
1936	55.5	4.6	95.4	58.2	41.8	28.9	71.1	58.8
1938	52.3	3.6	96.4	54.3	40.7	25.1	74.9	54.3
1940	52.0	2.5	97.5	53.3	43.2	21.4	78.6	55.0

listed as domestic servants; the respective figures for 1940 were 2.5 percent and 21.4 percent. No figures were available from the 1920 census or for any other year. Although the servant population had probably declined before 1930, the 1930 figure is offered as the best available estimate for the number of domestic servants in the 1920s. It is impossible to know the extent of decline over that period, but it was probably minor compared to the sharp drop during the Depression. Also, in using the 1930 figure for all elections in the 1920s, we err, if at all, on the conservative side; since there were probably more servants in the population in that period than the 1930 statistic would indicate, the estimates of participation in the 1920s would be on the low side of the truth, rather than exaggeratedly high. This is especially important to note because, even with admittedly low participation estimates for the 1920s, those levels still exceed voter activity in the 1930s. Finally, for the four elections between 1930 and 1940, linear interpolation was used, with the declining number of servants over the decade spread evenly over the five two-year intervals. With estimates of the number of servants in the male and female adult populations, the nonservant fraction of the population was easily obtained. Adjusted estimates of true participation levels, then, were calculated by dividing raw participation by the new estimates of the potential electorate. Those numbers are presented in table 5.4 and are graphed in figure 5.1.

As figure 5.1 shows, participation levels peaked just prior to 1932 and fell from that level during the critical years of the New Deal realignment. The trend is most obvious among men. With one exception, at least 61 percent of all Yankee men registered to vote in each of the elections between 1920 and

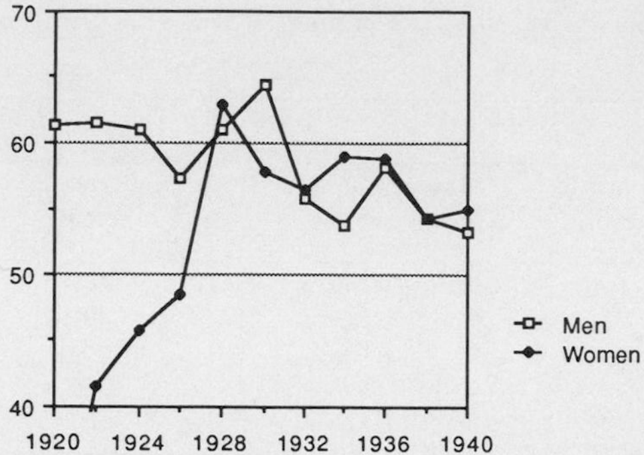

Figure 5.1 Total Registration in Yankee Precincts (as Percent of Nonservant Potential Electorate)

1930 inclusive. In 1930, male participation reached its highest level in the two decades, at 64.4 percent. Then, as other ethnic groups were mobilizing to vote, Yankee participation declined. After 1930, the number of registrants as a fraction of the population fell to a plateau of between 53.3 and 58.2 percent.

A similar pattern can be discerned from female registration figures. The important distinction between women and men, however, is that women in the 1920s were still entering the active electorate after their recent acquisition of the right to vote. Thus participation levels for women do not begin on a high level in the early 1920s. Rather, that decade represented a period of increasing registration and political involvement. In comparison with 1920, nearly twice as many Yankee women were registered to vote in 1926. By 1928, the number of registrants had soared to 62.8 percent of the nonservant population. That level of political mobilization—which may admittedly have been, but in that election only, slightly inflated by servants entering the active electorate to support Al Smith—was not exceeded in future years. The next four elections drew between 56.4 percent and 59.0 percent of Yankee women to register to vote. By 1938 and 1940, no more than 55.0 percent of that same population remained active, those two consecutive elections representing the lowest levels of participation since 1928. While the competing force of voter mobilization in the early 1920s makes the female case more subtle than the male, it is nevertheless clear that participation for women, too, had by the late 1930s fallen from a previously higher level.

Yankees, male and female, apparently deserted the active electorate in response to the sudden emasculation of the Republican party in national politics. Just as Yankees had withdrawn from city politics after the rise of Irish Democratic politicians, so now they became increasingly despairing as their influence, and the influence of their political party, waned in the face of the

New Deal realignment. James Sundquist argues, in his discussion of the 1930s upheaval, that the assumption "that *all* the new voters were mobilized by the Democrats cannot possibly be sustained. In a period of intense political controversy, when the country is polarized, both parties have a powerful attraction." His logic, reasonable at first glance, may bear further study. In Boston, in any event, there is strong evidence to the contrary. The Democrats in the 1930s mobilized a tremendous number of voters, and the Republicans, at least the one group examined, not only failed to mobilize new voters but actually lost supporters. By 1940, the year Erbring et al. suggest was a year of great Yankee interest as the final Republican attempt at an "anti–New Deal . . . counter-mobilization," Boston's Yankee men and women reached historic nadirs in political activity. The Republican party, in this most Republican group of individuals, had lost its ability to bring supporters to the polls.[33]

The events of the 1920s and 1930s, beginning with the encroachment of Irish Democrats into state politics and culminating with the New Deal realignment and the elections of Franklin Roosevelt, marked the denouement to the long-evolving Yankee withdrawal from the voting booth. The Republican party which they had so long supported and which they would continue to support well past 1940 had suddenly ceased to give direction to the American polity. As they were physically isolated from the rest of the city in the Back Bay and on Beacon Hill, so Boston's Yankees were by 1940 in a political wilderness. Deserted by Jews and blacks, they stood alone in the city in support of their party. The vote which Yankee women had won and wielded so successfully in the 1920s had by 1940 been turned against them by immigrant women, by Democrats. Once synonymous with Boston itself, the Yankees, in the words of one 1930 observer, had been reduced to a mere "numerical remnant, strongly intrenched in wealth and culture but hopelessly outnumbered and helpless in all contests in which mere numbers prevail."[34] And so, having been thoroughly defeated, the Yankee elite withdrew. No other group of men in the city had so few persons registered to vote in 1940. For many more years, Brahmins would continue to direct Boston's economy and provide leadership to its schools, its hospitals, and its cultural institutions. Many would even continue to run successfully for elective office, serving the Commonwealth ably in Boston and in Washington. Those seeking office, however, would have to emulate Leverett Saltonstall, who, running for governor in 1938, boasted with unconcealed delight of his Irish-looking, "South Boston face."[35] Yankee politicians, after all, could no longer depend on the votes of their own kind.

6
The Irish

Electoral participation in Boston's Irish neighborhoods was high in 1920 and grew even higher by 1940. Although the Irish appear to have been affected by the New Deal realignment, they were already so politically active prior to that era that no great increase in the size of the active electorate occurred. Thus, while in 1940 about 80 percent of all adult men were registered to vote, nearly two-thirds had been registered in 1920. Most women, too, had registered to vote by the mid-1920s, well before the era of general political upheaval.

As legend correctly has it, the Irish were throughout the period the sturdy foundation of the Democratic party in Boston. And, if anything, their commitment to the party of Al Smith and Roosevelt increased in intensity over time. In the city's lower-class Irish neighborhoods, Democrats constituted 94 percent of all registered voters in 1920 and 96 percent in 1940.

This was not a class-based phenomenon. All four socioeconomic classes isolated for this study moved together in direction and degree during the entire two decades. Whether rich or poor, the Bostonian of Irish descent was, for example, more likely to register Democratic in 1940 than in 1920 and more likely to vote for Roosevelt in 1932 than for John Davis in 1924. Socioeconomic status was, to be sure, an accurate indicator in these years of the depth of commitment to the Democratic party: the wealthier were consistently more likely to register and to vote Republican. But, significantly, that slight cleavage remained static and did not increase in the late 1930s, when appeals to class were supposedly at a historic high in American politics.

The Boston Irish, then, acted—at least in terms of their deep commitment to politics in general and to the Democratic party in particular—much like conventional accounts would suggest. Nationally, as in Boston, their attachment to the Democratic party was strong and deeply embedded. While blacks in the 1920s were still casting their votes based on cleavages from the 1860s, the roots of Irish partisanship actually antedated the Civil War. Irish immigrants, who began to arrive in large numbers in the 1840s, found in the United States two political parties: the Whigs, who were tainted by nativism and elitism and identified in cities such as Boston with the Yankee establishment, and the Jacksonian Democrats. Most Irish chose to support the Democratic party, often encouraged by the pressure and incentives of local machines. This decision was confirmed by events in the late 1850s, when the emergent Republican party drew support from former Know-Nothings and abolitionists, two groups toward which the Irish did not disguise their antipathy. As the divisions of the Civil War party alignment solidified, the Irish were distinguished for their strong identification with the Democrats. Thus, it was the Irish, the great Catholic immigrant group of the mid-century and a group caricatured for its indulgence in alcohol, at whom a clergyman supporting Republican James G. Blaine directed his infamous 1884 barb. Affirming his allegiance to the Republican party, Samuel Dickinson Burchard condemned the other party, ''whose antecedents have been Rum, Romanism, and Rebellion.'' Few Irish—or Southern whites, for that matter—were induced to switch parties after that remark.[1]

By the 1920s, then, Irish Democrats were practically as common as Irish Catholics. The 1928 candidacy of Al Smith and the ensuing New Deal realignment reinvigorated Irish identification with the Democratic party and ensured its continuance into the new party era inaugurated by Roosevelt. William V. Shannon argues that ''there was one institution other than the Catholic Church that retained and strengthened its hold on the loyalty of most Irish during the depression. That was the Democratic Party.'' As V. O. Key, Jr., has written, some observers came to regard ''the Democratic party as a private preserve of the Irish.'' Ironically, however, the relative numerical superiority of the Irish in the Democratic party was diminished with the formation of the New Deal coalition, grounded as it was on the mobilization and conversion of other groups. Still, in the North, the Irish continued to stand at the core of the party throughout the period, as they had since their initial arrival in the United States many decades before.[2]

The story of Massachusetts, no less than that of the rest of the continent, is the story of immigrants. Settlers came to the area like the ocean waves which they rode, gently lapping against the shore. But occasionally that rocky New England coastline has been battered by waves of terrifying ferocity, whipped up by storm and determined to encroach on the existing human settlement. The Great Migration, the initial influx of Puritan Yankees—some 20,000 settlers in all—to the nascent Massachusetts Bay Colony between 1630 and 1643, marked the establishment on the Shawmut peninsula of an enduring culture rooted ethnically in England.[3] Here was the original displacement, the removal of Indian by European. No future displacement would be so complete or have greater consequence for the region.

Yet, in terms of numbers, the Great Migration pales next to the Irish immigration to Massachusetts in the middle of the nineteenth century.

Between the early 1840s and late 1850s, 150,000 men, women, and children fled from the Emerald Isle to the Emerald City.[4] They came for food, escaping the devastating famine destroying their homeland; theirs, unlike the journey of the Puritans, was neither motivated by ideology nor was it primarily a quest for religious security. It was a trek for bare survival. And the America they found in Boston was an environment as hostile, arguably as alien, as that which confronted the Puritan fathers and mothers in the 1630s.

Significantly, however, the Irish, unlike the Yankees, were powerless to transform their frontier in meaningful ways. If population alone be the measure, the Englishman who had once displaced the Indian was now himself displaced by the Irishman. By the 1850s the Irish were on the verge of becoming a majority of all Boston residents; already, three out of every four foreign-born Bostonians had been born in Ireland. A certain Dr. Josiah Curtis, in his remarks on the 1855 Boston city census, may well have been the first to note the end to ''American'' numerical dominance, which, counting minor children of immigrants as also of foreign stock, had occurred in the five years since the federal census of 1850. He was alert enough, too, to suggest the future electoral consequences of that fact:

> The rate of increase in the foreign population . . . has been sufficient, as was anticipated, to change the majority of the whole population of our city from the American to the foreign side. . . . It will be very difficult to name a day in the future, when the number of American citizens, in the distinctive sense that this term is commonly used, will again constitute a majority of those who shall inhabit the present limits of Boston. It is also here worthy of remark, that while native voters have increased only 14.72 per cent. Since 1850, the foreign voters have increased threefold, or no less than 194.64 per cent.[5]

Still, the culture and society created by the English settlers did not disappear. Unlike the Indian civilization, long since vanquished or expelled, the institutions established in the wake of the Great Migration flourished, absorbing the Irish immigrants even while remaining aloof from them. The Irishman had come in a tidal wave, as later in the century the Jew and the Italian would come, but the city was not a sand castle. Boston was now a fortress, not easily penetrated by newcomers and impossible to destroy. Its government could, however, be taken over by a simple majority, and, that, at least, the Irish would achieve.

As the Irish swept ashore, they settled largely in two congested neighborhoods—the Fort Hill and Pearl Street district and the North End—which, under sheer force of numbers and poverty, quickly assumed the character of slums. ''By their immobility,'' Oscar Handlin argues in his 1941 book, *Boston's Immigrants,* ''the Irish crammed the city, recasting its boundaries and disfiguring its physical appearance.'' The two neighborhoods hugged the waterfront, sprawling on either side of Boston's commercial center. In these once-fashionable sections of the city, Walter Muir Whitehill notes, ''rural starvation in Ireland had been exchanged for urban misery.'' On Fort Hill, according to Firey, ''the mansions became tenement dwellings for immigrant families. . . . So dilapidated did the dwellings become . . . that there existed a positive health menace on the Hill.'' The North End, too, which had been declining in reputation since the Revolution, received its final shock with the arrival of Irish immigrants in the 1840s and 1850s. Any Yankees still remaining in either neighborhood quickly left and both areas, now segregated, were subsequently avoided by any residents of the city—except, of course, by some tens of thousands of poor Irish immigrants. Within a few decades, however, even the Irish were no longer inhabiting those neighborhoods. The Irish left the area around Fort Hill in the late 1860s, as their homes were razed and the hill removed. Movement out of the North End began in the 1880s, the Irish abandoning their community to newly arrived Italians and Jews.[6]

By the turn of the century, solid, largely second-generation Irish settlements had been established in a ring around the inner city, in what Woods and Kennedy termed the ''zone of emergence,'' an area encompassing much of Charlestown, South Boston, East Boston, Roxbury, and Dorchester. The physical, perhaps even superficial, contrast between those neighborhoods and the ''classic land of poverty'' downtown was obvious. As Woods and Kennedy observed in their study, written between 1907 and 1914:

> Though there are some exceptions, the neighborhoods of the Zone of Emergence impress one familiar with the downtown tenement communities as distinctly more habitable. The air is brighter, cleaner, and more vibrant; sunshine falls in floods rather than in narrow shafts; there is not so much dust and smoke; the streets are quieter; there is less congestion and more evident freedom of movement.

The Irish followed the movement of industries into these areas of the city, as the Yankees left. ''The American population retired,'' noted Woods and Kennedy, ''before the inroads of the transportation companies and the factories, on the one hand, and the proximity of unskilled foreigners which the new industries called for on the other.'' Now, in the 1910s, ''the Irish dominate; indeed the zone of emergence is the great Irish belt of the city. . . . In its conditions of living, its social and political organization, and all those subtle qualities which give the tone of the community, the zone is second-generation Irish.''[7]

Increasingly, however, with the passage of time, the Irish were being displaced in large sections of the "zone" by more recent immigrants. East Boston, for example, contained a substantial Italian community by the late 1910s, and Jews by then had settled over large portions of Dorchester and Roxbury. Many of the more successful Irish left. Those middle-class Irish made their homes farther out from the center of the city—in Brighton, which contained a large and ethnically homogeneous Irish community, and in the less ethnically distinct, heterogeneous neighborhoods of West Roxbury, Hyde Park, Jamaica Plain, and the Neponset section of Dorchester. Still, important Irish areas persisted in the zone. Even after losing many of the Irish who were rising in socioeconomic status, the neighborhoods of the zone included the largest and most visible pockets of Irish in the region.[8]

The bulk of Boston's Irish, whether in that zone or elsewhere in the city, had emerged from the wretched conditions of the North End and Fort Hill, but they had not, at least as a group, escaped a poverty which enveloped their present and cast a long shadow over their future. The ascribing of the word "emergence" to a zone, and, by extension, to its largely Irish population, most of which Woods and Kennedy were clearly convinced was mired in a seemingly perpetual state of bare subsistence, was an ironic form of mockery. Their concluding comments regarding Charlestown, Boston's most Irish neighborhood—that it had been transformed from a middle-class, dynamic area "into a section of the tenement-house frontier of a great city"—apply equally to their study of the zone in general. Stack finds that "the most striking feature of the zone of emergence was its pervasive mood of monotonousness and drabness." At least in the inner-city slums of the North End and Fort Hill, newly arrived immigrants could look forward with hope to a better future. That hope had been exchanged in the zone for a stagnant, inescapable poverty only slightly less intense than that of the inner city from which the Irish had run.[9]

Thernstrom, it will be recalled from the earlier discussion of the Italians, describes in great detail the extent of Irish poverty and social immobility in Boston. The city's Irish, he notes, were "the least successful of the 'old-immigrant' groups." For possible explanations, he suggests the insularity and cohesiveness of the Boston Irish community as well as the influence of values derived from their peasant past in Ireland. It was that set of values to which Bushee alludes when he states, in crude, turn-of-the-century fashion, that "the Irish have no natural instinct for economy"—they were characterized by a sacrifice of future achievement for present consumption; risk was generally avoided and education severely undervalued. Making a similar argument, Dennis P. Ryan believes that "the progress of the Irish was hampered most of all by their phenomenal success in politics and the Boston labor movement. . . . [T]he Irish politician channeled generations of Irish into secure but financially dead-end jobs as city clerks, firefighters, policemen, and utility and transit employees.'' As a result of these factors, Thernstrom finds, Irish Bostonians ''moved ahead economically only sluggishly and erratically.'' Indeed, according to Thernstrom, there was relatively little intergenerational advancement and even a ''dramatic tendency of Catholic youths who had begun their careers in nonmanual jobs to lose those jobs and to end their lives wearing a blue rather than a white collar,'' an ''apparent skidding syndrome.'' Decades earlier, Woods had made a similar observation in *The City Wilderness:*

> The Irish . . . are on the whole rising in the social scale, the second generation making a better showing than the preceding one; yet instances of deterioration are not infrequent. In certain localities the second generation tends to yield to the influences of idleness and evil surroundings. This double change, which is constantly going on in society, is very noticeable among the Irish people. As compared with the Jews, they seem like a people without ancestry. Each generation stands in its own strength. . . . The better class of Irish . . . are ambitious, imitative, and quick-witted. The majority of the Irish, however, have not yet revealed such progressive characteristics.

Such bluntly worded contemporary findings were, apparently, grounded in reality. The vast majority of Boston's Irish population were born poor and died poor and, when they died, they left children little better-off than they themselves had been.[10]

That most of Boston's Irish had yet to achieve middle-class status by the 1920s and 1930s is confirmed by census statistics and other measures of community socioeconomic levels. Of the homogeneous Irish neighborhoods in the city, only Brighton could be categorized as lower-middle-class. While to be sure, there were other middle-class Irish in the city, they were scattered among Yankees and other ethnic groups in areas such as Hyde Park and West Roxbury, as has already been mentioned. Besides lower-middle-class Brighton, three other groups of homogeneously Irish communities have been selected on the basis of socioeconomic level. Table 6.1 presents relevant census data from 1940, showing the main criteria for distinguishing among the four categories. The largest group studied is the lower-class Irish, found in South Boston, Uphams Corner, Charlestown, and much of Mission Hill. Communities on the rest of Mission Hill and in Forest Hills and parts of Dorchester constituted the working-class Irish, more successful socioeconomically than those in the lower class, but not yet middle-class. Finally, a small area in lower South Boston was selected as the poorest of any of the Irish sections of the city, as poor, in fact, as Boston's most miserable tenement districts. Four classes of Boston's Irish, then, have been isolated for the purposes of this study, categorized, respectively, as poor, lower class, working class, and lower middle class. One central criterion for the grouping of census tracts, an element that does not appear in table 6.1, was the ways in which precinct lines were drawn in the 1920s and 1930s. Sometimes the boundaries of voting precincts dictated that certain geographically contiguous census tracts be placed in one socioeconomic cluster; there were cases, including South Boston, where census data had to be consulted with precinct maps before neighborhoods could be usefully divided along socioeconomic lines.

Table 6.1 Socioeconomic Indices for Irish Neighborhoods in 1940, by Census Tract

	Census Tract	Median School Years Completed	% Professional Workers	Median Gross Monthly Rent, Dollars	% Mechanical Refrigerator	% Central Heating
Poor	M-2	7.9	1.2	21.46	9	4
	O-3	8.1	3.7	27.07	19	20
Lower Class	C-1	(Resident population too small. Census does not report figures.)				
	C-2	8.4	2.5	26.94	27	22
	C-3	8.5	3.9	31.18	29	35
	D-2	8.2	1.6	26.00	24	37
	D-3	8.6	6.9	25.41	35	36
	E-2	8.5	7.4	23.10	35	45
	N-1	8.1	3.5	25.50	24	16
	N-2	8.8	4.3	35.17	35	39
	N-3	8.5	6.1	36.03	35	44
	N-4	8.7	6.7	34.21	41	36
	P-1C	8.3	1.3	30.67	26	38
	S-6	8.4	6.6	32.22	29	56
Working Class	S-4	9.1	21.1	37.99	46	50
	T-2	8.8	5.4	38.93	41	79
	T-4A	8.8	7.2	38.78	37	65
	T-4B	9.4	5.0	40.65	47	95
	W-2	8.6	3.5	38.67	59	79
Lower Middle Class	Y-3B	10.7	15.3	40.75	71	93
	Y-4	10.7	8.3	45.08	60	95
	Y-5A	10.9	9.8	48.17	62	96

Source: United States Department of Commerce, Bureau of the Census, *16th Census of the United States, 1940, Population and Housing—Statistics for Census Tracts—Boston, Mass.* (Washington: United States Government Printing Office, 1942).

The poor Irish lived on the narrow streets of the lower end of South Boston (census tracts M-2 and O-3), on flat land historically subject to flooding. Thus Bushee could accurately observe that "the most congested portions of the Irish districts are in South Boston, . . . in the northern part of the island." As table 6.1 shows, indices of wealth and status attest to the very low status of the area's residents: the average adult had been in school only eight years and fewer than one in ten homes had either central heating or a mechanical refrigerator. Woods and Kennedy, writing in the 1910s, describe this neighborhood in vivid and pointed terms:

> The lower section of E Street from Second to Ninth Streets presents the congested tenement house area. . . . Most of the [older] houses . . . are no longer suitable for dwellings. They are stale with the dirt of the past. They are insufficiently equipped with sanitary conveniences. They are forlorn in appearance and invite careless, unwholesome living. . . . In these haunts of disease human life is sacrificed to the fetich of property. . . . [Such conditions] present to our observation the most menacing conditions which are to be found for human beings in city life.

This pocket of extreme poverty in the lower end of South Boston was, in short, according to Woods and Kennedy, an "unpleasant dream," an area "of unexampled unattractiveness." The residents of the area, then, who were overwhelmingly Irish, have been isolated for the purposes of this study as the city's poorest Irish.[11]

Still poor, but somewhat less desperate than the group just described, were the lower-class Irish communities of South Boston (census tracts N-1, N-2, N-3, N-4), Uphams Corner (P-1C), Charlestown (C-1, C-2, C-3, D-2, D-3, E-2), and Mission Hill (S-6). These neighborhoods were the vital core of Boston's Irish population; a solid majority of all the city's Irish living in homogeneous areas lived in one of these lower-class districts. Table 6.1 demonstrates the low socioeconomic character of these communities. In rough terms, median monthly rents did not exceed $36, no more than one-third of the homes had refrigerators, and less than half of the homes in any of the census tracts were centrally heated. The average level of education attained by this group was eighth grade. Not all of South Boston, of course, was lower-class Irish. Part of the peninsula was extremely poor and other portions of it were heavily populated with Poles, Italians, and Lithuanians.[12] Those South Boston precincts isolated as both Irish and lower-class were in the City Point neighborhood. Virtually all of Charlestown and all of Mission Hill, in contrast, were heavily Irish, although not all of Mission Hill's Irish were lower-class. A small Irish pocket existed, too, in Uphams Corner, where Dorchester borders South Boston.

In a study which otherwise celebrates and glorifies South Boston, John J. Toomey and Edward P. B. Rankin fear for the future moral health of people "who are living under depressing and demoralizing physical surroundings." Woods and Kennedy also sense an impending deterioration of the upper section of South Boston, which, compared to the miserable lower end, was at the time relatively pleasant. It "still has much open space within its limits besides park and playground areas. But ominously," they note, "the long lines of closely built wooden houses are creeping up and down [over?] the hill-side. Rear tenements are not unknown, foreshadowing future evils which even the breezes from off the harbor waters will not overcome." Charlestown, once an attractive, if not prestigious, neighborhood, had declined sharply since the middle of the nineteenth century. To Woods and Kennedy, "the housing portions of the district present the appearance of a mosaic of roofs, so closely do the dwellings seem to touch one another. Hardly an open space is visible." No longer is the neighborhood attracting residents with "thrift and ambition," like those Irish who began coming in the 1850s and 1860s. The Irish coming to Charlestown now "are ordinary laborers, whose removal here means no special rise in the social scale." Large sections of Mission Hill, too, had fallen sharply in status and living conditions since the nineteenth century. By the 1920s and 1930s, the magnificent Mission Church was surrounded on most sides by tenements. Homes originally built, as Warner has described, for the rising lower middle class, this "narrow and mean form of building" adapted itself quickly to the later influx of poorer Irish. The condition of the three-deckers in "this back eddy of the ward" made the residential neighborhood around the Mission Church "one of the most squalid sections of Roxbury," as Woods and Kennedy observe. These, then, were the circumstances of the lower-class Irish population in Boston.[13]

The working-class neighborhoods represented a noticeable improvement over the previous two classes. Including the Parker Hill section of Mission Hill (S-4), as well as parts of Dorchester (T-2, T-4A, T-4B) and Forest Hills (W-2), the Irish working class was, in terms of socioeconomic indices, at the median for the city as a whole. "The type of Irish who live on Parker Hill," according to Woods and Kennedy, "live in quite comfortable circumstances." Most of the men hold secure government jobs, and there is "a general air of prosperity," which is reflected in their substantial support for the Mission Church. Table 6.1 demonstrates that these neighborhoods represented an improvement, in socioeconomic terms, over the lower-class districts: a ninth-grade education was the norm, rents ranged between $38 and $41, nearly half the homes had refrigerators, and most of the dwellings were centrally heated. These neighborhoods were not, to be sure, especially advantaged, except when compared to most other Irish districts in the city.

Forest Hills, for example, was a working-class neighborhood, neither unusually poor nor middle-class. So, too, like their counterparts on Roxbury's Parker Hill, the working-class Irish in Dorchester gave considerable support to their parish churches. One of them, St. Peter's, standing at Meeting House Hill, was the center of perhaps the largest and most prosperous parish in the diocese. In general, the Irish neighborhoods in northeastern Dorchester—which included Meeting House Hill, Fields Corner, and Savin Hill—were populated by families which "constitute a fairly successful class whose children can start life on a normal, hopeful basis," according to Woods and Kennedy. Boston's working-class Irish at least had some reason to hope. They had achieved for themselves a measure of stability and security which, even in the 1920s and 1930s, was scarce among most of the city's Irish Catholics.[14]

The final group of Irish examined was made up of those who lived in the lower-middle-class community of northwest Brighton (Y-3B, Y-4, Y-5A). This population, straddling the parishes of St. Columbkille and Our Lady of the Presentation, had ascended into the ranks of the middle class without escaping from an ethnically homogeneous community. The origins of the area's composition lay in the nineteenth century, when "some of the more prosperous first- and second-generation immigrants found their way to the inviting semi-rural area of Brighton and slowly transformed this cattle and garden area into a suburb." With the increasing influence of Irish in its population, Brighton voted to annex itself to Boston in the 1870s. St. Columbkille's, constructed at that time, "became a magnet for the Boston Irish and was instrumental in changing the area's outlook from Yankee to Irish." In the 1920s and 1930s, a substantial pocket of lower-middle-class Irish remained in Brighton. As table 6.1 shows, this community was distinguished in many respects. Median monthly rents exceeded $40, two-thirds of the homes had refrigerators, and virtually all of the homes were centrally heated. The average adult, moreover, had received nearly eleven years of formal education. Probably the physical isolation of Brighton from the rest of the city contributed to the maintenance of this relatively successful community. Whatever the cause, the Irish neighborhood—bounded by Washington, Cambridge, and North Beacon Streets, and the city line—formed a cohesive and significant lower-middle-class enclave.[15]

In examining the electoral behavior of these four socioeconomic groups, it is immediately obvious that differences among them were not great; an emphasis on cross-cutting ethnic allegiances, then, is fundamental to predicting voting behavior. The Irish, quite simply, voted as Irish. While class was not unimportant, there was much more that united the four sets of Irish than divided them.

Boston's Irish were active political participants and staunch Democrats throughout the era studied. Table 6.2 details party registration figures by gender and class. Apparently, those events which led to a withering of Yankee interest in politics—the power of the Irish ward machines, the takeover of Boston government by the Irish, the increasing influence of the Irish and of the Democrats at the state level, and the creation of the majority New Deal coalition nationally—stimulated, even as they resulted from, intense political involvement by the city's Irish.[16] Whether by coercion or incentive, the Irish men and women provided the votes and the support upon which the Democratic political establishment in Boston rested. They, unlike the Yankees, did not desert the political sphere; rather, having conquered it, they continued to participate energetically.

The numbers of registered voters in Irish areas of the city attested to the high degree of Irish political activity. Although the Irish were, on average, lower on the socioeconomic scale than most other Bostonians, they were extremely well organized: the sizes of the Irish active electorates were unsurpassed by those of any other ethnic group at the time. "It goes without saying," notes Woods, "that the greatest degree of political activity is found among the Irish." As he observes in a separate study of Boston:

> The Irishman regards politics as a separate department of life. It is an end in itself. . . . The political interest of the Irish people is shown not only in the large proportion of the Irish voters, but also in the greater activity of those voters. They are not merely the most easily organized of any nationality, but they are the most capable organizers.[17]

Thus, in the early 1920s, as table 6.2 shows, about 70 percent of the male Irish population was registered to vote. Only the very poorest group of Irish men, with comparable figures ranging from 52 to 56 percent, failed to approach that level. That may well have resulted from the severity of poverty among that group and the transience of much of the population, both factors which would have mitigated against even the most earnest attempts to register voters. Two decades later, each of the active electorates had increased in size. Levels of participation among the vast majority of Irish men reached 80 percent by 1940, and more than 70 percent of the poorest group of men were politically active. If the poor Irish in lower South Boston are excepted for the moment, only upper-middle-class Jews were registered in 1920 at the same level as the city's Irish, and by 1940 even they had been surpassed by the intensity of Irish political action.

The data in table 6.2 reveal a similar phenomenon among Irish women. By 1926, six years after the passage and implementation of the Nineteenth Amendment but still prior to the campaign by Al Smith and the later realignment, a solid majority of women in the Irish neighborhoods had already registered to vote. As was true for men, the poorest women were the exception, with only 36.6 percent registered in that year. Among the three other socioeconomic groups, however, the size of the female electorate ranged from 52.4 to 54.3 percent. No other ethnic group in the city attained even the level of 36.6 percent achieved by the poor Irish, which was itself low compared to the political participation rates of the other Irish women in the city. At the end of the era, in 1940, the active electorate had expanded to about 70 percent of the Irish population, with the poorest group reaching a level of 57.5 percent. Again, even that low figure was higher than the number of women registered to vote in any other ethnic group in Boston. Exceptionally large numbers of Irish men and women, then, were participating in the political process in the early 1920s and even more were doing so after the historic elections of the late 1920s and 1930s.

Table 6.2 Party Registration Figures in Irish Precincts as Percent of Total Potential Electorate

	Poor Men				Poor Women			
	All Reg.	Dem.	Rep.	Ind.	All Reg.	Dem.	Rep.	Ind.
1920	52.2	40.1	1.9	10.2	10.6	9.5	0.4	0.7
1922	55.9	48.4	2.5	5.0	25.8	18.6	0.7	6.5
1924	52.0	40.8	2.2	9.0	29.1	22.4	1.3	5.4
1926	55.9	49.8	1.1	5.0	36.6	27.0	1.1	8.5
1928	60.2	49.5	1.5	9.2	45.2	38.5	1.1	5.6
1930	63.3	50.7	1.4	11.2	51.2	38.4	1.2	11.6
1932*	61.9				47.5			
1934	69.9	60.7	0.8	8.3	54.5	43.0	0.8	10.7
1936	69.1	59.3	1.4	8.4	53.6	48.8	0.9	3.9
1938	73.1	63.5	1.3	8.4	57.6	52.1	1.0	4.5
1940	70.7	61.6	1.4	7.8	57.5	52.8	1.3	3.5
	Lower Class Men				Lower Class Women			
	All Reg.	Dem.	Rep.	Ind.	All Reg.	Dem.	Rep.	Ind.
1920	64.6	50.6	3.4	10.6	18.2	10.0	0.8	7.3
1922	68.5	55.4	3.8	9.3	44.5	31.7	1.6	11.2
1924	65.4	54.7	3.7	7.0	46.6	36.1	2.4	8.1
1926	67.0	56.2	3.5	7.3	52.4	39.2	2.0	11.2
1928	72.3	58.1	3.5	10.6	60.5	47.1	2.5	10.9
1930	75.5	59.6	3.3	12.6	60.6	48.4	2.5	9.6
1932*	74.6				62.5			
1934	77.8	67.2	2.9	7.7	64.3	57.6	2.4	4.2
1936	76.6	68.4	2.8	5.4	68.4	59.1	2.4	6.9
1938	79.1	70.1	3.0	6.1	70.4	63.6	2.4	4.4
1940	82.9	70.5	2.9	9.5	70.8	62.5	2.5	5.8

Table 6.2 (cont'd)

	Working Class Men				Working Class Women			
	All Reg.	Dem.	Rep.	Ind.	All Reg.	Dem.	Rep.	Ind.
1920	65.7	41.3	6.0	18.4	16.7	6.6	1.2	8.9
1922	70.9	53.2	6.8	10.9	41.9	22.0	2.5	17.4
1924	69.4	49.6	7.7	12.2	43.3	27.2	3.9	12.1
1926	68.9	54.5	5.9	8.6	54.3	34.2	2.7	17.4
1928	71.9	55.5	5.2	11.2	59.9	44.0	3.7	12.2
1930	72.7	53.6	4.5	14.6	60.0	43.1	3.2	13.8
1932*	74.9				56.7			
1934	77.0	63.9	4.0	9.1	62.5	51.5	3.0	8.0
1936	78.8	66.2	3.7	8.9	64.6	52.9	2.9	8.8
1938	81.1	66.2	3.3	11.5	66.2	56.4	3.1	6.7
1940	81.5	66.5	3.6	11.4	66.4	55.3	3.1	8.0

	Lower Middle Class Men				Lower Middle Class Women			
	All Reg.	Dem.	Rep.	Ind.	All Reg.	Dem.	Rep.	Ind.
1920	72.1	36.8	12.8	22.4	24.3	7.9	3.3	13.0
1922	66.3	51.5	11.9	2.9	48.8	19.5	5.7	23.6
1924	69.0	49.6	12.3	7.0	49.6	33.0	7.1	9.5
1926	67.4	53.8	8.6	5.0	52.4	27.4	5.5	19.5
1928	74.6	51.7	9.0	13.8	58.0	41.4	5.9	10.7
1930	76.9	45.5	8.0	23.4	59.8	38.9	5.4	15.5
1932*	66.8				56.8			
1934	68.2	46.0	5.9	16.3	59.5	39.9	4.7	14.9
1936	78.8	57.9	7.6	13.2	66.7	49.2	6.1	11.4
1938	79.8	61.3	7.4	11.1	71.3	53.4	6.9	11.1
1940	79.5	59.0	6.7	13.9	71.7	52.3	6.4	13.0

*Party enrollment figures are not available for 1932.

For all Irish, the increase in voter activity was gradual. With the partial exception of 1928, there is no evidence in registration figures of any sharp surge in the size of the active electorate concentrated over a single period, largely because so many Irish were already active before the onset of the realignment years. Women do appear, however, to have mobilized primarily over the elections of 1928 and 1936. As illustration, the number of lower-class Irish women registered to vote rose from 52.4 percent in 1926, to 60.6 in 1930, to 64.3 in 1934, and, finally, to 70.4 in 1938. While the election of 1932 created 3.7 new voters per 100 women, that of 1928 mobilized 8.2 and that of 1936 mobilized 6.1. Across all classes of Irish women, the gains in registration made in 1928 and 1936 were more significant than those in 1932. And it appears that the 1928 increases were especially important, generally exceeding those of 1936. No such definite pattern can be discerned across the groups of men. The relatively small increases in the numbers of registered men between the mid-1920s and 1940 apparently occurred slowly and without noticeable discontinuities, although the peculiar dip in the lower-middle-class Brighton figures in the early 1930s deserves an explanation that I am at a loss to offer. One observation which can be stated with some accuracy is the uniform importance of the 1928 election for men. The year that Al Smith sought the presidency is the only period in which significant increases were recorded across all four groups. While for any one male socioeconomic group, 1928 may not have been the most decisive year, it did at least have some measurable impact on each of the groups. One should stress, though, the subtlety of these distinctions. There was no great mobilization of Irish voters. The minor mobilization that did occur peaked, but only slightly, in 1928; the elections of 1932 and 1936 were important as well. More so than for other ethnic groups, however, Al Smith motivated many previously apathetic Irish to register. As Huthmacher describes the 1928 campaign, with some hyperbole, "the task among Irish-Americans was primarily one of registration, and Democratic politicians in the Irish wards of Boston . . . virtually fell over one another adding names to the voting lists."[18] And, significantly, as was not the case for Italians, women responded to Al Smith's appeal with the same force as men.

Certainly the Irish community in Boston was not shaken by party realignment: Republicans were practically as rare in 1920 as they would be in 1940. Huthmacher refers to Boston's Irish as "the backbone of the [Democratic] party, . . . [t]he bedrock of the new alignment."[19] Of those enrolled in one of the major parties, 95 percent of the poorest Irish were Democratic in 1920 and 98 percent were Democratic two decades later. The trend was the same for the other socioeconomic groups. Thus, at the other end of the scale, lower-middle-class Irish increased their commitment to the Democratic party from 73 percent to 89 percent over the same period. As table 6.2 shows, at no time were Irish Democrats threatened with extinction, and, indeed, their ranks expanded over time.

Men shifted most strongly toward a more intense Democratic tie with the 1932 election, an election of much less importance for women. Between 1930 and 1934, then, nearly 10 percent of the Irish male electorate added their names to the list of Democratic registrants. The only group in which there was no such gain was the lower middle class; there, however, the number of Democrats remained stable in 1932 even as the total number of registered voters plummeted sharply. It is interesting to note in passing the role, albeit minor, played by the conversion of Republicans in the gains accrued by

Democrats. Among all four groups of men, but especially among the working class and the lower middle class, Republicans suffered clear desertions over the twenty-year period. By 1940, the number of Republican men had withered to as little as half of its former strength. Women in each of the groups, on the other hand, were mobilized more than men but not converted, and they entered the ranks of the Democratic party in substantial numbers throughout the entire period. No single election was of unusual importance for them. Among men, it seems, Roosevelt registered as Democrats those whom Al Smith had first attracted as independents as well as those who were registering for the first time in 1932, a pattern by now familiar from the experience of other ethnic groups in Boston. While Smith contributed to increased electoral interest and to great gains in turnout, it was the election of Roosevelt that converted those temporary supporters into registered and active Democrats. The election of 1932, for men, and the elections of 1932 and 1936, for women, were of central importance in consolidating the place of additional Irish in the emergent Democratic coalition of the New Deal era, a process which had begun, for the Irish, with the initial mobilizations of 1928.

Table 6.3 Vote in Irish Precincts for President, Representative in Congress, and Senator in General Court as Percent of Potential Electorate

	Poor President			Poor Congressman		Poor State Senator	
	Dem.	Rep.	Other	Dem.	Rep.	Dem.	Rep.
1920	16.7	8.8	2.3	21.0	3.5	24.8	3.3
1922				27.4	3.0		
1924	19.7	6.3	7.9	32.5	3.8	29.6	2.8
1926						32.8	1.5
1928	52.2	2.3		48.1	2.8	45.9	3.9
1930				39.0	2.3	32.5	9.5
1932	43.7	2.3		42.1	1.9	39.4	5.0
1934				45.9	2.3		
1936	44.2	4.7	5.7	43.2	11.2*	43.4	7.6
1938				51.3	4.0		
1940	45.8	11.7		49.4	5.1	48.9	4.0

	Lower Class President			Lower Class Congressman		Lower Class State Senator	
	Dem.	Rep.	Other	Dem.	Rep.	Dem.	Rep.
1920	26.1	12.7	1.9	29.8	10.3	34.2	5.8
1922				35.5	6.8		
1924	28.9	10.2	8.7	44.9	6.5	40.4	5.6
1926						38.7	3.5
1928	61.1	5.5		55.7	7.0	56.9	4.7

Table 6.3 (cont'd)

	Lower Class President			Lower Class Congressman		Lower Class State Senator	
	Dem.	Rep.	Other	Dem.	Rep.	Dem.	Rep.
1930				42.2	6.8		
1932	54.9	5.2		50.2	6.7	50.2	5.2
1934							
1936	49.5	7.7	8.0	49.7	12.6*	46.9	12.9
1938							
1940	51.8	17.4		55.9	11.4	57.6	7.6

	Working Class President			Working Class Congressman		Working Class State Senator	
	Dem.	Rep.	Other	Dem.	Rep.	Dem.	Rep.
1920	23.4	20.3	2.0	26.7	12.3	29.8	10.8
1922				34.4	9.6		
1924	28.4	15.8	10.1	40.8	13.5		
1926							
1928	60.6	7.8		54.0	11.6	55.4	7.5
1930				37.2	11.5		
1932	52.4	7.0		43.5	14.5		
1934						49.2	5.8
1936	45.7	10.2	10.6	37.2	29.4*	52.6	9.8
1938				43.9	20.9		
1940	46.6	23.1		46.9	20.8	55.8	8.6

	Lower Middle Class President			Lower Middle Class Congressman		Lower Middle Class State Senator	
	Dem.	Rep.	Other	Dem.	Rep.	Dem.	Rep.
1920	22.5	27.7	2.0	26.5	20.9	25.5	21.3
1922						34.3	12.7
1924	28.2	21.7	8.2	36.3	16.6	42.4	9.5
1926				35.9	9.7	34.5	8.8
1928	59.9	12.3		55.6	11.4	55.1	11.2
1930				41.8	7.9	43.0	7.1
1932	51.2	12.1		51.1	9.9	50.9	11.8
1934				49.7	7.4	46.7	9.9
1936	44.5	16.1	10.3	50.2	17.4*	52.2	14.7
1938				53.1	14.3	49.9	16.0
1940	43.6	29.0		56.8	14.5	50.3	16.4

*Republican vote for Congress in 1936 includes votes cast for third-party candidates.

Inspection of table 6.3, then, which displays, as percentages of the potential electorate, Irish voting behavior between 1920 and 1940, yields a curious puzzle. The reaffirmation of Democratic support reflected in registration figures coincided with a desertion of the national party's candidate. Large numbers of Irish were rejecting President Roosevelt's bids for reelection, even though the number of Democratic registrants was increasing significantly.

The roots of this tendency are apparent even in the 1920 election. Indeed, it is not at all clear that the elections of 1928 and 1932, when the Irish overwhelmingly supported the Democratic nominees for president, were not themselves the exceptions to what, in other years, was lukewarm support at best for the national candidate. In 1920, when, among the Irish, registered Democrats vastly outnumbered Republicans, Warren Harding carried one group and was competitive in the others. Harding received one-third of the vote cast by the lower-class Irish of South Boston, Uphams Corner, Charlestown, and Mission Hill at a time when only 6 percent of those identifying with a party considered themselves Republican. Similarly, in lower-middle-class Brighton, Harding received 53 percent of the vote cast, carrying a population three-quarters of whose party enrollees were registered Democrats. John Davis, as table 6.3 shows, did no better in 1924 than had James Cox in 1920. In both years, and among all four socioeconomic groups, Democratic candidates for president failed to attract the support of large numbers of nominal Democrats, running well behind candidates for Congress, who themselves fared slightly worse than candidates for seats in the state senate.

A similar pattern reemerged in 1936 and 1940, when ties to the Democratic party in terms of registration figures were at even higher levels than before. Although Democrats running for Congress and for the state senate, at least in 1940, continued to attract support commensurate with the number of registrants in the active electorate, Roosevelt had lost the favor of many Boston Irish. Between 1932 and 1936, his share of the poor vote fell from 95 to 81 percent of those cast; of the lower-class vote, from 91 to 76 percent; of the working-class vote, from 88 to 69 percent; and of the lower-middle-class vote, from 81 to 63 percent. His share of the total vote declined even further in 1940. The losses he suffered were substantial and not reflected in party registration data.

Behind the rejection of Roosevelt by such large numbers of Irish were reasons quite similar to those for the parallel desertions of the Democratic nominee in 1920. Perhaps most importantly, the Irish in both periods were repudiating policies which they perceived as pandering to British imperialist interests. In 1920, the Democratic party inherited from Woodrow Wilson a commitment to the Treaty of Versailles and the League of Nations. Boston's Irish gave their warm endorsement to the League as originally conceived in the context of the Fourteen Points but found its realization intolerable: Wilson had neglected his original commitment to self-determination, thus sacrificing a free Ireland, in exchange for an international compact to protect the British empire. That the Irish could not tolerate. As a result, they grew fiercely isolationist, and their activity served as well to legitimate political claims arising from ethnic identities. Once the Irish Free State was granted independence in 1922, resentment toward the national Democratic party began to diminish.[20]

In ensuing years, though, two important third-party candidacies emerged, siphoning off support from the Democratic nominees. Robert M. La Follette, running as a Progressive, received considerable backing in Boston's Irish neighborhoods in 1924, doing as well as he had among the Italians but falling short of the strong vote accorded him by most Jews. His credentials were attractive. According to Huthmacher, he was a well-known supporter of an independent Ireland and a vocal opponent of the Ku Klux Klan, American entry into World War I, and future American intervention in European affairs.[21] That year, poor Irish gave La Follette 23 percent of all votes cast for one of the three major-party candidates, lower- and working-class Irish gave him just over 18 percent of their votes, and lower-middle-class Irish gave him 14 percent of their votes. Among the poorest group, La Follette even outpolled Calvin Coolidge. Indeed, the support received by La Follette and Coolidge brought Davis's share of the total vote down to a level as low as Cox's had been in 1920.

The other significant third-party movement of this period, inspired primarily by Father Charles E. Coughlin, contested the elections of 1936. Coughlin—whose enormous popularity rested on a mixture of reactionary politics, isolationism, Anglophobia, and, above all, anti-Semitism—combined forces with others alienated from the Roosevelt presidency to create the Union party, which offered William Lemke and Thomas C. O'Brien as candidates for president and vice president, in addition to supporting several candidates for Congress.[22] From a national perspective, no major city was more receptive to Coughlin's appeal and to the Lemke candidacy than was Boston and no ethnic groups in the country were more enthusiastic than were the Irish and German Catholics.[23] Lemke received between 10 and 16 percent of the total Irish votes cast for president, with greater support in the working- and lower-middle-class Irish neighborhoods than in the two poorer groups. In each of the areas except lower-middle-class Brighton, Lemke's support was greater than that for Alf Landon. He did, as has long been suspected, far better among Boston's Irish than among any other of its major ethnic groups. It was not a spectacular showing, to be sure, but nevertheless unsettling to those unsympathetic to Coughlin's fears and threatened by his appeal.

Many of the grievances expressed by Irish Bostonians in 1936, and then again in 1940, had been anticipated in the 1920 election. Roosevelt was accused of being a British sycophant and of fostering American intervention in the crisis which, even in the mid-1930s, was already developing in Europe. More importantly, perhaps, before the outbreak of war, Roosevelt and his influential advisers appeared to be serving the interests of the left, a perspective increasingly offensive to the bulk of Irish Catholics. The Spanish Civil War was a watershed event in American politics: where American liberals saw a battle between democracy and fascism, the Irish saw a great struggle between the forces of godlessness and those of the church. Roosevelt's failure to support Germany and Italy in their defense of Franco angered many. Communism, in this view, had insidiously penetrated deep into the domestic and international spheres. Persecution of Catholics in Spain and Mexico and American recognition of the Soviet government were, for the Irish, paramount issues. Even the administration in Washington was tainted by a liberal cast. Men and women like Felix Frankfurter, Rexford Tugwell, Harry Hopkins, and Frances Perkins were viewed by many Irish as too powerful. As their great leaders, Al Smith and William Cardinal O'Connell, rebelled against Roosevelt's policies, many Irish grew wary of the president whom they had supported with such vigor in 1932. By 1936, with alternatives in Lemke and Landon, the Irish vote for Roosevelt fell sharply, as did the vote for several congressional candidates. Four years later, Lemke and Coughlin were no longer contesting the presidency, but the residue of the bitterness which they had reflected lingered. Many Irish prominent in the administration—Joseph P. Kennedy, James A. Farley, Thomas G. Corcoran, and Frank Murphy, for example—had begun to leave their positions, further undermining the president's popularity with Irish voters. That was compounded by the war in Europe and Roosevelt's active assistance to the Allies and, especially, to Britain, which was benefiting from an exchange of American destroyers for the use of British naval bases. Again, as it had two decades earlier, the cause of isolationism energized the Irish community. Roosevelt, opposed in 1940 by a single candidate, received an even smaller share of the total vote cast by the Boston Irish than he had received in his first campaign for reelection. One-quarter of the Irish lower class cast ballots for Willkie.[24]

Between the rebellions of 1920 and, to a lesser extent, 1924, and those of 1936 and 1940, the Boston Irish gave extraordinary support to the Democratic candidates for president. Voter turnout between 1924 and 1928 increased sharply. And, in 1928, and again in 1932, the majorities accorded the Democratic nominees were enormous. As shares of all votes cast, Smith and

Roosevelt received, respectively, 96 and 95 percent of the poor Irish vote; 92 and 91 percent of the lower-class Irish vote; 89 and 88 percent of the working-class Irish vote; and 83 and 81 percent of the lower-middle-class Irish vote. Indeed, turnout and Democratic support were both so enormous in those years that, with one exception, actual majorities of the entire adult population of each of the groups cast votes for the Democratic candidates; in 1928, in fact, 60 percent of the potential Irish electorates, except for the poorest group, turned out in support of Al Smith.

Al Smith was as close to a favorite son of the Boston Irish as any New Yorker could aspire to be. ''My beloved friends of Massachusetts,'' began his emotional 1932 speech on behalf of Roosevelt's candidacy, delivered in Boston at the end of October, ''I am home. I am home in every sense that it means.'' Indeed, not until Roosevelt had already received the nomination of the Democratic National Convention in 1932 had the Massachusetts delegation ended its drive to recall Smith as the party's candidate. And it was in all likelihood the decision of Smith to return to Boston before the election and to campaign vigorously for Roosevelt that accounted for the solid Democratic majorities of 1932 among the Boston Irish.

Those halcyon days of sweeping Democratic victories appear, in retrospect, as but a brief interlude in a period of, if not dissatisfaction with, at least tepid support for, the Democratic candidates for president. The slight mobilization and registration of Irish voters on behalf of the Democratic party that Smith inspired and Roosevelt realized may have primarily benefited the party locally. It is conceivable that, on the national level, the Irish were responding strictly to the personal appeal of Al Smith, an Irish and a Catholic with whom they could identify, and to his subsequent endorsement of Roosevelt. As Robert K. Massey, Jr., suggests, Smith's role in the 1932 campaign was crucial. ''Without his blessing, political observers predicted [in early October], Franklin Roosevelt could not carry Massachusetts.'' Perhaps there was no permanent attachment to Roosevelt himself or to his New Deal. What did persist throughout this period, however, was a general Irish commitment to the Democratic party.

Even that belief, though—that the Irish remained strong Democrats throughout this period—has not gone unchallenged. Erbring et al. argue that ''the lore that has the Irish as part of the New Deal realignment is without foundation. . . . [T]he Irish clearly didn't like Roosevelt—he turned them off their one-time Democratic loyalty.'' Such a change ''at the individual level,'' they continue, ''must have involved genuine partisan change by way of alienation and, ultimately, conversion; and . . . most of it happened early on.'' That hypothesis is directly contradicted by the data collected in Boston, the city cited, incidentally, in rhetorical support of their assertions. Tables 6.2 and 6.3 show that the city's Irish did, if anything, grow more Democratic over time; their reluctance to support Roosevelt in 1936 and 1940 was, notably, remarkably similar to their desertions of 1920 and 1924. Thus, while support of the presidential nominee remained low in both decades, loyalty to the Democratic party, at the level of local offices and registration, did not dissipate and, indeed, grew deeper in the 1930s.[25]

Figure 6.1, which illustrates the vote for the Republican candidate for president, and figure 6.2, which traces the share of the partisan active electorate registered in the Republican party, vividly show the divergence between election returns and party identification over the twenty-year period as well as the role of class distinctions. The U-shaped figure 6.1 contrasts clearly with the more linear, downward sloping, figure 6.2. While Irish support for the national Democratic nominees peaked in 1928 and 1932 and then fell in succeeding elections, registration figures were unaffected. The two variables appear to have shifted independently of one another.

An especially interesting feature of Irish political activity in the 1920s and 1930s was its class dimension. Numerous scholars have converged on the view that, not only did the Irish vote along class lines, but class-based politics became especially sharp by 1936 and 1940. "In drawing the line of cleavage between worker and 'economic royalist,' " explains Lubell, "Roosevelt unquestionably sharpened the sense of class division in American society." Fuchs observes that "differences in Democratic strength within all religious groups except the Jews could be attributed to differences in economic status." And this general reasoning has often been specifically applied to the voting behavior of the Irish. Erbring et al. speculate that "middle class Irish Americans were likely to look upon what Roosevelt and the New Deal came to represent with no less aversion, and with no lesser sense of class interest, than many other middle class Americans." According to Trout in his study of Boston, by 1940, as "low-income Italo-Irish neighborhoods began to fall

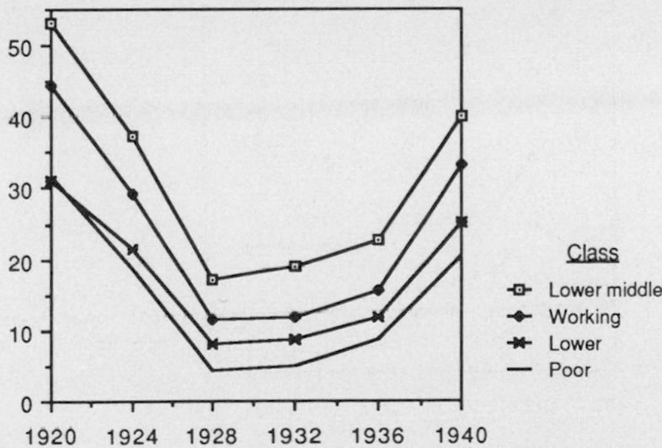

Figure 6.1 Vote in Irish Precincts for Republican Candidate for President, by Class (as Percent of All Votes Cast)

away'' from their previously high levels of support for Roosevelt, ''more affluent Irish and Italian voters defected to an even greater degree.'' One major flaw in Trout's logic—and in the logic of many others who claim to have found similar economic-based divides in the later elections of James Michael Curley—is the assumption that the city's middle-class wards were as ethnically homogeneous as its lower- and working-class wards. Although it is not inconceivable that Curley or Roosevelt's support diminished more among middle-class Irish than among lower-class Irish, that conclusion cannot be drawn from simple comparisons of Hyde Park or West Roxbury, both heavily Yankee, with Irish Charlestown. Here is a particularly clear instance of the value of precinct-level research and analysis. In sum, though, the belief is pervasive that, locally as well as nationally, the 1930s witnessed the ''disintegration of Irish political homogeneity,'' supplanting an ethnic cue with socioeconomic motivation.[26]

That realignment along class lines, so deeply ingrained in the political science literature, did not occur within Boston's Irish community. Inspection of either figure 6.1 or figure 6.2 renders that conclusion inescapable. Whether in terms of vote for president or in terms of registration, there was no widening of class divisions in the mid- or late 1930s in Boston. To be sure, the Irish consistently split along class lines throughout the decades, so that by any measure and at every point in time, the poorer groups socioeconomically were also the more Democratic. Significantly, however, the size of those cleavages remained constant: the impacts of the elections of 1936 and 1940 on class division were no different from those of any preceding elections. Whatever drift occurred in the 1930s, whether it was away from Roosevelt in figure 6.1 or toward more Democratic registration in figure 6.2, was uniform across all four classes. Middle-class or poor, Boston's Irish were responding

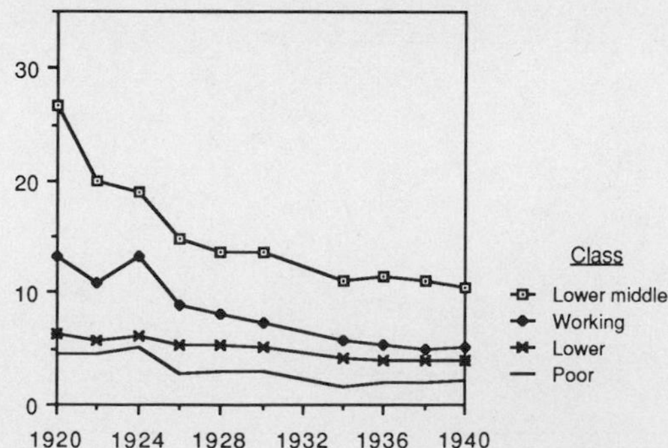

Figure 6.2 Republican Registration in Irish Precincts, by Class (as Percent of Total Two-party Enrollment)

to the same forces. Differences from year to year resulted from appeals to ethnicity rather than to class. The vote for Willkie in 1940 was inspired by issues that united the Irish, such as antagonism toward Britain and the European war, and not by issues that divided the Irish into discrete socioeconomic groups.

As the New Deal alignment coalesced in the 1930s, then, Boston's Irish continued to provide the foundation of the city's Democratic base. Spurred by the candidacy of Al Smith in 1928 and the subsequent rise to national dominance of the Democratic party, the Irish renewed their century-old standing commitment. Voting returns and registration statistics both confirm the mobilization of new Irish voters and their overwhelming tendency to identify with the Democratic party. Turnout rates in the 1930s reached new, higher levels, reflecting the intense Irish interest in political affairs. Even as disenchantment with Roosevelt emerged, Boston's Irish continued to vote heavily, to register as Democrats, and to support Democrats for lower offices. And, defying the dictates of political theory, the Irish reacted to events as an ethnic group instead of as four groups with divergent class interests. They did not suddenly split in the late 1930s along socioeconomic lines. Rather they stood together. The Irish, by far the largest and most powerful community in the Boston political arena, had achieved consensus both on an underlying Democratic commitment and on short-term issues affecting the depth and expression of that learned loyalty.

7

Making New Deal Democrats

The remaking of the Democratic party in the 1930s was no doubt an important event in the party history of this century. ''The election of 1932 deserves to be called a 'revolution,' '' E. E. Schattschneider has written, ''because it destroyed something very much like a permanent Republican lease of power; it was no ordinary election, and the overthrow of the Republican party was no ordinary alternation of the parties in power.'' And that upheaval in the system of party competition coincided with a shift in public policy which, in Schattschneider's estimation, was unparalleled in all of American history.[1] Peacefully and with great dignity, millions of men and women changed an established political order in order to make it more capable of coping with unprecedented economic crisis. Their quiet decisions created a new Democratic coalition and redefined the party system.

As this study of the individual political actor in Boston has shown, the processes undergirding the New Deal realignment were complex and subtle, and they occurred against a backdrop of some continuity. No simple mechanism can adequately summarize the fine detail of the actual transformation. Women often acted differently from men, poorer individuals often acted differently from wealthier individuals, and ethnicity remained throughout the source of great distinctiveness between groups. Close examination of homogeneous precincts for five important ethnic communities in a major city leaves the student of realignment impressed most by the variegation of a phenomenon which, at a distance, appeared to have been sharp and tidy. The picture of the realignment cannot be painted with broad, sweeping strokes. Rather, were one to seek to illustrate on canvas the making of New Deal Democrats, the medium best suited to the task would be pointillism.

Still, in political activity as in pointillism, the countless specks of color are not wholly random. The painter arrays his myriad dots to conform to a carefully designed whole. While no one so directs the votes of most individuals, nevertheless their individually conceived decisions do evince certain overarching patterns. That, indeed, is a basic premise of this project, and the organization of the book by ethnic group is that premise's most obvious manifestation. Our search for order, however, must be conducted with a suitable respect for the constant strain of disorder and for the disconnected decisions that ran through the era.

A cross-sectional perspective confirms the suspicion that discernible patterns existed across all individuals studied, regardless of ethnicity. Four of the more important of those patterns are the subject of this chapter. In general, it appears, first, that men realigned before women. Second, within groups where both processes occurred, conversion preceded mobilization. The third pattern relates to the differential impact of national and local forces on political change within each group. Fourth, the degree of party discipline emerges as an important variable in understanding the shape of political participation along socioeconomic lines. In brief, certain truths emerge from comparative analysis of the five ethnic groups in the city and the individuals composing them. Those patterns suggest some thoughts about the period of realignment which we have studied; the summary thoughts appear at the end of the chapter.

That women lagged after men in their enthusiasm and support for the Democratic party is an interesting finding. It has long been believed that women, especially foreign-stock women, contributed disproportionately to the great Democratic successes of 1928 and 1932 in urban centers such as Boston. Those women, who only recently had acquired the right to vote in state and national elections, ostensibly mobilized in response to the candidacy of Al Smith. Foreign-stock and black men, in contrast, it is believed, having long been active in the political system, could not have had as strong a numerical impact on events. To simplify without grossly distorting this view, while both men and women could have converted or crossed party lines to vote for Al Smith in 1928, only women at the same time possessed the ability and will to newly mobilize in large numbers. The dramatic increase in voter turnout in 1928, Sundquist writes, "was probably due mainly to the motivation of many women, who though enfranchised in 1920 had never voted, to cast their ballots for the first time." It is a view shared by many other scholars, including Lubell, Burner, Huthmacher, and Andersen. So, although in the early and mid-1920s immigrant and black women and their daughters were especially likely to forgo their newly acquired franchise, they suddenly in 1928 realized their latent power and registered and voted for Al Smith, mobilizing in large numbers in anticipation of the erupting realignment. This is a popular historical description of events of that era, but its basis in fact is weak.[2]

Rather, as has already been shown several times, women became Democrats only after men had initiated the realignment. Figure 7.1 illustrates this pattern of successive movement. It displays, for men and for women, the timing of increases in Democratic party enrollment. Only the three groups that were transformed by the events of the 1920s and 1930s—Jews, blacks, and Italians—have been selected for this purpose. (Throughout this chapter, Italians are represented graphically by the East Boston community and Jews are represented by their lower-middle-class stratum; in each case, the specific group chosen is the largest and most representative segment of the ethnic community as a whole.) What is graphed, for the period between 1926 and 1940, is the percentage of the total increase in Democratic party registration that occurred in each two-year interval. The six years prior to 1926 are omitted both because women were mobilizing and registering in those years for reasons entirely unrelated to the impending realignment and because the first potentially critical election did not occur until 1928. What this presentation of the data permits is an emphasis on the years of the most intense increases in Democratic registration, calculated separately for men and for women, as fractions of their total Democratic gains over the fourteen-year period.

Italian women in East Boston, for example, experienced their greatest surges in 1936 and 1938. In 1926, only 8.8 percent of the population was enrolled in the Democratic party. By 1940, fully 36.2 percent were so registered, a gain of 27.4 points. Of that total increase of 27.4 points, 8.7 points were recorded between 1934 and 1936, when the number of registered Democratic women rose from 22.6 to 31.3 percent of the population. That gain of 8.7 for the two-year interval ending in 1936 represented nearly one-third, or 31.8 percent, of the entire increase of 27.4 points over the fourteen years. In contrast, the rise in Democratic participation and identification between 1926 and 1928 was only 2.4 points, or 8.8 percent of the total increase during the realignment. Nearly four times as many Italian women registered and became Democrats in 1936 as in 1928. An incumbent President Roosevelt, and not Al Smith, was ultimately the beneficiary of the gradually mobilizing pool of Italian women voters. Contrary to supposed patterns and perhaps even to intuition, foreign-stock women did not begin to vote in unusually large numbers in 1928. They did not exercise a still unfamiliar political right even to express enthusiasm for the first Catholic to be nominated by a major party for the presidency. Rather, as figure 7.1 shows, Italian women, compared to Italian men, embraced the Democratic party with their greatest enthusiasm relatively late. The years when the greatest relative accretions by men were made to the ranks of the Democratic party were 1932 and 1934: over half of the total increase in male Democratic registrants in these fourteen years occurred between 1930 and 1934.[3]

A partisan analysis by gender, then, yields particularly clear results in the Italian case. Democratic gains peaked first among men, in 1932 and 1934, and

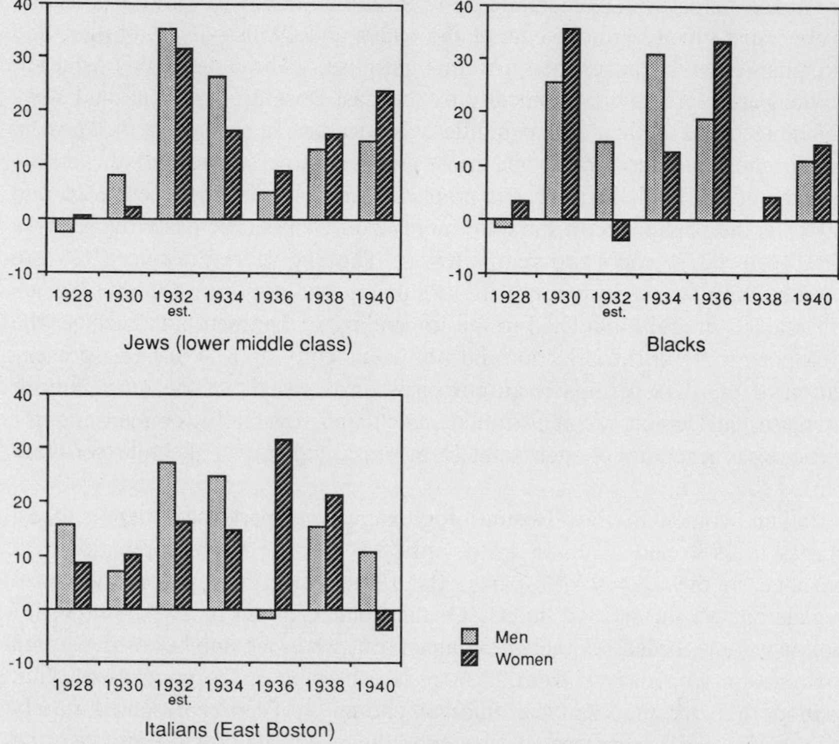

Figure 7.1 Gains in Democratic Registration, by Gender (for Two-year Periods Ending in Year Indicated, as Percent of Total Increase for 1926–40 Period)

only later, in 1936 and 1938, among women. This pattern of Democratic attachments is reinforced by the examination in Chapter 3 of the overall level of political activity, which shows male mobilization occurring primarily in 1928 and 1932 and female mobilization occurring mainly in 1932 and 1936. Men, perhaps prepared by Al Smith's candidacy in 1928, became Democrats with the accession of Roosevelt to the presidency, while women, conditioned both by the success of the New Deal and perhaps by the activity of Italian men, waited until the reelection campaign and the second administration to express their emerging partisanship and politicization.

Similar, if less dramatic patterns, can be observed in the behavior of the black and Jewish communities. Black men, as has earlier been noted, became progressively more Democratic in the years between 1928 and 1936, with their greatest gains in 1930 and, especially, 1934. Black women, on the other hand, entered the Democratic party in two great surges, one in 1930 and the other in 1936. The tremendous movement in 1930 is as difficult to explain here as it was in Chapter 4: with this single, puzzling exception, there is no evidence that blacks were fundamentally realigned before the election of Roosevelt and the implementation of the New Deal in the following years. It is much easier, of course, to account for the peak in 1936. In that year, 33.5 percent of the Democratic gain over the entire period was recorded. Whatever occurred in 1930, it is improbable that women were responding at that time to the issues which would define the New Deal coalition. Those issues were, however, at the heart of the 1936 conflict. While men in black precincts slowly attached themselves to the Democratic party throughout the early and mid-1930s, black women finally responded in 1936 with their own mobilization. It is not inconceivable that women, new to registration and voting, took their partisan cues from men during the era of realignment. Like the pattern displayed in Italian East Boston, the city's black women lagged after men in their own movement toward the Democrats.

Jewish women, in subtle contrast to their counterparts in the black and Italian neighborhoods, acted in greater concert with Jewish men. Thus, increased support for the Democratic party peaked for both sexes in 1932. That year, though, was of greater relative importance for men than it was for women. Democratic support then continued to increase sharply for men into 1934. Indeed, the six years between 1928 and 1934 accounted for 69.8 percent of the Democratic gains among Jewish men. In contrast, gains among women in those years represented 50.6 percent, or just half, of their total for the whole period. Women in the Jewish community did not move toward the Democratic party in 1934 with the same force as men. Rather, women became more Democratic at a steadier rate, with a large increase in 1940 and smaller gains in 1934, 1936, and 1938. For men, the number of Democratic registrants was concentrated in the late 1920s and early 1930s. Female gains were significant in that period, but not as heavily skewed in that direction; substantial movement continued into the mid and late 1930s among Jewish women.

Although the three graphs in figure 7.1 stand out strongly for their radical differences one from the other, one trend is clearly apparent. With only the most minor exceptions, until 1934 increased male support for the Democratic party as a share of the whole period consistently outpaced female support. Conversely, after 1934 female support was the more important. Democratic gains among men were more concentrated in the early years of the realignment, while those among women were more concentrated in the later years. Accounting for this pattern is not difficult. Women had, after all, received the vote only in 1920, and thus were much less familiar with the political system. Some of those who did register initially may have eschewed party identification, lacking a history of partisan political activity. Further, certainly among the immigrant groups but probably among blacks as well, cultural characteristics may have acted to discourage political participation of women even after it had become legal. Less comfortable with the political system than men, women were slower to enter it. Only in the latter half of the 1930s, after men had experienced the bulk of their movement into the Democratic coalition, did women make their greatest contributions to Democratic success.

The second major pattern visible upon inspection of voter behavior in this period is related to the timing of voter conversion and mobilization. At least for the two communities that were realigned through a combination of the two processes, change from within the system preceded change from without. This might be expected, considering the relative costs of the two mechanisms: while mobilization required the political activation of former nonvoters and their attraction to one of the partisan alternatives, conversion required only a different vote from existing members of the active electorate. Conversion of existing voters to the Democratic party occurred among blacks and Jews earlier than a mass mobilization of former nonvoters.

In earlier chapters, different estimates were made of the relative import of mobilization and conversion to the formation of the New Deal coalition. The accuracy of those estimates, presented in the context of examining registration data, depends on basic assumptions of voter behavior at the time. Three such assumptions have been offered. The first case assumes that any Republican registrant who left his party adopted a Democratic identification; that is, former Republicans did not become independents. The third case, in contrast, measures the amount of voter conversion that would have occurred if all former Republicans had become independents rather than Democrats. Both those cases, of course, attempt to measure defections from the Republican party to the Democratic party. While that movement represents the most dramatic form of voter conversion, it is—as the necessity of those two polar assumptions shows—extremely difficult to quantify. The presence of independents, of large numbers of persons enrolled in neither of the two parties, renders it impossible to trace movement between the ranks of identifiable Republicans and Democrats.

Of all measures of voter conversion utilized in this book, it is the second of the three cases presented in tables 2.5 and 4.4 that is arguably the most useful and interesting. Indeed, that case yields the only solid figures on the importance of conversion and mobilization to the realignment; it, unlike the other two cases, does not rest on unverifiable hypotheses. What the second case does demand, however, is a particular definition of conversion and mobilization: conversion is understood as the action of any former non-

Democratic registrant who at some point declares his support for the Democratic party, while mobilization is viewed as the entrance into the active electorate as Democrats of former nonregistrants. Where the first and third cases define conversion as a shift from Republican to Democratic identification, the second case terms conversion any movement to the Democratic party by either former Republicans or former independents. Thus the body of independents no longer represents an obstacle to estimating the degree of conversion; rather, they are incorporated into the definition. Whether new Democrats come from within the active electorate or are mobilized from outside of it is the particular issue addressed with great precision in the second case. Certainly this represents a fundamental aspect of the debate over conversion and mobilization.

For lower-middle-class Jews, as table 2.5 shows, conversion was the dominant process in the early years of the realignment, while mobilization did not assume overwhelming importance until the late 1930s. The Jewish shift toward the Democratic party occurred in two stages. In 1932, with the election of Roosevelt, Jews began to alter their pattern of party allegiances. This stage was characterized by a substantial amount of genuine voter conversion. Between 1930 and 1934, conversion of existing registrants represented from 53 to 67 percent of all Democratic gains among men and from 17 to 44 percent of all such gains among women, depending on the partisan composition of entering voters. In the second stage of the Jewish realignment, in 1936–38, conversion suddenly became negligible. In the period between 1934 and 1940, mobilization accounted for all of the Democratic gains among women and at least 87 percent of the increased level of Democratic support among men. Whereas in the early 1930s conversion was the main process by which men become Democrats and an important vehicle for women as well, its role in the realignment had been virtually eliminated by the prominence of mobilization after the middle of the decade.

Table 4.4 demonstrates for Boston's blacks a similar temporal precedence for conversion, although voter conversion was not as important in the realignment of blacks as it was among Jews. The black community as a whole had decisively realigned by 1936, supporting by a comfortable margin the reelection effort of Roosevelt. None of the substantial Democratic gains achieved in that year came from within the existing electorate. Rather, among both men and women, mobilization of new voters accounted for the whole of the increase in Democratic enrollment between 1934 and 1938. Prior to that period, however, the effect of conversion cannot be so easily discounted. As much as 55 percent of the 1930 Democratic surge among women and 25 percent of the gains among men between 1928 and 1936 may have resulted from conversion of existing political participants. Mobilization of black Democrats was of unambiguously greater importance in 1936 than it had been in the early years of the formation of the New Deal coalition.

Members of the active electorate, then, were more important in the initial stage of the realignment than they would be later. As a review of relevant data from the experiences of blacks and Jews shows, mobilization of new voters became the sole mode of realignment only after conversion had run its course. Not until the new cleavages were set did the vast pool of nonvoters in the potential electorate assert with full force its long-dormant power.

The form that the realignment assumed for each ethnic group on the national and local levels was determined by the relative salience of the two levels to the interests of each group. There were, in principle, of course, at least two possible realignments. While not wholly independent of each other, the decisions to support the Democratic party on the national level and to support it on the local level were based on quite different sets of issues. To speak of realignment, then, as an indivisible phenomenon is misleading. In actuality, several realignments simultaneously were occurring or, alternatively, not occurring, on various planes in the federal system. Even when Democratic support rose and fell in similar ways for different political offices, it is probable that important issues on a single level provided the major incentive for partisan change, which, with a lag, was then translated into transformations on other levels of government.

Locating the probable engine, the level which exerted the driving force of realignment, is a task which demands attention to differences among each of Boston's five ethnic groups. Figure 7.2 offers such detail. In it are graphed, for each group, two separate lines, one measuring the group's support for the national Democratic party and the other measuring its loyalty to the local organization. National support is represented by the percentage of the two-party vote cast for the Democratic candidate for president. Local support is the Democratic percentage of the two-party vote for state senator. While the two decades from 1920 to 1940 are graphed, the set of local statistics is often incomplete, the consequence of eliminating from study uncontested state senate races.

Two principal patterns emerge. The New Deal realignment in the clusters of homogeneous precincts for the Jewish, black, and, on a necessarily milder level, Yankee communities, was apparently led by national issues. After the late 1920s, the vote for president was consistently higher than that for state senator. Further, the national identification with the Democratic party seems to have gradually led to increased support for local candidates. In the Irish and Italian communities, a nearly opposite process occurred. It would appear that commitment to the local organization was the underlying loyalty of Italians and Irish. While national events in the late 1920s and early 1930s encouraged

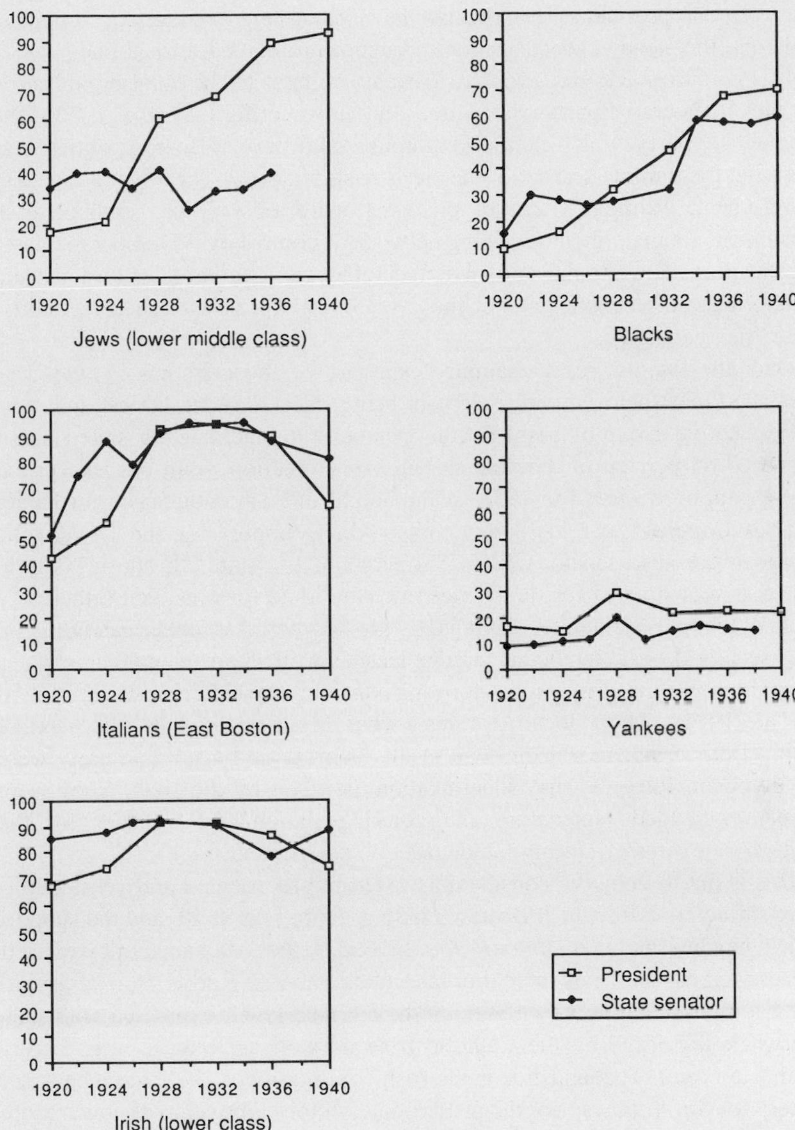

Figure 7.2 Vote for Democratic Candidates for President and State Senator (as Percent of Two-party Vote)

the vote for president to approach the normal level of support for state senators, the steadier identification throughout remained a local one.

It is no surprise to discover that Irish attachment to the local organization of the Democratic party was fierce and unwavering. By the 1920s, the Democratic party, which exercised thorough control over Boston politics, was itself but the humble servant of the city's Irish majority. The Irish ran the city government. While the era of powerful ward bosses was ending, Irish Bostonians retained their sprawling network of control over Democratic party organizations down to the ward and precinct levels. And, at least for local and state offices, the beneficiaries of those votes, delivered with such regularity, were Irish candidates.

Over the twenty years examined, support of those in Irish lower-class precincts (that socioeconomic segment being chosen as the largest and most representative group of Irish) for the Democratic candidate for state senator exceeded 85 percent of the vote cast in every election, with one exception. The exception occurred in 1936, at the height of Irish enthusiasm for Father Charles Coughlin and William Lemke, when support for the Democratic candidate for state senator fell to 78.4 percent. As figure 7.2 shows, only in that year was support for the Democratic candidate for president, albeit as a share of the two-party vote, significantly greater than that for the candidate for state senator. Local Democrats fared at least as well as presidential candidates throughout the entire period, performing considerably better until 1928 and in the late 1930s. Those local loyalties—what Trout has called "the habit of voting Democratic, developed before the Depression began"[4]—surely were the dominant form of party identification assumed by the Irish. They were deeply embedded, antedating and coloring national preferences for the Democrats expressed during the decade of realignment.

This is not to deny the considerable, even unprecedented and yet unduplicated, affection with which Boston's Irish regarded Al Smith and the support which they lavished upon him in 1928. Indeed, James Michael Curley himself was ostracized four years later after his endorsement of Roosevelt over Smith. Yet that unusual support for Smith on the national level, expressed with such overwhelming force by the Catholic Irish as well as Italians, was largely candidate-based. The landslide in the Irish community of 1928 was a personal victory for Smith; it was not the institutional victory enjoyed with much more predictability by local Irish candidates. Irish support for the national party seemed ultimately the consequence of the interaction of national issues with the basic, underlying attachment to the local Democratic party.

A similar, if somewhat less strong, pattern of attachment apparently characterized the Italian community as well. Bound by the ties of religion and co-opted politically by Irish Democratic power, Boston's Italians acquiesced in a fairly stable allegiance to the local Democratic party. Frederick A. Bushee commented in 1903 on the divided partisanship that he observed in Boston's Italian community. Often inclined to avoid political activity altogether, the Italian, when he voted, tended to support Republicans on the national level. "In local matters, however," noted Bushee, "the situation at the North End of Boston requires him to vote for one or another leader in the Democratic party."[5] The "situation" to which Bushee alluded was, of course, the discipline enforced by the local, Irish-dominated political machine. Figure 7.2 illustrates the importance of local ties. Except in 1920—when Italian bitterness with the national party apparently affected even local elections—the Democratic vote for state senator in East Boston consistently represented at least three-quarters of all votes cast for a major-party candidate.

Support for local figures in Italian precincts was significantly deeper than that for the candidate for president. Even in the days of greatest excitement for the national party, between 1928 and 1936, Italians did not express greater enthusiasm for Smith or Roosevelt than they did for their local state senator. And prior to 1928 as well as after 1936, Italian support for the national party remained well below that for the local party. Throughout the realignment, the national vote fluctuated much more than the local vote. While the candidacy of Al Smith and the programs of the New Deal would reinforce and help to nationalize earlier loyalties, the partisan identification of Italians remained firmly grounded in local politics and organization. It was in Boston's Irish ward bosses—and not in Al Smith—that the Italian commitment to the Democratic party originated and was sustained.

At the other end of the spectrum, ideologically and motivationally, were the Yankees. They, in vivid contrast to most other Bostonians, maintained throughout the 1920s and 1930s an abiding faith in the Republican party. That support, while strong in national elections, was especially fierce in local contests, in which the mutual animosity between the Yankee establishment and the Irish machine was most clearly manifested. Indeed, Edward C. Banfield and Martha Derthick recount the frustration of the reform-oriented Committee of One Hundred, who, in their efforts to change the city charter in 1909, sought to divorce local from national influences. At least many Yankees who voted for the Democratic candidate for president were sophisticated enough to support the Republican party locally; presumably, the reformers reasoned, others in the city could be persuaded to follow that example. By creating nonpartisan mayoral elections, "the reformers wanted to join to the Republican minority the 'better class' of Democrats who were voting Democratic on the local level because of state or national issues."[6] Irish control of the Democratic party in Boston, which probably was responsible for the local foundation of Italian partisanship, was equally the cause of the thorough Yankee rejection of Democratic candidates for local offices.

Of the few Yankees who voted Democratic in national elections, perhaps as many as one in three deserted that party's candidate for state senate. The remarkable consistency of that ticket-splitting is visible in figure 7.2. When, in the late 1920s and early 1930s, more Yankees began to cast ballots for the Democratic candidate for president, a commensurately larger share gave their support to local Democrats. Still, local support, while following the national vote, always remained substantially beneath it. Boston's Brahmins, argues John Stack, "overwhelmingly rejected Irish political leadership."[7] A party barely palatable on the national level was anathema in the context of the ethnic warfare being waged with such ferocity in Boston between the Irish and the Yankees.

Jews shared the Yankee resentment against the local Democratic organization. While the Jewish grievance was not as ancient, it was similarly unshaken even by the upheaval of the 1930s. No group in Boston was at once more thoroughly transformed at the national level and more intractable, at least in the short run, at the local level. Between 1920 and 1940, the Democratic share of the lower-middle-class Jewish vote for president soared from 17.5 to 93.0 percent of all votes cast for one of the two major parties. At the same time, fragmentary evidence suggests that support for Democrats running for the state senate was unchanged, at just over one-third of the vote from 1920 until 1936, the last contested election in the period.

Much of the continued Jewish support for Republicans in local contests surely reflected the character of the races, which, by the early 1930s, were predictably fought between Jewish Republicans (Ulin, Fox, Brackman, Spigel) and Irish Democrats (White, Gallagher, Coughlin, Buckley, Burke, McHugh, Duffy). That Jews continued to support other Jews for office, especially given the alternatives, is not illogical, even after they had transferred their support to Democrats nationally. Indeed, the very choices confronting the Jews attested to their total exclusion from the local Democratic party. "The Democratic party in Jewish Ward 14 was," as Stack suggests, "a closed Irish political club. It was only through the Republican party that Jews could become involved in city politics on a local level." Reviewing the list of state committeemen from Dorchester and Mattapan, Lawrence Fuchs finds that the local Democratic organization remained closed to Jews in the 1930s—even in a ward nearly homogeneously Jewish. "Despite the shift of Jewish voters to the Democratic Party in 1932, all Democratic State Committeemen from districts embracing Ward 14 were Irishmen, while all of their Republican rivals were Jews."[8]

For a variety of reasons, then, Jewish Bostonians did not change their local voting patterns when they shifted nationally. Figure 7.2 shows the steep rise in support for the Democratic candidate for president occurring simultaneously with no change in the vote for state senator. Even when Jews were not themselves candidates for office, Jewish voters systematically rejected the approach to government generally favored by Irish politicians. Specifically, Jews, especially in the 1930s and 1940s, sought a policy of vigorous internationalism abroad and liberalism at home. Irish candidates for the United States Senate—typically isolationist and resistant to major aspects of the New Deal, and further tainted by the vague sense of anti-Semitism pervading the Irish community—fared poorly in Jewish neighborhoods. Fuchs has documented that phenomenon in Boston. In 1940, when David I. Walsh was challenged by Henry Parkman, Jr., a Republican, "probably four out of ten Boston Jews who voted for Roosevelt also voted for Parkman." And, when in 1944, Leverett Saltonstall ran against Democrat John Cocoran for the United States Senate, "probably more than five out of every ten Jewish voters in Ward 14 cast ballots for Roosevelt and Saltonstall."[9] That represented ticket-splitting on a massive scale. Not until later did Jews translate their support for the national Democratic party to that party's candidates for local and state office.

Facilitating the continued Jewish loyalty to local and statewide Republican candidates was, of course, the nature of their community's initiation into the New Deal coalition. Large numbers of the new Jewish Democrats, those who gave such massive support to the national party, were converts from the Republican party. Residual Republican loyalties remained even after presidential voting patterns had been transformed. Their status as converts helped make their realignment gradual. Like a caboose suddenly wrenched loose from its engine, local Jewish Republicanism lingered into the New Deal era. The national Democratic party was obviously the agent of change. Before it could affect the local vote, however, especially one so heavily determined by recent converts, the city organization would have to be opened to Jews and its candidates would have to approach closer to the ideal of liberal internationalism favored by the Jewish community and by the national Democratic leadership. Only then could Jews be expected to change their local voting behavior.

Such a process of local change did, indeed, characterize Boston's blacks. Their support for local Democrats rose throughout the 1930s, reflecting their growing attachment to the national party under Roosevelt. It is particularly interesting that their vote for state senator exhibited such clear movement toward the Democratic party. Blacks were, after all, no more welcome in local Democratic machines than were Jews, and they, too, had reason for great commitment to the pursuit of liberal policies. Perhaps the best explanation for their increasing loyalty to the Irish political organization in Boston was the nature of their community's realignment. Voter conversion was much less important in the black community than it had been among Jews. Most of their Democratic gains had come from the mobilization of new voters. Mobilized as New Deal Democrats, these blacks did not have to contend with competing, vestigial party loyalties. They registered as Democrats because of Roosevelt and the New Deal, but they easily translated that partisan identification into votes for local offices. Unlike many Jews, torn between prior Republican bonds and emergent national Democratic support, blacks—mobilized, not converted—more naturally voted straight tickets.

Figure 7.2 shows what, among blacks, was apparently a steady upward tug exerted by national Democratic support on local candidates. Thus, in 1928, presidential candidate Smith received 31.9 percent of the two-party vote cast, while the Democratic candidate for state senate received 27.5 percent. By 1940, the black community's support for Democrats on all levels of government had increased substantially, more than doubling to 69.8 percent for Roosevelt and 59.3 percent for state senator. Throughout the period, local attachments lagged behind national levels of support, even while growing constantly stronger. The source of change in the black community, while it cannot of course be conclusively proved, seems to have been the New Deal and the national party.

As the salience of issues on the local and national levels differed tremendously across the ethnic groups in Boston, so did the course of their realignments toward the Democratic party. In every case but one—the exception were the Yankees, who never realigned—local Democratic strength exceeded national support during much of the 1920s. For two groups, that relationship remained essentially intact after the intervening critical period between 1928 and 1936. The Irish and Italian commitments to the Democratic party were in place prior to the New Deal realignment as local loyalties and, while reinforced by national events, retained their foundation at the level of the local political organization. For the other groups, however, the national events of the 1930s disrupted and overturned the earlier arrangement. National support for the Democratic party among Jews and blacks exceeded local support levels for the first time in 1928; then, during the 1930s, as national support continued to rise, the local vote apparently followed among blacks but not among Jews. The Yankees, basically Republican, had always been especially hesitant to support the local Democratic organization.

Transforming the configuration of the Boston political community, realignment assumed shapes peculiar to each group.

Local and national differences constituted just one of two important results associated with the political machine: the other characteristic of political organization, and the final point to be discussed in this chapter, was its relationship to political participation, and especially to the level of participation across socioeconomic levels. Fortunately, the two ethnic groups in Boston whose size and diversity allowed examination by socioeconomic group—the Irish and the Jews—were also at opposite extremes in terms of degree of political organization by the local Democratic party. While many other changes did occur, it is significant that the basic organizational bases of the two groups—and, consequently, the levels of participation within them—persisted intact in their 1920s form through the realignment.

Recent academic literature offers some insight into natural rates of political participation by socioeconomic level and the effect of political organization on those rates. Philip E. Converse demonstrates the correlation between higher socioeconomic levels and more ideologically constrained belief systems. The upper classes, he suggests, are more aware of their interests and exhibit self-discipline in their voting behavior. For them, external organization is superfluous: they will vote and vote "correctly" without being instructed to do so. Lower socioeconomic groups, in contrast, must be carefully organized if they are to express their interests in political terms with the force of the upper classes. "Asymmetrical elite strategies therefore emerge," argues Converse. "They are best summed up perhaps in terms of an increasingly *overt* stress on group loyalty and cohesion *per se* as one moves from right to left across party spectra in most political systems." When controlled by individual motivation alone, upper-class persons are more successful in articulating and supporting their interests than are members of the lower classes. That inequity finds compensation in the greater stress on partisan-based organization of lower socioeconomic levels.[10]

Perhaps the most thorough work in this area has been that conducted by Sidney Verba, Norman H. Nie, and Jae-On Kim. In their 1972 work, *Participation in America,* Verba and Nie first documented the close connection between socioeconomic status and level of political participation. They then broached the possibility that intervening organizational structures might act to lessen or even eliminate that relationship. Going beyond Converse's observation that socioeconomic level affected the consistency of partisan support, Verba and Nie suggest that status and class are intimately linked even with voter turnout and other indices of participation. Such is the paradox, they note, that "class relates strongly to participation rates" in a nation which so carefully avoids the organization of interests along class cleavages. Verba and Nie offer a possible explanation:

> It is just the absence of an explicit class basis of politics in an institutional or an ideational sense that explains the close relationship in the behavioral sense. If there were more class-based ideologies, more class-based organizations, more explicit class-based appeal by political parties, the participation disparity between upper- and lower-status citizens would very likely be less. . . . The absence of institutions and ideas associated with social status makes, paradoxically, such status a more potent force in American politics.

To test that hypothesis, Verba, Nie, and Kim proceeded to conduct a seven-nation study of political participation, which in 1978 was published as *Participation and Political Equality.* With that book, they confirm their earlier suspicion that the peculiar absence of class-based organization in the United States permitted the expression of socioeconomic status in participation rates. "There is a fairly clear contrast between the United States and the other nations in relation to voting. The comparative weakness of institutions in the United States is reflected in the fact that among [all] citizens . . . those higher on the [socioeconomic] scale are more active." And that situation differs considerably from the rest of the nations studied, in each of which "institutions are dominant. . . . If one has strong ties to political institutions, one's voting participation is high no matter what one's level of socioeconomic resources. Conversely, if one is not affiliated with any political institution, one's voting participation is low no matter what one's position on the [socioeconomic] scale." Cross-nationally, then, the existence of mobilizing political institutions is "necessary and sufficient" to eliminate the class bias in participation arising from individual motivation.[11]

That this is true within countries as well is a natural extension of the basic logic. In the nineteenth century, for example, urban political machines were extremely effective in encouraging political participation among the poor. Their methods may have been questionable, but their success in registering members of the lower classes and inducing high levels of turnout for the dominant party is undisputed. Certainly part of the reason for the contemporary socioeconomic gradient in voting in the United States is the disintegration of this sort of political organization.

Boston in the 1920s and 1930s presents itself as an unusually valuable arena for the effect of machine discipline on the level of political participation. There were in the city two ethnic groups, the Irish and the Jews, that can be examined internally along socioeconomic lines through clusters of homogeneous precincts. The Irish achieved in their neighborhoods a particularly efficient and disciplined organization on behalf of the local Democratic party.

Jews, on the other hand, spurned not only Irish political leadership but the necessity of machine politics. If the academic literature is correct, Irish electoral activity should have been high and unrelated to socioeconomic level, while Jewish activity should have been skewed in favor of upper-income individuals.[12] Both patterns did, indeed, occur.

Boston's Irish political leadership attained an extraordinary level of organization in Irish neighborhoods. From delivered votes flowed jobs, patronage, and city services. "Votes are his business," remarked Robert A. Woods in his description of the Irish ward boss, "they mean money, power. The boss can never be a disinterested member of society. He is forced to make men act and vote with him. . . . The only morality he seeks in men is loyalty to him." Of all virtues, observed Woods in a separate study, loyalty to the boss, and particularly to the party he represents, is supreme. "Ward politics is built up out of racial, religious, industrial affiliations; out of blood kinship; out of childhood associations, youthful camaraderie, general neighborhood sociability. Party regularity is simply the coalescence of all these." Nowhere was such virtue and such behavior better realized than in the city's Irish community. The Irish, remarked Bushee, "are the great political organizers, and the rank and file of the Irish voters are the most easily organized of all nationalities."[13]

Boston's Jewish community emulated the Irish in few areas, and least of all in political organization. Woods understood and vividly conveyed the refusal of Jews—describing in this passage, it must be stressed, those who had some minimal contact with the machine—to succumb to tight, Irish discipline:

> They are very difficult material for the politician. They are individualists, quarreling constantly among themselves, each demanding to have as good a share as the most favored one. They do not act in a mass under impulses of loyalty. They are of that very uncomfortable sort who "have to be seen often." They demand stated and regular returns for political allegiance, or else their allegiance is gone.

Jews prided themselves on their independence from party and, especially, from its manifestation in the Irish political machine. As Bushee observed even in 1903—when Jews were still new to the political system and most vulnerable to Irish efforts to discipline their vote— "the Jews are not wedded to any party or faction, and the handling of their vote is a strain on the sagacity of even an Irish politician." They frustrated the designs of Irish ward bosses and refused to succumb to basic conventions of political behavior. Members of the Jewish community, according to Woods, formed nonpartisan clubs to discuss political issues and become informed voters; the Irish were incredulous, unable to understand the logic of any but the most partisan political organization. In their attempt to mediate factional quarrels among Jewish leaders, "the Irish step in and attempt a task which proves a strain even to their ingenuity." Resisting cooperation with the dominant political forces in the city, the Jew stood alone among recent immigrants in his antagonism toward the Irish-dominated machine. "The Jew," concluded Woods, "is a thorn in the flesh to the Irish politician."[14]

How these two strikingly different attitudes toward political organization affected participation by socioeconomic level is apparent in figure 7.3. What is graphed is the size of the active electorate as a proportion of citizens in the potential electorate. That statistic is averaged over two periods, 1920–30 and 1932–40, and then graphed for each of the two ethnic groups against socioeconomic status. In 1920, for example, 39.7 percent of all adults in working-class Irish precincts were registered to vote. Of that particular base population, however, about 10.0 percent consisted of immigrants who were not yet naturalized citizens. To control for such temporarily ineligible members of the potential electorate, the number of registered voters—39.7 per 100—is recalculated over an electorate of 90.0, yielding a final figure of 44.1 percent. Among working-class Irish in 1920, 44.1 percent of all adult citizens were registered to vote and, hence, members of the active electorate. By 1930, as similar calculations would show, 73.2 percent of the citizenry had become active political participants. The average of such figures over the ten-year period, using the figures from 1920 and 1930 and the four interim election years, was 63.5 percent, which is graphed in figure 7.3 for the Irish working class.

Inspection of the Irish graphs reveals the absence of any relationship between socioeconomic level and voter activity. At any given time, the

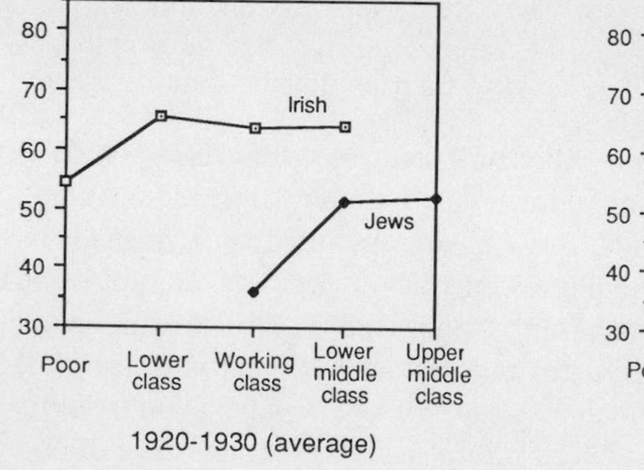

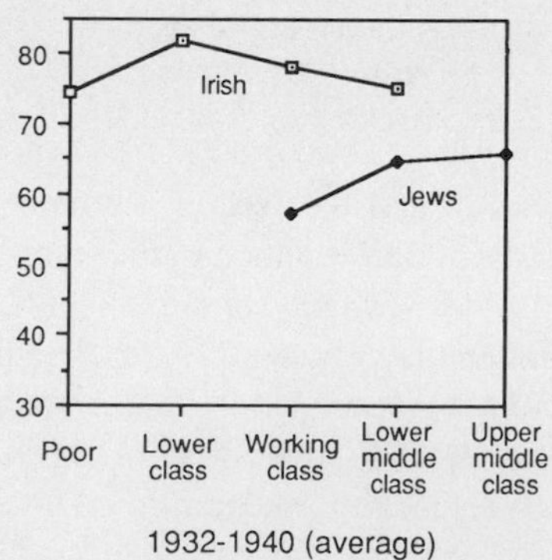

Figure 7.3 Total Registration in Irish and Jewish Precincts, by Class (as Percent of Adult Citizens Only)

number of registered voters is undifferentiable across classes. In the average of the years from 1920 to 1930, the politically active fractions of the population, listed from poor to lower middle class, ranged from 54.3 to 65.4 to 63.5 to 64.0 percent. Rates of political participation by 1940 had increased for all Irish without disturbing the underlying uniformity among socioeconomic segments, which, again listing numbers of registered voters from poor to lower middle class, ranged from 77.9 to 86.5 to 81.4 to 81.5 percent. For the poorest Irish alone, participation levels were visibly lower than those of the other three classes. That group of Irish was, however, bogged down in a degree of poverty and material misery unusual even in a city where Irish poverty was the norm. Many of those in the poorest group were transients; most others were struggling to attain a level of bare subsistence. Yet even that group managed to register at rates which, especially by the 1930s, approached those of the bulk of the city's Irish. With that one caveat, as figure 7.3 shows, the three major groups of Irish registered to vote at remarkably high rates, and their degree of participation was wholly unrelated to socioeconomic status. Between 1920 and 1930, the Irish line is flat across all groups (except for the poor), and by the 1930s, the relationship between status and political integration might even be described as an inverse correlation. The thoroughness of Irish political machines effected a genuine equality in political participation in Boston's Irish community, so that the lower class of South Boston, Charlestown, and Mission Hill voted, as a fraction of their population, in numbers no smaller than the lower-middle-class Irish in Brighton.

A very different pattern is manifested in the behavior of the Jewish community. Throughout the 1920s and 1930s, participation of working-class Jews lagged substantially behind the levels of the two middle-class groups. In this case, certainly, there is no dismissing the relationship of class to levels of political participation: working-class Jews, unlike poor Irish, did not live on the margins of the socioeconomic scale. Rather, Jewish registration rates represented the natural result of mobilization based wholly on individual motivation. Those rates are uniformly lower than those achieved by the disciplined Irish and show a sharp positive relationship with income and class. The socioeconomic gradients in the Jewish community foreshadowed the shape of contemporary American participation as described by Verba and Nie. In the 1920s, for example, 36.1 percent of the working class was registered to vote, compared to 51.5 percent of the lower middle class and 52.2 percent of the upper middle class. While the gap had narrowed by 1940, the basic relationship appeared to remain intact. Apparently, a threshold existed beyond which increased income and status did not have an impact on the extent of electoral activity. Thus the two middle classes voted at virtually identical rates over the two decades, at a level significantly higher than that for the working class. It would be interesting to speculate, further, on reasons for the steady closing of the gap between the working class and the middle classes. Most likely, perhaps, is the development by the late 1930s of a Jewish political organization capable of mobilizing voters and inducing them to vote. Such activity, centered around Jewish concern over events in Europe and liberalism at home, could conceivably have been initiated in imitation of, and in reaction to, the Irish. Whether such issues and corresponding political activity were sufficient after 1940 to eliminate the socioeconomic disparity in participation deserves further study. Jews, however, throughout the 1920s and into the late 1930s, acted in a manner consistent with weak organization and fierce voter independence from political bosses. Class, before and after the realignment, was strongly correlated with the level of participation. Individual motivation, untempered by Irish machines, was expressed in the Jewish community by a clear socioeconomic division in registration rates throughout most of the period.

Where machines were powerful, as in Irish neighborhoods, potential voters entered the active electorate in large numbers and without regard for socioeconomic divisions. Class did not affect registration levels of the Boston Irish because the institutions of political organization intervened. Jews, on the other hand, resisted the discipline of machine politics. Consequently, their participation rates reflected class distinctions. Throughout the period, Jewish political participation was less intense than Irish participation and more closely tied to individual motivation and resources.

It is tempting now, after having outlined four interesting but seemingly disparate aspects of the New Deal era, to stand in awe of the marvelous intricacy of the realignment and finally concede that the phenomenon defies summary characterization. Of nothing are we so sure as the complexity of the process. We stare intensely at each of the precious dots of the pointillist and are overwhelmed by the blur and sheer amorphousness of the sight that we behold. We take a step back and are reassured, but only partly. Pieces of images grow before our eyes: a dog, a pink ribbon, a face, a blade of grass. But still the design of the artist, the unified vision which we seek, remains elusive. Only when we see the painting at a distance does the coherence of the whole finally assert itself.

There is, of course, no promise of such a satisfying framework in the decisions of millions of individual actors. Politics is not the grand design of some artist. Still, the search for some larger perspective is never a wholly thankless task. We have seen the dots up close in the study of individuals as they each became Democrats or remained Republicans in different ways, at different times, responding to different forces. We have seen, too, in this chapter some larger images of those decisions. The activity of men and voter conversion were more important in the earlier stages of the realignment; the activity of women and the mobilization of new voters were more important in the later stages. As we also found, the shape that the realignment assumed for each of the ethnic groups was, it appears, dictated by the salience of local and national issues at the very inception of the critical era. Political participation by class in the 1930s looked much like it had in the 1920s, the consequence of the degree of party organization. Even if the hope of discovering any larger vision is illusory, we have seen several patterns which surely deepen our understanding of the course of realignment and further demonstrate the richness of its mechanics.

Yet a certain logic does indeed exist, overarching individual activity and lending coherence to the several points just outlined. From those four patterns, it is clear that, at least in this set of Boston precincts, the formation of the New Deal coalition occurred in two distinct stages. It was initiated and led by persons already active in the political system: men and converted voters. Not until later in the realignment, in the second stage, did women and mobilization peak in significance. The formative moment of the realignment was the achievement of those most familiar with the existing party system, and the new Democratic coalition emerged in the 1930s defined and shaped by older patterns of behavior. Thus the linkage between socioeconomic status, political organization, and the intensity of voter registration continued, as did the relative and differential impact of local and national issues. Much was old in the creation of a new party order.

Samuel Lubell was among the first and most astute observers of the radical cast of the Democratic coalition that emerged during the Great Depression, of what he termed "the really revolutionary surge behind the New Deal." As he argued, "No segment of the population was more ready for 'a new deal' than the submerged, inarticulate urban masses. They became the chief carriers of the Roosevelt Revolution."[15] And Lubell was correct. Throughout the 1930s the coalition was sustained by the constant infusion into the political system of women, of blacks, of recent immigrants and their children, of so many persons to whom registering and voting were unfamiliar and new.

Still, those same participants remained, as Lubell suggested, mere "carriers" of the revolution. Others had led the revolution. The overwhelming defeat of Herbert Hoover in 1932 was an instance of retrospective voting. "The election was not," argues V. O. Key, "a revolt of the downtrodden."[16] Others had forged the coalition, supported Al Smith, and elevated Roosevelt to the presidency. The political neophytes, those previously uninterested in politics and unmoved by the cleavages of the 1920s, just followed. While history would accord to them the central role in the remaking of the Democratic party, they were merely reacting to and reinforcing events which had already occurred. Habitual patterns of involvement, political experience, and familiar issues drove the early years of the realignment and shaped the direction that it would take. The party system as it finally emerged was at once new and antique. Reshaped by old actors and defined by familiar patterns of behavior, the changed party system by the mid and late 1930s rested upon the will of a new generation fused in agony and hope.

8

Conclusion

Maybe Charles A. Beard and his contemporaries were not so mistaken after all. Maybe the emergence of realignment theory in the 1950s in the writing of Lubell, Key, and Schattschneider did not provide a complete solution to the study of American political history. And maybe Burnham's famous conception of a stable party system agitated only periodically by change needs substantial revision. For we have discovered that even in Boston—a city struck with special ferocity by the upheaval of the late 1920s and 1930s—there was, in the era we have studied, nothing that could be called a single, massive electoral realignment. Certainly changes associated with traditional models of realignment did occur in Boston: many new voters were mobilized into the active electorate, many old voters switched parties, and the Democratic party expanded and diversified its base of support. But these changes were less the result of a great mass movement than they were the accumulation of many smaller events. We have long regarded the New Deal realignment as a special moment, qualitatively different and in some way aloof from the rest of party history in this century. That is wrong. It was not special in any qualitative sense. All that set those years apart from periods before and after was the quantity of small changes compressed into a short period of time. Changes in patterns of political participation and party identification characterized the years before 1928 and have characterized every decade since the 1930s. And even the intense upheavals in the electorate during the New Deal era, which did have major consequences for the relative strength of the two major parties and for the direction of national policy, did not create anything resembling a wholly new party system. The realignment perspective has been a valuable one for the study of political history, but it should not elevate the disruption and change of the 1930s above greater continuities. We should stop waiting for the next realignment or wondering if it has already occurred. There is no ''it'': we live in realignment constantly and have been doing so since at least the turn of this century.

This book has neither in intent nor in execution been an ethnic study, although one suspects the basic format may occasionally have deceived the reader. Rather, the central object examined has been the actual behavior of homogeneous precincts and the inferred behavior of individuals composing them. V. O. Key, Jr., argued correctly that a full understanding of the process of realignment requires a deep examination of the individual political actor. In "A Theory of Critical Elections" he qualified his own characterization of voter behavior by noting that it was always hazardous to ground such conclusions in aggregate statistics. "To interpret properly the behavior," Key wrote, "one would need a voting history of individual voters over a period of several elections, a body of data not readily available."[1] For the 1920s and 1930s, that information, that body of data, can never be recovered. The construction of individual voting histories became possible only with the advent of survey research. What has been assembled for this particular project, however, is a data set which permits with reasonable accuracy the tracing of individual activity in that otherwise-lost period. Boston precincts were selected and clustered in ethnically and socioeconomically homogeneous groups in an attempt to more nearly approach the true electoral mechanics of realignment. In the process of establishing the relative importance of the mobilization of new voters and the conversion of Republicans to the emergence of the New Deal coalition, the richness and detail of the process of realignment were made manifest.

Of the five groups studied in Boston, Jews were the most sharply realigned. Democrats in 1920 represented only 18 percent of all lower-middle-class Jews enrolled in one of the two major parties. By 1940, that same community would give Roosevelt 93 percent of its two-party vote. Something dramatic had obviously happened, since all available registration and voting evidence, at least on the national level, confirms the shift suggested by those numbers. It is much harder to discern any trends in the votes cast for state senator and for representative in Congress, although we do know that by the 1950s Jewish support for the Democratic party was reflected in support for local as well as national Democratic candidates and that patterns of registration reflected that permanent shift.[2]

Not only had Jews in general transferred their allegiance from the Republican to the Democratic party, but, in this group shift, intragroup socioeconomic distinctions suddenly ended. Figure 2.1 illustrates the destruction of class cleavages among Jews. Whereas the presidential elections of 1928 and 1932 exhibited marked division along socioeconomic lines—which would survive in the vestigial form of party registration into the 1940s—that class division disappeared by 1936 and 1940. Boston's Jews had emerged from the realignment fused into a solid ethnic bloc.

The critical years of the realignment for Jews were 1932 and 1936–1938. Perhaps surprisingly, the 1928 candidacy of Al Smith, which received the support of most of the city's Jews, had no effect on their partisan identification. Had his election not been followed immediately by the Depression and the rise of Roosevelt, it would clearly have been a deviating election in Jewish precincts. Only because that deviation occurred as the final event before the realignment has it been widely viewed as the beginning of the shift. At best, it was a precursor to the realignment—but, in truth, it was merely another election in an old system of party attachments which then unexpectedly proceeded to crumble.

Conversion of existing members of the active electorate played an important role in the transformation of the Jewish community, as did mobilization of new voters. Partly because such a high percentage of them were already politically active in the 1920s, men were converted in substantially greater numbers than were women in the subsequent years of realignment. Also, it is clear that most of the Democratic recruitment from previously non-Democratic registrants occurred in 1932. Mobilization, on the other hand, could have accounted for a large portion of the Democratic gains in 1936–38, as any decline in Republican support in that period was largely offset by increased numbers of unenrolled voters. Although mobilization was certainly important, conversion played a central role in the realignment of Boston's Jews. In none of the other communities studied in Boston would conversion be nearly so fundamental to an understanding of electoral change.

Indeed, the city's Italians were not even realigned in the conventional sense. Of all registered voters, seventeen in twenty were Democrats in 1920, while nineteen in twenty were Democrats by 1940. There was thus a perceptible drift throughout the period in the direction of the Democratic party, but hardly a critical realignment. In the Italian community, Republicans had virtually disappeared years before Al Smith's candidacy or the Great Depression.

What the events of the late 1920s and 1930s did achieve, however, was a massive mobilization of new voters. Between 1924 and 1940, the number of Italian registrants almost quadrupled in the North End and increased 130 percent in East Boston. Those new voters were important because of their numbers. While the Italian community was overwhelmingly Democratic before it absorbed any new registrants, it was in the 1920s the most politically apathetic of any of the city's major ethnic groups. The infusion of thousands of former nonvoters into the active electorate gave Italians the political strength and influence they had previously lacked.

Almost all of Boston's new Italian Democrats were newly mobilized participants in the political system, but the pace and timing of that mobilization varied within the community. Probably the most critical election for Italian Bostonians was in 1932. Although the 1928 campaign was also important among Italians and helped to trigger the wave of mobilization in East Boston and the North End, it did not affect the population uniformly. In particular, women did not begin to mobilize in large numbers until 1932 and 1936. Men, in contrast, appear to have mobilized earlier, primarily in 1928 and 1932. By 1940, Italians were registered in roughly the same numbers as the city's working-class Jews, the poorest of the three Jewish groups examined but still socioeconomically well above either of the two Italian neighborhoods studied.

Blacks, like the Italians, exhibited fascinating gender-based differences in political behavior. Indeed, it was the rapid mobilization of new women voters in 1936 which gave that election its critical character for Boston's entire black community. Voting data indicate that mobilization accounted for the great bulk of Democratic gains among blacks in the 1930s, although conversion did occur, while registration data suggest that it was primarily a surge of women in 1936 which gave Roosevelt his large measure of support that year. Men did not enter the electorate suddenly at that or any other time, but rather mobilized slowly in the decade after 1928.

Because of that striking mobilization of women, 1936 appears to have been the crucial election for the city's black community. Not only was it the first time, at least since 1920, that the Democratic candidate for president won the support of a majority of the city's blacks, but Roosevelt actually received two out of every three votes cast. Boston's blacks, who in the 1920s had been strongly Republican, had, by 1940, shifted their support to the Democrats.

Although they moved in the same direction as the city's Jews, blacks as a group did not realign as sharply. Jews had been as Republican as blacks in the 1920s and, by the late 1930s, were voting in substantially greater numbers than Boston's blacks for national Democratic candidates. Since many Jews had converted, such a drastic transformation was possible in an electorate which was already fairly active. Blacks, however, were realigned primarily through the mobilization of new voters. Thus, most of the black Republicans in the 1920s retained their old party ties through the 1930s. Only because so many new voters were mobilized as Democrats was the Democratic party able to overcome the obstacle of entrenched Republicans in the community. In 1920, 23.8 percent of the black potential electorate was registered to vote—a level equivalent to that for the city's working-class Jews. Two decades later, though, 56.3 percent of all blacks were registered, a figure exceeding the bare majorities who were registered in the Italian and working-class Jewish communities and nearly comparable to the level of registration among lower-middle-class Jews. Interestingly, too, that 1940 figure, when broken down by gender, shows that while black men had just kept pace with working-class Jewish men, black women were actually registered in numbers equivalent to upper-middle-class Jewish women. Enough new blacks entered the active electorate in the 1930s to transform the Democrats into the majority party in black precincts without converting large numbers of former Republicans.

Boston's Yankees, in contrast, did not abandon their traditional commitment to the Republican party. A partisan commitment born of ethnic, regional, and class conflict was not easily shaken, and, if anything, was reconfirmed by the events of the late 1920s and 1930s. In 1920, Harding received 83.3 percent of the two-party Yankee vote cast, and Republican candidates for representative in Congress and for state senator received 88.8 and 90.9 percent, respectively. The state senate seat was uncontested in 1940, but in 1938 the Republican candidate won 85.3 percent of the vote, while two years later Willkie received the support of 78.3 percent and the congressional candidate that of 82.8 percent. Party enrollment figures confirm this continued Yankee loyalty to Republicanism.

To be sure, there were some on Beacon Hill and in the Back Bay who were persuaded in this era to transfer their support to the Democratic party. Their numbers, however, were few. The movement is visible in the unusually strong support given by Yankees to Al Smith and other Democrats in 1928 as well as by a plateau of Democratic registration slightly higher in the 1930s than it had been in the previous decade. As registration patterns indicate, the Democratic shift occurred over the 1932 election. Yankees affected by the changing political environment, like members of other ethnic groups in the city, made permanent in the early 1930s what had been merely tentative in 1928.

Much more important than the relatively insignificant segment of Democratic Yankees was the apathy which pervaded the entire community. Considering their high socioeconomic status and familiarity with American political norms, Yankee Bostonians participated in surprisingly low numbers throughout these years. A relatively small number of men, for example, was registered to vote in 1920; even fewer were in the active electorate by 1940. Alone among the major groups in the city, the Yankees experienced political demobilization.

The Irish, like the Yankees, were but barely affected by the events of the 1920s and 1930s. Their deeply ingrained support for the Democratic party did not waver. Indeed, it grew stronger over time. In 1920, of all registered voters enrolled in one of the two major parties, 93.6 percent of the lower-class Irish and 86.7 percent of the working-class Irish were Democrats. By 1940, those proportions had risen to 96.1 percent and 94.8 percent. With powerful machines enforcing what ward bosses delicately termed "party harmony," Irish voters recognized their interest in expressing support for the Democratic party.[3] Voting returns attested further to that underlying loyalty.

Not only did the Irish give great support to Democratic candidates, they did so at a remarkably high level of participation. Although they were relatively poor, the Irish were well-organized and eager actors in the political system. Nearly two-thirds of all Irish men, with the exception of those in the poorest group, were registered to vote in 1920, and, by 1940, over 80 percent were members of the active electorate. Women were scarcely less enthusiastic. A majority of Irish women, again except in the poorest segment, had registered to vote by the mid-1920s, while over two-thirds had done so by 1940. His ability to deliver the vote was one of the notable achievements of the Irish ward boss operating in his own community.

The strong Irish commitment to the Democratic party did not fracture along class lines during the 1930s. Poorer Irish, of course, were more Democratic than middle-class Irish in the 1920s, and they continued to be so in ensuing years. But the gap between the four socioeconomic groups did not widen in 1936 or 1940. Irish drifted toward or away from the Democratic party and its candidates as a unified ethnic group, with the same issues affecting different social strata in similar ways. No class cleavage suddenly arose in the Irish community as a result of the New Deal realignment.

As this review of some of the book's findings suggests, there was no single year of realignment. It is clear, for example, that even in Boston's homogeneous precincts, the process that we call realignment extended well beyond the 1928 election. Other scholars have been correct in arguing that Al Smith received historically high levels of support from groups that dominated a city such as Boston: blacks, Jews, Irish, Italians. Among Catholics, in particular, the vote for Smith was overwhelmingly favorable and strong. Where such scholars erred, however, was in the assertion that the presidential vote for Smith among these groups represented the critical election in the period of intense realignment. That belief is expressed in the work of Key and Sundquist, among others. J. Joseph Huthmacher refers to "the fact that the Bay State's conversion took place in 1928," an event which he attributes to the formation of a "new coalition" of Irish and new immigrants. Kristi Andersen, in her study of Chicago "foreign-stock" areas, similarly notes that "it is clear that the key Democratic advantage was gained in the 1928 election." "Before the Roosevelt Revolution," according to the famous aphorism of Samuel Lubell, "there was an Al Smith Revolution."[4]

But the story of the 1928 election is more complex. By relying solely on presidential returns, many of these scholars could not distinguish between temporary and lasting changes in electoral support. Major groups of the New

Deal coalition did support Smith in 1928, but, as registration figures show, they did not all suddenly begin to realign at that time. As Allan J. Lichtman argues from county-level data, ''Party registration seems to have been unaffected by Al Smith's candidacy. Both metropolitan and nonmetropolitan counties emerged unscathed from the 'Revolution of 1928.' Changes in the percentage of registered Democrats and in the composition of party coalitions began to take place only after 1930.'' Lutz Erbring et al. as well as Jerome M. Clubb and Howard W. Allen report similar results. And Massey suggests that the support for Smith was primarily the result of ethnic and religious attachments, substantively different from the basis of the lasting coalition which would form in Massachusetts in the 1930s.[5] Surely those are the conclusions contained in the preceding chapters of this book. The election of 1928 was not obviously critical for blacks. It was of somewhat greater importance for the Irish. Italians, who voted in large numbers for Al Smith and in so doing helped prepare themselves for later realignment, nevertheless recorded their sharpest and most uniform gains in mobilization toward the Democratic party in 1932. For Jews and for that small minority of Yankees who did become Democrats, the argument is unambiguous. Their partisanship was completely unmoved by their vote for Smith. The appeal of Al Smith was the appeal of a person. Lasting realignment was initiated not just by his candidacy but also by ensuing events.

Deserving of passing acknowledgment in this regard is the relationship between turnout in 1928 and that in 1932. For that relationship has been integral to the usual argument, based on the vote for president, that Smith's candidacy was the linchpin of realignment in certain cities. There is no question that Smith drew voters to the polls. A simple inspection of the voting data contained in preceding chapters confirms the common belief that turnout rose sharply in 1928 over the preceding two presidential contests, and that Roosevelt did not in 1932 improve on Smith's level of support. Indeed, in that basic fact is contained the source of the assertion that the election of 1928 was the true watershed in the development of Democratic support among ethnic groups in major cities. As has been shown, though, partisanship was not affected in 1928 among all groups of political actors; only in the 1930s did registration data begin to more generally reflect the development of a new Democratic coalition.

What did occur in 1928 was a campaign that tapped so deeply the emotions of members of the active electorate that a stunning number of those who were registered to vote that year actually cast ballots for president in November. ''When the polls closed,'' states Huthmacher, ''93.5 percent of the registered voters in Massachusetts had exercised the franchise, breaking all records.'' In Boston itself, an even higher proportion of registrants actually voted in 1928.

The candidacy of Roosevelt in 1932 resulted in substantial increases in the number of registered voters and in the number of those formally enrolled in the Democratic party. But Roosevelt himself did not engender the enthusiasm in Boston that surrounded Smith's campaign. While more people were eligible to vote in 1932, a smaller proportion of the active electorate cast ballots. "Thus," as Huthmacher remarks, "the total number who went to the polls in 1932 was slightly smaller than the number called out by the rousing battle four years earlier." Smith had succeeded in generating massive participation of those already active politically. Electoral support for Roosevelt, as a proportion of all registered voters, was less impressive. Roosevelt, however, accelerated in 1932 the process of creating new voters and new Democrats.[6]

Many of those persons who entered the Democratic coalition in the 1930s had undoubtedly been influenced by the candidacy of Al Smith, since their later decision to register as Democrats was surely eased by the election of 1928. In general, party identification as reflected in registration data must follow, or at least coincide with, choices made in the voting booth. Votes cast for Al Smith certainly disturbed basic commitments to the Republican party and made the initiation of many men and women into the New Deal coalition less traumatic, as forces for political change intensified. But each cluster of precincts responded in its own peculiar way to the events of the era. Many were unaffected, and of those which did experience change, some had not decisively realigned until the mid or late 1930s.

I suggested in Chapter 1 that the relationship between registration and voting decisions is valuable for discerning the mechanics of individual realignment. Cases of pure mobilization should be characterized by immediate translation of voting patterns into changes in registration figures. That, of course, occurred in the Italian community and, to a large degree, in the black community. Drawn into the electorate to vote for Democratic candidates for national or local offices, newly mobilized voters logically enrolled as Democratic registrants. There was no significant time lag between increases in the Democratic vote and in the roster of party enrollees because of the overwhelming importance of mobilization in the realignment. The Jewish community, in contrast, exhibited a high instance of voter conversion: many of the new members of the Democratic coalition had once been members of the Republican party. As was predicted, then, an important time lag existed between changes in the vote and commensurate changes in party registration statistics. The movement of converts into the Democratic party as voters did not simultaneously appear as changes in party enrollment. Converted Jews, unlike mobilized Italians, were not immediately aware that they had become Democrats.

As the New Deal coalition formed in the 1930s, no class cleavages erupted in Boston within or among any of the groups studied. The wealthier, at least in Boston, did not rebel against Roosevelt in 1936 or 1940, as so many other students of the realignment have found. Key maintains, for example, that in 1936 "cries of 'traitor to his class' and assertions of the wickedness of instigating class warfare were heard on the hustings. They had basis in the facts of electoral behavior if not justification in political morality." Lubell similarly finds "class warfare" an accurate characterization of the new party system. By 1940, he reports, "the division between worker and 'economic royalist' was . . . sharply drawn," while Erbring et al. set the beginning of class voting in 1938. In sum, as descriptions of the realignment generally argue, the emergence of the New Deal coalition coincided in the late 1930s with an exacerbation of class cleavages in voting patterns. "The party system," reasons James L. Sundquist, "undoubtedly reflected some degree of class bias before the realignment, but there can be little doubt that it was accentuated by the event."[7]

Whether the voters examined by this study are simply unrepresentative in this respect cannot be determined. What is clear is that at no point in the creation of the New Deal coalition in Boston did ethnic groups in homogeneous precincts diverge along class lines. We would expect, if class were the source of increasing division by 1940, that wealthier voters became more Republican and that poorer voters voted more strongly Democratic in the contest that year between Roosevelt and Willkie in comparison with how they voted four or eight years earlier. Yet the most affluent group in Boston, the Yankees, cast, as a proportion of all votes, nearly as many Republican ballots in 1936 as they would in 1940. Italians, an extremely poor group, actually revolted against Roosevelt in 1940, for reasons discussed in Chapter 3. The Democratic vote among blacks, which had risen sharply in 1936, did not increase substantially over the next four years. But the most persuasive evidence of the absence of class cleavages in Boston comes from the Irish and the Jews, two groups that were broken down for this study into various socioeconomic strata. Poorer Irish had always tended to be slightly more Democratic than wealthier Irish. As figures 6.1 and 6.2 show, however, that underlying pattern was wholly unaffected by the elections of 1936 or 1938 or 1940. Issues and candidates affected all Irish equally; sudden cleavages along class lines never emerged. For Jews in Boston, the conclusion is even more dramatic. Jews in the 1920s and early 1930s had, at least as much as the Irish, been divided in their partisan attachments along class lines. The effect of the elections of 1936 and 1940, however, was to end that class division. By the end of the formative period of the coalition, the expression in voting preferences of socioeconomic interests had in the Jewish community been wholly destroyed. The residue of earlier, class-based partisanship, as well as the end of that motivation is apparent in figures 2.1 and 2.2. Bostonians, then, did not respond to the development of the New Deal coalition along class lines. Each of the major groups in the city apparently acted in the late 1930s in consonance with perceived ethnic interests and not with the dictates of socioeconomic status.

New Deal Democrats emerged in Boston through an intricate and fascinating process. The result of that process is illustrated in figure 8.1, which displays the fraction of all adults registered to vote for each of the ethnic groups in the city. It should be noted, first, that much of the increase in the size of the active electorates in the 1920s reflected the gradual assumption of the franchise by women. More relevant for our purposes, then, is the trend of each line beginning with the election of 1928. Simple inspection reveals the effect of the changes in the party system on political participation. Four of the five major groups had by the mid-1930s become pillars of the New Deal Democratic coalition; one had not. Yankee exceptionalism manifested itself in a sturdy commitment to the Republican party even after that party had lost control of the federal government. While each of the other ethnic groups was encouraged by Democratic victories, the Yankees grew increasingly apathetic. The only group in the city whose active electorate did not grow in the 1930s, Yankees participated at a level that by 1940 was the lowest for any measured community. Electoral success evidently bred confidence and enthusiasm among Democrats and potential Democrats, lassitude within the ranks of the Republican party.

Figure 8.1 suggests, too, the roles played by voter mobilization and conversion in the realignment. For the four groups in the new Democratic coalition, voter activity rose sharply in two and much more moderately in the two others. The slightness of the increase in Irish registration naturally reflects the high plateau it had reached before the onset of the realignment. There was, in short, little room for growth in the size of the Irish active electorate. Some mobilization of new Democrats did occur, as the gradual upward movement in the Irish graph shows. Among blacks and Italians, however, mobilization was the central process of realignment. The slopes of the Italian and black curves, consequently, are quite steep. Much of the movement of those groups toward the Democrats, after all, was simply the accretion of new voters to the active electorate. Finally, the Jewish graph shows the much different path taken by that community toward the Democratic party. Jews were sharply realigned in the 1930s, but much of that realignment occurred within the active electorate, the result of voter conversion. Unlike for blacks or Italians, mobilization of new voters was not of overwhelming importance to the Jewish realignment. As we might expect, then, the slope of the Jewish curve is not so steep. While many Jews were mobilized into the active electorate, many others already politically active simply changed their partisan affiliation. Four of the city's five groups, then, moved toward the Democratic party in the 1930s or reconfirmed their loyalty to it. Yankees alone stood by their historic Republican allegiance, their low level of political activity attesting to their demoralization in an age of Democratic ascendancy.

Events conspired between 1920 and 1940 to reshape the nation's party system. Not since the Civil War had American politics been so thoroughly altered. In the three presidential elections just prior to 1930, the Republican party won three overwhelming victories; the next three contests were landslides for Democratic candidate Franklin Delano Roosevelt. "The Democrats did not simply win a routine victory in 1932; they weakened mightily, if they did not destroy, the coalition that had ruled the country."[8] So wrote Key twenty years later. Massachusetts—since the early days of the Republic a bastion of Federalism, then Whiggery, then Republicanism—was one of only two non-Southern states to support Al Smith in 1928. In Boston, which had gone Republican in 1920 and 1924, Smith won with a margin of 99,000 votes. Although no one could know at the time, that election marked the end of Massachusetts's historic role as one of the most secure of Republican states. As Robert K. Massey, Jr., describes, incumbent president Hoover chose not to come to Massachusetts in 1932. "His advisers believed that his presence was more sorely needed elsewhere, and, besides, Massachusetts appeared to be safely in the Hoover column."[9] While Hoover's advisers underestimated the magnitude of the impending Roosevelt landslide, they were accurate in their assessment that Massachusetts was significantly more Republican than the nation as a whole. Still, Hoover lost the state, as Massachusetts embarked on her steady drift toward the Democratic party. Over the ensuing decades, Massachusetts slowly distinguished herself for her growing Democratic loyalty. In the final few days of the 1984 presidential campaign, Walter Mondale and President Reagan both visited Boston and actively solicited support. They came, though, for reasons quite different from those motivating Hoover's decision in 1932. Massachusetts in 1984 was, compared to the country, neither unusually Republican nor even generally competitive; it was a dependable source of Democratic votes. What Reagan sought in his Massachusetts visit, and what Mondale was attempting to prevent, was a fifty-state sweep. Mondale ultimately carried only his home state of Minnesota, but, of the other forty-nine, Massachusetts provided Reagan his narrowest margin of victory. Dwight D. Eisenhower and Ronald Reagan have been the only Republicans since Calvin Coolidge to win the Commonwealth's votes in the electoral college.

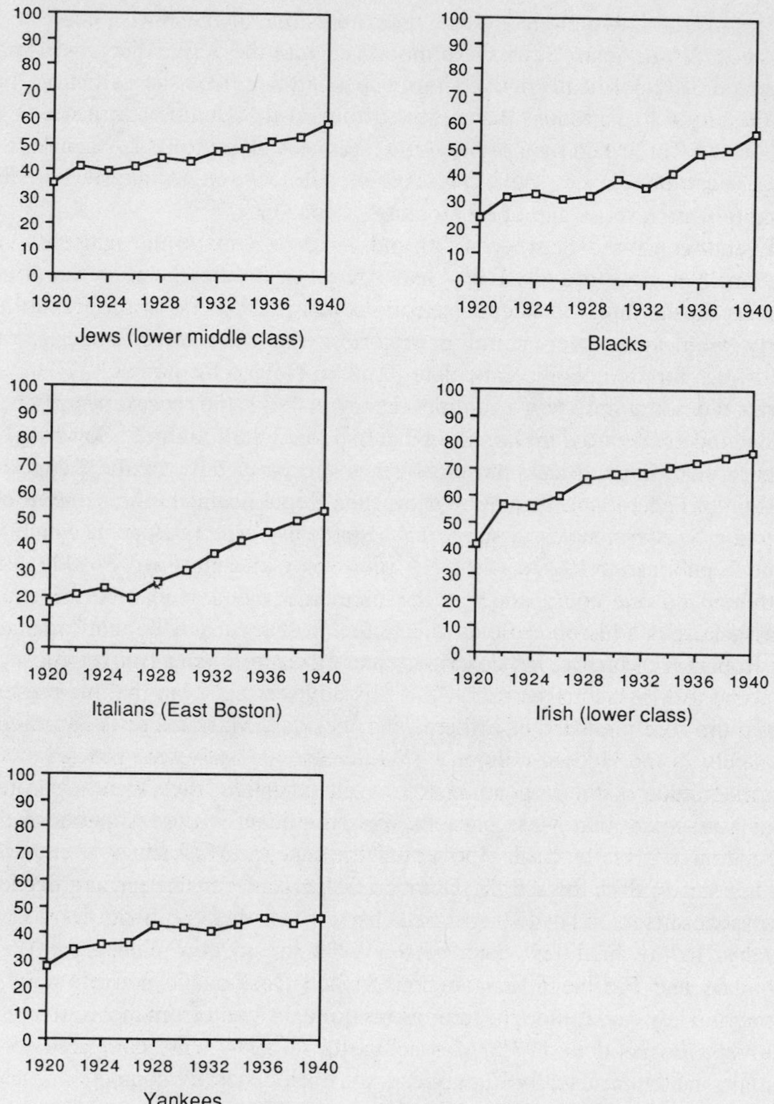

Figure 8.1 Total Registration (as Percent of Potential Electorate)

In the 1920s and 1930s, the great partisan balance in America changed. Franklin Roosevelt and the Democratic party succeeded in articulating the concerns of a people mired in severe economic depression. Despair alone would have been sufficient to defeat Herbert Hoover in 1932. But it was with a sense of relief that many Americans permanently vested their support in the Democratic party, as that party vindicated the hope and the trust placed in it. On every level of the country's vast and complex political system realignments occurred. Political change in the cities and towns transformed states, which in turn transformed the nation. Ultimately, however, that sweeping force originated in the independent decision made by each of millions of individual citizens.

So stunning was the reestablishment of a Democratic majority in that era that political scientists developed a new theory to describe it. The seminal literature on political realignment grew directly out of attempts to fit the political upheaval of the 1930s into the history of the American party system. As Lubell wrote in 1952, "The distinctive feature of the political revolution which Franklin D. Roosevelt began . . . lies not in its resemblance to the political wars of Andrew Jackson or Thomas Jefferson, but in its abrupt break with the continuity of the past." Key, in his 1955 article, regarded the 1928 presidential election as the very model of a critical election. He identified critical realignments as moments "in which more or less profound readjustments occur in the relations of power within the community and in which new and durable electoral groupings are formed." While Key's 1959 article recognized the gradualness of much political change, it also reaffirmed the notion that such change was distinct from the "abrupt changes" and "more durable shifts" which characterized critical elections. "Any working definition of the concept 'critical realignment,' " Burnham argued in 1970, "must, practically speaking, eliminate both deviating election situations . . . and gradual secular realignments." A realignment perspective, in other words, regards realignments as sharp breaks from the normal pattern of politics.[10]

That perspective branded older approaches to party history as unhistorical and insensitive to the significance of major change. "Conceptions of the party system characteristically do not explicitly include a time dimension," Key wrote in 1959. "Most writing about politics seeks to establish a pattern of continuity between the present and past," argued Lubell. "American political history readily lends itself to being pictured as a succession of struggles revolving around the same, recurring themes—the Hamiltonian versus Jeffersonian tradition, the 'people versus plutocracy', capital pitted against labor, agrarians against the city, states rights against federal centralization." The aim of the scholars who helped develop the notion of critical realignment was to correct those readings of American history. In fact, realignment theory emerged to stress above all the discontinuity and periodic, sudden change in the evolution of the party system in the United States. "Such a theory," Burnham understood, "must inevitably emphasize the elements of stress and abrupt transformation in our political life at the expense of the consensual, gradualist perspectives which have until recently dominated the scholar's vision of American political processes and behavior.'' Although some recent scholarship has modified this stress on discontinuity, that emphasis lies at the very heart of any concept of realignment.[11]

What scholars like Burnham, Lubell, and Key rejected was the story of American party history as one long train of constancy, the story which was told until the 1950s by Binkley, Key himself, and other students of the party system and which was contained in Charles A. Beard's once-influential 1928 book, *The American Party Battle.* There Beard asserted that since the establishment of the national government under the Constitution, ''there has been no sharp break in the sources of party strength, in policy, or in opinion. On the contrary,'' he continued, ''[The various alignments of political parties] have been merely phases of one unbroken conflict originating in the age of George Washington and continuing without interruption to our own time.'' Beard traced the basic division between parties to the sources of faction outlined by James Madison in the tenth number of *The Federalist,* to what Beard termed ''the possession of different kinds and amounts of property.'' It is an argument easily caricatured and attacked, but Beard's formulation was more sophisticated than that general statement indicated.[12]

There was, in Beard's theory, some accommodation for political change. He argued, for example, that ''political democracy, subject to some limitations, has become accepted'' by all Americans. While ''economic Federalism of the Hamilton type . . . has continued steadily to the present time'' as the basis of one major party, ''political Federalism of the Hamilton type,'' the notion that masses should defer to elites, had, according to Beard, long since disappeared. What bound one party together was its devotion to government support for ''business enterprise,'' although that party departed from its main principles insofar as it acquired a Western agrarian wing in 1860. The other party had been dominated since its formation by agrarian interests, united in the belief that the descendants of Hamilton were ''engaged in enriching capitalistic classes at the expense of the masses.'' But Beard realized that the age of agrarian dominance over the affairs of its own party was closing. Andrew Jackson had ''added an army of mechanics'' to the agrarian party, and those ''mechanics''—city residents—were prepared one century later to seize control of the party. ''With the growth of the industrial population, the center of gravity in the Democratic party is passing, has already passed, from the open country to the cities,'' wrote Beard early in 1928. ''It is perhaps no exaggeration to say that the Democratic party, founded by Jefferson to represent the agricultural interest, has become the organ of 'the mobs of the great cities' which he feared and despised, thus to a large extent the organ of industrial masses of alien origin or immediate alien descent. As the party accustomed to pummelling the people of 'wealth and talents,' the Democrats also draw to their ranks recruits from the lower middle classes.'' And, Beard knew, the agrarian wing of the party was powerless to resist its fall from power. Southern whites had to acquiesce in the changing balance within the Democratic party. ''The power of the cotton planters sinks relatively in the scale,'' Beard contended. ''Chained to the Democratic party by their antagonism to the negro, they cannot force concessions by threats of desertion and retaliation.''[13]

Beard's theory was flawed, but it was decidedly not static. While it emphasized the lines of continuity between the past and present, the perspective Beard brought to the study of party history also recognized moments of abrupt change in the national party balance—such as 1800 and 1860 and, surely, had the book been written later, 1932—which had great consequences for the direction of national policy. Beard understood the special importance of certain moments: of 1787–88, ''when the federal Constitution was adopted, giving an immense impetus to business enterprise''; of 1800, ''when the agricultural party was put into power and proceeded to acquire all the land between the Mississippi River and the Pacific''; of the ''upheaval of 1828,'' when the agricultural party acquired ''an active mechanic-labor wing''; of 1860, when ''the planters were unhorsed and subjugated to businessmen and farmers,'' as the capitalistic party assumed majority status and incorporated ''freehold farmers, North and West,'' into its electoral base; of 1896, the year of the Republicans' ''great victory over the easy money party''; of 1928, when the book was written and when control of the Democratic party was passing decisively to its urban wing. But Beard's perspective had serious limitations, too. It could not, for example, explain ''the great body of social legislation enacted during the last thirty years,'' the age of Progressive reform, within the context of a party system split between business and agrarian interests. More importantly, the basic premise of *The American Party Battle* was the unchanging line of division between the sets of interests composing American society. Yet Beard, to accurately describe American party history, acknowledged that the business party acquired a large agrarian wing in 1860 and that the party of agricultural interests was about to be eaten whole by Northern cities in 1928.[14]

Just as discontinuity is the essence of realignment theory, continuity is the essence of the approach Beard brought to the study of the party system. Neither perspective is entirely satisfactory. Beard, as hard as he might have tried, could not account for basic changes in American political parties. And, without betraying itself, the body of realignment scholarship could not acknowledge that the great political upheaval of the 1930s was, at least in the electorate, qualitatively indistinguishable from the course of party evolution in the rest of this century.

It is the contention of this book that a new and subtler understanding of the development of the American party system is needed. The American people have been tinkering with their political parties throughout the twentieth century. Our emphasis on the tinkering that occurred between the late 1920s and the late 1930s, indeed the creation of a perspective designed explicitly to account for that remarkable decade, has caused an unfortunate neglect of the currents of change and continuity which have coursed through the party system all during the century.

We have found, through the examination of homogeneous voting precincts in Boston, that real change did occur in the New Deal era. Large numbers of Jewish voters abandoned the Republican party and developed new Democratic attachments. Other Jews entered the active electorate for the first time in that era, most as Democrats. Blacks, too, shifted as a group toward the Democratic party, but their shift was due primarily to newly mobilized voters; it is likely that most black Republicans remained loyal to their party. And we have learned that, in those years, the number of Italians actively participating in the political system swelled enormously. Most of those changes occurred between 1928 and 1938.

But there were, too, real continuities in that era. While those living in Irish and Yankee precincts did experience some slight changes in political activity and party attachment, those changes were incremental. The basic partisan loyalties of Boston's Irish and Yankees did not shift in this era, nor were there substantial transformations in patterns of participation. Similarly, we have established that probably the main body of black and Italian voters in the mid-1920s retained their old party identifications intact through the entire period that followed. Other fundamental characteristics of the electorate, such as the relative salience of local and national issues as well as the relationship between party organization and patterns of political participation by class, were, as Chapter 7 argues, substantially unaffected by the intervention of political upheaval in the 1930s.

In fact, even the genuine change telescoped into the decade after 1928 was effected by disparate processes occurring at different times. Some men and women who eventually became Democrats were drawn in by Al Smith; others voted for Al Smith but without otherwise indicating any alienation from the Republican party; others voted for Herbert Hoover; and still others did not vote at all. Depending on gender, ethnicity, socioeconomic status, and idiosyncrasy, the year of fundamental change in party allegiances occurred in either 1928, 1932, 1934, 1936, or 1938. The reasons for attraction to the

Democratic party were local in some cases and national in others. If the issue was national, it was primarily because of Al Smith's ethnic appeal or because of the Great Depression or because of the New Deal or because of Roosevelt's leadership ability or because of liberalism or because of economic programs or because of events in Europe. Some voters, including almost all Italians and Irish as well as most blacks, expressed their support for the Democratic party with straight tickets, while others, including many Jews, had not as late as 1940 reconciled their firm national attachment to the Democratic party with their inconsistent support for that party's candidates for local offices. There were, in sum, many realignments in the period we have studied. They occurred at different times in response to different stimuli and through different behavioral mechanics.

And there have been many realignments since. White Southerners, who remained at least as loyal to the Democratic party as Boston's Irish from the days of Reconstruction through the 1930s, have been voting Republican in presidential elections for well over a generation—and early hints of that realignment are rooted as deep in the past as 1928 and 1948. Many Catholic and working-class voters began to desert the Democratic party, at least in national elections, in the late 1960s. On the other hand, blacks today are more Democratic as a group than they ever were in the Roosevelt years, and Northeastern Yankees have been moving away from their traditional Republican allegiances. Vast regional shifts have occurred, too, reflecting the changing bases of the parties. That Hoover considered Massachusetts safely Republican in 1932 and that both Reagan and Mondale viewed the state as among the most Democratic in 1984 reflects that broader transformation. The Northeast, the most Republican section in the country in the 1930s, is now its most Democratic section; the South, the most Democratic section in the 1930s, is now the country's most Republican region in presidential elections. Such dramatic changes have occurred across decades during which there was no decisive disintegration of the Democratic coalitional base. Many groups won to the Democratic party in the 1930s generally still identify with it.

Not only does the country constantly experience realignment, but the nature of political change and of partisan identification reflects the trend toward weakened parties that began at the turn of the century. Our study of homogeneous voting precincts in Boston reveals that the bonds of party were already loosening in the 1920s and 1930s, as Burnham and McCormick have argued. Italians, Irish, and blacks tended to give to local candidates of one party the same level of support they gave to that party's national candidates, but there were times when discrepancies were exposed in the votes for different levels of offices. Yankees and especially Jews showed little regard for the consistency of party support in their voting behavior. Not until the

1940s and 1950s did the Jewish movement to the Democratic party in Boston express itself in registration figures and votes for candidates for local office. Similarly, citing states like Iowa and the results there of the 1948 election, Key reported that "any appraisal of the character of the new Democratic party has to take note of the fact that in former Republican territory it is to a high degree a presidential party." The partisan transformation of the white South, too, has been most dramatic in the vote for national candidates; in terms of local political leaders, the South remains overwhelmingly Democratic. Thus, while in 1984 and 1988 the Republican candidate for president easily won the electoral votes of every one of the former Confederate states, Democratic majorities continue to dominate each of the eleven state legislatures. That striking divergence between local and national partisan success can no longer be considered temporary. It has been normal behavior now since the mid-1960s, lasting nearly as long as any of the party systems isolated in realignment theory. What Southern white political schizophrenia represents is both a set of durable party attachments radically different from those which survived the New Deal era and a changed political environment in which split tickets present no contradiction to be eventually resolved.[15]

The electoral mechanics which produced the party upheaval of the 1930s are no different from those which were reshaping political parties in the first three decades of this century and have continued to reconstitute electoral bases and to change the party balance in the last five decades. All that distinguished the "New Deal realignments" was the fact that enough changes were compressed into a sufficiently short period of time to effect a sudden shift in the balance between the two major parties. Changes no less profound than the movement of Jews and blacks to the Democratic party in the 1930s—such as the movement of white Southerners, whose partisan ties were unshaken in the New Deal era, toward national Republican candidates—have occurred many times in the years since. It is not even clear that the lines of cleavage and policy issues that excited the 1930s and 1940s had a greater impact on their time than did the Progressive reforms earlier in the century or the divisions that were exposed by the civil rights movement in the 1960s. Certainly, the shift in national policy was less after 1896 than it was in either the 1910s or the 1960s.

A riddle was posed in the opening pages of this book. We are finally in a position to solve it. As the Civil War was, according to Beard, the "Second American Revolution," so Lubell termed the political upheaval which resulted from the turmoil in the late 1920s and 1930s the "Third American Revolution."[16] From a realignment perspective, it is difficult to understand why that "Third American Revolution" was so utterly incapable of reversing the decline of political parties which had begun in the early 1900s. To many scholars, it has been puzzling that so great a boulder could be hurled against the party system without wreaking institutional change of lasting consequence. Neither Schattschneider nor Burnham offered explanation, and McCormick's recent work did not investigate the electoral mechanics underlying the New Deal upheaval. Now, having conducted that investigation, we have uncovered the foundation of the fabled realignment, and it is atomistic. What was hurled in the 1930s was no great chunk of stone but only a few fistfuls of sand. The party system paused, rubbed its eyes, and then moved on along a changed course, much as it has always done when pelted with sand and much as it likely will continue to do far into the future.

Only because normal patterns of constant change were concentrated into a few brief years and because those changes gave a special advantage to one party has the 1930s long seemed so unusual. Even during the "party period," assuming that this characterization of politics has some application to the nineteenth century, such moments of intensified change were infrequent. The first occurred with the birth of mass democracy, in the 1830s; the second occurred on the eve of the Civil War, in the 1850s; and the third occurred with the final effort to arrest the industrialization and urbanization of American society, in the 1890s. To account for the cataclysmic forces sufficient to cause such a compression of political changes in the 1930s, we must look to the confluence of several events: the candidacy of Al Smith, the first Catholic to run for the presidency and a powerful symbol for the urban masses with recent immigrant pasts; the Great Depression; the unprecedented expansion of government programs as part of the New Deal; and the crisis in Europe which by 1939 had erupted in a Second World War. Together these events affected enough members of the electorate to cause a relatively sudden shift in the partisan balance. Key, writing in 1952, indicated that "a theory of the relation of disaster and party alignment" linked the 1850s and 1860s with the 1930s. The "catastrophe" of civil war, he argued, had "burned into the American electorate a pattern of partisan faith that persisted in its main outlines until 1932." And, continued Key, a "second catastrophe, the Great Depression," combined with "the Roosevelt Revolution in national policy" and the legacy of the 1928 campaign, had decisively altered that prior system of allegiances. Despite the operation of such powerful forces, Key admitted as late as 1952, the "new" party divisions were not so radically different from the old ones. By the mid-1930s, Roosevelt had nearly "fuse[d] together a new party from among the resentful, the disinherited, and the old Democrats"; and, while the "old Democrats" remained in the new Democratic party, "the upper-class supporters of Roosevelt in 1932 tended to return . . . to the party of their fathers," the Republican party. "The imprint of the 1860's," he wrote, "remains to this day on the map of our politics. . . . The Great Depression and the Roosevelt Revolution modified the pre-existing partisan division by the recruitment of great numbers of Democrats notably in the industrial and metropolitan centers,'' wrote Key, emphasizing the incremental nature of the New Deal changes three years before introducing a formal realignment perspective on the era. ''Another stratum was deposited on the accumulated historical precipitate that seems to condition, if not fix, the shape of our party groups.''[17]

That view of political change, expressed by one who was still struggling to resolve the tensions between Beard's view of party history and his own developing ideas of party realignment, represents a synthesis that is worth rediscovering. Of course there was great change in the 1930s. But, just as surely, much did not change in those years, and the nature of political change during the ''New Deal realignments'' was no different except in quantity from the change which has shaped our politics ceaselessly for generations. Whereas substantially new party systems might have been born in the 1830s and 1850s—there were no ''old Republicans,'' for example, in the Republican party of 1856—the changes which occurred in the 1930s, and probably, too, in the 1890s, were incremental, accretions to and decrements from previously existing electoral coalitions. Key came closest to articulating this view when he referred to party coalitions as ''accumulated historical precipitate'' and when he later enunciated a concept of gradual, ''secular realignment''; but Key's adoption of critical election theory in 1955 caused him to regard certain eras, such as the late 1920s and 1930s, as exceptions from those usual processes.[18] The New Deal realignment, it is true, is just one realignment, and Boston is just a single city. That realignment, however, provided the model for the perspective on party development that emerged in the 1950s, and much of the scholarship on the realignment grew out of the experiences of cities like Boston. Given the variegation that we have found in Boston's homogeneous precincts, we can state with some confidence that the notion of realignment can be no more than a descriptive label for many quite different but contemporaneous changes, and that those changes are no different from those occurring in other years. It is clear, too, that such periods of frenzied, intensified activity are triggered by momentous events. And because of the erosion in the role played by parties in the political system since the turn of the twentieth century, America's next great national crisis will probably trigger a less decisive and less sweeping series of realignments than past eras of upheaval; constant change will persist as parties are continuously redefined, and frayed and vacillating party loyalties will continue to characterize the behavior of American voters. The party system has not been stagnating since the 1930s, waiting for that infusion of new ideas and new supporters that ostensibly comes only in brief spurts of realignment. Our parties are ever-changing and they are reborn daily, but they sever only at glacial pace every tie with their pasts.

Appendix 1

Research Method and Sources

Voting precincts are the smallest units for which cities and towns report party registration and election statistics. Boston, in the years between 1920 and 1940, was divided into as few as 221 precincts and as many as 388. Although ward lines in Boston were redrawn just once in those years, precinct lines were redrawn several times. Wards in this era were composed of between 6 and 22 precincts, depending on the number of voters in a ward at a given time. Precinct boundaries were constantly changing in order to reflect population movements as well as increases or decreases in political participation. The city's precincts were drawn on the basis of active, not potential, electorates; precincts contained roughly the same number of registered voters, but different numbers of adults and different population sizes. Generally, each precinct contained a few hundred voters. Almost never were there more than one thousand voters in a precinct. Because they were relatively small aggregate units in a city of ethnically homogeneous neighborhoods, many of Boston's precincts contained populations which were homogeneous ethnically and socioeconomically. This book is grounded on such homogeneous precincts, on those parts of Boston in which one ethnic group represented at least 80–85 percent of the whole population. A list of those precincts is presented in Appendix 2.

Central to this book, indeed upon which much of its argument ultimately rests, are the precincts selected for analysis. This study is in part an effort to approach the level of individual behavior. It is, however, impossible to know how individuals actually voted, and public opinion polls are unavailable for these years. So we must rely on aggregate data. I have chosen to isolate precincts which are ethnically and socioeconomically homogeneous, the assumption being that the political behavior of such units most accurately reflects the decisions of the individuals within it. The selection of voting precincts was undoubtedly the most time-consuming and demanding of all the challenges which had to be confronted in producing this work.

Before precincts could be chosen, the distribution of ethnic groups between 1920 and 1940 in Boston had to be established. That meant going far beyond such general descriptions as "South Boston has always been Irish" to learning just how concentrated a particular ethnic group was in a certain area, what the exact boundaries of that area were, and when and for how long that specific area contained that high concentration of that ethnic group; answers to those questions in many cases required information down to the level of the city block. While conducting that inquiry, it was equally important to reconstruct the boundaries of voting precincts as they existed throughout the period. Only with both pieces of information, of course, could I proceed to study voting behavior.

The first—and, in retrospect, the single most valuable—method for identifying homogeneous ethnic pockets was to consult all relevant documents from the state and federal censuses. Determining which census materials would be useful and then locating them were not simple jobs. The federal census schedules, the actual handwritten sheets on which the census-taker recorded each person's name and address and any information obtained from that person for a particular census, are opened to the public only after the lapse of seventy-two years. Thus the latest census for which such schedules are available today is that of 1910. For subsequent years, the years examined in this book, published summaries of each federal census had to be located.

State censuses in Massachusetts were conducted in 1925 and 1935 independent of the federal census. But those two censuses, at least from the perspective of a political historian, are pathetic documents. Apparently compelled by a state legislature eager to cut costs and publish only the most "necessary" of statistics, the secretary of the Commonwealth managed to summarize into thirty pages each the essential results of the 1925 and 1935 censuses. The only information reported for wards, a level which was at least documented quite thoroughly by the federal censuses of that period, was total population and the number of legal voters. Perhaps those two skimpy reports resulted from negative reaction to the extraordinarily detailed published state census of 1915. That document not only provided a tremendous amount of material at the ward level but even included precinct breakdowns. The great irony, though, was that Boston in 1915 had just redrawn ward lines and was in the process of creating new precincts within those wards. Rather than report information for obsolete wards and precincts, the state census for 1915 chose to report breakdowns in Boston at the ward level only. There is, in the opening pages of the 1915 report, an allusion to an enumeration of the population of the City of Boston by blocks for the purposes of that census. No statistics from that block enumeration were included, however, and, if they did at any time actually exist, they have apparently long since disappeared.

It was to the federal censuses, then, that attention was directed. In its reports for 1920 and 1930, the federal Bureau of the Census published statistics that could help determine the ethnicity of a certain population:

country of birth of foreign-born whites, number of blacks in the population, number of native-born whites in the population, number of foreign-born whites in the population. Unfortunately, however, the smallest populations for which such published breakdowns were reported in 1920 and 1930 were at the ward level. The city's wards—which numbered 26 in the early 1920s and have numbered 22 ever since 1925—were large and generally heterogeneous units. Information reported at that level could at best indicate if a population of a given ethnic group resided within ward boundaries; what ward-level statistics could not relate is where within each ward such groups were concentrated. Since the voting precinct is a subdivision of the ward, it was acutely necessary to know which of those subdivisions were ethnically homogeneous and which were not.

The first published descriptions of Boston's population in groupings smaller than the ward (at least in census documents for the period examined) were contained in two reports compiled from the 1940 federal census. In 1940, an exhaustive summary of Boston by census tract was released, as was a housing survey by city blocks. The block statistics apparently were compiled for the first time in that year. While most of the information given for city blocks is related strictly to the condition of the housing stock, two variables were included that proved valuable to this study. Most important was a breakdown by city block of the number of dwelling units occupied by whites and the number occupied by nonwhites. Boston's black population at the time of this study was so small that such information came to be essential to the selection of black precincts: nonwhites could be identified at the block level, and other census reports showed that, for most sections of Boston with large concentrations of nonwhites, virtually all nonwhites were black. The other category utilized at the block level was average monthly rent, which was one indicator of an area's socioeconomic status. Because voting precincts never overlapped perfectly with units for which a number of such class variables were available, it proved useful to know at least this minimum of economic information at the block level.[1]

In addition to this volume of block statistics, the Bureau of the Census in 1940 published a report organized by census tract. Much smaller than wards and usually larger than voting precincts, census tracts were formed by boundaries wholly unrelated to those marking the city's political divisions. The introduction to the 1940 report described the guidelines used for drawing tract boundaries:

> Census tracts are small areas, having a population usually between 3,000 and 6,000, into which certain large cities . . . have been divided for statistical and local administrative purposes. . . . The tract areas are established with a view to approximate uniformity in population, with some consideration of uniformity in size, and with

> due regard for natural barriers. Each tract is designed to include an area fairly homogeneous in population characteristics. . . . The tracts are intended to remain unchanged from census to census and thus to make possible studies of changes in social and economic characteristics of the population within small sections of the city.

Organized by census tract was a rich body of statistics, including several important ethnic and socioeconomic characteristics. Boston in 1940 was divided into 156 such census tracts; in the same year, the city contained 386 voting precincts. The census tracts were crucial in locating solid ethnic concentrations. Not only were their boundaries uniform over time, but the tracts had been purposely and often successfully designed to identify ethnically and socioeconomically homogeneous sections of the city.[2]

An intriguing question and a challenge were contained in the 1940 tract report. ''The Census Bureau made tabulations of 1910 data by census tracts not only for New York, but also for the 7 other cities having a population of over 500,000,'' the introduction to the report stated. ''Tract data were tabulated for the same 8 cities in 1920, but this number was increased to 18 in 1930 . . . [and] to 60 cities in 1940.'' If statistics for the nation's eight largest cities had been compiled by census tract decennially since 1910, it is logical to assume that such data had been prepared for Boston. Boston was, after all, in both 1900 and 1910, the fifth-largest city in the country, with a 1910 population of 670,585. Only New York, Chicago, Philadelphia, and St. Louis were larger.[3] Somewhere, in some form, then, those pre-1940 census tract reports for Boston must once have existed. The important question for one studying the period between 1920 and 1940 was to determine if that supposition was indeed true, and, if true, whether such reports had survived to this day.

In attempting to locate census tract information from 1920 or 1930, I scoured libraries as well as public and private organizations. The Bureau of the Census was unaware of any census tract breakdowns for Boston prior to the 1940 published report. After repeated inquiries, all they could finally suggest was that, had such reports ever existed, they would have been forwarded to ''Boston's planning commission'' upon completion. But Boston's City Planning Board was dissolved a generation ago. The Boston Redevelopment Authority, the agency which assumed many of the old planning board's functions, emphatically denied any organizational link to the long-defunct board and maintained that they had inherited none of that department's records. Many other organizations were contacted in search of the old census tract data, but without success. No federal, state, county, or city agency was aware of any census tract report for Boston prior to the 1940 document, nor was any private historical group. And, if census tracts had been analyzed for the City of Boston prior to 1940, no such reports had survived in any of the major public or private libraries in the Boston area.

What were, however, found scattered among the libraries were three publications whose common parent was a 1930 census tract report. Those three derivative studies proved that there had been at least one major canvas of Boston by census tract prior to the published 1940 study. *The People of Boston* (1939), prepared by the City Planning Board, used figures from the 1930 census to identify the census tracts in which most of the city's blacks lived; the document also provided a breakdown by age group and gender for each of the census tracts and blocks in Boston.[4] A publication of the Boston Health League, *Alphabetical Street Index and Basic Demographic Data for the City of Boston by Census Tracts* (1931) reported population, geographic area, and density by census tract, using statistics from the 1930 census. According to *Alphabetical Street Index,* information had been collected by census tract since 1910, and two agencies, the Massachusetts Board of Probation and the Boston City Health Department, were making use of that data in their work in 1931. A map of the city divided into census tracts was included in the booklet, and copies of the map were, at least in 1931, available from the Boston Council of Social Agencies.[5] The most thorough and informative of the three publications was the report issued by that same Boston Council of Social Agencies, *Social Statistics by Census Tracts in Boston* (1933). Part of the importance of *Social Statistics* lay in its introduction, which reviewed the history of data collection by census tract in Boston through 1930. "In some cities," the report stated, "federal census material has been available by census tracts since 1910 or 1920. Although population figures for Boston on this basis were available in 1920, it was not until 1930 that . . . eleven tables by census tracts were made available through the efforts of the Boston Health League and a generous grant of money from the City Health Department." The eleven tables, only the titles of which were contained in this publication, apparently provided at least as much information about ethnic and socioeconomic variables as were later included in the 1940 published report. While *Social Statistics* included a number of maps and graphs summarizing the results of the 1930 census tract report for Boston, the study contained no raw data.[6] It was still necessary to locate the document upon which this and the two other publications had been based, a 1930 report by census tract for Boston composed of eleven tables. There was no longer any purpose in pursuing similar reports from 1910 or 1920. Except as simple population counts, they had never existed.

An effort was immediately made to contact the agencies mentioned in those three publications. All of the organizations had, though, long since disbanded or been radically reorganized. For clues to the fate of the 1930 census tract report, I read through surviving papers and newsletters issued by the defunct agencies. From a series of bulletins published by the Boston Council of Social Agencies between 1930 and 1935, I learned that this organization was central to the collection and dissemination of 1930 census tract statistics in Boston. The 1930 bulletins discussed extensively the benefits of dividing the city into census tracts: lecturers on the topic had actually come to Boston at the invitation of the council. In October 1931, it was reported that "planographs"—copies of the original census tract sheets prepared by the Census Bureau—had been bound into a volume available for inspection at the Boston Health League office. Copies of the volume could be purchased for $50 each. The Health League remained custodian for the census tract reports until February 1933, when the Boston Council of Social Agencies assumed responsibility.[7]

So, to locate the original bound census tract information, I began to search for existing organizations that might trace their roots to the Boston Council of Social Agencies. One of the organizations contacted was the United Community Planning Corporation, a research organization for social service groups. An official there was not sure, but he vaguely remembered having heard of the Boston Council of Social Agencies as one of the ancestors of the United Community Planning Corporation. He agreed to check on that connection, as well as to investigate the possibility that the 1930 census tract document was buried somewhere among the United Community Planning Corporation's inherited papers. A few days later he called back. His agency was indeed descended from the Boston Council of Social Agencies. Even more, he had, after having spoken to a retired colleague, succeeded in locating the document as well as some related papers. The volume was, he said, extremely fragile and water-damaged; it was also priceless and irreplaceable, the most detailed portrait of Boston prepared from the 1930 census. Copies of that volume were soon acquired by both the Boston Public Library and the Harvard University Library. And, when last contacted, the Census Bureau, too, was considering purchasing a copy of its own report.[8]

The next task was to compare information from the 1930 and 1940 census tracts and to illustrate on a map of the city those tracts that were ethnically homogeneous throughout the 1930s. Italians and Jews were especially easy to locate. From inspection of the two censuses, a number of tracts were conspicuous for extraordinarily high concentrations of those two groups. Since no ethnic ancestry table was included in those censuses, the main statistics utilized were those indicating country of origin for the foreign-born and the children of foreign-born. Where that information indicated that an overwhelming majority of those two groups were Italian, it seemed likely that the census tract's population was generally of Italian stock. Census tracts with large numbers of Russians, Poles, and others of Eastern or Central European origin were tentatively classified as Jewish. Boston received relatively few non-Jewish immigrants from Eastern Europe, and those it did receive tended to live among Irish or Italians rather than among Jews. At this preliminary stage, those areas of the city with relatively large numbers of Irish immigrants were also marked, although in no census tract did persons born in Ireland dominate as did Jews and Italians in their sections of the city. The bulk of Boston's Irish had entered the city in the middle of the nineteenth century and thus their descendants by 1930 and 1940 appeared in the census as American children of American parents. Tracts with heavily native-born white populations were noted, too.

Blacks were a little more difficult to identify from census tracts. There were at the time so few blacks in Boston that in 1930 only seven census tracts were at least 20 percent black and just one tract in the entire city had a population which was majority black. For blacks, then, it became necessary to refer to the 1940 statistics by city block. This was possible because the block data broke down white and nonwhite population by city block, and, importantly, the same census tracts which contained large numbers of blacks in 1940 were identical to those which had large black populations in 1930. The only necessary assumption, which appeared reasonable, was that blacks and whites living in the same numbers in the same census tract in 1930 and 1940 were distributed throughout that tract in roughly the same way throughout the period.

Once ethnic concentrations in the city had been preliminarily identified, the next major project was to reconstruct precinct divisions. No authority existed which detailed changes in precinct lines between 1920 and 1940. To establish the timing of such changes, it became necessary to scrutinize a variety of overlapping sources. Four sets of precinct maps from the period were located. Arranged in large atlases which devoted one or two pages to each of the city's wards, three sets (1916, 1925, and 1935) were held in the Special Collections of the Massachusetts State Library, and one set (1921) was found in the Government Documents room of the Boston Public Library. I examined a bound volume of material dealing with precinct changes from 1895 to 1935, which was also in the Boston Public Library's Government Documents room; that volume provided information on three precinct changes affecting the 1920s and 1930s. The 1925 *Annual Report of the Board of Election Commissioners* discussed the recent ward and precinct redistricting in its introduction. And additional precinct information was contained on a sheet on file in the Government Documents room of the Boston Public Library, which purported to list precinct changes during this period based on an analysis of old city documents.

No source, however, was complete in itself. Not only did none mention even most of the changes contained in other sources, but information in one source might be flatly contradicted in another. Confusion was especially compounded by the Boston *Municipal Register,* an annual city publication. Through the late 1910s and early 1920s, the *Register* appeared to carefully document any changes as they occurred in the boundaries of the city's voting precincts. But beginning in the mid-1920s, the *Register,* while continuing to include precinct information, lapsed into carelessness and error. Rather than updating changes in precinct boundaries each year, the *Register* simply began to reprint the previous year's entry, extending outdated and incorrect information into perpetuity. It was, in retrospect, an especially dangerous series to consult. As a report issued annually, the *Municipal Register* had a veneer of completeness and seemed constantly up-to-date. Yet it was the most inaccurate of all the documents.

What proved the best means of discovering changes in precinct lines as they occurred was the *Annual Report of the Board of Election Commissioners.* While the *Annual Report,* except in 1925, never actually discussed precinct line redrawings, those changes were implicit in every page of election statistics. Since most election results were presented in the *Annual Report* by ward and precinct, it became a straightforward if tedious matter to review those actual returns for the period between 1915 and 1940. I examined election results at this stage of research, then, only as a means of discovering the number of precincts being reported for each ward in a particular year. Whenever the number of precincts in a given ward changed, it was clear that the ward's precinct lines had been recently redrawn. Similarly, with five exceptions as explained below, a constant number of precincts in a ward from one year to the next was taken as evidence that no redivision had occurred.[9]

Between 1920 and 1940, I concluded, the city operated under what can be described as two ward systems and five precinct systems. New ward lines went into effect in 1916 and 1925. Similarly, precinct lines were redrawn for the entire city five different times, effective in 1916, 1921, 1925, 1932, and 1936. Within each of those five precinct systems, smaller changes were occasionally implemented at the ward level, but no citywide redivisions occurred. This scheme fit perfectly all the extant sources, with the exception of the now obviously incorrect *Municipal Register*. Every change which had been mentioned by other sources showed up in this study of the *Annual Report of the Board of Election Commissioners*; there was no evidence of lines being redrawn without the number of precincts changing except in the original creation of the five systems. With some effort, city documents could be found to substantiate the changes suggested by the *Annual Report* and to describe, in words, the precinct boundaries. Creating a full set of precinct maps remained, though, a formidable task. Of the five citywide redrawings, only three basic systems could be located in the form of maps. The Massachusetts State Library contained precinct atlases for 1916 and 1925, while an atlas for 1921 was available at the Boston Public Library. Thus two complete precinct systems—those created in 1932 and 1936—as well as five, smaller, ward-wide redistrictings, had to be fashioned into maps from verbal descriptions contained in city documents.[10]

Preliminary ethnic distributions were compared with precinct boundaries, and the two were then verified against other available evidence of ethnic concentrations in this period. One important issue that remained to be tested was the correspondence between the location of ethnic groups in 1920 and the census tracts identified for 1930 and 1940. That correspondence could be checked in part by comparing populations within ward boundaries in 1920 against populations in census tracts and city blocks reported for 1930 and 1940. For that purpose, census tracts and city blocks were pieced together, in jigsaw-puzzle style, to form the geographic area encompassed by each of the twenty-six 1920 wards. Then the ethnic group population reported for each ward in the 1920 census was checked against the population living there in the 1930s. The assumption made was that an ethnic group's pattern of distribution within a given ward was relatively constant over the two decades if the size of its population in that ward did not change. If there were, for example, as many Jews living in Roxbury's Ward 16 in 1920 as there were in the same area in 1930, it is assumed—unless information to the contrary was found—that those Jews lived in the same census tracts within the 1920 ward that they dominated in 1930 and again in 1940.

In sections of the city with significant black populations, voting precincts were broken down into their constituent city blocks. Exact measures of the black population of those precincts in 1940 were then extracted from the 1940 census block report. For measures of the percentage of black residents of precincts between 1920 and the late 1930s, distributions at the block level in 1940 were consulted alongside 1930 census tract figures, 1920 ward figures, and several studies done between the early 1910s and the 1930s describing black residential patterns in Boston. Those sources allowed the designation of certain voting precincts as homogeneously black at different points in time.

Similar techniques were used in identifying homogeneous precincts for the city's other ethnic groups. Information from the federal censuses was supplemented by contemporary community studies, accounts of life in different sections of Boston, histories, government reports, and many other books and documents from the period. Informal guidelines for choosing precincts had evolved into a requirement of a specific ethnic concentration of at least 80–85 percent of the total population and geographical continuity over the twenty years. Since, for example, the black inroads into upper Roxbury occurred only after the late 1920s, that neighborhood was not studied at all, even in the 1930s, because there were no black precincts in that geographic area in the early 1920s. West End Jews, too, so important in 1920, were not included in this study because no Jewish precincts remained in the West End by the late 1930s. Based on those guidelines and the accumulated ethnic data, a tentative list of ethnically homogeneous precincts was drawn up. Areas of the city with especially low numbers of foreign-born residents, as determined by the census, were broken down into precincts in an effort to determine if any of those areas were solidly Irish or solidly Yankee. And the *Social Register* was consulted in the effort to locate concentrations of wealthy Yankee residents in Boston in the 1920s and 1930s.

''Police lists''—lists of residents arranged by streets within each precinct, bound into separate volumes for each ward, and compiled annually by the city's Police Department—were the basis for final judgments of the ethnicity of each precinct.[11] Every precinct under consideration was evaluated by an examination of the names of its residents. Used alone, this was an imperfect method of identifying Italians, Irish, Jews, and Yankees. But, employed as the final step in a long process, it did provide one last, and rather good, method of verifying the ethnic homogeneity of precincts. The screening process consisted of reading through the police lists for at least five different years in the twenty-year period. So many independent readings permitted sensitivity to significant ethnic shifts and to the constantly redrawn precinct lines. No effort was made, for obvious reasons, to validate black precincts in this manner. It was a happy circumstance, then, that blacks, alone among ethnic groups, could be identified in 1940 at the level of the city block. This information, combined with several accounts of Boston's blacks written in the earlier decades of the century, provided reasonable assurance that blacks, too, were represented in their precincts in numbers greater than 80–85 percent.

With a list of precincts for each ethnic group completed and verified, those units were examined for intragroup socioeconomic differences, using various measures from the 1930 and 1940 censuses. Income and wealth were not reported in those years. In their place were such measures as the value of owned homes, the monthly rent of rental units, the numbers of families owning mechanical refrigerators, the number of homes centrally heated, the level of education attained by adults in each district, and the occupations of each area's residents. Like measures of ethnicity, these socioeconomic variables were drawn from the 1930 and 1940 reports by census tract and the 1940 report by city block, and were reinforced by earlier census information at the ward level, several other studies and documents from those years, and occupational data reported in the police lists.

At last, with a surety born of careful research, it was possible to study the political choices made in each set of precincts. The same *Annual Report of the Board of Election Commissioners* which had proved so valuable in reconstructing precinct lines could now be put to its intended use.[12] From it came most of the original data contained in this study. Among the measures provided by the report were adult population by gender, number of registered voters by gender, number of registrants enrolled in each of the political parties by gender, vote for senator in the Massachusetts General Court, vote for representative in Congress, and—for 1920, 1924, and 1928—vote for electors of president and vice-president. All these statistics (with the exception noted at the end of Appendix 3) were reported at the level of the voting precinct. Oddly, however, the election report did not provide precinct-level results of the vote for president in 1932, 1936, or 1940. To say the least, that omission was disturbing to someone engaged in a study of the Roosevelt revolution at the level of the precinct. A number of frantic inquiries ensued in an effort to find that information. Finally, after thumbing through the back issues of a number of newspapers, I discovered the vital data: the *Boston Globe*—at least in 1932, 1936, and 1940—reported the vote for president at the precinct level for the entire city of Boston.[13] With results from the *Globe* supplementing the great wealth of statistics in the *Annual Report of the Board of Election Commissioners,* probably all the information one could reasonably expect at the precinct level was available for this study of Boston. Now the analysis of the data and the writing could begin.

So had gone the research. From the beginning, integrity of data was accorded the highest attention. It would have been worse than meaningless to have spoken of the Italian vote or the black vote if the precincts being studied had not been thoroughly investigated and proved homogeneously Italian or black. No effort was spared to eliminate that danger in this work. If I have accomplished nothing else, I have identified precincts in Boston which, between 1920 and 1940, were ethnically and socioeconomically homogeneous. Of that at least I am confident, and I ask the reader's indulgence when, in each of the main ethnic chapters, substantial space is accorded to discussion of the distribution of that group in Boston. For, without that evidence and that justification for the specific precincts selected, the study of voting and partisanship lacks foundation.

Appendix 2
The Precincts

The method for selecting precincts is described in Appendix 1; the process for extracting registration and voting data from these precincts and tabulating those data is described in Appendix 3. It is worth reminding the reader that precinct lines were frequently redrawn in the 1920s and 1930s. What was called, for example, Precinct 3 in Ward 14 in one year might represent an entirely different geographic area from Precinct 3 in Ward 14 in another year. Single precincts rarely persisted intact for more than a few years before being redrawn. The groupings of precincts shown below each represent a certain section or sections of the city which remained ethnically and socioeconomically homogeneous over the two decades. While populations in those precinct clusters might have expanded or contracted between 1920 and 1940 and while the names of precincts constituting such clusters might have changed completely over time, the types of people living in the area did not change considerably and the geographic area itself remained intact as a center of a homogeneous community. Any neighborhood included at one point in a given category is represented at every point of time; neighborhoods which were not composed of the same ethnic group over the twenty years or were not constantly ethnically homogeneous are never included.

What follows below is a complete list of the precincts which were analyzed in this study. Precincts are grouped by year and by ethnic group and, within certain of the ethnic groups, are further grouped by neighborhood or by socioeconomic status. The groupings shown here correspond exactly to the categories of ethnicity, class, and neighborhood which appear throughout this book. Wards are listed first, just before the colon. After each colon appear all the precincts in that ward identified as ethnically homogeneous for the year or years indicated. Thus, in 1920, there were five precincts identified as Jewish and as lower middle class: Precinct 7 in Ward 16 (16: 7); Precincts 3, 4, and 5 in Ward 19 (19: 3, 4, 5); and Precinct 1 in Ward 21 (21: 1). All results from those five precincts have been added together to obtain voting and registration figures for Boston's lower-middle-class Jews living in homogeneous precincts in 1920. Now the list:

JEWISH PRECINCTS

1920

working class	18: 2
lower middle class	16: 7
	19: 3, 4, 5
	21: 1
upper middle class	16: 9

1921–1924

working class	18: 2
lower middle class	16: 8, 9
	18: 1
	19: 3, 4, 5
	21: 1
upper middle class	16: 11

1925–1931

working class	14: 1
lower middle class	12: 13, 14, 15
	14: 2, 3, 4, 8, 9, 10, 14, 16
upper middle class	12: 16

1932–1935

working class	14: 1
lower middle class	12: 13, 14, 15
	14: 2, 3, 4, 8, 9, 10, 12, 13, 14, 16, 17, 18, 19
upper middle class	12: 16, 17

1936–1940

working class	14: 1
lower middle class	12: 13, 15
	14: 2, 3, 4, 8, 9, 10, 11, 12, 13, 14, 15, 16, 17, 18, 19, 20, 21
upper middle class	12: 16, 17, 18

ITALIAN PRECINCTS

1920–1924

East Boston	2: 6, 7
North End	5: 1, 2

1925–1931

East Boston	1: 2, 4
North End	3: 1, 2

1932–1933

East Boston	1: 2, 4, 20
North End	3: 1, 2

1934–1935

East Boston	1: 2, 4, 20
North End	3: 1, 2, 12, 13, 14

1936–1940

East Boston	1: 1, 2, 4, 5, 20, 21
North End	3: 1, 2, 12, 13, 14

BLACK PRECINCTS

1920	13: 2, 3
1921–1924	13: 2, 4
1925–1935	9: 5, 6, 7
1936–1940	9: 5, 6, 7, 9

YANKEE PRECINCTS

1920	8: 4, 6, 7
1921–1924	8: 4, 7, 9
1925–1935	5: 4, 7, 8, 10
1936–1940	5: 4, 8, 10

IRISH PRECINCTS

1920

poor	9: 3
	10: 1
lower class	3: 2, 3, 5, 6, 7
	4: 2, 3, 4, 5, 6, 7
	9: 8, 9
	10: 9
	11: 4
	14: 3, 4, 5
working class	11: 8, 9
	14: 6
	17: 8
	18: 5, 6, 7
	22: 4, 6, 8
lower middle class	26: 4, 6

1921–1924

poor	9: 3
	10: 1
lower class	3: 2, 3, 5, 6, 7
	4: 2, 3, 4, 5, 6, 7
	9: 8, 9
	10: 8, 9
	11: 4
	14: 4, 5, 6
working class	11: 8, 10
	14: 7, 9
	17: 11
	18: 8, 9, 10, 11
	22: 9, 10
lower middle class	26: 5, 6, 9

1925–1931

poor	6: 3
	7: 7
lower class	2: 2, 3, 4, 5, 6, 7, 10, 11, 13, 14, 16
	6: 9, 13, 14
	7: 2, 13
	10: 4, 5, 6
working class	10: 3, 7, 8
	11: 12, 13
	13: 10, 14
	15: 7, 12, 15
lower middle class	22: 6, 7, 13

1932–1935

poor	6: 3
	7: 7
lower class	2: 2, 3, 4, 5, 6, 7, 10, 11, 13, 14, 16
	6: 9, 13, 14
	7: 2, 13
	10: 4, 5, 6
working class	10: 3, 7, 8
	11: 12, 13
	13: 10, 14
	15: 7, 12, 15
lower middle class	22: 6, 7, 10, 13, 15

1936–1938

poor	6: 3
	7: 7
lower class	2: 2, 3, 4, 5, 6, 7, 10, 11, 13, 14, 16
	6: 9, 13, 14
	7: 2, 13, 17
	10: 4, 5, 6

working class	10: 3, 7, 8
	11: 12, 13
	13: 10, 14
	15: 7, 12, 15
lower middle class	22: 6, 7, 13, 15
1940	
poor	6: 3
	7: 7
lower class	2: 3, 5, 6, 7, 10, 11, 13, 14, 16
	6: 9, 13, 14
	7: 2, 13, 17
	10: 4, 5, 6
working class	10: 3, 7, 8
	11: 12, 13
	13: 10, 14
	15: 7, 12, 15
lower middle class	22: 6, 7, 13, 15

Appendix 3

Party Registration and the Vote: The Process of Tabulation

This book is built around a core of ten basic tables. For each of the five ethnic groups, two tables are presented: one reports voting patterns and the other reports party registration figures. Appendix 1 discusses the method used to select the homogeneous precincts whose behavior is summarized in the tables, while the list of those precincts appears in Appendix 2. With that list of precincts, any researcher with the interest and some degree of patience should be able to reproduce each of the tables in this book. Nearly all registration and voting statistics by precinct are contained in Boston's *Annual Report of the Board of Election Commissioners*. The only information not available in the election report are the precinct-level votes for electors of president and vice president in 1932, 1936, and 1940; those figures are drawn from the *Boston Globe*. For a fuller discussion of those sources, the reader is referred to Appendix 1.

Several steps were involved in the process of converting raw precinct data into finished table entries. What follows below is a review of that process. That review will be done by describing the genesis of a single line of entries in the two types of tables: the 1928 patterns of voting and party registration for Italians in the North End. The decision to use 1928 and to use North End Italian precincts for the purposes of illustration is a wholly arbitrary one; we could just as easily derive results for 1926 North End Italians or 1922 lower-middle-class Jews or 1940 Yankees or 1932 working-class Irish. Every entry in each of the book's ten tables has been derived in a manner consistent with that shown below.

Our first task is to identify the relevant homogeneous precincts. According to Appendix 2, there were in 1928 two voting precincts which were homogeneously Italian and in the North End. They were Precincts 1 and 2 in Ward 3 (listed as 3: 1, 2). Those two precincts are the source of all the data for the entries being discussed.

Next we calculate the potential electorate. The potential electorate is defined as the number of adult men and women residing in each precinct, as determined in the final "police list," which includes the preliminary as well as supplementary count of residents of voting age. From the *Annual Report of the Board of Election Commissioners,* we obtain these figures:

Ward Pct.	Men	Women	All
3: 1	3,487	2,465	5,952
3: 2	3,006	2,158	5,164
Total	6,493	4,623	11,116

This group of 6,493 men and 4,623 women represented the entire voting-age population of these two heavily Italian, North End precincts in 1928. All of those men and women, whether or not they were citizens and immediately eligible to register and vote, were at least potential members of the active electorate.

The size of the active electorate (for reasons that should be clear in the next paragraph) is defined by the number of men and women registered to vote in the 1928 state primary. For the Italian precincts of the North End, the *Annual Report* listed the following numbers of registered voters:

Ward Pct.	Men	Women
3: 1	836	161
3: 2	881	182
Total	1,717	343

At the time of the state primary, then, the active electorate—the registered voters—of the two precincts consisted of 1,717 men and 343 women.

The *Annual Report* included additional information on these registrants. Drawing on check lists used at the state primary, the *Report* listed, by gender, the number of enrolled members of each political party. This was not a list of those who had actually voted in one or the other party primary, but rather a list of those who were registered to vote at the time of the state primary and had chosen to associate themselves with either the Democratic or Republican party. Patterns of party registration for men and for women in Italian precincts in the North End in 1928 were:

	Men		Women	
Ward Pct.	Dem.	Rep.	Dem.	Rep.
3: 1	478	77	120	8
3: 2	573	54	122	9
Total	1,051	131	242	17

Only for the state primary did the *Report* reveal the stated partisan preferences of Boston's registered voters.

Thus it is the number and composition of registered voters at the time of the state primary which form the foundation of the registration tables in this book. Knowing the total number of voters registered for the state primary and the number of those voters enrolled in either the Democratic or Republican party, we can easily calculate the number of registered voters formally identifying with neither major party. At the state primary in 1928, there were 1,717 men registered to vote in one of the two Italian precincts in the North End; if 1,051 of those men were enrolled as Democrats and 131 were enrolled as Republicans, then there must have been 535 independents, men who were registered to vote but unenrolled in a major political party. Similarly, if 343 women were registered, and 242 of them were Democrats and 17 were Republicans, then 84 women in those precincts were independents.

Since our goal is to express these results as fractions of a potential electorate, we must divide each of those numbers by the total number of voting-age adults in the two precincts. The potential male electorate numbered, it will be recalled, 6,493 persons. Dividing 1,717 registrants, 1,051 Democrats, 131 Republicans, and 535 independents by a potential electorate of 6,493 yields the following result, with all numbers expressed as percentages:

North End Men

Year	All Reg.	Dem.	Rep.	Ind.
1928	26.4	16.2	2.0	8.2

We follow the same procedure for women in these North End precincts, expressing as fractions of a potential electorate of 4,623 women the reported registrants and their party enrollments—343 total registrants, composed of 242 Democrats, 17 Republicans, 84 independents. Thus:

North End Women

Year	All Reg.	Dem.	Rep.	Ind.
1928	7.4	5.2	0.4	1.8

Both sets of numbers, those for men and those for women living in Italian precincts in the North End in 1928, correspond exactly to the appropriate line of entries in table 3.1. We have, then, completed the process of generating one set of entries, expressed as percentages of the potential electorate, for a party registration table.

So now we turn to the table reporting voting returns. We will continue to use the same set of precincts for this example. Again, of course, our potential electorate numbered 11,116 men and women. Unlike registration data, voting data do not discriminate between women and men; only the total vote of the precinct is known.

From the *Annual Report,* we gather the raw votes by precinct for electors of president and vice president in 1928. The vote was reported only for the two major candidates in that election. It was:

Ward Pct.	Hoover/Curtis Rep.	Smith/Robinson Dem.
3: 1	71	1,131
3: 2	67	1,167
Total	138	2,298

To obtain finished table entries, we must divide each of those totals by the potential electorate of 11,116, yielding:

North End Vote for President			
Year	Dem.	Rep.	Other
1928	20.7	1.2	n/a

This is the set of entries in table 3.2 describing the vote for presidential and vice-presidential electors in Italian precincts in the North End in 1928 as a percentage of the potential electorate.

Similar procedures are followed in tabulating the votes for state senator and for the district's representative in Congress. Raw votes are collected from the *Annual Report*:

	Vote for Congressman		Vote for State Senator	
Ward Pct.	E. Donnelly Rep.	J. Douglass Dem.	J. Buckley Dem.	L. Rivoire Rep.
3: 1	73	1,078	1,054	64
3: 2	76	1,072	1,079	61
Total	149	2,150	2,133	125

And, in finished form, with raw vote totals converted into percentages of the potential electorate of 11,116:

	North End Vote for Congressman		North End Vote for State Senator	
Year	Dem.	Rep.	Dem.	Rep.
1928	19.3	1.3	19.2	1.1

These, of course, with the vote for presidential electors, represent a full set of entries in the North End section of table 3.2.

With this discussion, we have succeeded in replicating a sample of each of the main entries composing the ten voting and registration tables in this book. The reader, if she so wishes, should now be able to reconstruct those tables.

There are some exceptions, apparent in the tables themselves, from the relatively straightforward procedure followed in the above model; those exceptions fall into two classes. First, no known record exists of party enrollment figures by precinct in 1932. Curiously, for that year only, the *Annual Report* listed numbers of partisan registrants at the ward, but not precinct, level. Where ethnically homogeneous precincts constituted a substantial part of a single ward—specifically, Ward 14 (Jewish) and Ward 5 (Yankee)—1932 party registration figures are estimated for precincts, using precinct data from 1930 and 1934 and ward data from 1930, 1932, and 1934. In all other cases, no attempt is made to estimate the partisan composition of the body of registered voters in 1932. The second exception concerns the vote in any year when a candidate in part or all of a cluster of precincts ran unopposed. In such cases, no entries appear in the part of the table directly affected. Hence, for example, the gaps in table 3.2: candidates for Congress in both East Boston and the North End ran unopposed in 1926, 1934, and 1938, and a candidate for the state senate in those areas ran unopposed in 1938. Including the votes cast for them in the tables would have obscured long-term trends in the relative appeal of the two parties. That the reader is aware that such gaps represent temporary collapses of two-party competition should be sufficient for the larger purposes of this study. In other cases, such as the vote for congressman among lower-class Irish in 1934, which is omitted from table 6.3, the omission resulted from a situation in which candidates faced opposition in some precincts (in one congressional district) but other candidates ran unopposed in other precincts (in a separate congressional district). Again, a decision was made to report results only when all precincts in a given group had the opportunity to vote for at least two opposing candidates.

That such decisions had to be made is the nearly inevitable result of an attempt to investigate actual voting decisions. The final tables were prepared with care for the data underlying them. As I discuss in the text, there were instances, such as in Jewish precincts during this period, when little can be discerned from particular two-party pairings, and there were instances when two-party pairings were nonexistent. Any statistical portrait of the real world is rife with idiosyncrasy. I have not shielded the reader from that idiosyncrasy, but neither have I abdicated judgment in cases when such circumstances rendered results irrelevant and unintelligible.

Appendix 4

A Note on the Presentation and Analysis of Statistical Data

Research and statistics presented in these pages have allowed us, in the context of electoral realignment, to study differences between men and women, to investigate the relevance of class and ethnicity, to examine the connection between votes for local and for national candidates, and to establish a relationship between patterns of voting and patterns of registration. But there are questions which this book has left unanswered. I am as frustrated as any reader by the limitations that the data set has imposed on certain forms of inquiry and analysis. My purpose in this appendix is simply to acknowledge the validity of such concerns and to describe, for one last time, the original data set. Even as it has been capable of recalling in vivid detail a lost moment in our political history, secrets remain that that data set cannot divulge.

Two basic factors account for these limitations. First, we know almost nothing about each precinct qua precinct. And second, we do not know everything about the larger homogeneous districts of which precincts were a part. While conceptually distinct, the problems overlap considerably in the original sources of data.

In the effort to identify Boston voting precincts that were at once ethnically homogeneous and socioeconomically homogeneous, I was able to locate measures of those variables that, for the 1920s and 1930s, were quite strong and mutually reinforcing. Among the more important resources were censuses; lists by street address of every resident in the city; and community, settlement house, and autobiographical studies. Used together, those sources allowed the identification of small areas within the city of unmistakable homogeneity. From close reading of the data, a general cut-off criterion of 80 or 85 percent seemed to represent accurately the lowest number of Jews or blacks or Italians or Irish or Yankees living in their respective precincts at any point between 1920 and 1940. All precincts were classified as homogeneous or not homogeneous, with no attempt made to fashion a continuous scale between the two poles.

More precise measurements of the relative homogeneity of precincts (whether the comparison is made across time or space) could not be made without straining the bounds of a reasonable use of historical sources. The censuses never measured ethnicity per se. Available surrogates included breakdowns of the population into native-born whites, foreign-born whites, and blacks, and the country of birth for those whites born abroad. And even those data at the level of the census tract are available only for 1930 and 1940—and never are they available at the precinct level. Hence, from censuses, exact measurement of an area's ethnic homogeneity is possible only for blacks in 1930 and 1940, and that possibility cannot be realized because of the incongruence between census tract and precinct lines as well as the fact that too few blacks lived in Boston at the time to be significant in number at the level of the census tract. Only the 1940 census by city block contains enough detail to allow us to know exact proportions of blacks within a given precinct, but we lack such measures for any other year and, standing alone as an explanatory variable, it cannot sensibly be used to explain electoral differences among the four black precincts in 1940. "Police lists" were published annually throughout this period, but from them could be extracted only last names and occupations. To reinforce other sources and provide independent verification of precincts I had chosen or was still considering, the street lists proved quite valuable for each of the white ethnic groups. Still, I do not believe that lists of last names are amenable to the strict quantification of ethnicity. The remaining studies, each done at different times by different groups and in different areas of the city, again provided solid support for my search for homogeneous units but were unsuitable for comparative purposes.

This discussion serves as explanation and excuse for the failure of this work to indicate exactly how homogeneous each of the precincts was at every point in time. It proved possible to filter out homogeneous precincts but not to offer refined measures of degrees of homogeneity. Consequently, we are unable to set up statistical models to measure the effect of slight changes in ethnic concentrations over time or even between different precincts at a single point in time. And the socioeconomic categories, like the distinction between homogeneous and nonhomogeneous precincts, relied on a variety of measures, none of which was ever measured with precision at the precinct level (except for average monthly rent, reported in the 1940 block census) and none of which was measured at any other useful level of aggregation for the full twenty-year period. We do not know enough about individual precincts to distinguish them, on ethnic or socioeconomic terms, from like precincts. What we must be satisfied with is the identification of groups of like precincts. And little evidence exists which would suggest that any group of precincts chosen became substantially more or less homogeneous between 1920 and 1940 or that class divisions within ethnic groups in those precincts were at all correlated to differences in ethnic homogeneity. Although I cannot prove it beyond doubt, I do not believe, for example, that middle-class Irish or Jewish precincts were any less homogeneous than ethnically equivalent working-class precincts. Throughout the process of choosing precincts for analysis, the fact of ethnic homogeneity was established before any attempt was made to place precincts in class-based categories. The classification of precincts as ethnically homogeneous is a project in which I have enormous confidence. We cannot, however, use the vast array of disjointed sources on which I have relied for that project in order to estimate slight differences in the degree of homogeneity over a two-decade period now more than half a century past.

I am also frustrated by the inability of the data to account for residential mobility or to distinguish between generational replacement and the mobilization of former nonvoting adults. Both phenomena are obscured in aggregate data, even when the aggregate is as small as a voting precinct. I do not think, however, that either problem seriously detracts from the conclusions reached in this study.

People, of course, were constantly moving into and out of the precincts under examination. The implicit assumption of the analysis, however, is that such movement, if anything, reinforced the homogeneity of the precinct. People moving into lower-middle-class Jewish precincts tended, I believe, to be lower-middle-class Jews, and those moving out tended to be Jews relocating either to poorer areas of the city or, more likely, to the wealthier suburbs. It is my belief, for which I have located much circumstantial but little quantifiable evidence, that geographic mobility reflected socioeconomic mobility, that the unceasing shifting of populations served to maintain homogeneous aggregates. In political terms, I have assumed that, whatever the changes in individuals who compose otherwise homogeneous precincts, no change in partisan complexion results simply from residential mobility. To assume otherwise would be to measure, not the impact of voter conversion and voter mobilization within homogeneous units, but rather the overwhelming but irrelevant influence of new residents within the boundaries of precincts, which themselves were constantly shifting.

Similarly, at any level of aggregation, generational replacement cannot be differentiated from voter mobilization. What I assume throughout the book is that there is a constant, "regular" level of generational replacement which does not necessarily upset the existing political balance. Only when voters are entering the electorate in greater than that "regular" number or when they are entering with partisan affiliations different from those of voters already in or leaving the active electorate is mobilization, in the sense in which it is used in this book, occurring. I am not interested in those processes by which twenty-one-year-old black Republicans replaced dying black Republicans, as I am not interested, in part because the data are not available, in the processes by which one family of black Republicans moved into a neighborhood of existing families of identical ethnic, socioeconomic, and political characteristics. Our object of investigation is the genuine political change occurring at the aggregate level, which helps us understand better the sorts of changes that could reasonably occur at the level of the individual.

Presumably the phenomena of residential mobility and generational replacement were as important in the 1920s as they were in the 1930s. Yet there is little evidence of political upheaval before 1928 and much evidence of political change in the following decade. Young voters were certainly an important force in the Democratic coalition that took form in the 1930s, but those voters were only one part of a larger story of mobilization and conversion which resulted in that realignment. As residential and generational changes did not disturb the stable political arrangements which still prevailed into the 1920s, so they probably did not directly effect the realignments of the 1930s.

For a generation of political scientists raised in the age of the Gallup poll and the exhaustive, detailed federal census, my estimates of ethnic concentration and socioeconomic status must appear somewhat crude. They are admittedly blunt instruments in a field now used to greater sophistication. In an ideal world, we would have at our disposal carefully calibrated measurements, taken annually, of a variety of variables. But records of the past are rarely so obliging. Ethnicity—as well as socioeconomic status and neighborhood—could not be measured along a scale of values. This is a weakness of an attempt to isolate homogeneous voting units rather than to perform regression analysis over many unsifted units. It is, too, of course, the great strength of the work. The use of homogeneous precincts has permitted us to view actual, rather than inferred, voting behavior, and to probe deeply the environments in which many, often similar, individual decisions were being made.

Notes

Chapter One

1. Walter Dean Burnham, ''The Changing Shape of the American Political Universe,'' *American Political Science Review,* vol. 59, no. 1 (March 1965), pp. 22–23.

2. Burnham, ''Changing Shape,'' pp. 12, 10, 23; Walter Dean Burnham, *Critical Elections and the Mainsprings of American Politics* (New York: W. W. Norton, 1970), p. 71.

3. See Richard L. McCormick, *The Party Period and Public Policy* (New York: Oxford University Press, 1986).

4. See ibid.; quotes are from pp. 200, 202.

5. Ibid., p. 182.

6. See V. O. Key, Jr., ''A Theory of Critical Elections,'' *Journal of Politics,* vol. 17, no. 1 (February 1955).

7. V. O. Key, Jr., *Politics, Parties, and Pressure Groups* (New York: Thomas Y. Crowell, 1942), pp. 263, 270, 272. On p. 270, Key quotes from A. N. Holcombe in Logan, *The American Political Scene,* rev. ed. (New York: Harper, 1938), p. 280.

8. Key, *Politics, Parties, and Pressure Groups,* 1st ed., p. 263n; Charles A. Beard, *The American Party Battle* (New York: Macmillan, 1928), pp. 6, 29, 140, 135–36, 146.

9. Cortez A. M. Ewing, *Presidential Elections* (Norman: University of Oklahoma Press, 1940), pp. 41, 1, 15.

10. Wilfred E. Binkley, *American Political Parties* (New York: Alfred A. Knopf, 1943), pp. viii, 378, 381, 385, also 379.

11. Samuel Lubell, *The Future of American Politics* (New York: Harper and Brothers, 1952), p. 3.

12. Ibid., pp. 2, 1, 2–3, 4.

13. Ibid., pp. 29, 35, 43. Samuel J. Eldersveld had earlier recognized the importance of major cities to the success of the Democratic party in presidential elections since 1932. See Eldersveld, ''The Influence of Metropolitan Party Pluralities in Presidential Elections since 1920,'' *American Political Science Review,* vol. 43, no. 6 (December 1949), pp. 1189–1206.

14. V. O. Key, Jr., ''The Future of the Democratic Party,'' *Virginia Quarterly Review,* vol. 28, no. 2 (Spring 1952), pp. 161, 163.

15. Ibid., pp. 165, 166, 164.

16. Key, ''Critical Elections,'' pp. 4, 4n, 11.

17. Ibid., pp. 4, 7, 9, 16, 11n.

18. Ibid., pp. 4, 16n.

19. E. E. Schattschneider, "United States: The Functional Approach to Party Government," in *Modern Political Parties: Approaches to Comparative Politics*, ed. Sigmund Neumann (Chicago: University of Chicago Press, 1956), pp. 214, 215.

20. Ibid., pp. 196–97, 206, 201–2, 208. Quotation from p. 208 is italicized in original.

21. V. O. Key, Jr., "Secular Realignment and the Party System," *Journal of Politics*, vol. 21, no. 2 (May 1959), pp. 198–99, 208–9.

22. Wilfred E. Binkley, *American Political Parties*, 3d ed. (New York: Alfred A. Knopf, 1958), pp. 395–96; V. O. Key, Jr., *Politics, Parties, & Pressure Groups*, 5th ed. (New York: Thomas Y. Crowell, 1964), pp. 170, 187.

23. Key, "Critical Elections," p. 17n.

24. Angus Campbell, Philip E. Converse, Warren E. Miller, and Donald E. Stokes, *The American Voter* (New York: John Wiley and Sons, 1960), pp. 531, 532–33, 534, 535–36; Angus Campbell, Philip E. Converse, Warren E. Miller, and Donald E. Stokes, *Elections and the Political Order* (New York: John Wiley and Sons, 1966), pp. 63–77; Gerald Pomper, "Classification of Presidential Elections," *Journal of Politics*, vol. 29, no. 3 (August 1967), pp. 537, 562.

25. William Nisbet Chambers, "Party Development and the American Mainstream," in *The American Party Systems*, ed. William Nisbet Chambers and Walter Dean Burnham (New York: Oxford University Press, 1967), pp. 4, 7; Walter Dean Burnham, "Party Systems and the Political Process," in Chambers and Burnham, *American Party Systems*, pp. 277, 278.

26. Burnham, *Critical Elections*, pp. 32–33, 181.

27. Duncan MacRae, Jr., and James A. Meldrum, "Critical Elections in Illinois: 1888–1958," in *Electoral Change and Stability*, ed. Jerome M. Clubb and Howard W. Allen (New York: The Free Press, 1971), pp. 67, 53, 61; John M. Allswang, *A House for All Peoples* (Lexington, Kentucky: University Press of Kentucky, 1971), p. 207; Carl N. Degler, "American Political Parties and the Rise of the City: An Interpretation," in Clubb and Allen, *Electoral Change and Stability*, p. 135; John L. Shover, "Was 1928 a Critical Election in California?" in Clubb and Allen, *Electoral Change and Stability*, pp. 218, 232; Jerome M. Clubb and Howard W. Allen, "The Cities and the Election of 1928: Partisan Realignment?" *American Historical Review*, vol. 74, no. 4 (April 1969), p. 1218.

28. Allan J. Lichtman, "Critical Election Theory and the Reality of American Presidential Politics, 1916–1940," *American Historical Review*, vol. 81, no. 2 (April 1976), p. 320; Walter Dean Burnham, Jerome M. Clubb, and William H. Flanigan, "Partisan Realignment: A Systemic Perspective," in *The History of American Electoral Behavior*, ed. Joel H. Silbey, Allan G. Bogue, and William H. Flanigan (Princeton: Princeton University Press, 1978), p. 49; Lee Benson, Joel H. Silbey, and Phyllis F. Field, "Toward a Theory of Stability and Change in American Voting Patterns: New York State, 1792–1970," in Silbey et al., *History of American Electoral Behavior*, pp. 81, 103; Jerome M. Clubb, William H. Flanigan, and Nancy H. Zingale, *Partisan Realignment* (Beverly Hills: Sage Publications, 1980), p. 31.

29. David Burner, *The Politics of Provincialism* (New York: Alfred A. Knopf, 1967), p. xi; James L. Sundquist, *Dynamics of the Party System* (Washington, D.C.: The Brookings Institution, 1973), pp. 200, 203, 202; Everett Carll Ladd, Jr., with Charles D. Hadley, *Transformations of the American Party System* (New York: W. W. Norton, 1975), pp. 31–87; Lubell, *Future of American Politics,* p. 29.

30. Key, ''Future of the Democratic Party,'' pp. 166, 165; Degler, ''American Political Parties,'' p. 141; Charles Sellers, ''The Equilibrium Cycle in Two-Party Politics,'' in Clubb and Allen, *Electoral Change and Stability,* p. 159; Burner, *Politics of Provincialism,* pp. 228, 229.

31. Burnham, *Critical Elections,* pp. 6, 92; Sundquist, *Dynamics,* 1st ed., p. 181; James L. Sundquist, *Dynamics of the Party System,* rev. ed. (Washington, D.C.: The Brookings Institution, 1983), pp. 197, 230, 199.

32. Ladd and Hadley, *Transformations,* 1st ed., pp. 78, 82; Kristi Andersen, ''Generation, Partisan Shift, and Realignment: A Glance Back to the New Deal,'' in Norman H. Nie, Sidney Verba, and John R. Petrocik, *The Changing American Voter,* enlarged ed. (Cambridge: Harvard University Press, 1979), p. 75.

33. Kristi Andersen, *The Creation of a Democratic Majority, 1928–1936* (Chicago: University of Chicago Press, 1979), p. xiii.

34. Andersen, ''Generation, Partisan Shift, and Realignment,'' pp. 75n, 74–75; Andersen, *Creation,* pp. xii, 4, 16, 4–5.

35. Andersen, *Creation,* p. 117.

36. Andersen, *Creation,* p. 97; Lawrence H. Fuchs, *The Political Behavior of American Jews* (Glencoe, Ill.: The Free Press, 1956), p. 209; Sundquist, *Dynamics,* rev. ed., pp. 235n, 239; Clubb and Allen, ''Cities and the Election of 1928,'' p. 1219.

37. Lubell, *Future of American Politics,* pp. 4, 6, 51, 52, 54.

38. See Key, ''Critical Elections''; Key, ''Secular Realignment.''

39. Burner, *Politics of Provincialism,* pp. 242–43, 253–55; [United States Department of Commerce, Bureau of the Census, and?] Boston Health Department, ''Census Tract Data [for Boston]: 1930 Census.'' Compare precincts examined by Burner with those listed in Appendix 2.

40. See Allswang, *House;* quotes are from p. 3.

41. See Andersen, *Creation,* esp. pp. xv, 87, 93, 100, 106–10, 116–20.

42. Ibid., p. 101.

43. See Key, ''Critical Elections''; Lubell, *Future of American Politics,* pp. 35, 40, 50.

44. Two good studies of Boston politics in that era are J. Joseph Huthmacher, *Massachusetts People and Politics, 1919–1933* (Cambridge: The Belknap Press of Harvard University Press, 1959) and Charles H. Trout, *Boston, the Great Depression, and the New Deal* (New York: Oxford University Press, 1977). Many other sources are referred to in the text or included in the bibliography.

Chapter Two

1. ''Jews in a New World,'' *Boston Globe,* 17–21 February 1985, rpt., p. 6.

2. Fuchs, *Political Behavior,* p. 210; Key, ''Secular Realignment,'' p. 207; Everett Carll Ladd, Jr., with Charles D. Hadley, *Transformations of the American Party System,* 2d ed. (New York: W. W. Norton, 1978), p. 61.

3. United States Department of Commerce, Bureau of the Census, *Fourteenth Census of the United States, Taken in the Year 1920,* vol. 3, *Population, 1920—Composition and Characteristics of the Population, by States* (Washington, D.C.: Government Printing Office, 1922), p. 457; "Census Tract Data: 1930 Census," Tables I and II; United States Department of Commerce, Bureau of the Census, *16th Census of the United States, 1940, Population and Housing—Statistics for Census Tracts—Boston, Mass.* (Washington, D.C.: Government Printing Office, 1942), pp. 4, 26, hereafter cited as Census, *1940—Census Tracts* [United States Department of Commerce, Bureau of the Census, and Boston Council of Social Agencies?], "Country of Origin of Foreign Stock, Boston: 1940" (1944).

4. Isaac M. Fein, *Boston—Where It All Began* ([Boston?]: Boston Jewish Bicentennial Committee, 1976), p. 36; Francis Russell, *The Great Interlude* (New York: McGraw-Hill, 1964), p. 92; *American Jewish Yearbook,* 5679 (Philadelphia: The Jewish Publication Society of America, 1918), p. 49; *American Jewish Yearbook,* 5689 (1928), p. 108; Jewish Welfare Board, "Study of the Jewish Community of Greater Boston, Massachusetts" (New York: Jewish Welfare Board, 1940), Table 2 on p. 37. Compare Jewish Welfare Board, "Study of the Jewish Community," pp. 6–7, to Bureau of Jewish Social Research, "Jewish Communal Survey of Boston" (New York: Bureau of Jewish Social Research, 1930), pp. 1–3. The population estimates for 1930 and 1940 presented in the text are not drawn directly from the community studies published in those years. As the authors of the 1940 study revised, with the benefit of greater information, the calculations of ten years before, so does hindsight allow critical evaluation of that second study. The basis for the new figures are data from the federal censuses and the community studies reporting the number of schoolchildren in the population. Using census data from tracts T-6, T-7, and U-6 (all homogeneously Jewish and containing the heart of Boston's Jewish community), it was found that the proportion of the population between ages 5 and 14 declined from 16.5 percent in 1930 to 13.7 percent in 1940. This information, combined with the number of absences from school on Yom Kippur as contained in the 1940 study, yielded the figures in the text. Compared with the estimates in the 1940 study, the figure for 1930 remains practically intact, while that for 1940 is revised upward.

5. Huthmacher, *Massachusetts People and Politics,* pp. 9; "Jews in a New World," p. 5; John F. Stack, Jr., *International Conflict in an American City: Boston's Irish, Italians, and Jews, 1935–1944* (Westport, Conn.: Greenwood Press, 1979), pp. 153, 35.

6. Fein, *Boston—Where It All Began,* p. 50; Robert A. Woods, ed., *Americans in Process* (1902; rpt. New York: Arno Press and The New York Times, 1970), pp. 40, 44, map after 40; Paula J. Todisco, *Boston's First Neighborhood* (Boston: Boston Public Library, 1976), pp. 29, 30; William M. DeMarco, *Ethnics and Enclaves* (Ann Arbor: UMI Research Press, 1981), pp. 27–28; City of Boston, City Planning Board, *East Boston,* 1915 Public Document no. 116, ed. George Gibbs, Jr. (Boston: City of Boston Printing Department, 1916), p. 57; Robert A. Woods and Albert J. Kennedy, eds., *The Zone of Emergence,* abridged and edited by Sam B. Warner, Jr. (Cambridge: Harvard University Press, 1962), pp. 109, 161; Robert A. Woods, ed., *The City*

Wilderness (Boston: Houghton Mifflin 1898), pp. 36, 39–41; Frederick A. Bushee, *Ethnic Factors in the Population of Boston* (New York: Macmillan, 1903), p. 25.

7. Woods, *Americans in Process,* pp. 40, 43, 265, 381, and map after p. 46; Fein, *Boston—Where It All Began,* p. 50; Thomas H. O'Connor, *Bibles, Brahmins, and Bosses: A Short History of Boston* (Boston: Trustees of the Public Library of the City of Boston, 1976), p. 94; John Daniels, *In Freedom's Birthplace: A Study of the Boston Negroes* (1914; rpt. New York: Arno Press and The New York Times, 1969), pp. 144–45; Bushee, *Ethnic Factors,* pp. 25, 30; Boston Tercentenary Committee, *Fifty Years of Boston: A Memorial Volume,* ed. Elisabeth M. Herlihy (Boston: [Boston Tercentenary Committee?], 1932), p. 63.

8. [United States Department of Commerce, Bureau of the Census, and Boston Council of Social Agencies?], "Census Tract Population—Boston, [1910–1940]"; O'Connor, *Bibles, Brahmins, and Bosses,* p. 94; Woods and Kennedy, *Zone* (1962), pp. 120–21; Russell, *Great Interlude,* pp. 88, 92–94; Maurice Baskin, "Ward Boss Politics in Boston: 1896–1921," A.B. thesis, Harvard University (March 1975), p. 19; Huthmacher, *Massachusetts People and Politics,* p. 9; Fein, *Boston—Where It All Began,* p. 50; Bureau of Jewish Social Research, "Jewish Communal Survey," p. 3; Sam Bass Warner, Jr., *Streetcar Suburbs,* 2d ed. (Cambridge: Harvard University Press, 1978), p. 113.

9. Ben Rosen, *The Trend of Jewish Population in Boston* (Boston: Federated Jewish Charities, 1921), pp. 12, 18; Woods, *Americans in Process,* p. 44; Todisco, *Boston's First Neighborhood,* pp. 29–30, 33; Bureau of Jewish Social Research, "Jewish Communal Survey," pp. 1–3; Boston, City Planning Board, *East Boston,* pp. 57–59; Woods and Kennedy, *Zone* (1962), pp. 85, 90–91, 161, 174; Census, *1920,* p. 457; Daniels, *In Freedom's Birthplace,* pp. 145–47.

10. Baskin, "Ward Boss Politics," p. 103; Huthmacher, *Massachusetts People and Politics,* p. 9; Rosen, *Trend of Jewish Population,* pp. 12–13, 18; Boston Tercentenary Committee, *Fifty Years of Boston,* p. 63; Census, *1920,* p. 457; Bureau of Jewish Social Research, "Jewish Communal Survey," pp. 1–3; Jewish Welfare Board, "Study of the Jewish Community," Table 2 on p. 37; City of Boston, Listing Board, *List of Residents 20 Years of Age and Over,* 1920–1940 (Boston: City of Boston Printing Department, 1920–1940), 1940, Wards 3 and 5.

11. The Combined Jewish Appeal, *Fifty Years of Jewish Philanthropy in Greater Boston, 1895–1945* (Boston: The Combined Jewish Appeal, 1945), pp. 11–13, 35, 45, 51; Fein, *Boston—Where It All Began,* p. 61; *American Jewish Yearbook,* 5680 (1919), pp. 388–90.

12. Rosen, *Trend of Jewish Population,* pp. 11–13, 17–18, 21, 25; Boston, Listing Board, *List of Residents,* 1920–1940; Bureau of Jewish Social Research, "Jewish Communal Survey," pp. 2–3.

13. Russell, *Great Interlude,* pp. 88, 94, 96, 100, 102; Fuchs, *Political Behavior,* p. 84. See also Russell, *Great Interlude,* pp. 1–2, 86–88, 92–103, 109.

14. These figures are based on census data from 1920, 1930, and 1940, for the census tracts enclosed within 1920 ward lines. For this analysis, Ward 16 is "Roxbury," Wards 18 and 19 together are "northern Dorchester," and Ward 21 is "southern Dorchester and Mattapan." Since the overwhelming majority of Jews living

within those ward lines were residents of the area from which precincts were chosen, it seems fair to use the ward estimate of Jewish population as an approximation for that part of the ward actually of interest. To determine the Jewish populations of the three districts, several sets of data and a variety of sources were consulted. Especially important were the 1930 and 1940 studies of Boston's Jewish community. Although the final population estimates contained in those studies were not used, their method and raw statistics greatly influenced the numbers cited in the text. From the two studies and from federal censuses were drawn total populations of homogeneous census tracts, school-age populations within the districts, public school absences on Yom Kippur in 1929 and 1938, persons born in Eastern Europe, and a variety of other cross-reinforcing measures. See Census, *1920,* p. 457; "Census Tract Data: 1930 Census," Table II; Census, *1940—Census Tracts,* Table 3, pp. 26–52; Jewish Welfare Board, "Study of the Jewish Community," pp. 2–15, esp. 12, Table 2 on p. 37; Russell, *Great Interlude,* p. 109; Rosen, *Trend of Jewish Population,* p. 18; Bureau of Jewish Social Research, "Jewish Communal Survey," pp. 1–3; Boston Tercentenary Committee, *Fifty Years of Boston,* p. 63. See also note 4 above.

15. Jewish Welfare Board, "Study of the Jewish Community," pp. 17–23, esp. 20; Russell, *Great Interlude,* pp. 94–103, 109; Rosen, *Trend of Jewish Population,* pp. 11–12, 17–18; Stack, *International Conflict,* pp. 35, 57, 100, 153; Fuchs, *Political Behavior,* p. 84; Stephan Thernstrom, *The Other Bostonians* (Cambridge: Harvard University Press, 1973), pp. 136–37, 152, 171–75.

16. "Census Tract Data: 1930 Census"; Census, *1940—Census Tracts;* Russell, *Great Interlude,* pp. 93–94. For exact precincts chosen (which obviously did not coincide perfectly with census tract boundaries), another report was consulted for statistics on average monthly rent: United States Department of Commerce, Bureau of the Census, *16th Census of the United States, 1940, Housing—Block Statistics—Boston,* Supplement to the First Series/Housing Bulletin for Massachusetts (Washington, D.C.: Government Printing Office, 1942), hereafter cited as Census, *1940—Blocks.*

17. "Census Tract Data: 1930 Census"; Census, *1940—Census Tracts;* Warner, *Streetcar Suburbs,* pp. 53, 69, 106–16, esp. 106, 114. See footnote 16 above for method of choosing precincts.

18. For discussion of role played by Irish anti-Semitism in causing Jews to become Republicans, see Russell, *Great Interlude,* p. 97; Woods, *Americans in Process,* p. 159; Fuchs, *Political Behavior,* pp. 57, 209; Stack, *International Conflict,* pp. 57, 70, 153. For more general treatment of Jewish realignment and causes behind it, see Burner, *Politics of Provincialism,* pp. 239–42; Ladd and Hadley, *Transformations,* 2d ed., pp. 61–64, 85, 115; Fuchs, *Political Behavior,* pp. 50–51, 72–73; "Jews in a New World," pp. 6, 8; Allswang, *House,* p. 52; Campbell et al., *American Voter,* pp. 159–60.

19. Lubell, *Future of American Politics,* p. 52; Ladd and Hadley, *Transformations,* 2d ed., pp. 63–64, 116; Fuchs, *Political Behavior,* pp. 74, 76.

20. Fuchs, *Political Behavior,* p. 84; Ladd and Hadley, *Transformations,* 2d ed., p. 115; Norman H. Nie, Sidney Verba, and John R. Petrocik, *The Changing American Voter* (Cambridge: Harvard University Press, 1976), p. 229; "Jews in a New World," p. 7.

21. Allswang, *House,* pp. 183, 186–87.

22. Woods, *Americans in Process*, p. 160.

23. Woods and Kennedy, *Zone* (1962), p. 122.

24. Key, ''Critical Elections,'' p. 4.

25. Ladd and Hadley, *Transformations*, 2d ed., pp. 61–62; Burner, *Politics of Provincialism*, p. 240; Fuchs, *Political Behavior*, pp. 129–30; Allswang, *House*, p. 56; Key, ''Critical Elections,'' pp. 5–6; Andersen, *Creation*, pp. 103–5.

26. See Andersen, *Creation*, p. 118, and Sundquist, *Dynamics*, rev. ed., p. 233. Five percent over four years as a mortality estimate falls between their two assumptions and actually would strengthen both their calculations in their own favor.

27. Key, ''Critical Elections,'' pp. 3–11, 16; Burner, *Politics of Provincialism*, pp. 240–42; Andersen, *Creation*, p. 100; Sundquist, *Dynamics*, rev. ed., p. 219; Huthmacher, *Massachusetts People and Politics*, p. 260.

28. Lutz Erbring, Norman H. Nie, and Edward Hamburg, with Nancy Dobrozdravic, ''Realignments in the American Party System,'' paper presented to the American Political Science Association Meeting, Chicago, August 1983, p. 25. ''NEW ETHNIC'' is capitalized in original.

29. *Boston Herald*, 7 November 1928, as cited in Huthmacher, *Massachusetts People and Politics*, p. 190.

Chapter Three

1. Allswang, *House*, pp. 55, 77–79; Sundquist, *Dynamics*, rev. ed., p. 219.

2. Lubell, *Future of American Politics*, pp. 40, 68, 70–71, 73.

3. Boston Tercentenary Committee, *Fifty Years of Boston*, p. 68; Stack, *International Conflict*, p. 37; Huthmacher, *Massachusetts People and Politics*, pp. 10, 13; Gustave Ralph Serino, ''Italians in the Political Life of Boston,'' Ph.D. thesis, Harvard University, pp. 17–18, 20–21.

4. Stack, *International Conflict*, p. 31; Huthmacher, *Massachusetts People and Politics*, pp. 93–94; Burner, *Politics of Provincialism*, p. 17.

5. Huthmacher, *Massachusetts People and Politics*, p. 11; DeMarco, *Ethnics and Enclaves*, p. 45; Archdiocese of Boston, Church Census, selected parishes, 1910–1940; Woods, *Americans in Process*, pp. 268, 270–72.

6. Thernstrom, *Other Bostonians*, pp. 135–36, 140, 162–63, 168–71; Stack, *International Conflict*, pp. 37, 149.

7. Woods, *Americans in Process*, p. 268.

8. City of Boston, City Planning Board, *The North End*, 1919 Public Document no. 40 (Boston: City of Boston Printing Department, 1919), p. 1; Todisco, *Boston's First Neighborhood*, pp. 29, 33; Woods, *Americans in Process*, pp. 40, 44; Serino, ''Italians,'' p. 22; DeMarco, *Ethnics and Enclaves*, pp. 1, 107; John Anthony Piccione, ''Naturalization, Ethnic Intermarriage, and Education as Measures of Acculturation: The Italian-American Community in Boston, 1890–1940,'' A.B. thesis, Harvard University (March 1980), p. 1.

9. DeMarco, *Ethnics and Enclaves*, pp. 21, 23–24, 29, 107–8; Woods, *Americans in Process*, pp. 40, 44, 381; Bushee, *Ethnic Factors*, pp. 25–26, 28; O'Connor, *Bibles, Brahmins, and Bosses*, p. 94; Todisco, *Boston's First Neighborhood*, pp. 33, 45; ''Census Tract Data: 1930 Census,'' Table I; Census, *1940—Census Tracts*, Table

1 on p. 4; Serino, ''Italians,'' pp. 10, 11; Piccione, ''Naturalization,'' p. 3; Rosen, *Trend of Jewish Population,* p. 18; ''Census Tract Population—Boston, [1910–1940].''

10. Huthmacher, *Massachusetts People and Politics,* p. 9; Piccione, ''Naturalization,'' pp. 3, 12; Boston, City Planning Board, *East Boston,* pp. 57–58; Woods and Kennedy, *Zone* (1962), pp. 159–61, 174; Serino, ''Italians,'' p. 24.

11. Woods and Kennedy, *Zone* (1962), pp. 158–61, 165–66, 179; Boston, City Planning Board, *East Boston,* p. 58; Federated Jewish Charities, *Annual Report,* 1918–1919 (Boston: Federated Jewish Charities, 1919), scanned list of contributors for those with East Boston addresses; Serino, ''Italians,'' pp. 11, 24, 27; Boston Tercentenary Committee, *Fifty Years of Boston,* p. 63; Rosen, *Trend of Jewish Population,* p. 18. Population estimates based on Census, *1920,* p. 457; ''Census Tract Data: 1930 Census,'' Tables I and II; Census, *1940—Census Tracts,* Table 1, on p. 4, and Table 3, on pp. 27–28.

12. O'Connor, *Bibles, Brahmins, and Bosses,* pp. 104, 107–8; Huthmacher, *Massachusetts People and Politics,* pp. 15–16; Russell, *Great Interlude,* pp. 166, 169–70, 173; Serino, ''Italians,'' pp. 24–25, 39.

13. Huthmacher, *Massachusetts People and Politics,* pp. 15–16; Serino, ''Italians,'' pp. 40–42; Woods, *Americans in Process,* p. 158.

14. Woods, *Americans in Process,* pp. 64, 159; Serino, ''Italians,'' pp. 46, 74; Baskin, ''Ward Boss Politics,'' p. 103.

15. Lubell, *Future of American Politics,* pp. 34–35; Andersen, *Creation,* pp. 100, 109; Sundquist, *Dynamics,* rev. ed., p. 215; Allswang, *House,* pp. 56, 207; Serino, ''Italians,'' pp. 42, 45, 48, 69; Burner, *Politics of Provincialism,* p. 242; Huthmacher, *Massachusetts People and Politics,* pp. 164–67, 173, 260; Key, ''Critical Elections,'' pp. 4–5, 7, 9.

16. Lubell, *Future of American Politics,* p. 40; Burner, *Politics of Provincialism,* p. 229; Andersen, *Creation,* p. 9.

17. Burner, *Politics of Provincialism,* pp. 242–43; Stack, *International Conflict,* pp. 83, 115–16; Lubell, *Future of American Politics,* pp. 52, 212; Erbring et al., ''Realignments,'' p. 26; Serino, ''Italians,'' p. 78.

18. Burner, *Politics of Provincialism,* pp. 236, 242–43.

19. See, for a similar point nationally, Lutz Erbring, Norman H. Nie, and Edward Hamburg, with Nancy Dobrozdravic, ''Electoral Participation in America: Looking Back,'' paper prepared for the Conference on Analyzing Declining Voter Turnout in America, at the University of Chicago, April 1984, p. 14.

20. Piccione, ''Naturalization,'' p. 2; Bushee, *Ethnic Factors,* p. 36; Woods, *Americans in Process,* p. 51.

21. Key, ''Critical Elections,'' p. 4.

22. Key, ''Secular Realignment,'' pp. 208–9; Lubell, *Future of American Politics,* pp. 73–74; Massachusetts Acts of 1936, Chapter 180, as cited by the Office of the Secretary of the Commonwealth.

Chapter Four

1. Daniels, *In Freedom's Birthplace,* p. 293.
2. Ibid., pp. 294–95.

3. Ibid., pp. 294, 295, 298.

4. Ladd and Hadley, *Transformations,* 2d ed., pp. 58–60, 85. See also Campbell et al., *American Voter,* p. 160.

5. Burner, *Politics of Provincialism,* pp. 237–39, 241–42.

6. Lubell, *Future of American Politics,* pp. 48, 53.

7. Andersen, *Creation,* pp. 100–101, 105–6; Sundquist, *Dynamics,* rev. ed., p. 232.

8. Erbring et al., ''Realignments,'' p. 36; Sundquist, *Dynamics,* rev. ed. p. 219.

9. Erbring et al., ''Realignments,'' pp. 36–37. ''BLACK'' is capitalized in original.

10. Erbring et al., ''Electoral Participation,'' p. 15.

11. Thernstrom, *Other Bostonians,* pp. 178–80.

12. Elizabeth Hafkin Pleck, *Black Migration and Poverty: Boston, 1865–1900* (New York: Academic Press, 1979), pp. 77–80; Woods, *City Wilderness,* p. 44.

13. Bushee, *Ethnic Factors,* pp. 25–27; Adelaide Cromwell Hill, ''The Negro Upper Class in Boston—Its Development and Present Social Structure,'' Ph.D. thesis, Radcliffe College (1952), p. 374; Rheable M. Edwards and Laura B. Morris, with Robert M. Coard, *The Negro in Boston* (Boston: Action for Boston Community Development, 1961), pp. 7–18; Pleck, *Black Migration,* pp. 31–33, 79–80; Woods and Kennedy, *Zone* (1962), pp. 85, 89; Woods, *Americans in Process,* p. 45; Woods, *City Wilderness,* pp. 44–45; O'Connor, *Bibles, Brahmins, and Bosses,* pp. 143–44; Daniels, *In Freedom's Birthplace,* pp. 143–49, 152, 192–97, 231.

14. Daniels, *In Freedom's Birthplace,* pp. 146–47; Robert A. Woods and Albert J. Kennedy, *The Zone of Emergence,* abridged and edited by Sam Bass Warner, Jr., 2d ed. (Cambridge: M.I.T. Press, 1969), p. 125; Russell, *Great Interlude,* p. 88; Boston Tercentenary Committee, *Fifty Years of Boston,* p. 63; Census, *1920;* ''Census Tract Data: 1930 Census''; Census, *1940—Census Tracts.*

15. Thernstrom, *Other Bostonians,* p. 194; ''Census Tract Data: 1930 Census.''

16. Edwards and Morris, *Negro in Boston,* p. 18; Pleck, *Black Migration,* p. 80; Woods and Kennedy, *Zone* (1962), p. 89; O'Connor, *Bibles, Brahmins, and Bosses,* p. 143; Daniels, *In Freedom's Birthplace,* pp. 145–49, 152, 192–97, 231; Census, *1940–Blocks.*

17. For Congress, the Republican candidate received a 20.3 percent share of the potential electorate in 1932 and a 26.2 percent share in 1936. (He was unopposed in 1934.) Republican support for the state senate fluctuated wildly throughout the two decades, but there is no noticeable loss of support in the 1930s. The Republican share was 17.6 percent in 1932, 12.1 percent in 1934, and 15.5 percent in 1936.

18. Daniels, *In Freedom's Birthplace,* p. 284.

Chapter Five

1. Michael E. Hennessy, *Four Decades of Massachusetts Politics, 1890–1935* (Norwood, Mass.: The Norwood Press, 1935), pp. 27, 59, 140, 142, 145, 147, 242, 285, 292, 299, 314; Huthmacher, *Massachusetts People and Politics,* pp. 34–40; Walter Firey, *Land Use in Central Boston* (Cambridge: Harvard University Press, 1947), pp. 71–72; Cleveland Amory, *The Proper Bostonians* (New York: E. P.

Dutton, 1947), pp. 12–13; *Social Register: Boston, 1920,* vol. 34, no. 5 (New York: Social Register Association, November 1919); *Social Register: Boston, 1930,* vol. 44, no. 5 (New York: Social Register Association, November 1929); *Dictionary of American Biography* (New York: Charles Scribner's Sons, 1928 to date).

2. Hennessy, *Four Decades,* pp. 298–301, 318–22.

3. Hennessy, *Four Decades,* pp. 314–15, 330, 343–48, 358–60, 387, 397–98, 416, 427, 532; Huthmacher, *Massachusetts People and Politics,* pp. 16–17; Amory, *Proper Bostonians,* p. 142; Russell, *Great Interlude,* p. 206. Ancestries and standing in society are confirmed in the *Social Register, Dictionary of American Biography,* and *The National Cyclopedia of American Biography* (New York and Clifton, N.J.: James T. White, 1898 to date).

4. This characterization of Beacon Hill and the Back Bay, as the discussion below will demonstrate, applies most accurately to that portion of the population most likely to register and vote.

5. Russell, *Great Interlude,* pp. 162–64; Peter K. Eisinger, *The Politics of Displacement: Racial and Ethnic Transition in Three American Cities* (New York: Academic Press, 1980), pp. 29–30, 34–35, 40–41; Helen Howe, *The Gentle Americans, 1864–1960: Biography of a Breed* (New York: Harper and Row, 1965), p. 98; William V. Shannon, *The American Irish,* rev. ed. (New York: Macmillan, 1966), p. 183; Huthmacher, *Massachusetts People and Politics,* p. 7; O'Connor, *Bibles, Brahmins, and Bosses,* pp. 86–87; Boston Tercentenary Committee, *Fifty Years of Boston,* p. 83; Walter Muir Whitehill, *Boston in the Age of John Fitzgerald Kennedy* (Norman: University of Oklahoma Press, 1966), pp. 21, 35; Works Progress Administration, Federal Writers' Project, *Massachusetts: A Guide to Its Places and People,* American Guide Series (Boston: Houghton Mifflin, 1937), p. 136; Raymond E. Wolfinger, "The Development and Persistence of Ethnic Voting," *American Political Science Review,* vol. 59, no. 4 (December 1965), pp. 897–98.

6. Russell, *Great Interlude,* p. 164; Eisinger, *Politics of Displacement,* p. 30; Oscar Handlin, *Boston's Immigrants, 1790–1865: A Study in Acculturation* (Cambridge: Harvard University Press, 1941), p. 183; Shannon, *American Irish,* p. 183; Huthmacher, *Massachusetts People and Politics,* p. 12; Stack, *International Conflict,* pp. 21–23; Barbara Miller Solomon, *Ancestors and Immigrants: A Changing New England Tradition* (Chicago: University of Chicago Press, 1956), p. 60; Arthur Mann, *Yankee Reformers in the Urban Age* (Cambridge: The Belknap Press of Harvard University Press, 1954), p. 7; Amory, *Proper Bostonians,* pp. 23, 248–49; John P. Marquand, *The Late George Apley: A Novel in the Form of a Memoir* (Boston: Little, Brown, 1938), pp. 98, 323.

7. Russell, *Great Interlude,* pp. 91, 165–212, esp. 193; O'Connor, *Bibles, Brahmins, and Bosses,* pp. 93–97, 117–23, esp. 122; Boston Tercentenary Committee, *Fifty Years of Boston,* p. 83; Eisinger, *Politics of Displacement,* pp. 17, 29–54; Trout, *Boston,* pp. 21, 27–28, 43, 275; Shannon, *American Irish,* p. 198; Stack, *International Conflict,* pp. 22, 29, 33, 151–52; Solomon, *Ancestors and Immigrants,* p. 153; Ronald P. Formisano and Constance K. Burns, eds., *Boston, 1700–1980: The Evolution of Urban Politics* (Westport, Conn.: Greenwood Press, 1984), pp. 115, 266–68, 275; Robert A. Dahl, *Who Governs? Democracy and Power in an American*

City (New Haven: Yale University Press, 1961), pp. 64, 66, 68, 233–34, 237; Wolfinger, "Ethnic Voting," p. 899; Marquand, *The Late George Apley,* pp. 149, 181–85; Samuel Eliot Morison, *One Boy's Boston, 1887–1901* (Boston: Houghton Mifflin, 1962), pp. 64, 68–69; Whitehill, *Age of JFK,* pp. 21, 41; Amory, *Proper Bostonians,* pp. 14–15, 30; Peter R. Knights, *The Plain People of Boston, 1830–1860: A Study in City Growth* (New York: Oxford University Press, 1971), p. 120.

8. Trout, *Boston,* p. 10; Russell, *Great Interlude,* p. 164; Boston Tercentenary Committee, *Fifty Years of Boston,* p. 64. See also Trout, *Boston,* p. 14; Brett Howard, *Boston: A Social History* (New York: Hawthorn Books, 1976), p. 82; Mann, *Yankee Reformers,* p. 5; Stack, *International Conflict,* p. 30.

9. Amory, *Proper Bostonians,* p. 249; Walter Muir Whitehill, *Boston: A Topographical History,* 2d ed., enlarged (Cambridge: The Belknap Press of Harvard University Press, 1968), pp. 59–65; Whitehill, *Age of JFK,* pp. 14, 39; Firey, *Land Use,* pp. 87–90, 114; Marquand, *The Late George Apley,* pp. 29–30; J. Ross McKeever, "Beacon Hill . . . A Thesis in Site Planning," thesis, School of Architecture, Massachusetts Institute of Technology (1935), pp. 15, 7–8; Howard, *Boston: A Social History,* p. 35; Handlin, *Boston's Immigrants,* pp. 18–19; O'Connor, *Bibles, Brahmins, and Bosses,* p. 40; Formisano and Burns, *Boston, 1700–1980,* p. 61.

10. Whitehill, *Topographical,* pp. 151–64, 235; Whitehill, *Age of JFK,* pp. 30, 39; Firey, *Land Use,* p. 263; Handlin, *Boston's Immigrants,* p. 100.

11. Robert A. Woods and Albert J. Kennedy, eds., "The Zone of Emergence" (c. 1907–1914), chap. 1 (p. 1).

12. Firey, *Land Use,* pp. 68, 263; Whitehill, *Age of JFK,* p. 30; Amory, *Proper Bostonians,* p. 31; Howard, *Boston: A Social History,* p. 100; Whitehill, *Topographical,* pp. 164, 151, 158–59, 178; Warner, *Streetcar Suburbs,* pp. 2, 32, 53, 144; Marquand, *The Late George Apley,* p. 99; Works Progress Administration, *Massachusetts,* p. 136.

13. McKeever, "Beacon Hill," pp. 17, 35; Works Progress Administration, *Massachusetts,* p. 152; Woods, *Americans in Process,* map after p. 46; Firey, *Land Use,* pp. 123, 88–90, 95–96, 112, 115; Howe, *Gentle Americans,* p. 171; Amory, *Proper Bostonians,* p. 31; Charlotte Greene, *While on the Hill: A Stroll Down Chestnut Street* (Boston: The Four Seas, 1930), p. 10, as quoted in Firey, *Land Use,* p. 96; Abbie Farwell Brown, *The Lights of Beacon Hill* (Boston: Houghton Mifflin, 1922), p. 11, as quoted in Firey, *Land Use,* p. 95.

14. Firey, *Land Use,* pp. 68, 70, 88, 117–19, 265–69; Whitehill, *Topographical,* pp. 164–73, 178; Whitehill, *Age of JFK,* p. 39; Morison, *One Boy's Boston,* pp. 24, 35, 63; Marquand, *The Late George Apley,* pp. 25–26;1 McKeever, "Beacon Hill," pp. 19–20; Handlin, *Boston's Immigrants,* p. 100; Mann, *Yankee Reformers,* p. 5; Warner, *Streetcar Suburbs,* pp. 144, 17; Woods, *City Wilderness,* pp. 5, 29, 31, 112; Mary Antin, *The Promised Land* (Boston: Houghton Mifflin, 1912), pp. 295, 360–61.

15. Firey, *Land Use,* pp. 70, 117, 119–24, 332–34; Howe, *Gentle Americans,* pp. 4, 167, 171; Whitehill, *Age of JFK,* p. 44; Morison, *One Boy's Boston,* pp. 21–24; Amory, *Proper Bostonians,* p. 144; McKeever, "Beacon Hill," pp. 10, 12, 19–20, 50; Works Progress Administration, *Massachusetts,* pp. 150–52.

16. Firey, *Land Use,* pp. 70–71, 114–15, 122, 134, 242–45, 263, 269–89, 338; *Back Bay Ledger and Beacon Hill Times,* editorial, 11 January 1940, as quoted in Firey, *Land Use,* p. 273; Whitehill, *Topographical,* pp. 184, 189, 193; Whitehill, *Age of JFK,* pp. 43–44; Amory, *Proper Bostonians,* p. 343; Marquand, *The Late George Apley,* p. 327; Trout, *Boston,* pp. 250, 255, 257, 268, 269; V. O. Key, Jr., *American State Politics: An Introduction* (New York: Alfred A. Knopf, 1956), p. 155; City of Boston, City Planning Board, "Building Accommodations in Boston's Downtown–Back Bay Business District: Spring, 1953" (Boston: Boston City Planning Board, 1953), Map A.

17. See Firey, *Land Use,* pp. 71–72, 115; Amory, *Proper Bostonians,* pp. 12–13.

18. Firey, *Land Use,* pp. 99, 103, 263, 265, 287, 334; Whitehill, *Topographical,* p. 193; Howe, *Gentle Americans,* pp. 97–98, 387, 393; Amory, *Proper Bostonians,* pp. 11, 31, 90, 95–96, 142; McKeever, "Beacon Hill," pp. 7–8, 10, 12, 50; Trout, *Boston,* pp. 255, 14, 16, 26; Works Progress Administration, *Massachusetts,* pp. 149–52; Stack, *International Conflict,* pp. 30, 158; Formisano and Burns, *Boston, 1700–1980,* p. 61. Percentages are based on the number of occupied dwelling units as listed in "Census Tract Data: 1930 Census" and Census, *1940—Census Tracts.*

19. Firey, *Land Use,* pp. 88, 114–15, 117, 133–34, 263, 269–70, 333–34; Whitehill, *Age of JFK,* pp. 43–44.

20. All census figures used throughout this chapter are drawn from the following sources: "Census Tract Population—Boston, [1910–1940]"; "Census Tract Data: 1930 Census"; Census, *1940—Census Tracts;* Census, *1940–Blocks.*

21. Firey, *Land Use,* pp. 99–100, 278–79.

22. Firey, *Land Use,* pp. 104–6, 99, 134, 279; Eleanor Early, *And This is Boston!* 2d ed. (Boston: Houghton Mifflin, 1938), p. 53, as quoted in Firey, *Land Use,* p. 106; Amory, *Proper Bostonians,* pp. 138–39; Howe, *Gentle Americans,* pp. xiii, 106, 185–86, 188–89, 354.

23. For references to pervasiveness of Irish servants, see Eisinger, *Politics of Displacement,* p. 42; Howard, *Boston: A Social History,* p. 120; Dennis P. Ryan, *Beyond the Ballot Box: A Social History of the Boston Irish, 1845–1917* (Rutherford: Fairleigh Dickinson University Press, 1983), pp. 41–45, 149; Handlin, *Boston's Immigrants,* pp. 66–67, 193; Solomon, *Ancestors and Immigrants,* p. 153; Morison, *One Boy's Boston,* pp. 16–20; Bushee, *Ethnic Factors,* pp. 67–68, 71, 77–78; Howe, *Gentle Americans,* pp. 50, 100–101; Firey, *Land Use,* pp. 104, 107, 270. For references to decline in 1930s, see Trout, *Boston,* p. 26; Whitehill, *Age of JFK,* p. 43; Whitehill, *Topographical,* p. 184.

24. Firey, *Land Use,* p. 83, reinforces this description of Beacon Hill and the Back Bay as extraordinarily affluent areas. Tract K-3, he notes, contained in 1940 fewer working-class persons than any other in the city, and the three census tracts combined are surpassed only by tract Y-5C, in the Aberdeen district of Brighton. See also Firey, *Land Use,* pp. 103, 106–7, 269–70.

25. Ryan, *Ballot Box,* pp. 41–45, 149; Handlin, *Boston's Immigrants,* pp. 66–67, 120, 193; O'Connor, *Bibles, Brahmins, and Bosses,* p. 88; Solomon, *Ancestors and Immigrants,* p. 153; Marquand, *The Late George Apley,* p. 115; Morison, *One Boy's Boston,* pp. 17–18; Firey, *Land Use,* pp. 124–28, 213. That voting lists from the

1920s and 1930s no longer exist was ascertained by an exhaustive search of the records of the Boston Election Department, including their holdings in dead storage in the basement of the School Department building on Court Street.

26. Ronald Story, *The Forging of an Aristocracy: Harvard & the Boston Upper Class, 1800–1870* (Middletown, Conn.: Wesleyan University Press, 1980), pp. 6, 15, 36, 96, 162, 172; Russell, *Great Interlude,* pp. 86–87, 91; Lubell, *Future of American Politics,* pp. 39, 51–52, 132–33; Huthmacher, *Massachusetts People and Politics,* pp. 14–15; Formisano and Burns, *Boston, 1700–1980,* pp. 136, 88–89, 266–67; Sundquist, *Dynamics,* rev. ed., pp. 90–91, 104; Ladd and Hadley, *Transformations,* 2d ed., pp. 52, 54–57, 70, 122; Harold F. Gosnell, *Machine Politics: Chicago Model* (1937; rpt. New York: Greenwood Press, 1968), p. 47; V. O. Key, Jr., *The Responsible Electorate: Rationality in Presidential Voting, 1936–1960* (Cambridge: The Belknap Press of Harvard University Press, 1966), pp. 34–35; Key, "Critical Elections," pp. 7, 16; Campbell et al., *American Voter,* p. 156; Key, *Politics, Parties, & Pressure Groups,* 5th ed., pp. 218–19; Wolfinger, "Ethnic Voting," p. 907; Dale Baum, *The Civil War Party System: The Case of Massachusetts, 1848–1876* (Chapel Hill: University of North Carolina Press, 1984), pp. 97–98, 75, 83, 85–86, 212–13; Erbring et al., "Electoral Participation," p. 10; Erbring et al., "Realignments," pp. 18–19, 42.

27. Gosnell, *Machine Politics,* pp. 122, 125, 38–39; Trout, *Boston,* pp. 34–35, 296; Howard, *Boston: A Social History,* p. 85; Nie et al., *Changing American Voter,* enlarged ed., pp. 217, 223–24, 383; Huthmacher, *Massachusetts People and Politics,* pp. 14–15; Amory, *Proper Bostonians,* p. 161; Howe, *Gentle Americans,* p. 239; Stack, *International Conflict,* p. 34; Key, *American State Politics,* pp. 122, 155; Ladd and Hadley, *Transformations,* 2d ed., pp. 52, 54–57, 67–71, 122; Erbring et al., "Realignments," p. 38; Marquand, *The Late George Apley,* pp. 43, 222–24, 242–43, 270.

28. Quote attributed to Professor Burnham is drawn from extensive discussions with the author at his office in Cambridge, 1985–1986. See also Lawrence G. McMichael and Richard J. Trilling, "The Structure and Meaning of Critical Realignment: The Case of Pennsylvania, 1928–1932," in Bruce A. Campbell and Richard J. Trilling, eds., *Realignment in American Politics: Toward a Theory* (Austin: University of Texas Press, 1980), p. 46; Trout, *Boston,* pp. 20, 102, 116, 125, 269–70, 296; Lubell, *Future of American Politics,* pp. 40, 51–52; Paul Kleppner, *Who Voted? The Dynamics of Electoral Turnout, 1870–1980* (New York: Praeger, 1982), p. 103; John M. Allswang, *The New Deal and American Politics: A Study in Political Change* (New York: John Wiley and Sons, 1978), pp. 60–61; Key, *Responsible Electorate,* pp. 34–35; Huthmacher, *Massachusetts People and Politics,* pp. 14, 162–63, 174–75, 253; Story, *Forging of an Aristocracy,* p. 172; Shannon, *American Irish,* pp. 188–89, 197; Formisano and Burns, *Boston, 1700–1980,* pp. 88–89, 136, 266–67; Eisinger, *Politics of Displacement,* pp. 32, 45, 51; Howard, *Boston: A Social History,* p. 85; Robert K. Massey, Jr., "The Democratic Laggard: Massachusetts in 1932," *New England Quarterly,* vol. 44, no. 4 (December 1971), p. 572; Wolfinger, "Ethnic Voting," p. 899; Erbring et al., "Electoral Participation," pp. 10, 13; Erbring et al., "Realignments," pp. 42–44, 53; Whitehill, *Age of JFK,* pp. 41–43; Amory, *Proper*

Bostonians, pp. 161, 164–65; Morison, *One Boy's Boston,* pp. 59–61; Howe, *Gentle Americans,* pp. 98–99, 130–33, 164–65, 168, 239, 249–51, 341–42; Hennessy, *Four Decades,* pp. 397–98.

29. Howe, *Gentle Americans,* pp. 98–99.

30. Huthmacher, *Massachusetts People and Politics,* p. 181; Massey, ''Democratic Laggard,'' p. 572.

31. Huthmacher, *Massachusetts People and Politics,* p. 253; Massey, ''Democratic Laggard,'' p. 572; Howe, *Gentle Americans,* pp. 132–33, 342.

32. Sheila M. Rothman, *Woman's Proper Place: A History of Changing Ideals and Practices, 1870 to the Present* (New York: Basic Books, 1978), pp. 127–29; Burner, *Politics of Provincialism,* pp. 69–70; Burnham, *Critical Elections,* p. 77; Huthmacher, *Massachusetts People and Politics,* p. 34; Gosnell, *Machine Politics,* p. 98; ''Women Voters Lead in 3 Wards,'' *Boston Herald* (18 October 1929); article fragment, *Boston Herald* (23 October 1920).

33. Sundquist, *Dynamics,* rev. ed., p. 238; Erbring et al., ''Electoral Participation,'' p. 13.

34. Boston Tercentenary Committee, *Fifty Years of Boston,* p. 66.

35. O'Connor, *Bibles, Brahmins, and Bosses,* p. 123; Russell, *Great Interlude,* p. 206.

Chapter Six

1. Handlin, *Boston's Immigrants,* pp. 202, 212, 214; Ryan, *Ballot Box,* p. 85; Baum, *Civil War Party System,* pp. 53, 93–95, 99–100, 108–9, 177, 215; Eisinger, *Politics of Displacement,* p. 35; Huthmacher, *Massachusetts People and Politics,* pp. 14–16, 260; Formisano and Burns, *Boston, 1700–1980,* p. 114; Campbell et al., *American Voter,* pp. 159–60; Ladd and Hadley, *Transformations,* 2d ed., pp. 46–53, 271; Lubell, *Future of American Politics,* pp. 79, 225; Shannon, *American Irish,* pp. 49–50, 54–55; Key, *American State Politics,* p. 241; Nie et al., *Changing American Voter,* enlarged ed., pp. 214–15; Burner, *Politics of Provincialism,* p. 15; Kleppner, *Who Voted?* pp. 45–46, 56, 105; Daniels, *In Freedom's Birthplace,* p. 281.

2. Shannon, *American Irish,* pp. 305, 313, 327; Key, *Politics, Parties, & Pressure Groups,* 5th ed., p. 253. See also Stack, *International Conflict,* p. 34; Fuchs, *Political Behavior,* p. 77; Huthmacher, *Massachusetts People and Politics,* p. 260; Campbell et al., *American Voter,* p. 159; Ladd and Hadley, *Transformations,* 2d ed., pp. 50–53, 71, 84–86, 271; Dahl, *Who Governs?* pp. 38–39; Key, *American State Politics,* pp. 236, 241–42; Nie et al., *Changing American Voter,* enlarged ed., p. 214. Also, for the argument that the Irish rejected Roosevelt and the New Deal coalition, see Erbring et al., ''Realignments,'' pp. 34–35.

3. Bernard Bailyn et al., *The Great Republic,* 3d ed. (Lexington: D. C. Heath, 1985), vol. 1, p. 40; William L. Langer, ed., *An Encyclopedia of World History,* 5th ed. (Boston: Houghton Mifflin, 1972), p. 549.

4. The figure in the text represents an estimate of the number of Irish immigrants to Massachusetts in the period stated. Aggregate census data did not report country of birth until 1850. In 1850, there were 115,917 Massachusetts residents who had been born in Ireland. In 1860, there were 185,434 Massachusetts residents who had been

born in Ireland. At mid-decade, in 1855, the state census counted 181,304 Massachusetts residents who had been born in Ireland. And it was noted in the 1855 census that immigration between 1845 and 1850 had been much more substantial than that since 1850. Further, in 1855, there were 21,707 Massachusetts residents who had been born in British North America and 27,969 Massachusetts residents who had been born in Great Britain. Since, prior to the early 1840s, Irish immigration to Massachusetts had been relatively slight, especially compared to British immigration, it seems reasonable to say that the combined total of persons who had been born in Britain and in British North America certainly outnumbered, even overwhelmed, those who had been born in Ireland. If, then, there had been even as many as 30,000 Irish in Massachusetts before the early 1840s, at least 150,000 more arrived as immigrants over the following decade. See [United States Government],*The Seventh Census of the United States: 1850* (Washington, D.C.: Robert Armstrong, Public Printer, 1853), p. xxxvii; United States Department of the Interior, *Population of the United States in 1860; compiled from the original returns of the Eighth Census* (Washington, D.C.: Government Printing Office, 1864), p. xxix; Secretary of the Commonwealth of Massachusetts, *Census of Massachusetts, 1855* (Boston: William White, Printer to the State, 1857), pp. 132, 233, 235–36.

5. Massachusetts, *Census, 1855*, pp. 126, 236.

6. Handlin, *Boston's Immigrants,* pp. 93–99, 105–6; Whitehill, *Age of JFK,* pp. 21, 20; Firey, *Land Use,* pp. 43–45, 51–52, 58–59, 114, 181. See also O'Connor, *Bibles, Brahmins, and Bosses,* pp. 86–87, 92–93; Bushee, *Ethnic Factors,* pp. 2, 23, 25, 36; Whitehill, *Topographical,* pp. 112, 174, 281; Ryan, *Ballot Box,* pp. 21–22, 137, 140; Howard, *Boston: A Social History,* pp. 66, 91; Woods, *City Wilderness,* pp. 54–55; Eisinger, *Politics of Displacement,* p. 33; Woods, *Americans in Process,* pp. 41–42, 44; Robert H. Lord, John E. Sexton, and Edward T. Harrington, *History of the Archdiocese of Boston, 1604–1943,* vol. 3 (New York: Sheed and Ward, 1944), p. 243; Epworth League House, *A Religious Social Study* ([Boston?]: Epworth League House Commission, 1894), pp. 2, 91; Russell, *Great Interlude,* pp. 166–67; Boston Tercentenary Committee, *Fifty Years of Boston,* p. 63; Woods and Kennedy, "Zone," chap. 2 (pp. 5–6), chap. 6 (p. 4); Knights, *Plain People,* p. 120; Todisco, *Boston's First Neighborhood,* p. 29.

7. Woods and Kennedy, "Zone," chap. 1 (pp. 2, 6, 4, 8). See also ibid., chap. 1 (pp. 1–15); O'Connor, *Bibles, Brahmins, and Bosses,* pp. 92–93.

8. Woods and Kennedy, "Zone," chap. 1 (pp. 4, 8, 10–11); Thernstrom, *Other Bostonians,* pp. 165, 208; Boston, Listing Board, *List of Residents,* 1920–1940; Boston 200 Corporation, *Brighton* (Boston: Boston 200 Corporation, 1975), pp. 1, 13, 20–21.

9. Woods and Kennedy, "Zone," chap. 2 (p. 20); Stack, *International Conflict,* p. 40. See also Shannon, *American Irish,* pp. 183–87; Warner, *Streetcar Suburbs,* pp. 87, 97; Woods and Kennedy, "Zone," chap. 2 (pp. 7–9, 14), chap. 5A (p. 17), chap. 6 (pp. 5–10); John J. Toomey and Edward P. B. Rankin, *History of South Boston (Its Past and Present) and Prospects for the Future, with Sketches of Prominent Men* (Boston: John J. Toomey and Edward P. B. Rankin, 1901), p. 466; Trout, *Boston,* pp. 11–14, 175.

10. Thernstrom, *Other Bostonians,* pp. 186, 167–68, 250, 152–160; Bushee, *Ethnic Factors,* p. 31; Ryan, *Ballot Box,* pp. 105–6; Woods, *City Wilderness,* pp. 39–40. See also Bushee, *Ethnic Factors,* pp. 36, 150; Ryan, *Ballot Box,* p. 104; Thernstrom, *Other Bostonians,* pp. 132–33, 135–38, 143, 170–71; O'Connor, *Bibles, Brahmins, and Bosses,* pp. 87–88; Shannon, *American Irish,* pp. 24–28, 183–87; Woods, *City Wilderness,* pp. 42–43; Stack, *International Conflict,* pp. 7, 27–28, 36, 40, 152–53. For dissent, presented in the context of New Haven, see Dahl, *Who Governs?* p. 41.

11. Bushee, *Ethnic Factors,* p. 30; Woods and Kennedy, "Zone," chap. 6 (pp. 8–10, 6, 5). See also Woods and Kennedy, "Zone," chap. 6 (pp. 4–18).

12. "Census Tract Data: 1930 Census," Table II; Census, *1940—Census Tracts,* Table 3; Woods and Kennedy, "Zone," chap. 6 (pp. 12, 14–15); Commonwealth of Massachusetts, Bureau of Statistics, *The Immigrant Population of Massachusetts* (Boston: Wright and Potter, State Printers, 1913), p. 27.

13. Toomey and Rankin, *South Boston,* p. 466; Woods and Kennedy, "Zone," chap. 6 (p. 10), chap. 2 (pp. 8–9, 14), chap. 5A (p. 17); Warner, *Streetcar Suburbs,* p. 87. See also Firey, *Land Use,* pp. 184, 216; Bushee, *Ethnic Factors,* p. 25; Handlin, *Boston's Immigrants,* pp. 102, 171; O'Connor, *Bibles, Brahmins, and Bosses,* pp. 90, 92–93, 103–4; Woods, *City Wilderness,* pp. 41, 117, 308–9; Toomey and Rankin, *South Boston,* p. 468; Lord et al., *History of the Archdiocese,* pp. 243–46, 682; Stack, *International Conflict,* pp. 32, 37–38, 40, 55; Russell, *Great Interlude,* p. 88; Warner, *Streetcar Suburbs,* pp. 68–69, 86–88, 93–97; Boston 200 Corporation, *Charlestown* (Boston: Boston 200 Corporation, 1976), pp. 3–5; Boston 200 Corporation, *Mission Hill* (Boston: Boston 200 Corporation, 1976), pp. 1–2, 5, 7, 11, 15, 26; Trout, *Boston,* pp. 10–14, 175; Woods and Kennedy, "Zone," chap. 2, chap. 5A, chap. 6.

14. Woods and Kennedy, "Zone," chap. 5A (p. 19), chap. 5C (p. 6). See also O'Connor, *Bibles, Brahmins, and Bosses,* pp. 103–4; Woods, *City Wilderness,* pp. 308–9; Lord et al., *History of the Archdiocese,* pp. 246–51, 254–57, 683–86; Warner, *Streetcar Suburbs,* pp. 43, 68–69, 73–74, 79–88, 93–97; Boston 200 Corporation, *Dorchester* (Boston: Boston 200 Corporation, 1976), pp. 7–9, 14–15, 17, 19; Boston 200, *Mission Hill,* pp. 1–2, 5, 7, 11, 15, 26; Woods and Kennedy, "Zone," chap. 5A, chap. 5C, chap. 6 (p. 22).

15. Boston 200, *Brighton,* pp. 13, 20–21. See also Firey, *Land Use,* p. 70; Lord et al., *History of the Archdiocese,* pp. 261, 689; Warner, *Streetcar Suburbs,* p. 163; Boston 200, *Brighton,* pp. 1–2, 4–7, 12–13, 20–21.

16. Bushee, *Ethnic Factors,* pp. 124, 132, 151; Shannon, *American Irish,* pp. 62–63, 183, 197–200; Woods, *City Wilderness,* pp. 126–27, 134; Woods, *Americans in Process,* p. 63; Toomey and Rankin, *South Boston,* p. 475; Stack, *International Conflict,* p. 151; Woods and Kennedy, "Zone," chap. 1 (pp. 13–14); Eisinger, *Politics of Displacement,* p. 34; Russell, *Great Interlude,* pp. 185–86.

17. Woods, *City Wilderness,* p. 134; Woods, *Americans in Process,* p. 63.

18. Huthmacher, *Massachusetts People and Politics,* p. 164.

19. Ibid., pp. 214, 260.

20. Huthmacher, *Massachusetts People and Politics,* pp. 23–31, 33, 42, 47, 50, 74; Lord et al., *History of the Archdiocese,* pp. 610–15; Stack, *International Conflict,* pp. 63–64; Fuchs, *Political Behavior,* p. 18; Burner, *Politics of Provincialism,* pp. 235, 242.

21. Huthmacher, *Massachusetts People and Politics,* pp. 99–102. See also Burner, *Politics of Provincialism,* pp. 128–41, 235.

22. Trout, *Boston,* p. 259; Lubell, *Future of American Politics,* pp. 89, 142; Shannon, *American Irish,* pp. 296, 303–6, 310–19; Stack, *International Conflict,* pp. 50–54, 128–29.

23. Stack, *International Conflict,* pp. 54–57, 70, 92–93, 98–99, 129–34, 152–54; Trout, *Boston,* pp. 288–90, 292; Lubell, *Future of American Politics,* pp. 143, 212; Shannon, *American Irish,* pp. 303, 313.

24. Trout, *Boston,* pp. 259–61, 288, 293–96, 300; Lubell, *Future of American Politics,* pp. 142–43; Shannon, *American Irish,* pp. 222–29, 296, 303–6, 315–19, 331–32, 336, 347–66; Stack, *International Conflict,* pp. 58–70, 116–27, 153; Fuchs, *Political Behavior,* p. 18; Campbell et al., *American Voter,* p. 159; Erbring et al., ''Realignments,'' p. 35.

25. *Boston Post* (28 October 1932) and *New York Times* (28 October 1932), as quoted in Massey, ''Democratic Laggard,'' p. 570; Massey, ''Democratic Laggard,'' p. 567; Erbring et al., ''Realignments,'' pp. 34–35 (''IRISH'' is capitalized in original). See also Massey, ''Democratic Laggard,'' pp. 553–74; Lubell, *Future of American Politics,* pp. 34–35, 40, 50, 212–13; Shannon, *American Irish,* pp. 177–81, 220–21, 305, 327, 331–32, 336, 347–48, 352; Stack, *International Conflict,* p. 34; Huthmacher, *Massachusetts People and Politics,* pp. 163–64, 181–82, 244, 251, 260; Campbell et al., *American Voter,* p. 159; Russell, *Great Interlude,* pp. 185–87, 200–201; Fuchs, *Political Behavior,* p. 77; Nie et al., *Changing American Voter,* enlarged ed., pp. 89, 214; Burner, *Politics of Provincialism,* pp. 229, 235–36, 242; Lord et al., *History of the Archdiocese,* p. 636; Trout, *Boston,* pp. 103, 107–9, 112, 116; Bruce M. Stave, *The New Deal and the Last Hurrah: Pittsburgh Machine Politics* ([Pittsburgh?]: University of Pittsburgh Press, 1970), p. 18; Ladd and Hadley, *Transformations,* 2d ed., pp. 50–53, 71, 84–86, 271; Key, *American State Politics,* p. 242; Lichtman, ''Critical Election Theory,'' pp. 323, 327–28, 331; Sundquist, *Dynamics,* rev. ed., pp. 192–93, 215; Hennessy, *Four Decades,* pp. 384, 470–71, 521, 528–29; Dahl, *Who Governs?* pp. 49–50; Key, ''Critical Elections,'' p. 4.

26. Lubell, *Future of American Politics,* p. 50; Fuchs, *Political Behavior,* pp. 75–76; Erbring et al., ''Realignments,'' p. 35 (''IRISH'' is capitalized in original); Trout, *Boston,* p. 296; Erbring et al., ''Electoral Participation,'' p. 15 (''IRISH'' is capitalized in original). See also Shannon, *American Irish,* pp. 225, 228–30; Lubell, *Future of American Politics,* pp. 51, 212; Fuchs, *Political Behavior,* pp. 77, 84; Trout, *Boston,* pp. 47, 116; Ladd and Hadley, *Transformations,* 2d ed., p. 271; Campbell et al., *American Voter,* p. 156; Allswang, *New Deal,* pp. 41, 60–61; Edward C. Banfield and Martha Derthick, eds., ''A Report on the Politics of Boston, Massachusetts'' (Cambridge: Joint Center for Urban Studies of the Massachusetts Institute of Technology and Harvard University, 1960), p. I-15; Peter Anthony Biagetti, ''Person-

alism, Localism, and Nativism: An Analysis of Boston Politics from the Rise of James Michael Curley to the Fall of Louise Day Hicks,'' A.B. thesis, Harvard University (March 1978), pp. 33, 43, 128.

Chapter Seven

1. Schattschneider, ''United States: The Functional Approach,'' p. 208.

2. Sundquist, *Dynamics,* 1st ed., p. 177n; Lubell, *Future of American Politics,* p. 40; Burner, *Politics of Provincialism,* p. 229; Andersen, *Creation,* p. 9; Huthmacher, *Massachusetts People and Politics,* p. 44.

3. Party enrollment figures for 1932 are estimates, based on total registration figures for 1930, 1932, and 1934, and party breakdowns for 1930 and 1934.

4. Trout, *Boston,* p. 302.

5. Bushee, *Ethnic Factors,* p. 133.

6. Banfield and Derthick, ''Report on the Politics of Boston,'' p. II-2.

7. Stack, *International Conflict,* p. 34.

8. Stack, *International Conflict,* p. 34; Fuchs, *Political Behavior,* p. 56.

9. Fuchs, *Political Behavior,* p. 138.

10. Philip E. Converse, ''The Nature of Belief Systems in Mass Publics,'' in *Ideology and Discontent,* ed. David E. Apter (New York: The Free Press, 1964), p. 248.

11. Sidney Verba and Norman H. Nie, *Participation in America: Political Democracy and Social Equality* (New York: Harper and Row, 1972), pp. 339–40; Sidney Verba, Norman H. Nie, and Jae-On Kim, *Participation and Political Equality: A Seven-Nation Comparison* (New York: Cambridge University Press, 1978), pp. 120–21, 124.

12. Support for the reasoning underlying this proposition can also be found in Erbring et al., ''Electoral Participation,'' pp. 16–17, 19.

13. Woods, *City Wilderness,* pp. 126–28; Woods, *Americans in Process,* pp. 149–50, 157; Bushee, *Ethnic Factors,* p. 130.

14. Woods, *Americans in Process,* pp. 160, 64; Bushee, *Ethnic Factors,* p. 132.

15. Lubell, *Future of American Politics,* p. 29.

16. Key, *Politics, Parties, & Pressure Groups,* 5th ed., p. 524. See also Key, ''Future of the Democratic Party,'' pp. 163–64.

Chapter Eight

1. Key, ''Critical Elections,'' p. 9n.

2. Key, ''Secular Realignment,'' p. 207.

3. Woods, *Americans in Process,* pp. 126–27.

4. Huthmacher, *Massachusetts People and Politics,* p. 260; Andersen, *Creation,* p. 100; Lubell, *Future of American Politics,* p. 35. See also Sundquist, *Dynamics,* rev. ed., pp. 193, 215; Shannon, *American Irish,* pp. 180–81; Key, ''Future of the Democratic Party,'' p. 166.

5. Lichtman, ''Critical Election Theory,'' p. 337. See also Erbring et al., ''Electoral Participation,'' p. 14; Erbring et al., ''Realignments,'' p. 25; Massey, ''Democratic Laggard,'' pp. 568–71; Lichtman, ''Critical Election Theory,'' pp. 320,

323, 327–28, 331, 335–37, 341–42, 344; Clubb and Allen, "Cities and the Election of 1928," pp. 1207, 1215–16, 1218–20.

6. Huthmacher, *Massachusetts People and Politics,* pp. 180, 250–51; Hennessy, *Four Decades,* p. 396. See also Trout, *Boston,* pp. 116–17; Massey, "Democratic Laggard," p. 571.

7. Key, "Future of the Democratic Party," p. 165; Lubell, *Future of American Politics,* p. 51; Erbring et al., "Realignments," pp. 42–44; Sundquist, *Dynamics,* rev. ed., pp. 217–18. See also Key, *Politics, Parties, & Pressure Groups,* 5th ed., p. 532; Erbring et al., "Realignments," pp. 34–35.

8. Key, "Future of the Democratic Party," p. 163.

9. Massey, "Democratic Laggard," p. 571.

10. Lubell, *Future of American Politics,* p. 3; Key, "Critical Elections," p. 4; Key, "Secular Realignment," p. 198; Burnham, *Critical Elections,* p. 6.

11. Key, "Secular Realignment," p. 198; Lubell, *Future of American Politics,* p. 198; Burnham, *Critical Elections,* pp. 3–4.

12. Beard, *American Party Battle,* pp. 29, 6.

13. Ibid., pp. 134–37, 146–47.

14. Ibid., pp. 143–44, 112, 144. See also ibid., pp. 136, 146–47.

15. Quote is from Key, "Future of the Democratic Party," p. 168. See, for recent work on the changing electoral bases of parties as well as on the decline of political parties in general: Nie et al., *Changing American Voter,* enlarged ed.; Ladd and Hadley, *Transformations,* 2d ed.; John R. Petrocik, *Party Coalitions* (Chicago: University of Chicago Press, 1981); and Martin P. Wattenberg, *The Decline of American Political Parties, 1952–1984* (Cambridge: Harvard University Press, 1986).

16. Lubell, *Future of American Politics,* p. 3.

17. Key, "Future of the Democratic Party," pp. 161, 163, 164, 165, 166. See also Clubb, Flanigan, and Zingale, *Partisan Realignment,* chap. 3.

18. See Key, "Future of the Democratic Party," "Critical Elections," and "Secular Realignment." Quote is from "Future of the Democratic Party," p. 166.

Appendix 1

1. Census, *1940—Blocks,* esp. pp. 2–4.

2. Census, *1940—Census Tracts,* esp. pp. 1–3.

3. Census, *1940—Census Tracts,* pp. 1–3; United States Department of the Interior, Census Office, *Twelfth Census of the United States, Taken in the Year 1900: Census Reports,* vol. 1, *Population*—Part 1 (Washington, D.C.: United States Census Office, 1901), p. lxix; United States Department of Commerce, Bureau of the Census, *Thirteenth Census of the United States, Taken in the Year 1910,* vol. 1, *Population, 1910—General Report and Analysis* (Washington, D.C.: Government Printing Office, 1913), p. 79.

4. City of Boston, City Planning Board, *The People of Boston,* vol. 1, *Population Distribution,* W.P.A. Project no. 17567 (Boston: City Planning Board, August 1939).

5. Boston Health League, compiled for the Boston Health Department, *Alphabetical Street Index and Basic Demographic Data for the City of Boston by Census Tracts* (Boston: City of Boston Printing Department, 1931).

6. Boston Council of Social Agencies, Bureau of Research and Studies, *Social Statistics by Census Tracts in Boston* (Boston: Boston Council of Social Agencies, April 1933), esp. p. 2.

7. Boston Council of Social Agencies, *Bulletin,* vol. 10, no. 3 (March 1930), pp. 12–13; vol. 9, no. 5 (May 1930), pp. 8–9; vol. 9, no. 9 (November 1930), cover, pp. 3–4; vol. 10, no. 8 (October 1931), p. 14; vol. 11, no. 1 (January 1932), pp. 3–4; vol. 12, no. 1 (February 1933).

8. The UCPC also located a summary of Boston's population by census tract for 1910, 1920, 1930, 1934, and 1940. The 1910 numbers were, apparently, for tracts with slightly different boundaries from those later used. See "Census Tract Population—Boston, [1910–1940]." Three months later, a second copy of the "Census Tract Data: 1930 Census" volume was located at the Boston Redevelopment Authority. About to be discarded by the BRA library as a worthless leftover from the old City Planning Board, it was saved by a member of the Research Division.

9. See City of Boston, Board of Election Commissioners, *Annual Report,* 1915–1940, Public Document no. 11 (Boston: City of Boston Printing Department, 1916–1941).

10. The atlases used were City of Boston, "Division of Wards into Voting Precincts," 1916, 1921, 1925. The 1935 atlas reflects neither the original system of 1932 nor that of 1936; it shows, rather, the 1932 system amended as of 1935. Boston City Documents used included 1914 #121; 1915 #68; 1918 #120; 1920 #40; 1924 #97; 1925 #77; 1931 #92; 1933 #83; 1935 #73; 1938 #57; 1939 #47; and, for 1921, "Division of Wards into Voting Precincts by Board of Election Commissioners," document dated 28 March 1921.

11. Boston, Listing Board, *List of Residents,* 1920–1940.

12. Boston, Board of Election Commissioners, *Annual Report,* 1920–1940.

13. "Vote of Boston," *Boston Evening Globe,* 9 November 1932, p. 12; "Vote of Boston," *Boston Evening Globe,* 4 November 1936, p. 16; "Boston Vote," *Boston Daily Globe,* 6 November 1940, p. 12.

Bibliography

Unpublished and Rare Sources

Unpublished documents, dissertations, theses, and other studies are included in this section. In addition, government publications, maps, and other works that have not been found in more than one location—and may thus well be unique copies now—are also included. Immediately after each entry, in parentheses, is an abbreviation for the name of the institution or collection in which the work in question can be found. These abbreviations follow. Unless otherwise indicated, cities and towns named are in Massachusetts.

AJHS	American Jewish Historical Society, Waltham
ArchdBos	Archives, Archdiocese of Boston, Brighton
BPLGov	Government Documents, Boston Public Library
BPLRare	Rare Book Collection, Boston Public Library
BRA	Research Division, Boston Redevelopment Authority
BUMugar	Mugar Memorial Library, Boston University
BurCens	Bureau of the Census, Washington, D.C.
HUArchv	Harvard University Archives
HULoeb	Loeb Library, Harvard University
HUMaps	Harvard University Map Collection
HUWid	Widener Library, Harvard University
HebColl	Hebrew College Library, Brookline
MITRotch	Rotch Library, Massachusetts Institute of Technology
MSL	Special Collections, Massachusetts State Library
UCPC	United Community Planning Corporation, Boston

Archdiocese of Boston. Church Census (cards). Selected parishes, 1910–1940. (ArchdBos)

Banfield, Edward C., and Martha Derthick, eds. ''A Report on the Politics of Boston, Massachusetts.'' Cambridge: Joint Center for Urban Studies of the Massachusetts Institute of Technology and Harvard University, 1960. (HUArchv)

Baskin, Maurice. ''Ward Boss Politics in Boston: 1896–1921.'' A.B. thesis. Department of History, Harvard University, March 1975. (HUArchv)

Biagetti, Peter Anthony. ''Personalism, Localism, and Nativism: An Analysis of Boston Politics from the Rise of James Michael Curley to the Fall of Louise Day Hicks.'' A.B. thesis. Department of Government, Harvard University, March 1978. (HUArchv)

Boston, City of. "Division of Wards into Voting Precincts" (atlas). 1916, 1925, 1935. Bound volumes of precinct maps. (MSL)

______. "Division of Wards into Voting Precincts" (atlas). 1921. Bound volume of precinct maps. (BPLGov)

______. "Division of Wards into Voting Precincts." Bound volume of selected documents detailing precinct-line redrawings, 1895–1935. Incomplete. (BPLGov)

______. *Municipal Register.* 1915–1940. Boston: City of Boston Printing Department, 1915–1940. (BPLGov)

Boston, City of. Board of Election Commissioners. *Annual Report.* 1915–1940. Public Document No. 11. Boston: City of Boston Printing Department, 1916–1941. (BPLGov)

Boston, City of. City Planning Board. "Building Accommodations in Boston's Downtown–Back Bay Business District: Spring, 1953." Boston: Boston City Planning Board, September 1953. (HULoeb)

______. Map of City of Boston. 1925, 1926 copy, 1932. (HUMaps)

______. Map of City of Boston. 1926. (BPLRare)

Boston, City of. Listing Board. *List of Residents 20 Years of Age and Over.* 1920–1940. Boston: City of Boston Printing Department, 1920–1940. (BPLGov)

[Boston, City of. Public Library.] "List of References in Public Documents to Precinct-line Redrawings." Incomplete. (BPLGov)

Boston Council of Social Agencies. *Bulletin.* 1930–1941. Incomplete. (HUWid)

Bureau of Jewish Social Research. "Jewish Communal Survey of Boston." New York: Bureau of Jewish Social Research, 1930. (HebColl)

Combined Jewish Appeal, The. *Fifty Years of Jewish Philanthropy in Greater Boston, 1895–1945.* 1945 Combined Jewish Appeal Year Book. Boston: The Combined Jewish Appeal, 1945. (AJHS)

Ennice, Ruth. "Back Bay." M.A. thesis. Boston University Graduate School, 1941. (BUMugar)

Erbring, Lutz, Norman H. Nie, and Edward Hamburg, with Nancy Dobrozdravic. "Electoral Participation in America: Looking Back." Paper prepared for the Conference on Analyzing Declining Voter Turnout in America, at the University of Chicago, April 1984.

______. "Realignments in the American Party System." Paper presented to the American Political Science Association Meeting, Chicago, August 1983.

Federated Jewish Charities. *Annual Report.* 1918–1919, 1922–1923, 1924–1925, 1925–1926, 1927–1928. Boston: Federated Jewish Charities, 1919, 1923, 1925, 1926, 1928. (AJHS)

Greater Boston Community Council, Community Studies Research Bureau. *What Do You Know about South Boston and Its Neighborhoods: Andrew Square, City Point, Old Harbor Village, Telegraph Hill, West Broadway?* Boston: Greater Boston Community Council, November 1944. (HULoeb)

Harper, Richard Charles. "The Catholic Church and the Democratic Party in Boston, 1924–1936." A.B. thesis. Committee on Degrees in Social Studies, Harvard University, March 1975. (HUArchv)

Hill, Adelaide Cromwell. "The Negro Upper Class in Boston—Its Development and Present Social Structure." Ph.D. thesis. Department of Social Relations, Radcliffe College, 1952. (HUArchv)

Jewish Welfare Board. "Study of the Jewish Community of Greater Boston, Massachusetts (With Special Reference to the Resources and Needs for Jewish Center Work)." New York: Jewish Welfare Board, 1940. (AJHS)

McCaffrey, George Herbert. "The Political Disintegration and Reintegration of Metropolitan Boston." Ph.D. thesis. Department of Government, Harvard University, March 1937. (HUArchv)

McKeever, J. Ross. "Beacon Hill . . . A Thesis in Site Planning." Degree of Master in City Planning thesis. School of Architecture, Massachusetts Institute of Technology, 30 January 1935. (MITRotch)

Neusner, J. Jacob. "The Rise of the Jewish Community of Boston, 1880–1914." A.B. thesis. Department of History, Harvard University, April 1953. (HUArchv)

Piccione, John Anthony. "Naturalization, Ethnic Intermarriage, and Education as Measures of Acculturation: The Italian-American Community in Boston, 1890–1940." A.B. thesis. Department of History, Harvard University, March 1980. (HUArchv)

Serino, Gustave Ralph. "Italians in the Political Life of Boston: A Study of the Role of an Immigrant and Ethnic Group in the Political Life of an Urban Community." Ph.D. thesis. Department of Government, Harvard University. Deposited, 1950. (HUArchv)

United States Department of Commerce, Bureau of the Census. *Population and Housing Units by Census Tracts: 1940—Boston, Massachusetts.* Bulletin. Series PH-2, no. 32. 24 April 1941. (BurCens)

[United States Department of Commerce, Bureau of the Census, and Boston Council of Social Agencies?]. "Census Tract Population—Boston." 1910 (different boundaries), 1920, 1930, 1934, 1940. (UCPC)

______. "Country of Origin of Foreign Stock, Boston: 1940." Information broken down for foreign-born white and native white of foreign or mixed parentage. Copies prepared 25 May 1944, 3 April 1951. (UCPC)

______. "Mother Tongue, Boston: 1940." Information broken down for foreign-born white, native white of foreign or mixed parentage, and native white of native parentage. (UCPC)

[United States Department of Commerce, Bureau of the Census, and?] Boston Health Department. "Census Tract Data [for Boston]: 1930 Census." (BRA and UCPC)

Woods, Robert A., and Albert J. Kennedy, eds. "The Zone of Emergence." Photocopy of original typescript now at the South End House, 20 Union Park, Boston. Original prepared c. 1907–1914. (HUWid)

Published Sources

Allswang, John M. *A House for All Peoples: Ethnic Politics in Chicago, 1890–1936.* Lexington, Kentucky: University Press of Kentucky, 1971.

______. *The New Deal and American Politics: A Study in Political Change.* Critical Episodes in American Politics. Robert A. Divine, series ed. New York: John Wiley and Sons, 1978.

American Jewish Yearbook. 5679–5691. Harry Schneiderman, ed., for the American Jewish Committee. Vols. 20–32. Philadelphia: The Jewish Publication Society of America, 1918–1930.

Amory, Cleveland. *The Proper Bostonians.* New York: E. P. Dutton, 1947.

Andersen, Kristi. *The Creation of a Democratic Majority, 1928–1936.* Chicago: University of Chicago Press, 1979.

______. "Generation, Partisan Shift, and Realignment: A Glance Back to the New Deal." In Nie, Verba, and Petrocik, *Changing American Voter,* enlarged ed.

Antin, Mary. *From Plotzk to Boston.* Boston: W. B. Clarke, Park Street Church, 1899.

______. *The Promised Land.* Boston: Houghton Mifflin, 1912.

Baum, Dale. *The Civil War Party System: The Case of Massachusetts, 1848–1876.* Chapel Hill: University of North Carolina Press, 1984.

Beard, Charles A. *The American Party Battle.* New York: Macmillan, 1928.

Benson, Lee, Joel H. Silbey, and Phyllis F. Field. "Toward a Theory of Stability and Change in American Voting Patterns: New York State, 1792–1970." In Silbey, Bogue, and Flanigan, *History of American Electoral Behavior.*

Binkley, Wilfred E. *American Political Parties: Their Natural History.* New York: Alfred A. Knopf, 1943.

______. *American Political Parties: Their Natural History,* 3d ed. New York: Alfred A. Knopf, 1958.

Boston, City of. City Planning Board. *East Boston: A Survey and a Comprehensive Plan.* 1915 Public Document No. 116. George Gibbs, Jr., ed. Boston: City of Boston Printing Department, 1916.

______. *The North End: A Survey and a Comprehensive Plan.* 1919 Public Document No. 40. Boston: City of Boston Printing Department, 1919.

______. *The People of Boston.* Vol. 1. *Population Distribution.* W.P.A. Project No. 17567. Boston: City Planning Board, August 1939.

Boston Council of Social Agencies, Bureau of Research and Studies. *Social Statistics by Census Tracts in Boston: A Method of Neighborhood Study.* Boston: Boston Council of Social Agencies, April 1933.

Boston Health League, compiled for the Boston Health Department. *Alphabetical Street Index and Basic Demographic Data for the City of Boston by Census Tracts.* Boston: City of Boston Printing Department, 1931.

Boston Tercentenary Committee, Subcommittee on Memorial History. *Fifty Years of Boston: A Memorial Volume. Issued in Commemoration of the Tercentenary of 1930.* Elisabeth M. Herlihy, ed. Boston: [Boston Tercentenary Committee?], 1932.

Boston 200 Corporation. *Brighton.* Boston 200 Neighborhood History Series. Boston: Boston 200 Corporation, 1975.

______. *Charlestown.* Boston 200 Neighborhood History Series. Boston: Boston 200 Corporation, 1976.

______. *Dorchester.* Boston 200 Neighborhood History Series. Boston: Boston 200 Corporation, 1976.

______. *East Boston.* Boston 200 Neighborhood History Series. Boston: Boston 200 Corporation, 1976.

______. *Hyde Park.* Boston 200 Neighborhood History Series. Boston: Boston 200 Corporation, 1976.

______. *Jamaica Plain.* Boston 200 Neighborhood History Series. Boston: Boston 200 Corporation, 1976.

______. *Mission Hill.* Boston 200 Neighborhood History Series. Boston: Boston 200 Corporation, 1976.

______. *The South End.* Boston 200 Neighborhood History Series. Boston: Boston 200 Corporation, 1975.

______. *West Roxbury.* Boston 200 Neighborhood History Series. Boston: Boston 200 Corporation, 1976.

''Boston Vote [by Precinct—1940].'' *Boston Daily Globe,* 6 November 1940, p. 12.

Burner, David. *The Politics of Provincialism: The Democratic Party in Transition, 1918–1932.* New York: Alfred A. Knopf, 1967.

Burnham, Walter Dean. ''The Changing Shape of the American Political Universe.'' *American Political Science Review,* vol. 59, no. 1 (March 1965), pp. 7–28.

______. *Critical Elections and the Mainsprings of American Politics.* New York: W. W. Norton, 1970.

______. ''Party Systems and the Political Process.'' In Chambers and Burnham, *American Party Systems.*

Burnham, Walter Dean, Jerome M. Clubb, and William H. Flanigan. ''Partisan Realignment: A Systemic Perspective.'' In Silbey, Bogue, and Flanigan, *History of American Electoral Behavior.*

Bushee, Frederick A. *Ethnic Factors in the Population of Boston.* Publications of the American Economic Association, Third Series, vol. 4, no. 2 (May 1903). New York: Macmillan, 1903.

Campbell, Angus, Philip E. Converse, Warren E. Miller, and Donald E. Stokes. *The American Voter.* New York: John Wiley and Sons, 1960.

______. *Elections and the Political Order.* New York: John Wiley and Sons, 1966.

Campbell, Bruce A., and Richard J. Trilling, eds. *Realignment in American Politics: Toward a Theory.* Austin: University of Texas Press, 1980.

Chambers, William Nisbet. ''Party Development and the American Mainstream.'' In Chambers and Burnham, *American Party Systems.*

Chambers, William Nisbet, and Walter Dean Burnham, eds. *The American Party Systems: Stages of Political Development.* New York: Oxford University Press, 1967.

Clubb, Jerome M., and Howard W. Allen. ''The Cities and the Election of 1928: Partisan Realignment?'' *American Historical Review,* vol. 74, no. 4 (April 1969), pp. 1205–20.

______, eds. *Electoral Change and Stability in American Political History.* New York: The Free Press, 1971.

Clubb, Jerome M., William H. Flanigan, and Nancy H. Zingale. *Partisan Realignment: Voters, Parties, and Government in American History.* Sage Library of Social Research, vol. 108. Beverly Hills: Sage Publications, 1980.

Converse, Philip E. "The Nature of Belief Systems in Mass Publics." *Ideology and Discontent,* ed. David E. Apter. New York: The Free Press, 1964.

Cook, Frederic W. *The Massachusetts Voter: His Rights and Duties of Citizenship in State, County, City, and Town.* Boston: Ginn, 1928.

Dahl, Robert A. *Who Governs? Democracy and Power in an American City.* New Haven: Yale University Press, 1961.

Daniels, John. *In Freedom's Birthplace: A Study of the Boston Negroes.* 1914; rpt. New York: Arno Press and The New York Times, 1969.

Degler, Carl N. "American Political Parties and the Rise of the City: An Interpretation." In Clubb and Allen, *Electoral Change and Stability.*

DeMarco, William M. *Ethnics and Enclaves: Boston's Italian North End.* Studies in American History and Culture, no. 31. Robert Berkhover, series ed. Ann Arbor: UMI Research Press, 1981.

Dictionary of American Biography. New York: Charles Scribner's Sons, 1928 to date.

Edwards, Rheable M., and Laura B. Morris, with Robert M. Coard. *The Negro in Boston.* Boston: Action for Boston Community Development, 1961.

Eisinger, Peter K. *The Politics of Displacement: Racial and Ethnic Transition in Three American Cities.* New York: Academic Press, 1980.

Eldersveld, Samuel J. "The Influence of Metropolitan Party Pluralities in Presidential Elections since 1920: A Study of Twelve Key Cities." *American Political Science Review,* vol. 43, no. 6 (December 1949), pp. 1189–1206.

Epworth League House. *A Religious Social Study.* [Boston?]: Epworth League House Commission, 1894.

Ewing, Cortez A. M. *Presidential Elections: From Abraham Lincoln to Franklin D. Roosevelt.* Norman: University of Oklahoma Press, 1940.

Fein, Isaac M. *Boston—Where It All Began: An Historical Perspective of the Boston Jewish Community.* [Boston?]: Boston Jewish Bicentennial Committee, 1976.

Firey, Walter. *Land Use in Central Boston.* Cambridge: Harvard University Press, 1947.

Formisano, Ronald P., and Constance K. Burns, eds. *Boston, 1700–1980: The Evolution of Urban Politics.* Contributions in American History, no. 106. Jon L. Wakelyn, series ed. Westport, Conn.: Greenwood Press, 1984.

Fuchs, Lawrence H. *The Political Behavior of American Jews.* Glencoe, Ill.: The Free Press, 1956.

Goodwin, Doris Kearns. *The Fitzgeralds and the Kennedys: An American Saga.* New York: Simon and Schuster, 1987.

Gosnell, Harold F. *Machine Politics: Chicago Model.* 1937; rpt. New York: Greenwood Press, 1968.

Handlin, Oscar. *Boston's Immigrants, 1790–1865: A Study in Acculturation.* Cambridge: Harvard University Press, 1941.

Hennessy, Michael E. *Four Decades of Massachusetts Politics, 1890–1935.* Norwood, Mass.: The Norwood Press, 1935.

Howard, Brett. *Boston: A Social History.* New York: Hawthorn Books, 1976.

Howe, Helen. *The Gentle Americans, 1864–1960: Biography of a Breed.* New York: Harper and Row, 1965.

Hoyt, Homer. *The Structure and Growth of Residential Neighborhoods in American Cities*. Washington, D.C.: Federal Housing Administration, 1939.

Huthmacher, J. Joseph. *Massachusetts People and Politics, 1919–1933*. Cambridge: The Belknap Press of Harvard University Press, 1959.

Jaher, Frederic Cople. *The Urban Establishment: Upper Strata in Boston, New York, Charleston, Chicago, and Los Angeles*. Urbana: University of Illinois Press, 1982.

"Jews in a New World." *Boston Globe*. 17–21 February 1985; rpt.

Kaganoff, Benzion C. *A Dictionary of Jewish Names and Their History*. New York: Schocken Books, 1977.

Key, V. O., Jr. *American State Politics: An Introduction*. New York: Alfred A. Knopf, 1956.

______. "The Future of the Democratic Party." *Virginia Quarterly Review*, vol. 28, no. 2 (Spring 1952), pp. 161–75.

______. *Politics, Parties, and Pressure Groups*. New York: Thomas Y. Crowell, 1942.

______. *Politics, Parties, & Pressure Groups*, 5th ed. New York: Thomas Y. Crowell, 1964.

______. *The Responsible Electorate: Rationality in Presidential Voting, 1936–1960*. Cambridge: The Belknap Press of Harvard University Press, 1966.

______. "Secular Realignment and the Party System." *Journal of Politics*, vol. 21, no. 2 (May 1959), pp. 198–210.

______. "A Theory of Critical Elections." *Journal of Politics*, vol. 17, no. 1 (February 1955), pp. 3–18.

Kleppner, Paul. *Who Voted? The Dynamics of Electoral Turnout, 1870–1980*. New York: Praeger, 1982.

Knights, Peter R. *The Plain People of Boston, 1830–1860: A Study in City Growth*. New York: Oxford University Press, 1971.

Ladd, Everett Carll, Jr., with Charles D. Hadley. *Transformations of the American Party System: Party Coalitions from the New Deal to the 1970s*, 2d ed. New York: W. W. Norton, 1978.

Lichtman, Allan J. "Critical Election Theory and the Reality of American Presidential Politics, 1916–1940." *American Historical Review*, vol. 81, no. 2 (April 1976), pp. 317–51.

______. *Prejudice and the Old Politics: The Presidential Election of 1928*. Chapel Hill: University of North Carolina Press, 1979.

Lord, Robert H., John E. Sexton, and Edward T. Harrington. *History of the Archdiocese of Boston, 1604–1943*. Vol. 3. New York: Sheed and Ward, 1944.

Lubell, Samuel. *The Future of American Politics*. New York: Harper and Brothers, 1952.

Lukas, J. Anthony. *Common Ground: A Turbulent Decade in the Lives of Three American Families*. New York: Alfred A. Knopf, 1985.

McCormick, Richard L. *The Party Period and Public Policy: American Politics from the Age of Jackson to the Progressive Era*. New York: Oxford University Press, 1986.

McGerr, Michael E. *The Decline of Popular Politics: The American North, 1865–1928*. New York: Oxford University Press, 1986.

MacLysaght, Edward. *The Surnames of Ireland,* 3d ed. Dublin: Irish Academic Press, 1978.

McMichael, Lawrence G., and Richard J. Trilling. "The Structure and Meaning of Critical Realignment: The Case of Pennsylvania, 1928–1932." In Campbell and Trilling, *Realignment in American Politics*.

MacRae, Duncan, Jr., and James A. Meldrum. "Critical Elections in Illinois: 1888–1958." In Clubb and Allen, *Electoral Change and Stability.*

Mann, Arthur. *Yankee Reformers in the Urban Age*. Cambridge: The Belknap Press of Harvard University Press, 1954.

Marquand, John P. *The Late George Apley: A Novel in the Form of a Memoir.* Boston: Little, Brown, 1938.

Massachusetts, Commonwealth of. Bureau of Statistics. *The Immigrant Population of Massachusetts.*Part I of the Annual Report on the Statistics of Labor for 1912. Boston: Wright and Potter, State Printers, 1913.

Massachusetts, Commonwealth of. Secretary of the Commonwealth. *Census of Massachusetts, 1855*. Boston: William White, Printer to the State, 1857.

______. *Census of Massachusetts, 1860, from the Eighth U.S. Census*. Prepared by Geo. Wingate Chase. Boston: Wright and Potter, State Printers, 1863.

Massey, Robert K., Jr. "The Democratic Laggard: Massachusetts in 1932." *New England Quarterly,* vol. 44, no. 4 (December 1971), pp. 553–74.

Morison, Samuel Eliot. *One Boy's Boston, 1887–1901*. Boston: Houghton Mifflin, 1962.

National Cyclopedia of American Biography, The. New York and Clifton, N.J.: James T. White, 1898 to date.

Nie, Norman H., Sidney Verba, and John R. Petrocik. *The Changing American Voter,* enlarged ed. A Twentieth Century Fund Study. Cambridge: Harvard University Press, 1979.

O'Connor, Edwin. *The Edge of Sadness*. Boston: Little, Brown, 1961.

O'Connor, Thomas H. *Bibles, Brahmins, and Bosses: A Short History of Boston*. Lectures Delivered for the National Endowment for the Humanities, Boston Public Library Learning Library Program. Boston: Trustees of the Public Library of the City of Boston, 1976.

Petrocik, John R. *Party Coalitions: Realignment and the Decline of the New Deal Party System*. Chicago: University of Chicago Press, 1981.

Pleck, Elizabeth Hafkin. *Black Migration and Poverty: Boston, 1865–1900*. New York: Academic Press, 1979.

Pomper, Gerald. "Classification of Presidential Elections." *Journal of Politics,* vol. 29, no. 3 (August 1967), pp. 535–66.

Reid, Ira De A. *The Negro Immigrant: His Background, Characteristics and Social Adjustment, 1899–1937*. 1939; rpt. New York: Arno Press and The New York Times, 1969.

Rose, Philip M. *The Italians in America*. New York: George H. Doran, 1922.

Rosen, Ben. *The Trend of Jewish Population in Boston: A Study to Determine the Location of a Jewish Communal Building*. Monographs of Federated Jewish Charities of Boston, vol. 1, no. 1 (January 1921). Boston: Federated Jewish Charities, 1921.

Rothman, Sheila M. *Woman's Proper Place: A History of Changing Ideals and Practices, 1870 to the Present*. New York: Basic Books, 1978.

Russell, Francis. *The Great Interlude: Neglected Events and Persons from the First World War to the Depression*. New York: McGraw-Hill, 1964.

Ryan, Dennis P. *Beyond the Ballot Box: A Social History of the Boston Irish, 1845–1917*. Rutherford: Fairleigh Dickinson University Press, 1983.

Schattschneider, E. E. *The Semisovereign People: A Realist's View of Democracy in America*. Hinsdale, Ill.: The Dryden Press, 1975.

______. "United States: The Functional Approach to Party Government." *Modern Political Parties: Approaches to Comparative Politics*, ed. Sigmund Neumann. Chicago: University of Chicago Press, 1956.

Sellers, Charles. "The Equilibrium Cycle in Two-Party Politics." In Clubb and Allen, *Electoral Change and Stability*.

Shannon, William V. *The American Irish*, rev. ed. New York: Macmillan, 1966.

Shover, John L. "Was 1928 a Critical Election in California?" In Clubb and Allen, *Electoral Change and Stability*.

Silbey, Joel H., Allan G. Bogue, and William H. Flanigan, eds. *The History of American Electoral Behavior*. Princeton: Princeton University Press, 1978.

Social Register: Boston, 1920, vol. 34, no. 5 (November 1919). New York: Social Register Association, 1919.

Social Register: Boston, 1930, vol. 44, no. 5 (November 1929). New York: Social Register Association, 1929.

Solomon, Barbara Miller. *Ancestors and Immigrants: A Changing New England Tradition*. Chicago: University of Chicago Press, 1956.

Stack, John F., Jr. *International Conflict in an American City: Boston's Irish, Italians, and Jews, 1935–1944*. Contributions in Political Science, no. 26. Bernard K. Johnpoll, series ed. Westport, Conn.: Greenwood Press, 1979.

Stave, Bruce M. *The New Deal and the Last Hurrah: Pittsburgh Machine Politics*. [Pittsburgh?]: University of Pittsburgh Press, 1970.

Story, Ronald. *The Forging of an Aristocracy: Harvard & the Boston Upper Class, 1800–1870*. Middletown, Conn.: Wesleyan University Press, 1980.

Sundquist, James L. *Dynamics of the Party System: Alignment and Realignment of Political Parties in the United States*. Washington, D.C.: The Brookings Institution, 1973.

______. *Dynamics of the Party System: Alignment and Realignment of Political Parties in the United States*, rev. ed. Washington, D.C.: The Brookings Institution, 1983.

Thernstrom, Stephan. *The Other Bostonians: Poverty and Progress in the American Metropolis, 1880–1970*. Cambridge: Harvard University Press, 1973.

Todisco, Paula J. *Boston's First Neighborhood: The North End*. Boston: Boston Public Library, 1976.

Toomey, John J., and Edward P. B. Rankin. *History of South Boston (Its Past and Present) and Prospects for the Future, with Sketches of Prominent Men.* Boston: John J. Toomey and Edward P. B. Rankin, 1901.

Trout, Charles H. *Boston, the Great Depression, and the New Deal.* New York: Oxford University Press, 1977.

United States Department of Commerce, Bureau of the Census. *Fourteenth Census of the United States, Taken in the Year 1920.* Vol. 3. *Population, 1920. Composition and Characteristics of the Population, by States.* Washington, D.C.: Government Printing Office, 1922.

______. *16th Census of the United States, 1940. Housing—Block Statistics—Boston.* Supplement to the First Series/Housing Bulletin for Massachusetts. Washington, D.C.: Government Printing Office, 1942.

______. *16th Census of the United States, 1940. Population and Housing—Statistics for Census Tracts—Boston, Mass.* Washington, D.C.: Government Printing Office, 1942.

______. *Thirteenth Census of the United States, Taken in the Year 1910.* Vol. 1. *Population, 1910. General Report and Analysis.* Washington, D.C.: Government Printing Office, 1913.

United States Department of the Interior. *Population of the United States in 1860; compiled from the original returns of the Eighth Census.* Joseph C. G. Kennedy, Superintendent of Census. Washington, D.C.: Government Printing Office, 1864.

______, Census Office. *Twelfth Census of the United States, Taken in the Year 1900: Census Reports.* Vol. 1. *Population,* Part 1. Washington, D.C.: United States Census Office, 1901.

[United States Government.] *The Seventh Census of the United States: 1850.* J. D. B. DeBow, Superintendent of the United States Census. Washington, D.C.: Robert Armstrong, Public Printer, 1853.

Verba, Sidney, and Norman H. Nie. *Participation in America: Political Democracy and Social Equality.* New York: Harper and Row, 1972.

Verba, Sidney, Norman H. Nie, and Jae-On Kim. *Participation and Political Equality: A Seven-Nation Comparison.* New York: Cambridge University Press, 1978.

"Vote of Boston [by Precinct—1932]." *Boston Evening Globe,* 9 November 1932, p. 12.

"Vote of Boston [by Precinct—1936]." *Boston Evening Globe,* 4 November 1936, p. 16.

Warner, Sam Bass, Jr. *Streetcar Suburbs: The Process of Growth in Boston, 1870–1900,* 2d ed. Cambridge: Harvard University Press, 1978.

Wattenberg, Martin P. *The Decline of American Political Parties, 1952–1984.* Cambridge: Harvard University Press, 1986.

White, Theodore H. *In Search of History: A Personal Adventure.* New York: Harper and Row, 1978.

Whitehill, Walter Muir. *Boston: A Topographical History,* 2d ed., enlarged. Cambridge: The Belknap Press of Harvard University Press, 1968.

______. *Boston in the Age of John Fitzgerald Kennedy.* Norman: University of Oklahoma Press, 1966.

Whyte, William Foote. *Street Corner Society: The Social Structure of an Italian Slum.* Chicago: University of Chicago Press, 1943.

Wolfinger, Raymond E. "The Development and Persistence of Ethnic Voting." *American Political Science Review,* vol. 59, no. 4 (December 1965), pp. 896–908.

Wolfinger, Raymond E., and Steven J. Rosenstone. *Who Votes?* New Haven: Yale University Press, 1980.

Woods, Robert A., ed. *Americans in Process: A Settlement Study, North and West Ends, Boston.* 1902; rpt. New York: Arno Press and The New York Times, 1970.

______. *The City Wilderness: A Settlement Study.* Boston: Houghton Mifflin, 1898.

Woods, Robert A., and Albert J. Kennedy, eds. *The Zone of Emergence,* abridged and edited by Sam B. Warner, Jr. Cambridge: Harvard University Press, 1962.

Works Progress Administration, Federal Writers' Project. *Massachusetts: A Guide to Its Places and People.* American Guide Series. Boston: Houghton Mifflin, 1937.

Index